Hiking Virginia

Hiking Virginia

Third Edition

Bill and Mary Burnham

GUILFORD, CONNECTICUT
HELENA, MONTANA
AN IMPRINT OF GLOBE PEQUOT PRESS

To buy books in quantity for corporate use
or incentives, call **(800) 962-0973**
or e-mail **premiums@GlobePequot.com.**

FALCONGUIDES®

FalconGuides is an imprint of Globe Pequot Press.
Falcon, FalconGuides, and Outfit Your Mind are registered trademarks of Morris Book Publishing, LLC.

All interior photographs by Bill and Mary Burnham unless otherwise noted.
Maps © Morris Book Publishing, LLC

Project editor: David Legere
Layout: Sue Murray

Library of Congress Cataloging-in-Publication Data is available on file.

ISSN 1547-3406
ISBN 978-0-7627-7802-7

Printed in the United States of America

10 9 8 7 6 5 4 3 2 1

Contents

Acknowledgments ix
Preface x
How to Use This Guide xi
Introduction 1
Map Legend 8

The Hikes
Eastern Virginia
1. Chincoteague National Wildlife Refuge 12
2. False Cape State Park/Back Bay Wildlife Refuge 19
3. First Landing State Park 26
4. York River State Park 33
5. Belle Isle State Park 39
6. Newport News Park 44

Honorable Mentions
A. Great Dismal Swamp National Wildlife Refuge 49
B. Sandy Bottom Nature Preserve 49
C. Beaverdam Park 49
D. Hickory Hollow Natural Area Preserve 49
E. Caledon Natural Area State Park 65

Northern Virginia
7. Prince William Forest Park 54
8. Scotts Run Nature Preserve 61
9. Great Falls Park 67
10. G. Richard Thompson Wildlife Management Area 75
11. Rock Creek Park 81

Honorable Mentions
F. Mason Neck Wildlife Refuge/Mason Neck State Park 89
G. Bull Run-Occoquan Trail 89
H. Manassas National Battlefield Park 89
I. Wildcat Mountain Preserve 89
J. Sky Meadows State Park 90

Central Virginia
12. Trout Trail 94
13. Willis River Trail 101
14. James River State Park 110

Honorable Mentions
K. Belle Isle (Richmond) 115
L. Twin Lakes State Park 115

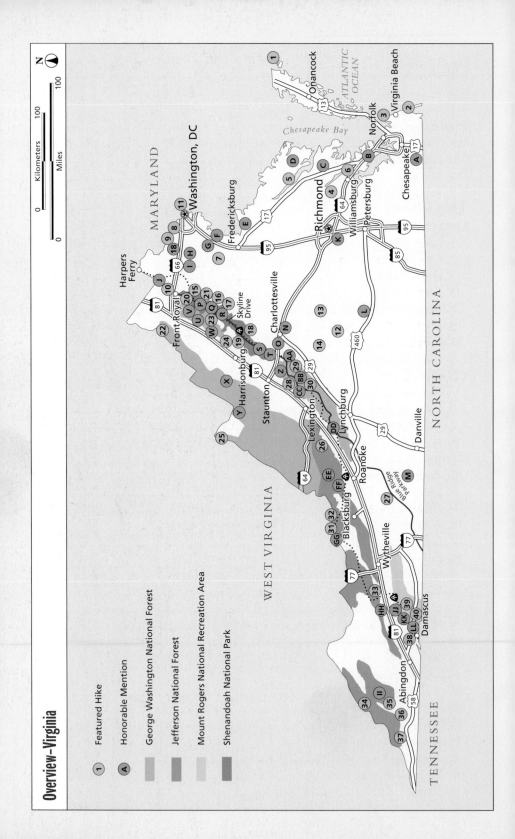

Overview–Virginia

Featured Hike

Honorable Mention

George Washington National Forest

Jefferson National Forest

Mount Rogers National Recreation Area

Shenandoah National Park

  M. Fairy Stone State Park 115

  N. Rivanna Trails 115

  O. Ragged Mountain Natural Area 116

Shenandoah National Park

  15. Mount Marshall Loop 120

  16. Hazel Mountain 127

  17. Old Rag 134

  18. Rocky Mount/Gap Run 141

  19. North Fork Moormans River 148

  20. Overall Run 155

  21. Piney River 160

  Honorable Mentions

  P. Jeremy's Run 166

  Q. Nicholson Hollow 166

  R. Whiteoak Canyon 166

  S. Big Run Portal–Rockytop Loop 166

  T. Riprap Hollow–Appalachian Trail Loop 166

Valley & Ridge

  22. Big Schloss 170

  23. Stephens Trail 177

  24. Fridley Gap 183

  25. Laurel Fork Area 189

  26. Roaring Run/Hoop Hole 195

  Honorable Mentions

  U. Shawl Gap–Massanutten East Trail 201

  V. Massanutten Mountain West/Signal Knob 201

  W. Massanutten Mountain East/Duncan Hollow 201

  X. Wild Oak National Recreation Trail 201

  Y. Shenandoah Mountain Trail/South 201

Blue Ridge Parkway

  27. Rock Castle Gorge 205

  28. St. Mary's Wilderness 210

  29. Three Ridges 216

  30. Mount Pleasant 222

  Honorable Mentions

  Z. Torry Ridge–Mill Creek Loop 227

  AA. Humpback Rocks 227

  BB. Crabtree Falls 227

  CC. Whetstone Ridge 227

  DD. Apple Orchard Falls–Cornelius Creek Loop Trail 227

Southwest Highlands

31. Huckleberry Loop 231
32. Mountain Lake Wilderness 237
33. Crawfish/Channel Rock 243
34. Pine Mountain Trail 250
35. Chief Benge Scout Trail 257
36. Devils Fork Loop 265
37. Stone Mountain Trail 270

Honorable Mentions

EE. Bad Mountain 277
FF. North Mountain–AT Loop 277
GG. The Rice Fields 277
HH. Hungry Mother State Park 277
II. Guest River Gorge Trail 278

Mount Rogers National Recreation Area

38. Feathercamp Ridge 282
39. Little Wilson Creek Wilderness 289
40. Mount Rogers Summit 296

Honorable Mentions

JJ. Four Trails Circuit 303
KK. Rowland Creek Falls Circuit 303
LL. Whitetop Laurel Circuit 303

The Great Escape: The Appalachian Trail through Virginia

Segment 1 – Damascus to Marion 308
Segment 2 – Marion to Roanoke 313
Segment 3 – Roanoke to Rockfish Gap 321
Segment 4 – Rockfish Gap to Chester Gap 328
Segment 5 – Chester Gap to Harpers Ferry 334

Great Day Hikes along the Appalachian Trail

Segment 1 – Damascus to Marion 340
Segment 2 – Marion to Roanoke 341
Segment 3 – Roanoke to Rockfish Gap 344
Segment 4 – Rockfish Gap to Chester Gap 346
Segment 5 – Chester Gap to Harpers Ferry 348

Contact Information (Statewide, National Forests, and National Parks) 349
Hike Index 350
About the Authors 352

Acknowledgments

We'd like to thank Scott Adams, our very first editor, who gave a pair of unknown writers a chance at their very first book. That book, *Hike America Virginia,* was the first edition of the book you now hold in your hands. Thanks, Scott! Hope to see you on the trail!

—Bill and Mary Burnham

Preface

Welcome to the third edition of *Hiking Virginia,* a book we first researched and hiked in the late 1990s before we had a GPS or a digital camera! For this edition, we re-hiked the trails, adding new color photographs, GPS coordinates for the trailheads, and information for people with disabilities. We've updated cues where trails have changed and added several new hikes, including new state parks that didn't exist a decade ago.

People collect stamps. People collect antiques. We collect special places. We pursue them as vigorously as a hobbyist does his or her passion. In doing so, we subscribe to the theory Richard Nelson eloquently expressed in *The Island Within:* "What makes a place special is the way it buries itself in the heart, not whether it is flat or rugged, rich or austere, wet or arid, gentle or harsh, warm or cold, wild or tame." In this spirit, we welcome you to *Hiking Virginia.*

Our book is about more than destinations. It is about experiences set amid Virginia's natural beauty. More and more, people seek out culture and history where they travel. Walking, whether up a mountain or down a quaint city street, offers a traveler no better way of achieving this (admittedly, we're biased—we LOVE hiking). A walk slows the world so sights, smells, and sounds may leave a mental imprint. *Hiking Virginia* is a trail of bread crumbs you can use time and time again to enjoy Virginia's beautiful landscapes, rich history, and kind people.

Virginia lends itself to the foot traveler. Higher mountains and larger expanses of preserved land may be found elsewhere, but in Virginia, the best parts of many worlds exist. Flat, low-lying coastal areas enjoy temperate ocean breezes. The Piedmont unfolds westward, one gentle hill after another, up to the steep flank of the Blue Ridge, an ancient mountain range of billion-year-old granite and prehistoric lava flows. Beyond the Blue Ridge and great valley lies the Allegheny chain of mountains, with distinct valleys and ridges tending northeast-southwest. In the state's far southwest corner, the land rises to its highest peaks of nearly 6,000 feet.

In Virginia, hikers find endless possibilities. They might walk beneath the broad sky of a high-altitude meadow, inhale the spruce scents of a remnant boreal forest, delight in the natural richness of an Appalachian cove forest, walk along tidal marshes, or play in the ocean surf. The sun rises over an Atlantic barrier island, while hundreds of miles inland in a mountain valley, sunlight creeps, inch by inch, down a forested ridge until it alights on the deepest, coolest parts of the earth. From coast to mountain, Virginia beckons. Answer her call, find your place, and make it special.

Thank you for purchasing the third edition of *Hiking Virginia.*

How to Use This Guide

Take a close enough look and you'll find that this little guide contains just about everything you'll ever need to choose, plan for, enjoy, and survive a hike in Virginia. We've done everything but load your pack and tie up your bootlaces. Stuffed with useful Virginia-specific information, *Hiking Virginia* features 45 mapped and cued hikes, 38 honorable mentions, 36 unique day hikes along the Appalachian Trail, and everything from advice on getting into shape to tips on getting the most out of hiking with your children or your dog. We've added accessible trails for people with disabilities, GPS coordinates for trailheads, and new color photographs. And you get the easy-to-understand color trail maps. With so much information, the only question you may have is: How do I sift through it all? Well, we answer that, too.

We've designed our guidebook to be highly visual, for quick reference and ease of use. What this means is that the most pertinent information rises quickly to the top, so you don't have to waste time poring through bulky hike descriptions to get mileage cues or elevation stats. They're set aside for you. Yet *Hiking Virginia* doesn't read like a laundry list. Take the time to dive into a hike description, and you'll realize that this guide is not just a good source of information—it's a good read. Here's an outline of the book's major components.

To aid in quick decision making, we start each hike chapter with a short summary to give you a taste of the hiking adventure to follow. You'll learn about the trail terrain and what surprises the route has to offer. If your interest is piqued, read on; if it isn't, skip to the next hike.

The hike specifications that follow are fairly self-explanatory. Here you'll find the quick, nitty-gritty details of the hike: where the trailhead is located, hike distance, approximate hiking time, difficulty rating, type of trail terrain, land status, the nearest town, what other trail users you may encounter, if there's any accessibility for people with disabilities, whether it's kid or pet-friendly, trail contacts (for updates on trail conditions), trail schedules, whether fees or permits are required, and available maps. Finding the trailhead provides dependable directions from a nearby city right down to where you'll want to park, with GPS coordinates.

The Hike is the meat of the chapter. Detailed and honest, it's our carefully researched impression of the trail. While it's impossible to cover everything, you can rest assured that we won't miss what's important. Miles and Directions provides mileage cues to identify turns and trail name changes, as well as points of interest. The Hike Information section at the end of each hike is a hodgepodge of information. Here we'll tell you where to stay, what to eat, and what else to see while you're hiking in the area.

The Honorable Mentions for each section detail hikes that didn't make the cut. In many cases it's not because they aren't great hikes, but they may be overcrowded or environmentally sensitive to heavy traffic. Be sure to read through these. A jewel might be lurking among them.

We don't want anyone to feel restricted to just the routes and trails that are mapped here. We hope you'll have an adventurous spirit and use this guide as a platform to dive into Virginia's backcountry and discover new routes for yourself. One of the simplest ways to begin this is to just turn the map upside down and hike the course in reverse. The change in perspective is often fantastic, and the hike should feel quite different. With this in mind, it'll be like getting two distinctly different hikes on each map.

For your own purposes, you may wish to copy the directions for the course onto a small sheet to help you while hiking, or photocopy the map and cue sheet to take with you. Otherwise, just slip the whole book in your backpack and take it all with you. Enjoy your time in the outdoors, and remember to pack out what you pack in.

How to Use the Maps

Overview Map

This map helps you find your way to the start of each hike from the nearest sizable town or city. Coupled with the detailed directions at the beginning of the cue, this map should visually lead you to where you need to be for each hike.

Elevation Profile

This helpful profile gives you a cross-sectional look at the hike's ups and downs. Elevation is labeled on the left, mileage is indicated on the top. Road and trail names are shown along the route, with towns and points of interest labeled in bold.

Route Map

This is your primary guide to each hike. It shows all of the accessible roads and trails, points of interest, water, towns, landmarks, and geographical features. It also distinguishes trails from roads, and paved roads from unpaved roads. The selected route is highlighted, and directional arrows point the way. Shaded topographic relief in the background gives you an accurate representation of the terrain and landscape in the hike area.

Introduction

Virginia Weather

Virginia's climate is a seasonal mixed bag. In winter, storms arrive from the west. In fall, tropical weather arrives from the Atlantic or, occasionally, from the Gulf of Mexico. When severe enough, these tropical storms become hurricanes. During summer, warm air settles over the state, resulting in hot days punctured by thunderstorms. Late fall and winter are wet-weather seasons, while summer and early fall are generally dry.

Along the coast—the state's warmest region—the Atlantic winds exert a moderating influence on temperatures, making highs and lows less extreme. Back Bay Wildlife Refuge, a coastal barrier island, averages 86°F in July. By contrast, the southern Piedmont city of Danville experiences an average temperature of 90°F in July. Likewise, in winter, temperatures on the coast average above freezing. Inland, on the Piedmont, temperature averages dip to the mid-20s.

Virginia's mountains and valleys produce wildly fluctuant temperatures and levels of precipitation. Virtually every state record—high and low temperature, high and low rainfall and snowfall—has occurred in the Blue Ridge Mountains and points west. Summer temperatures range from the mid 80s into the 90s. In winter, temperatures dip into the teens. Snow is common in the mountains, with average accumulations between 6 and 7 inches December through February.

When storms arrive from the west, the Allegheny Mountains cast a rain shadow over eastern mountain slopes and the Shenandoah Valley. When storms originate from the east, the Blue Ridge reverse the pattern, wringing moisture out on eastern slopes, leaving the western slopes and valleys dry. As a result, the Shenandoah Valley is the driest region of the state, averaging only 33 inches of rain annually. To the east, across the Blue Ridge, the city of Charlottesville averages 47 inches. And in far southwest Virginia, annual rainfall totals more than 60 inches.

Tropical storms and hurricanes deserve special mention in Virginia. They occur August through October and bring with them threats of high winds and flooding. A hurricane is defined as a storm with sustained wind gusts of 74 mph, but a tropical storm can be as harrowing an experience. Hurricanes are often thought of as coastal weather events, but Virginia's worst twentieth-century storm, Hurricane Camille in 1969, devastated Nelson County in the eastern Blue Ridge region. More recently, in 1996, Hurricane Fran caused mudslides and widespread flooding near Front Royal.

Virginia Flora and Fauna

Virginia's forests are comprised primarily of broadleaf, deciduous trees. Under this forest blanket exist plant communities specially adapted to the state's varying climates.

Grasses, salt meadow hay, and hearty shrubs such as wax myrtle populate coastal fringes of Virginia. These are some of the most resilient plants in the world, able to withstand harsh winds and saltwater conditions. Inland from the beaches and dunes, lagoons mix a daily tidal wash with mainland runoff. Fish spawn here and crustaceans such as fiddler crab live out early years on a nutrient-rich diet. On the mainland, forests of pines and oak typify the flat coastal region. In swampy areas, bald cypress and live oak are often draped with Spanish moss.

Pink lady's slippers are a special woodland treat.

Besides cushioning a daily onslaught of waves and wind, the Atlantic barrier islands of Virginia support breeding and migratory birds. From Assateague to False Cape, the arrival and breeding of songbirds, raptors, shorebirds, and wading birds of all shapes and sizes mark every season. As many as 400,000 birds of prey, representing twelve species, have been observed at Kiptopeke State Park on the Eastern Shore during a single fall count.

Virginia's Piedmont has traditionally supported agriculture. By the twentieth century, generations of farming left large swaths of barren land. Where forests returned, they are primarily black and white oak and Virginia and loblolly pine. In Virginia's state forests, oak and poplar are managed for harvest. Willow oak, river birch, hickory, and ash grow as well. Cumberland State Forest near Farmville marks the extreme western reach of the loblolly pine in Virginia. Turkey, fox, deer, raccoon, and squirrel populate these pockets of rejuvenated woodlands. Hunting has long been permitted, but state forests are a popular spot for hikers, horseback riders, mountain bikers, and campers as well.

The Appalachian oak-hickory forest rises to dominance within the Blue Ridge. Hickory is the successor of American chestnut. In the early twentieth century, it was estimated one of every four trees in the Appalachians was a chestnut. Today, few grow taller than 6 feet before

Mountain laurel are common throughout Virginia's woodlands.

succumbing to the chestnut blight. In the absence of chestnuts, oaks have assumed primacy in Virginia's western regions. Chestnut oaks are found on dry, rocky ridges, while white and red oak populate mountain slopes. In the forest understory, scrub oak and chinquapins grow.

In moist pockets below 4,500 feet elevation, the Appalachian cove forest holds more than twenty species of trees—beech, sugar, maple, and yellow poplar noticeable among these. Stands of eastern hemlock once made for impressive viewing. However, damage from the invasive woolly adelgid is now widespread in Virginia. Evidence of its handiwork is especially striking in Shenandoah National Park, where entire stands of hemlock are defoliated and dying. Even

Whitetail deer are common in Virginia.

so, quiet, cool pockets of this venerable evergreen may still be found along isolated mountain streams.

In the forest understory, dogwood and redbud bring colorful spring blossoms. Mountain laurel and rhododendron seem omnipresent on both dry, rocky ridges and in wet stream valleys. Wildflowers are profuse, from the common purple violets and white toothworts to the infrequently spotted Turk's cap lily. G. R. Thompson Wildlife Management Area, on the eastern slope of the northern Blue Ridge, is thought to hold the largest population of trillium wildflowers in North America. At Mount Rogers and Laurel Fork, the state's highest elevations, spruce and fir trees indicate a remnant boreal forest more typical of Canada.

Deer have rebounded from overhunting and habitat destruction of one hundred years ago to rank as almost a nuisance throughout Virginia. Black bears are found primarily in the western regions of the state, but may be spotted in the Great Dismal Swamp in southeast Virginia. Otherwise, Virginia's forests support small-game wildlife. A hiker's footsteps may flush turkey or grouse from the woods. Raccoon and other

Turk's cap lily blooming near Mount Rogers, Virginia's tallest peak.

nocturnal animals make hanging food a necessary part of any camping trip. Bobcats and coyotes are found statewide, but generally in larger areas of preserved forest.

The river systems of Virginia host a wide range of life, from the common brook trout to endangered freshwater mussels. The Clinch and Powell Rivers, flowing southwest to the Tennessee River, support a variety of the hard-shelled animals, many threatened or endangered due to sediment buildup and past toxic chemical spills. Salamanders and crayfish are present in Virginia's mountain streams.

NATIONAL FOREST WILDERNESS *sign shows the restrictions in these fragile areas.*

Throughout Virginia, there are 210 species of freshwater fish. Wild trout streams range from Big and Little Wilson Creeks in Mount Rogers National Recreation Area to North Fork Moormans River in Shenandoah National Park. In the coastal regions, crabs, clams, and other crustaceans inhabit muddy flats in the James, York, Rappahannock, and Potomac Rivers. Seasonal runs of rockfish, sea bass, croaker, and other fish have made sport fishing a popular pastime in the Chesapeake Bay and Atlantic Ocean.

Virginia has witnessed many successes under the federal Endangered Species Act, perhaps none as stirring as the return of a viable bald eagle population. Virginia is home to more than 225 active bald eagle nests. Mason Neck Wildlife Refuge, Caledon Natural Area, and other preserves along the lower Potomac River are renowned nesting and viewing areas for this bird of prey. Likewise, on the James River between Richmond and Isle of Wight County, more than 300 bald eagles have been counted in summer months. Best viewing times in any location are June through August and November through January.

Virginia Wilderness Restrictions/Regulations

In northern and southeast Virginia, public lands fall under three broad categories: federal parks, forests, and refuges; state parks and forests; and municipal parks. Keep in mind that wildlife refuges exist for the benefit of animals, not humans. Sections may be closed off to the public during breeding seasons. Conversely, federal, state, and municipal parks exist for humans, a fact reflected in their sometimes crowded conditions.

Virginia's two national forests cover 1.8 million acres of mountain forestland. The George Washington National Forest stretches from north of Winchester to just south of Lexington and Covington. The adjacent Jefferson National Forest

Fall foliage on a Virginia trail.

continues southwest to the Virginia-Tennessee border. Both are managed out of a single forest headquarters in Roanoke. While it is tempting to think the forests exist for hikers' enjoyment, they are in fact multiuse, with trails for horseback riders, cyclists, and all-terrain vehicles. Developed campgrounds and recreation areas are suitable for tents or motor homes. Hunting is permitted in season, and timber harvests are conducted regularly.

Virginia's national forests are divided into nine ranger districts, and each district is responsible for fire prevention, maintenance, and ecology within its boundary. Rangers and their assistants make excellent resources for hikers and can provide information on trails and weather. Mount Rogers National Recreation Area, which covers 117,000 acres of high country in southwest Virginia, is a specially managed component of the national forest and was created in 1965 with the intent of serving recreational needs of East Coast urban dwellers. Within it are 95 miles of trails for hikers, horseback riders, and cyclists.

Contained in Virginia's two national forests are twenty-four wilderness areas, which is an increase of seven since we wrote the first edition. The intent of wilderness is to allow land to return to a primitive state without interference from people. Motorized traffic and tools are not allowed, and trails may be unblazed and unmaintained. There are exceptions to every rule, however. In cases of emergencies, the Forest

Service or local emergency company may use vehicles, helicopters, chain saws, and other mechanical apparatus when responding in a wilderness area. Surprisingly, the wilderness designation does not automatically translate to remote. St. Mary's Wilderness Area, south of Staunton and Charlottesville, is blessed with an abundance of beautiful waterfalls; yet, because it's so easily accessed from I-81, it's more heavily used than some nonwilderness areas. That said, just as many of these areas feel truly remote. Many hikers have never heard of Beartown Wilderness, on the edge of Burke's Garden near Tazewell, or Kimberling Creek Wilderness, near Wytheville.

Appalachian Trail sign and white blaze. The AT is blazed white in Virginia.

Shenandoah National Park is Virginia's—and one of the nation's—most visited parks. There is an entrance fee; annual passes are available. Most visitors simply cruise Skyline Drive, a beautiful highway with scenic views that traces the ridgeline of the Blue Ridge. (South of the park, the road continues as the Blue Ridge Parkway, a scenic highway that ends in Great Smoky Mountains National Park in Tennessee.) It is said that a majority of travelers on Skyline Drive stray no more than a half mile from parking areas and pull-offs. Still, Shenandoah's backcountry receives a healthy number of visitors. Every hiker should be aware of the park's backcountry regulations, which govern issues from pets to fires to how to dispose of waste.

Getting Around Virginia

Area Codes

Virginia currently has seven area codes: 276 serves Martinsville, Bristol, Abingdon, and the rest of southwest Virginia; 434 serves Charlottesville, Lynchburg, and central Virginia; 540 covers Roanoke and western and northern Virginia, excluding Arlington; 571 overlays with 703 to serve the Washington, DC, suburbs and Arlington area; 757 serves Hampton Roads and the Eastern Shore; and 804 covers Richmond east to the Williamsburg area.

Roads

For current information on statewide weather and road conditions and closures, call the Virginia Department of Transportation (VDOT) 24-hour Highway Helpline at (800) 367-7623 (TTY users, call 800-432-1843) or visit www.vdot.state.va.us.

By Air

Dulles International Airport (IAD) is 23 miles northwest of downtown Washington, DC. Ronald Reagan Washington National Airport (DCA) is in nearby Alexandria. For full services, visit www.metwashairports.com. Richmond International Airport (RIC) is located 7 miles east of downtown Richmond. For full services, visit www.flyrichmond .com. Norfolk/Virginia Beach International (ORF) serves the Tidewater Region. For full services, visit www.norfolkairport.com.

Spring beauties.

Other major airports in Virginia include Roanoke Regional Airport (ROA), www.roanokeairport.com or www .roanoke.org/air.html; Shenandoah Valley Regional Airport (SHD), www.flyshd .com; Charlottesville Albemarle Airport (CHO), www.gocho.com; and Newport News–Williamsburg International (NNW), www.nnwairport.com.

To book reservations online, check out your favorite airline's website or search one of the following travel sites for the best price: www.cheaptickets.com, www .expedia.com, www.flycheap.com, www.priceline.com, www.travel.yahoo.com, www.travelocity.com, or www.trip.com—just to name a few.

By Train

Virginia is well served by AMTRAK. For information and/or reservations, visit them online at www.amtrak.com or call (800) 872-7245.

Virginia Railway Express (VRE) operates commuter rail service weekdays along two lines from Fredericksburg and Manassas to Union Station. For more information, call (800) RIDE-VRE or visit www.vre.org. Maryland Rail Commuter (MARC) operates commuter rail service weekdays along the Potomac River in Maryland. (An important stop for hikers is Harpers Ferry, West Virginia, where the Appalachian and C&O Canal Trails converge.) For more information, call (800) 543-9809 or visit www.mtamaryland.com.

By Bus

Greyhound serves most larger towns and cities in Virginia along with Dulles Airport several times a day. For information and/or reservations, visit them online at www .greyhound.com or call (800) 231-2222. Links to local transit operators in Virginia are available at www.apta.com/sites/transus/va.htm.

Visitor Information

For visitor information or a travel brochure, call the Virginia Tourism Corporation at (800) 321-3244 or visit their website at www.virginia.org.

Map Legend

Transportation

≡(81)≡ Interstate Highway

≡(460)≡ US Highway

≡(362)≡ State Highway

≡(613)≡ County/Forest Road

——— Local Road

⊢—⊢—⊢ Railroad

= = = = Unpaved Road

= = = = Jeep Trail

- - - - - - Featured Trail

- - - - - Trail

_🚲_ Bike Trail

_🐎_ Horse Trail

···🅐··· Appalachian Trail

Water Features

⬭ Body of Water

Marsh/Swamp

River/Creek

Intermittent Streams

⟋ Springs

≋ Waterfall

Land Management

- - - - - State Line

National Park/National Forest

National Wilderness Area

State or County Park

Natural Area

National Seashore

Symbols

▭▭▭ Boardwalk

⬲ Boat Launch

⏝ Bridge

🚌 Bus Stop

▲ Campground

⌒ Cave

→ Direction Arrow

▮ Gate

🅿 Parking

⤬ Pass/Gap

▲ Peak/Summit

🎪 Picnic Area

■ Point of Interest/Structure

▲ Primitive Campsite

📷 Ranger Station

🍴 Restaurant

🚻 Restrooms

▥▥▥ Steps

🗼 Tower

○ Town

① Trailhead

🚉 Train Station

📷 Viewpoint/Overlook

❓ Visitor Center

Eastern Virginia

Water, not the land, defines Virginia's eastern region. It washes up onto Atlantic barrier islands and rolls into the Chesapeake Bay, forming and shaping the coastline. It runs along a vast network of upland streams, molding river bluffs and carving small inlets and bays. It pours forth from western regions of the state, bursting into the estuarine lower reaches of the James, York, Rappahannock, and Potomac Rivers, giving shape to three large peninsulas that jut out into the Chesapeake Bay.

Water also redefines the landscape, as dramatically evidenced by Hurricane Isabelle in September 2003. One of the state's worst all-time storms in terms of damage inflicted, Isabelle hit state and city parks particularly hard, none more so than York River State Park. There an 8-foot storm surge destroyed footpaths and boardwalks and forced the closure of trails. Elsewhere, in Newport News Park and on the Eastern Shore's Chincoteague Wildlife Refuge, trails remained closed six months after the storm.

Over the long reach of geologic time, the influx and regress of water—sometimes gradual, sometimes dramatic—has been Eastern Virginia's legacy. The Chesapeake Bay itself is the drowned mouth of the Susquehanna River. In glacial times, when the ocean levels dropped some 400 feet, what we know today as the Chesapeake Bay was a wide river valley. The coastline stood 60 miles out into the present-day ocean. The sand beaches and brackish lagoons of today were, millions of years ago, forests and freshwater ponds.

Images of colonial Virginia ring out in accounts written by early explorers. The English, seeking permanent settlement of North America, came ashore in Virginia Beach, present-day Cape Henry. After months at sea, they were awestruck by an abundance of trees, plants, and animals. They saw dense swamps, where sheets of Spanish moss dangled from trees standing in knee-deep black water. Discarded oyster shells littered the beaches. Fish were abundant. Inland, near Tidewater, the Algonquin Indians had cleared only a fraction of the forest for their crops. Trees were tall and thickly trunked, and sheltered an abundance of wildlife.

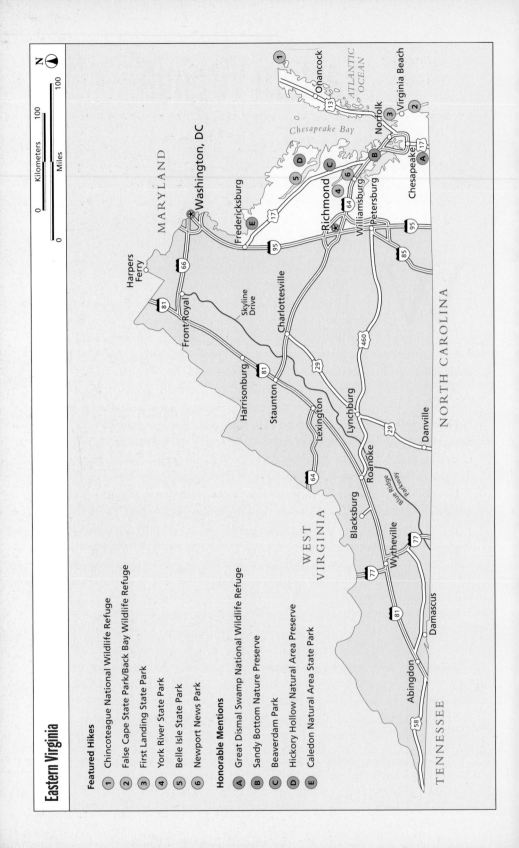

Eastern Virginia

Featured Hikes

1. Chincoteague National Wildlife Refuge
2. False Cape State Park/Back Bay Wildlife Refuge
3. First Landing State Park
4. York River State Park
5. Belle Isle State Park
6. Newport News Park

Honorable Mentions

A. Great Dismal Swamp National Wildlife Refuge
B. Sandy Bottom Nature Preserve
C. Beaverdam Park
D. Hickory Hollow Natural Area Preserve
E. Caledon Natural Area State Park

N

Kilometers
0   100

Miles
0   100

MARYLAND

WEST VIRGINIA

VIRGINIA

NORTH CAROLINA

TENNESSEE

ATLANTIC OCEAN

Chesapeake Bay

Washington, DC

Harpers Ferry

Front Royal

Skyline Drive

Charlottesville

Fredericksburg

Richmond

Petersburg

Williamsburg

Norfolk

Virginia Beach

Chesapeake

Onancock

Harrisonburg

Staunton

Lexington

Lynchburg

Danville

Roanoke

Blacksburg

Blue Ridge Parkway

Wytheville

Damascus

Abingdon

66

81

95

17

95

85

64

29

460

29

64

77

77

81

58

13

17

Eastern Virginia today harbors bits and pieces of this once-resplendent nature. Rare migratory birds winter over in the Dismal Swamp. Endangered turtles live in the swamps of First Landing State Park. In the harsh beach and dune environments, piping plovers struggle against predators large and small. Behind barrier islands, marshes perform the critical job of filtering land runoff while supporting a nursery of fish and shellfish. In hidden, secluded spots, rare orchids bloom and old-growth trees spread their branches, inviting you to rest in their shade. Bald eagles nest and roost on stretches of the James River between Richmond and Isle of Wight County.

Wherever you choose to explore, bring a pair of waterproof boots. Because no matter where you hike in eastern Virginia, you're bound to hit water.

The Hikes

1. Chincoteague National Wildlife Refuge
2. False Cape SP/Back Bay Wildlife Refuge
3. First Landing State Park
4. York River State Park
5. Belle Isle State Park
6. Newport News Park

Honorable Mentions

A. Great Dismal Swamp National Wildlife Refuge
B. Sandy Bottom Nature Preserve
C. Beaverdam Park
D. Hickory Hollow Natural Area Preserve
E. Caledon Natural Area State Park

1 Chincoteague National Wildlife Refuge

Every spring and fall, millions of birds migrate between cold, northern environs and temperate and tropical homes in Central and South America. En route, their needs are simple: an occasional place to rest and food to nourish. Wildlife biologists at Chincoteague National Wildlife Refuge, on the southern tip of Assateague Island, have engineered a deluxe ornithological wayside for the winged travelers. Entire sections of beach are closed during nesting season for such species as the endangered piping plover and Wilson's plover. On small, man-made earthen mounds rising in the middle of bayside lagoons, waterfowl perch and feed, protected from predators. As the human hand tinkers with wildlife balance, real drama plays out in the daily life of birds and land animals—and it's on display for all to see.

Start: Wildlife Pond/Beachfront Loop: Herbert H. Bateman Educational Center on Beach Road; Beachfront Backpack: Toms Cove Visitor Center

Distance: Wildlife Pond/Beachfront Loop: 7.5-mile loop; Beachfront Backpack: 25 miles out and back

Hiking time: Wildlife Pond/Beachfront Loop: about 3 hours; Beachfront Backpack: about 10 hours

Difficulty: Wildlife Pond/Beachfront Loop is easy. Beachfront Backpack is moderate due to length. Between May and Sept, mosquitoes, greenhead flies, deerflies, and ticks make exploration of Chincoteague's interior shrub and maritime forest inadvisable, especially at dawn and dusk. Long-sleeved shirts, pants, and bug netting, plus bug spray, can alleviate this problem.

Trail surface: Wildlife Pond/Beachfront Loop: A network of paved roads, dirt roads, and sand jeep trails lead hikers to a wide ocean beach, maritime forest of oak and pine, low dunes, and saltwater marsh. Beachfront Backpack: Sand and surf along a wide ocean beach.

Land status: National wildlife refuge and national seashore

Nearest town: Chincoteague, VA

Other trail users: Cyclists, anglers, over-sand vehicles, horseback riders, and hunters (in season)

Accessibility: Fully half of the refuge's trails are paved, including the Wildlife Loop, Swan Cove Trail, and Black Duck Trail.

Canine compatibility: Dogs not permitted, not even in the car

Trail contact: Chincoteague National Wildlife Refuge, 8231 Beach Rd., Chincoteague; (757) 336-6122; www.fws.gov/northeast/chinco

Schedule: Open daily, 5 a.m. to 10 p.m. May through Sept; 6 a.m. to 6 p.m. Nov through Mar; 6 a.m. to 8 p.m. Apr and Oct. Portions of beaches and trails may be closed for piping plover nesting in spring and summer and for hunting in Oct, Dec, and Jan. Call ahead for details.

Fees/permits: Entrance fee per vehicle; bicycles and pedestrians free. Backcountry permit required; register at the Toms Cove Visitor Center. Backpackers must depart with enough daylight to hike 12 miles to the State Line or Pope Bay backcountry campsites in Maryland. All freshwater must be carried in. Visit www.nps.gov/asis for camping rules and regulations.

Facilities/features: Restrooms, educational and visitor centers, lifeguarded beach, kayak launch, primitive camping across the Maryland border only

Maps: USGS Chincoteague East; refuge and park service maps available at visitors center

Finding the trailhead: From the new Chincoteague Bridge (VA 175): For the Wildlife Pond/ Beachfront Loop, stay straight to go on Maddox Boulevard (VA 2113). Drive 1.2 miles to a traffic circle and follow Maddox Boulevard through the circle. In 1.4 miles, reach the refuge entrance gate, where Maddox Boulevard becomes Beach Road. Enter the refuge and in 0.3 mile, turn left into the parking area for the Herbert H. Bateman Educational Center at 8231 Beach Rd. This new eco-friendly building serves as the visitor center, with nature exhibits inside. For the Beachfront Backpack, after entering the refuge, continue past the educational center and enter the Assateague Island National Seashore. In 1.5 miles, reach the Toms Cove Visitor Center on the right to obtain a backcountry permit. Visitor center GPS: N37 54.544' / W75 21.337'. *DeLorme: Virginia Atlas & Gazetteer:* Page 63, A5.

The Hike

Screams and cries rise off the oceanfront as hungry gulls and terns scavenge for food along the surf. Beyond Assateague Island's low sand and inland pine, snow geese float restlessly in a freshwater pool. Suddenly, on some silent, unseen signal, a single goose, then two, three—then the entire flock rises in flight. Their *whonk-whonk* joins with cries of shorebirds in a resounding cacophony.

An explosion of snow geese off the water draws the birder's eyes skyward. Here, a broad-winged raptor swoops high above the pond. Its brown wings tilt slightly left, then right in a jittery act of balance. The telltale white head and yellow, hooked bill soon come into focus. This bald eagle, its search for a meal frustrated, soars out of sight behind crowns of loblolly pine.

Hiking in the surf along Assateague Island National Seashore.

This winter struggle between prey and predator will end when snow geese fly north in spring. Closer to the ocean, a different life struggle begins in spring when piping plover descend upon Chincoteague National Wildlife Refuge on the southern tip of Assateague Island. After a brief courtship, breeding pairs build a nest in the sand. Up to four eggs will hatch within a month of being laid. For five critical days, the young chick's life consists of dodging predators and finding enough food to survive. Days turn to weeks, and the handful of chicks that survive face new dangers. Camouflage, the tiny, sand-colored plover's best defense, leads to unintended consequences: Humans inadvertently step on nests. Off-road vehicles run them over. Gulls harass adult plovers and carry away chicks. Other predators, raccoons and foxes among them, raid nests. Storms send tidal surges crashing over protective dunes—violent weather has destroyed entire nesting seasons at Chincoteague.

Animals fend for themselves on a daily basis in a never-ending search for an advantage—and a meal. Humans represent an interference in this delicate balance. The side of the scale on which we place our weight makes all the difference. In the case of the Delmarva fox squirrel, farming and homes had, by 1900, destroyed habitat in all but a tiny spot in Maryland. The balance tipped in the squirrel's favor in 1945, however, when Maryland set aside land for its protection. In 1971 it became illegal to hunt the large fox squirrel, which can weigh up to three pounds and measure 30 inches in length. On reserves in Virginia, Maryland, and Delaware, squirrel populations increased. From a population of 30 squirrels in 1970, Chincoteague now keeps its numbers around 350, shipping out squirrels to other suitable habitats if their numbers exceed this level.

Human intervention, often the cause of ailing animal populations, is just as often the cure. When plover chicks hatch in late May, refuge staff begin a sixteen- to eighteen-hour vigil over nesting sites. Nesting areas are signed and roped off, and occasionally beach roads are closed to vehicular traffic. In 2007 eighty plover chicks fledged, or were able to fly, on refuge islands, according to a shorebird productivity report. Assateague Island, along with neighboring barrier islands, account for the majority of the piping plover's breeding population in Virginia.

The Chincoteague refuge also played an instrumental role in the recovery of breeding peregrine falcons in Virginia. By the 1960s breeding peregrines had disappeared from the state, suffering from a fate similar to the bald eagles'—contamination from the pesticide DDT. Weakened eggshells broke, and chicks hatched prematurely. DDT was banned in 1972. In the late 1970s scientists began releasing pairs of peregrines in Virginia, both in coastal and mountain regions. In 1982 they hit gold when a pair of peregrine falcons was found nesting on Assateague Island, the first documented breeding pair in the state in nearly a half a century. As of 2010 Virginia supports twenty-three known breeding pairs of peregrine falcons, nearly all within the state's portion of the Eastern Shore. A delisting of the peregrine from an endangered species to a threatened species reflects national success in reintroducing breeding populations.

And yet even in a managed environment, disaster strikes. When several storms inundated the maritime forest of lower Assateague Island—which encompasses the whole of the Chincoteague refuge—volumes of salt water weakened the resident loblolly pines. The stress caused by a lack of freshwater made the pines susceptible to the southern pine beetle. Recovery from this trauma can be seen today along the Wildlife Loop Trail—where amid low shrubs and grass, pine saplings have made a vigorous comeback.

▶ **Kid Appeal: With rare exceptions, everyone wants to catch a glimpse of the famous Chincoteague wild ponies, which reside in the refuge and national seashore. The 1.6-mile Woodland Trail leads through a pine forest to an overlook where pony sightings are common. The new Bivalve Trail is a 0.2-mile spur off the Woodland Trail that leads to the shores of Toms Cove with a view of the old Assateague lifesaving station.**

For years, protection of Assateague Island extended to correcting nature itself. After every major storm, the park service rebuilt dunes with the goal of keeping an ocean ecology from slipping away. Littoral drift, the term for a shift in barrier islands westward, moves Assateague, on average, 30 feet every decade. But not everything needs protecting. Park managers have decided against rebuilding dunes and are now questioning the wisdom of building (and rebuilding) parking lots near the beach. Whatever conditions a storm leaves the barrier island, staff are now inclined to leave it untampered. Humans, and not the environment, will adapt to conditions. Briefly, balance tips back to Mother Nature.

The Sika deer, actually a Japanese Elk, inhabit Chincoteague National Wildlife Refuge.

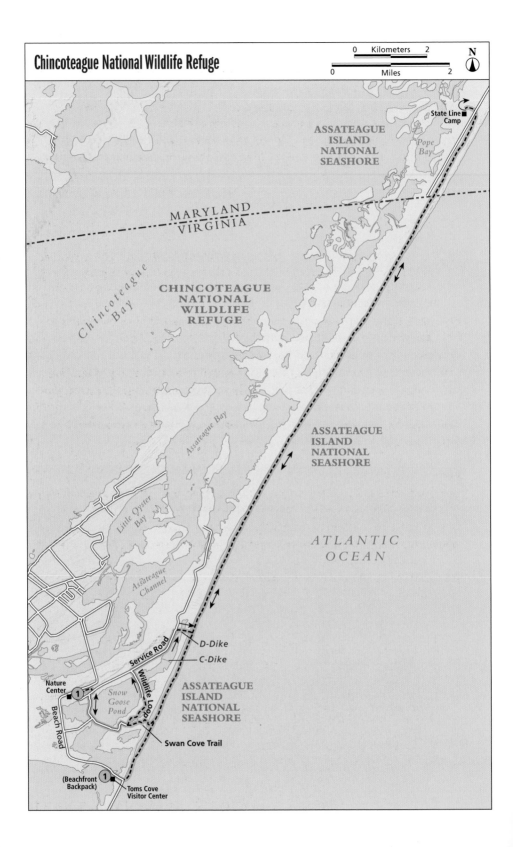

Chincoteague National Wildlife Refuge

0   Kilometers   2

0   Miles   2

N

State Line
Camp

ASSATEAGUE
ISLAND
NATIONAL
SEASHORE

*Pope
Bay*

MARYLAND
VIRGINIA

*Chincoteague
Bay*

CHINCOTEAGUE
NATIONAL
WILDLIFE
REFUGE

Assateague Bay

ASSATEAGUE
ISLAND
NATIONAL
SEASHORE

*Little Oyster
Bay*

*Assateague
Channel*

ATLANTIC
OCEAN

Service Road

D-Dike

C-Dike

Wildlife Loop

Nature
Center

1

*Snow
Goose
Pond*

ASSATEAGUE
ISLAND
NATIONAL
SEASHORE

Beach Road

Swan Cove Trail

(Beachfront
Backpack)

1

Toms Cove
Visitor Center

Miles and Directions

Wildlife Pond/Beachfront Loop

0.0 Start from the parking lot for the Herbert H. Bateman Educational Center. Opposite the visitor center, a boardwalk trail leads away through a pine forest.

0.3 Merge onto the paved Wildlife Loop road, which is open to vehicles from 3 p.m. to dusk, and continue straight. Views of Snow Goose Pool, a freshwater impoundment, open up on the left.

0.7 Continue straight on the Wildlife Loop road past the Black Duck Trail, which exits to the right and leads 0.5 mile to paved Beach Road.

1.4 Continue straight, past Swan Cove Trail, which exits to the right and is part of the return leg of this loop.

2.5 Cross Snow Goose Pool on a dike and turn right onto a gated dirt road, which is closed to public vehicle traffic except between Memorial Day and Labor Day, when sightseeing trams operate. **Option:** To return to the educational center, turn left at this T junction and follow the paved Wildlife Loop Road.

3.1 Continue straight on the gravel road past C-Dike. **Note:** This earthen embankment is closed and may not be used to access the beach.

3.6 Turn right onto D-Dike and hike 0.3 mile to the oceanfront.

3.9 Emerge from the dunes onto the beach. Turn right and head south along the beachfront.

5.5 Turn right and walk through the beach dunes onto Swan Cove Trail. **Note:** This trail may be closed during periods of high rainfall.

6.0 Swan Cove Trail ends at Wildlife Loop. Bear left to return to the educational center.

7.5 Arrive back at the Herbert H. Bateman Educational Center parking area.

Beachfront Backpack

0.0 Start from the Toms Cove Visitor Center, where you must obtain a backcountry permit and inquire where to park overnight. Head to the beachfront, turn left and walk north.

2.9 Pass a dune crossover to D-Dyke on the left. Continue straight.

9.4 Pass Old Fields crossover, a route leading left through the dunes to an interior service road. Continue straight.

11.0 Cross the Maryland state line and enter Assateague Island National Seashore. Continue straight.

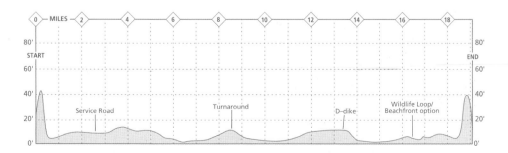

12.5 A tent sign in the dunes to the left indicates State Line campsites, primitive sites with no running water and chemical toilets. Camping is permitted amid dunes only. Turn around and return to the Toms Cove Visitors Center. **Note:** If State Line camp is booked, Pope Bay on the bayside of Maryland's Assateague Island is 0.5 miles north.

25.0 Hike ends at Toms Cove Visitor Center.

Hike Information

Local Information
Chincoteague Chamber of Commerce, (757) 336-6161, www.chincoteaguechamber .com

Local Events/Attractions
Annual Pony Swim and Penning, last Wed in July, Chincoteague, (757) 336-6161. An event of national renown, wild Chincoteague ponies are driven off the refuge across a small water passage and penned on Chincoteague Island for auction.

International Migratory Bird Celebration in May, National Wildlife Refuge Week in Oct, and Waterfowl Week in Nov, all at Chincoteague National Wildlife Refuge, (757) 336-6122

Lodging
The resort town of Chincoteague has a wide array of lodgings, from motels and B&Bs to rental homes. Visit www.chincoteaguechamber.com for listings.

There are several commercial campgrounds in Chincoteague, but backcountry camping is allowed only at Assateague National Seashore in Maryland.

Restaurants
More than 20 Chincoteague restaurants serve up fare ranging from seafood to the standard burger and fries.

Tours
Refuge staff lead walking tours throughout the year. Call (757) 336-6122 for information.

Organizations
Chincoteague Natural History Association (Friends of Chincoteague National Wildlife Refuge), (757) 336-6122

Other Resources
Eastern Shore of Virginia Tourism, (757) 787-8268, www.esvatourism.org

2 False Cape State Park/Back Bay Wildlife Refuge

Barrier islands serve as an ecological first line of defense for our shores. Storms batter them, waves wear them down, wind strips them clean. Tucked out of harm's way behind the islands lie sheltered bays and marshes teeming with grasses, shellfish, birds, and small animals. False Cape State Park and Back Bay National Wildlife Refuge showcase just one of Virginia's many barrier island and lagoon ecosystems, albeit a critical one. The preserves stand within striking distance of Hampton Roads' two million residents and all the incumbent pressures (pollution, development, overcrowding). Sprawl stops at the park boundaries, and hikers and bird watchers are assured a quiet afternoon with space to walk and think, or watch and listen.

Start: Little Island Park
Distance: 14.7-mile lollipop
Hiking time: About 7 hours
Difficulty: Moderate due to length
Trail surface: All aspects of seashore ecology are present, from the beach to dunes to maritime pine and oak forests. Between the barrier islands and mainland lie salt marshes and shallow bays replete with waterfowl.
Land status: National wildlife refuge and state park
Nearest city: Virginia Beach, VA
Other trail users: Cyclists, anglers, hunters (in season), and bird watchers
Accessibility: Back Bay NWR has an ADA-compliant visitor center, restrooms, and some boardwalks to wildlife-viewing stations and the beach. Due to its remote and primitive nature, there are no ADA facilities at False Cape State Park and the trails are all sand. In spring and summer, there is a tram to the park, accessible with advance notice.

Canine compatibility: Leashed dogs are permitted in False Cape State Park, but there's no access allowed through the Back Bay NWR, so they can only arrive by boat. Pets are not permitted in Back Bay NWR at any time.
Trail contacts: False Cape State Park, Virginia Beach, (757) 426-7128, www.dcr.virginia.gov/state_parks/fal.shtml; Back Bay National Wildlife Refuge, Virginia Beach, (757) 301-7329, www.fws.gov/backbay
Schedule: Back Bay NWR open daily dawn to dusk; interior trails closed Nov through Mar for bird nesting and in Oct for hunting. False Cape State Park is closed for a few days in Oct for a game-management program.
Fees/permits: Parking fee charged at Little Island Park Memorial Day to Labor Day
Facilities/features: False Cape State Park has pit toilets, drinking water, and primitive camping. Back Bay NWR has a visitor center, kayak/canoe launch, restrooms, and parking.
Maps: USGS North Bay, Knott Island; state park maps available at www.virginiaoutdoors.com

Finding the trailhead: From Virginia Beach, take the Indian River Road exit 286B off I-64. Proceed east on Indian River Road for 13.4 miles, then turn left onto New Bridge Road. In 1.3 miles, turn right onto Sandbridge Road. After 3.1 miles, turn right onto Sandpiper Road. Drive south on Sandpiper for 3.8 miles to Little Island Park on the left, where overnight parking is permitted. GPS: N36 41.588' / W75 55.473'. *DeLorme: Virginia Atlas & Gazetteer:* Page 35, C7.

Barrier islands are a habitat of extremes. The same beach where sunbathers flock for relaxation also harbors some of the earth's harshest living conditions. Waves beat upon it unceasingly, but those same waves bring ashore food that nourishes microorganisms, shellfish, birds, and small animals. Unfettered wind reduces shrubs and trees to bonsai proportions; wind also spreads beach grass and sea oat seeds, two species that help prevent sand-dune erosion. Then there is sand itself, barren of most nutrients, yet it creates the very reefs and dunes that preserve our coast.

A hiker must adapt to False Cape State Park and Back Bay National Wildlife Refuge (the park and refuge form a 20-mile contiguous stretch of protected coastal habitat between Virginia Beach and the North Carolina border). Forget mountain grandeur. Forget tall hemlocks or yellow poplar trees. Here, wind-lashed holly, oak, and pine eek out a precarious living. Deer, raccoons, opossums, and foxes rustle the shrubby thickets. Migratory birds capture the imagination—shorebirds in the spring, songbirds in spring and fall, and nesting birds in summer; in winter, it's the ducks and geese. Plant and animal life here have had more time to adapt than humans. Wax myrtle has a coating on its leaves that protects it against the relentless sun and moisture loss from high winds and salt exposure. Salt marsh cordgrass is able to overcome both the presence of salt water—which would kill less hardy plants—and a severe lack of oxygen in the dense, mushy marsh soil. It solves the problem of salt water through reverse osmosis, whereby it balances salt water intrusion with freshwater within its vascular cells. Oxygen, meanwhile, is pulled from the air and transported down the

Crossing the dune boardwalk at False Cape State Park.

Camp cooking at False Cape State Park.

stem to the roots. Look closely at the muddy fringe of a salt marsh at low tide and look for red stains in the otherwise black mud. This is a botanical version of rust, a by-product of oxygen mixing with iron sulfide.

Every dune, especially on the lagoon or wash side, features plants whose progression reveals their place in the ecology of the island. On the fringe grows sea rocket, a member of the mustard family. Higher on the dune, beach grass, native to northern barrier islands, and sea oats, commonly found on dunes from Virginia southward, coexist. In areas flooded daily by the tide, salt marsh cordgrass grows nearest to water, while salt marsh hay and black needlerush occupy higher areas of marsh. In the afternoon, at low tide on a clear day, the sun will glint off oxidized salt particles clinging to tall stems of these grasses, giving the impression of light bouncing off thousands of tiny mirrors. Beneath the grasses and puddles of brackish water, juvenile blue crabs reach maturity and fish spawn.

Plants that seem withered and dead during dry spells spring to life after rain. False heather jumps to life under moist conditions. Looking something like a small cedar, the heather's yellow flowers coat the ocean side of dunes. Because it grows low to the ground and spreads, heather helps stabilize the sand.

Down on the beach, sanderlings dart hither-and-dither, first chased by a crashing wave, only to turn and pursue it back into the ocean. This small bird pecks at the spongy sand, digging deep for shellfish. During the summer as many as thirty million clam larvae will occupy one square meter of surf. There are snails beneath the sand, too, and small crabs and worms. At nighttime, sandhoppers (small crabs) emerge from holes by the thousands to pick food from shells and seaweed coughed up by waves.

Luminescent and quick, the sandhopper has startled more than a few nighttime beach strollers. Rest assured, by the time you've figured out it's an animal and not a ghost, the critter is out of harm's way. It digs a hole in the sand at a speed of 6 feet in ten minutes, putting it well out of reach of prying eyes and bird beaks.

Given this diversity and complexity, it's worth considering how the wilds of False Cape and Back Bay might have developed were it not for the park and refuge. A few miles up the beach, Virginia Beach's boardwalk teems with humans on hot summer days. Sunbathers, surfers, and beach strollers crowd miles of white Atlantic beach. The city spends millions to preserve this, fighting nature with "beach replenishment projects," a process of pumping sand from offshore back onto shore.

The process they're fighting is the gradual drift of barrier islands (and our eastern coast, generally) to the south and west. Left to its own devices, the white sands of Virginia Beach would, in a couple hundred years, move, shifting south along the coast in the fashion of all barrier islands. Scientists call this *littoral drift*. Each wave picks up sand and transports it down the shoreline. A calm day or two will see tons of sand displaced. A hurricane or nor'easter will move those same tons in a few hours. The inlet below Ocean City, Maryland, which separates that resort town from Assateague Island, was carved by a single hurricane in 1933.

There was no dramatic event responsible for Back Bay and False Cape. In the 1800s some 300 people lived in the Wash Woods, a section of False Cape State Park. They fished for a living, and a few raised livestock and farmed. (Interestingly, Wash Woods settlers were survivors of a shipwreck off the coast; their first homes and church were built from what they could salvage from the ship.) Like the island itself, they lived at the mercy of the ocean. Over hundreds of years, farmland turned to marsh. Sand replaced fertile soil. Soon, sportsmen outnumbered inhabitants, and hotels and sporting clubs sprang up. Four-legged game was slim pickings. The waterfowl, on the other hand, were plentiful.

It can be taken as a sign of progress, then, that over time Virginia has moved from hunting wildfowl on this small barrier island to protecting them. Like other barrier islands up and down the East Coast, this island hosts neotropical birds migrating to Central and South America. Waterfowl nest here. In September, vireos, yellowthroats, and warblers arrive. By October, yellow-rumped warblers have alighted to spend winter. In all, bird spotters have recorded 288 bird species in the Back Bay refuge.

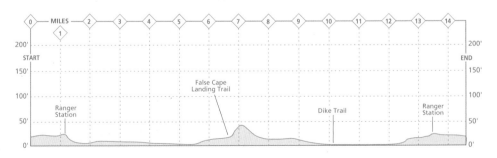

(This is typical of barrier islands lining the East Coast; Chincoteague National Wildlife Refuge on Virginia's Eastern Shore lists 300 bird species spotted.)

On these slivers of sand, the equivalent of an interstate highway rest stop, birds find the amenities they need: nesting spots, food, and, quite frankly, a spot to rest weary wings. And they seem to be more than willing to share it with hikers.

Miles and Directions

0.0   Start at Little Island Park. Walk to the south end of the parking lot. At a picnic pavilion, turn toward the beach and surf.

1.5   Hike straight along the beach, past a boardwalk that leads up into the dunes on the right. **Note:** The boardwalk leads to a Back Bay NWR ranger station and visitor center.

4.7   Reach the boundary of False Cape State Park. Continue straight on the beach.

5.0   A beach path leads right up into the dunes toward Barbour Hill primitive campsites and the state park's contact station, a turn-off marked by a small metal post with a yellow tent. From this junction, it is 0.7 mile across the island to the contact station. **Note:** If you are continuing farther down the beach, Barbour Hill is your last chance to supply drinking water; it is near the contact station and near the two camping areas there.

6.7   Turn right onto False Cape Landing Trail. **Note:** If you're walking in the surf far below the dune line, keep an eye peeled for a sign reading False Cape Landing Trail. There are primitive campsites in dunes after you turn onto the trail.

7.1   Turn right onto False Cape Main Trail, a wide dirt road. The ocean is now on your right, out of sight over the dunes. Back Bay is on your left. **Note:** Straight on False Cape Landing Trail, there is a boat landing in 0.3 mile, as well as bay-side campsites.

8.4   False Cape Main Trail arcs right at a junction with South Inlet Trail. Follow the road right. **Note:** South Inlet Trail leads left for 0.4 mile to a sheltered reach of water with scenic views.

9.0   Turn left onto Barbour Hill Beach Trail. There is a ranger station on the right side of the road. Past the ranger station, turn right onto Barbour Hill Interpretive Trail.

9.6   Pass an observation deck on the right side of the trail.

9.8   Leave False Cape State Park and enter Back Bay National Wildlife Refuge. Turn left onto the Dike Trail, which is a gravel and dirt road that runs alongside wildlife impoundments, large pools of water that attract waterfowl and migrating birds. This hike follows the western leg of the Dike Trail.

10.1   Where the trail forks, bear right onto the Dike Trail. **Note:** The left-bearing trail is a short spur to the bay.

10.9   Hike straight past a road that turns right and leads between two impoundments.

11.4   Follow the trail as it jogs left then right and continues its northward route. A road branches right, leading between impoundments. Within 0.2 mile, hike past a third road that branches right.

13.2   The Dike Trail merges with its eastern leg. Continue on past a pool on the right side of the trail.

13.4   Reach the Back Bay visitor center and ranger station. At the station, turn right onto the Seaside Trail boardwalk.

13.5   Descend off the boardwalk and dune and turn left. Head north along the beach.

14.7   Arrive back at Little Island Park.

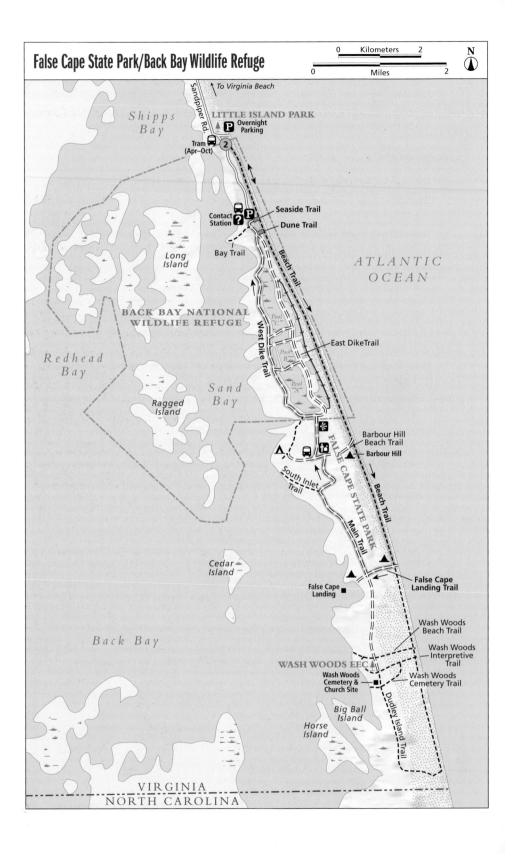

False Cape State Park/Back Bay Wildlife Refuge

Kilometers 0 — 2

Miles 0 — 2

N

To Virginia Beach

Shipps Bay

Sandpiper Rd

LITTLE ISLAND PARK

P Overnight Parking

Tram (Apr–Oct) 2

Contact Station

Seaside Trail

Dune Trail

Bay Trail

Long Island

Beach Trail

ATLANTIC OCEAN

BACK BAY NATIONAL WILDLIFE REFUGE

West Dike Trail

Redhead Bay

Pool "C"

East Dike Trail

Pool "B"

Sand Bay

Pool "A"

Ragged Island

Barbour Hill Beach Trail

Barbour Hill

FALSE CAPE STATE PARK

South Inlet Trail

Beach Trail

Cedar Island

Main Trail

False Cape Landing Trail

False Cape Landing

Back Bay

Wash Woods Beach Trail

Wash Woods Interpretive Trail

WASH WOODS EEC

Wash Woods Cemetery & Church Site

Wash Woods Cemetery Trail

Dudley Island Trail

Big Ball Island

Horse Island

VIRGINIA

NORTH CAROLINA

Hike Information

Local Information

Virginia Beach Convention & Visitors Bureau, (800) VA-BEACH (822-3224), www
.visitvirginiabeach.com

Local Events / Attractions

Winter Wildlife Festival, Jan, False Cape State Park, (757) 426-7128

Pungo Strawberry Festival, May, Virginia Beach, (757) 721-6001, www.pungo
strawberryfestival.info

The Virginia Aquarium & Marine Science Center, Virginia Beach, (757) 385-
FISH, www.virginiaaquarium.com. More than 800,000 gallons of aquariums with
sharks, sea turtles, and dolphins.

Lodging

There are 4 backcountry campgrounds with a total of 12 sites in False Cape State
Park. The closest is a 6.9-mile walk from Little Island Park, where campers must park.
*Campers must bring their own containers to transport water from the water sources, which are
all located in the Barbour Hill area of the park.* Water not suitable for drinking is available
in each camping area. There are also toilets. Camping is permitted for 4 to 6 people
per site. Call (800) 933-7275 for a reservation; same-day reservations are not accepted.

Restaurants

Virginia Beach has literally hundreds of restaurants. For a unique locals spot, close to
this hike, check out Blue Pete's Seafood & Steak Restaurant, Muddy Creek Road,
Pungo, (757) 426-2278. Specialties include fresh seafood, sweet potato biscuits, and
homemade desserts.

Tours

False Cape State Park conducts canoe, hiking, birding, and astronomy tours; call (757)
426-7128.

3 First Landing State Park

The ultimate surf-and-turf park, First Landing State Park is great for a tan—and far less crowded than the Atlantic beaches a few miles south. The "surf" is the mouth of the Chesapeake Bay, where it flows into the Atlantic Ocean; the "turf" is a landward trail network through an ecosystem that mixes southern plants with northern, temperate species. Spend an afternoon here among bald cypress swamps decked with Spanish moss, towering loblolly pines, and salt marsh. High, forested dunes offer great views of the water. Boardwalks take you safely through blackwater swamps, but at high tide be prepared to get your feet wet and muddy on more remote trails.

Start: Visitor center off Shore Drive

Distance: 6.5-mile loop

Hiking time: 2-3 hours

Difficulty: Easy due to flat terrain and a well-marked trail, with some difficult stretches along eroded trails and wet riverside routes

Trail surface: Dune trails, gravel roads, and boardwalks lead through marsh, beach, cypress swamp, and forested dunes with views of the bay

Land status: State park

Nearest town: Virginia Beach, VA

Other trail users: Cyclists, bird watchers, and joggers

Accessibility: The Chesapeake Bay Center and Trail Center are accessible, with accessible restrooms. The first loop of the Bald Cypress Trail has accessible boardwalks and bridges. There are paved walkways to the beach, and a beach wheelchair is available.

Canine compatibility: Leashed dogs permitted (leashes no longer than 6 feet)

Trail contact: First Landing State Park, 2500 Shore Dr., Virginia Beach; (757) 412-2300; www.dcr.virginia.gov/state_parks/fir.shtml. For camping reservations, call (800) 933-PARK or visit www.reserveamerica.com.

Schedule: Open year-round, 8 a.m. to dusk. The Trail Center and Chesapeake Bay Visitor Center are open Apr through Nov.

Fees/permits: Admission is free, but there is a parking fee.

Facilities/features: Environmental educational and trail centers, full-service campground and cabins, concessions at the Bay Store (groceries, snacks, camping supplies), beach (no lifeguards), picnic shelters, and boat launch

Maps: USGS Cape Henry; state park maps available at www.virginiaoutdoors.com

Finding the trailhead: From Norfolk, take exit 282 (Northampton Boulevard/US 13) off I-64 and drive 4.5 miles north on US 13. Follow signs for US 60 East (Shore Drive) and drive 4.5 miles on US 60 to the park entrance. At the traffic light at the park entrance, turn right into the park and follow the main park road straight into the parking lot for the Trail Center, where you can get information on park trails and what you can expect to see. Turn left at the light to reach the park office, camping, cabins, and the Chesapeake Bay Visitor Center. GPS: N36 54.916' / W75 02.485'. *DeLorme: Virginia Atlas & Gazetteer:* Page 35, A6.

The Hike

The 6th and 20th of April, about four o'clock in the morning, we described the land of Virginia . . . There we landed and discovered a little way, but we could find nothing worth the speaking of, but fair meadows and goodly tall trees, with such fresh waters running through the woods as I almost ravished at the first sight thereof.

So wrote George Percy, a Jamestown settler, recounting his first steps on North American soil in 1607. After a rough few days at sea, terra firma no doubt thrilled Percy's group, even if the landscape did not. They would name this point Cape Henry, christening forever present-day Virginia Beach's northernmost tip, where the Chesapeake Bay meets the Atlantic Ocean. Today the land inland from Cape Henry Lighthouse and Fort Story is called First Landing State Park, in their honor. Here hikers will find riches Percy and company found commonplace: maritime forest and southern swamp and beach ecology, all preserved for a walker's enjoyment.

By Percy's account, the landing at Cape Henry was rough. Native Americans attacked and two men were injured, one fatally. It was an inauspicious welcome that might have chased lesser men back to the Caribbean. There, at least, they had enjoyed hot spring baths, fish, and fowl to their satisfaction.

But these privateers, commissioned by the England-based Virginia Company, had other plans. Explorations by foot carried them inland from Cape Henry, through

A quiet shoreline in First Landing State Park within Virginia's most populous city, Virginia Beach.

land entangled in vines as thick as a man's thigh. They chased Native Americans off a pile of oysters roasting in a fire, and tasted a delicacy that would someday make the Chesapeake Bay famous around the world. By boat, they continued into the lower Chesapeake Bay and traveled to Hampton, Virginia, which they dubbed Point Comfort, met up with Kecoughtan Indians, and, instead of fighting, exchanged gifts.

When it came time to leave, the explorers staked a small cross to mark Cape Henry. Left behind were the "fair meadows and goodly tall trees," and for one reason or another, this coastal area never saw permanent settlement (save the military reservation occupying land around the lighthouse). As colonial Virginia grew in the 1600s, fishermen claimed it as common ground, launched boats, built small shelters, and laid out nets. In 1936 the state created Seashore State Park here. It was renamed First Landing in 1996.

What has been preserved? An ecology that mixes subtropical and temperate-zone plants for a species diversity one would normally find farther south. Loblolly, eastern, and pitch pines tower 100 feet and higher. Broad bald cypress stand in oily blackwater swamps, their small knees poking through primordial-like ooze. White sand dunes topped with clingy grasses. And bones. Archeologists unearthed remains of twenty-six Chesapean Indians here, predecessors of the Kecoughtan tribe that attacked Percy's group. The Smithsonian Institute housed the artifacts until 1998, when they were returned and reburied in a ceremonial mound near the park's visitor center.

You can start on an incredibly diverse hike at the Trail Center parking lot. The Bald Cypress/Long Creek/Osprey Trail loop takes you from cypress swamp through tidal marsh, bayside beach, dune forest, and back to swamp. Bring your binoculars. In one afternoon you're likely to see osprey nests, snowy egrets, and great blue herons.

On Bald Cypress Trail, Spanish moss hangs from the cypress. (This is the northernmost reach of the moss, a parasitic plant.) Larger specimens of this tree may date from 500 years ago. Around it, water lilies float on still water that reflects rainbow patterns—not from pollution, but from oils secreted by trees. It's possible, park interpreters say, that Captain John Smith and others replenished their casks of water here for a long return trip to England. The water, which colonists say tasted like strong ice tea, was so tannic, it could last six to eight weeks at sea.

Long Creek Trail takes you to the edge of Broad Bay and a view of large homes on the opposite bank—reminders of development this park escaped. Virginia Beach

First Landing's beach offers more than sunbathing, and summer isn't the only time to visit. Bird watchers with binoculars flock to Cape Henry in winter for views of Northern gannets that winter offshore in the mid-Atlantic region. During feeding, gannets tuck their wings and narrow themselves for a plunge of 100 feet or more into ocean depths. Also here, the chicken turtle ranks as a critically endangered species in Virginia, with five or fewer known to be in existence.

is the state's most populated city; First Landing is the state park system's most visited, attracting more than one million visitors annually. Yet it can handle the load. Solid trails built by Civilian Conservation Corps crews are well maintained, a considerable feat given the constant erosion. It helps that most people hike short interpretive trails near the visitor center, or hike and bike the wide Cape Henry Trail.

Hikers will find quieter moments on the hiker-only Long Creek Trail. Where the trail skirts White Hill Lake—more of a marsh than a true lake—American egrets and great blue herons wade in relative peace. Look for an osprey's huge nest atop dead loblolly and oak trees at the junction with the Osprey Trail. You might see muskrat and mink lodges in the tidal marshes. (You can identify muskrats by their flat, naked-looking tail.) If you're hiking early in the morning, sit for a while on the shore of Long Creek, near shallow or marshy water. A slick head will break the water's surface, swivel left and right, then disappear beneath the water. Each time it surfaces, it emits a hasping noise, as if it's clearing its nostrils. The muskrat survives primarily on aquatic vegetation, but its morning feeding ritual may yield clams, frogs, or an occasional fish.

Back on the trail, look for the partridgeberry, a trailing evergreen common in the park. The white pairs of tubular flowers bloom in June and July; the red berries and shiny green leaves are visible all winter. Curiously, partridges don't eat them, but Native American women drank a partridgeberry tea during the last weeks of pregnancy to lessen the pain of childbirth.

You can link again with Long Creek Trail by hanging a left at the end of Osprey Trail. This section gains a little elevation as you hike giant sand dunes covered with vegetation. It's the primary landform in the park—and it's constantly shifting, if ever so slowly.

Heads up: In warm months be prepared for ticks, mosquitoes, and snakes. During high tide, portions of the Osprey Trail may be messy, or even impassable. Be sure to stay on the trails, and ignore the bushwhacked side trails.

Miles and Directions

0.0   Start from the Trail Center parking lot. Walk down a wide gravel path that parallels the park entrance road. Walk straight past a footpath that breaks left and is a shortcut to the Cape Henry Trail.

0.05   Turn left onto the Cape Henry Trail, a wide multiuse trail is popular with bicyclists and joggers.

0.08   Turn right onto Bald Cypress Trail. The fence across the trailhead indicates this is a hiker-only trail.

0.1   Across the trail lies a nurse log, noteworthy for the shoots growing from the mossy, rotted lumber—shoots growing into small trees themselves. On your left is a sand dune thick with holly and pine. To your right is a cypress swamp. The chicken turtle (*Deitrochelys reticularia*), an endangered species, lives here, as do more common frogs and wading birds.

0.15   An unmarked path climbs the dune on your left. This is the first of many unmarked trails that spread like a spider web throughout the park. Hiking them might provide adventure, but it also contributes to erosion. Stay on the marked trails.

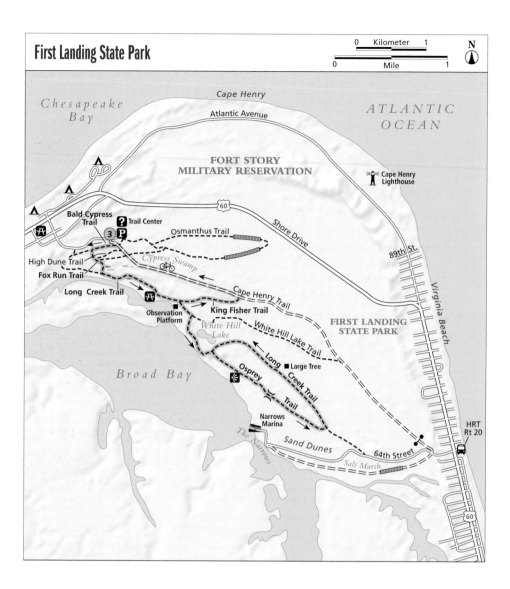

0   Kilometer   1

0   Mile   1

N

Chesapeake Bay

Cape Henry

Atlantic Avenue

ATLANTIC OCEAN

FORT STORY MILITARY RESERVATION

Cape Henry Lighthouse

60

Bald Cypress Trail

Trail Center

Osmanthus Trail

Shore Drive

89th St.

Cypress Swamp

High Dune Trail

Fox Run Trail

Long Creek Trail

Cape Henry Trail

King Fisher Trail

Observation Platform

White Hill Lake

White Hill Lake Trail

FIRST LANDING STATE PARK

Virginia Beach

Broad Bay

Long ■ Large Tree

Osprey Creek Trail

Trail

Narrows Marina

Sand Dunes

64th Street

HRT Rt 20

The Narrows

Salt Marsh

60

0.2 The Bald Cypress Trail makes a hard left. Climb five wooden steps, then turn left onto the Fox Run Trail. **Note:** A right turn leads to the park entrance road.

0.6 Cross a sand dune and come to a T intersection with the Long Creek Trail. Turn left onto Long Creek Trail.

0.7 Pass by a wide opening in the trees and underbrush with views onto Broad Bay.

0.8 Ignore two unmarked trails that split left off the Long Creek Trail. Long Creek Trail follows the riverside, separated from water by only marsh grass.

1.1 Top out on a sand dune with views over Broad Bay. This is a good spot for a picnic.

1.35 Stay straight on Long Creek Trail as King Fisher Trail enters on the left.

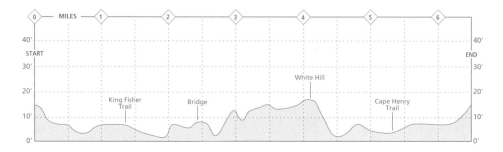

1.4 An observation deck on the right side of the trail allows for great views over the tidal wetlands that buffer Broad Bay. This structure marks the beginning of a series of boardwalks spanning sensitive habitat.

1.5 At a fork in the trail, bear right on Long Creek Trail. Cross a concrete spillway and skirt the south side of White Hill Lake.

1.8 Begin a brief steep climb to the top of the "white hill" sand dunes that lend the lake its name. Broad Bay is to the right.

2.0 Turn right and descend on the Osprey Trail. **Note:** The Osprey Trail skirts the water's edge. During high tide, it may be washed out. In all cases, prepare for wet hiking.

2.4 Cross a small wooden bridge.

2.7 Trail leaves behind its wet portions and climbs onto a low, wooded finger of land bounded by marsh.

3.1 Turn left onto Long Creek Trail.

4.3 Pass the Osprey Trail on the left.

4.5 Turn right onto King Fisher Trail. **Note:** Numerous unmarked paths lead off in different directions from this trail. Use the white blazes to keep you on track.

5.1 On the hillside to your left, notice the series of enormous loblolly pines. This species is a valuable commercial lumber. Native Americans called it the *loblolly*—meaning "mud puddle"—for the environment in which it grows well.

5.4 Turn left onto Cape Henry Trail.

6.3 A portion of the Bald Cypress Trail crosses the Cape Henry Trail. Continue straight on the Cape Henry Trail.

6.45 Reach the junction with the parking lot access trail. Turn right to return to the parking lot.

6.5 Arrive back at the parking lot.

Hike Information

Local Information

Virginia Beach Convention & Visitors Bureau, (800) VA-BEACH (822-3224), www.visitvirginiabeach.com

Local Events/Attractions

March for the Parks, held at the park in spring, (757) 412-2300. Hikers obtain pledges to help support trail maintenance.

Paddlefest, the area's biggest paddle sports event of the year, takes place at the park in mid-Sept.

The Chesapeake Bay Center (located on the Chesapeake Bay side of the park), (757) 412-2316. The center was completed in 1999 and houses exhibits on the First Landing in 1607, natural resource displays, the park's visitor information, and a Virginia Beach tourism information office.

Lodging

The park has 188 campsites, open Mar to Nov or Dec, depending on the weather. The 20 cabins are open year-round. For reservations and information, call (800) 933-7275 or visit www.reserveamerica.com.

Organizations

Friends of First Landing, Virginia Beach, (757) 412-2300

4 York River State Park

The worm-eating warbler, common to Virginia's Blue Ridge province, is also found in the coastal environment of York River State Park. After walking through the park's forests, thick with mountain laurel and holly, shaded by chestnut oaks and American beech, hikers will agree with the songbird: This park feels a lot like Virginia's mountain regions. Most paths here lead through mature hardwood forests to overlooks onto the York River. Land underfoot holds evidence—pottery shards, arrowheads—of settlement dating from tens of thousands of years ago. Perhaps the park's most interesting story is still being recorded—that of the Taskinas Creek Estuary, a vital marsh and hardwood swamp monitored by scientists as a gauge of the Chesapeake Bay's health.

Start: Park contact and fee station
Distance: 7.7-mile loop
Hiking time: 1-4 hours
Difficulty: Easy due to flat terrain, well-marked trails, and options for shorter hikes
Trail surface: Wooded paths, boardwalks, and gravel and dirt roads lead through marsh, fields, hardwood swamps, and upland forests.
Land status: State park
Nearest town: Williamsburg, VA
Other trail users: Cyclists and equestrians
Accessibility: Paved paths along native plant arboretum to canoe dock, 0.5-mile path around day-use area, and 0.75-mile ADA backwoods trail

Canine compatibility: Leashed dogs permitted (leashes no longer than 6 feet)
Trail contact: York River State Park, 5526 Riverview Rd., Williamsburg; (757) 566-3036; dcr.virginia.gov/state_parks/yor.shtml
Schedule: Open daily year-round, 8 a.m. to dusk. The visitor center is open year-round, but the visitor center office operates on a limited schedule from Nov to Mar.
Fees/permits: Per-vehicle entrance fee
Facilities/features: Visitor center, concessions, gift shop, ADA restrooms, picnic shelters, boat launch, and kayak and canoe rentals on a 7-acre pond and on Taskinas Creek
Maps: USGS Gressitt; state park maps available at www.virginiaoutdoors.com

Finding the trailhead: From I-64, take the Croaker exit 231B and go 1.2 miles north on Croaker Road/VA 607. Turn right onto VA 606—also called Riverview Road—and drive 1.7 miles to VA 696. Turn left onto VA 696 (York River Park Road). The fee station is in 2 miles. Parking lots for the visitor center, picnic area, and trails are just beyond the fee station. GPS: N37 24.718' / W76 42.847'. *DeLorme: Virginia Atlas & Gazetteer:* Page 50, A1.

The Hike

Offshore of Taskinas Creek Trail, salt marsh cordgrass sways with a stiff breeze. On the creek's muddy flats, spotted sandpipers and black-bellied plovers dart in earnest pursuit of food. A cluster of fiddler crabs scuttle for shelter. As you climb away from the creek on a trail beneath oak and beech trees, a great blue heron, startled, lumbers toward open water, letting loose a *gaaak* as a parting shot.

Boardwalk across tidal marsh at York River State Park.

How much, you might wonder, can these scenes differ from those of 300 years ago? The Native Americans of eastern Virginia were a riverine people; their lives revolved around what the rivers provided. Men hunted meadow and wood for white-tailed deer, turkey, and other prey, but the water provided all things necessary for life: food; fertile soil; shells for ornaments, tools, and trading; reeds for mats and baskets; and even transportation. At low tide, women foraged in freshwater marsh for arrow arum, whose root, tuckahoe, is edible when boiled. Thick-stemmed saltwort, pickled or preserved, made a tasty delicacy.

English settlers called it a "hand-to-mouth" existence, and yet their survival, too, depended on it. On a monthly—sometimes biweekly—basis, Native Americans sent gifts of food to the James Island fort in 1607–8, sustaining settlers during spring "starving times," when the previous fall's harvest had run out and new forest growth made hunting more difficult. When English farmers spread beyond fort walls onto the James/York River Peninsula, they found why the Native Americans could afford generosity: Chiskiack Indians planted maize, beans, and squash among burned tree stumps, remnants of field clearing. It was a high-yield, if not terribly efficient, farming system.

York River State Park's Powhatan Forks Trail crosses high peninsula meadows, then enters the shade of hardwood forest. A person who has spent time in Virginia's mountain woods may sense something familiar. The trees—chestnut oak, American beech, green ash—and a forest understory of mountain laurel, holly, and berry-producing shrubs thrive here thanks to soil conditions normally found in western Virginia. York River State Park soil contains marl, a limestone-heavy clay similar to soils of the Shenandoah Valley. Elsewhere in the park, the Yorktown rock formation sinks as deep as 150 feet or more underfoot. This is a calcium-rich soil, thick with deposits of ancient seashell and sand. Prehistoric seas washed over Virginia's coastal region several times. Erosion along the York River constantly churns up fossils pointing to past aquatic life. Unearthing five-million-year-old shells and whalebones is not an uncommon occurrence here.

Where the north branch of Powhatan Forks Trail drops into a marshy area, an expansive view of the river opens up. This approach is much gentler than the Riverview Trail's abrupt ending on high river bluffs a half mile downstream, yet both permit an unobstructed view of Purtan Bay on the opposite shore. Captain John Smith, hoping to save a struggling colony, took in a similar vista in the fall of 1608. (Today, homes dot that far shoreline and recreation boats bob in the water.) In Captain Smith's time, Purtan Bay was one home of Powhatan, chief of the eastern Native American empire that bore his name. His tribe, the Werowocomoco, built huts along the shallow bay and its three tributaries and used fragile bridges strung across tidal flats as links with each other.

In what must have been an embarrassing moment for the adventurous John Smith, he and a party of men crossed the York River to meet Powhatan, but landed in the wrong spot. Some men disembarked and tried crossing a stream by way of a bridge made of forked stakes and planks. It defeated the heavily clad men, and the Werowocomoco ferried them, a few at a time, across the creek. Later, after negotiating for corn, Smith and company tried returning to their ship, but his canoe ran aground on a mud flat. Powhatan's men trudged out to retrieve them; Smith asked instead for

Big cordgrass in a tidal marsh along the York River.

"some wood, fire, and mats to cover me." He spent the night thusly, waiting for the tide to return and float his boat off its hang-up.

Despite initial feebleness, the expanding colony soon had Powhatan's empire in retreat. Nathaniel Bacon Jr., a settler, led a group of armed, discontented landowners against the Native Americans in the summer of 1676. Miffed by the colonial governor William Berkeley's inability to keep Indian raiders in check, Bacon's men soon hounded the governor into hiding. Given virtually free reign, Bacon used outposts throughout the Tidewater to launch attacks. As a result, travelers today will see his name attached to innumerable homes, old forts, back roads, and "hideaways" throughout the region. York River State Park is no different. Near the park stands the Stonehouse site, a seventeenth-century military outpost during Bacon's Rebellion, now listed on the National Register of Historic Places. The Occoneechee tribe fell in May 1676, and the Pamunkey fell in August of that same year.

Bacon died of natural causes in October 1676 and Berkeley regained control of the Virginia colony. In February 1677, English settlers and Native Americans struck the Treaty of Middle Plantation. Besides war reparations—prisoners, land, weapons, tools— the treaty made remnants of a once-powerful Indian empire formal subjects to the king of England. It called for an annual tribute of three arrows and twenty beaver pelts in exchange for reservation land near West Point. More than 300 years later, the Treaty of Middle Plantation remains in force. Each autumn, Mattaponi (matta-PO-ni) and Pamunkey Indians trek to the governor's mansion to pay their rent for reservation land—a deer strung on a pole, with tribesmen dressed in full regalia supporting either end of the stick.

Miles and Directions

0.0 Start from the park contact and fee station. Follow a paved path alongside the park entrance road. In a few hundred feet, this paved path becomes a gravel-lined two-track path as it enters woods. There is a yellow sign on the right for the Backbone Trail. **Note:** Park trail maps identify this stretch as combined Backbone Trail/Woodstock Pond Trail.

0.16 Pass the Beaver Trail on the left. **Option:** Beaver Trail is a 0.6-mile alternative for circling Woodstock Pond. It ends near the York River at a junction with Woodstock Pond Trail. Use Beaver Trail to complete a shorter loop around the pond that will return you to the park visitor center.

0.4 At the junction of Woodstock Pond Trail, turn right on Backbone Trail, a hard-packed dirt road that runs 1.4 miles to the park's south boundary. Both cyclists and hikers use this trail. The Meh-Te-Kos bridle path (for horses) intersects it at numerous points. **Option:** Following Woodstock Pond Trail left leads to return to the visitor center in 0.8 mile.

1.2 Walk past the Pamunkey Trail, which branches left off Backbone Trail. **Note:** At this intersection, a power line cuts across Backbone Trail. Stick to the roadway bearing right.

1.4 Continue straight on Backbone Trail past a junction on the left for Powhatan Forks Trail.

1.6 Arrive at junction with Riverview and White-Tail Trails on the left. Veer left onto White-Tail Trail. (There's a picnic table here.)

1.65 Turn right onto Dogwood Lane Trail, a rutted narrow dirt road flanked by mountain laurel on the high-banked dirt roadsides.

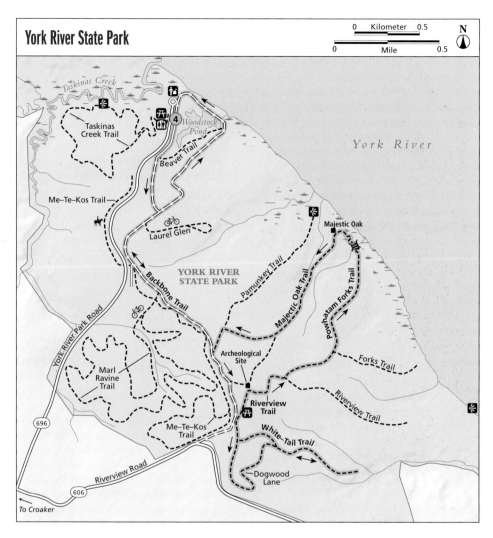

York River State Park

0   Kilometer   0.5

0   Mile   0.5

N

Taskinas Creek

Taskinas Creek Trail

Woodstock Pond

Beaver Trail

Me–Te–Kos Trail

York River

Laurel Glen

Majestic Oak

YORK RIVER STATE PARK

Backbone Trail

Pamunkey Trail

Majestic Oak Trail

Powhatan Forks Trail

York River Park Road

Marl Ravine Trail

Archeological Site

Forks Trail

Riverview Trail

696

Me–Te–Kos Trail

Riverview Trail

White-Tail Trail

Dogwood Lane

Riverview Road

606

To Croaker

2.0   Stay on Dogwood Lane Trail as a service road veers right. From here, Dogwood continues as a singletrack path through heavy woods flush with turkeys, pheasants, and deer.

2.4   Bear right onto White-Tail Trail.

2.8   White-Tail Trail ends in a large clearing that has limited winter and spring views of the York River. Turn around and retrace your steps along White-Tail Trail.

3.2   Continue straight on White-Tail Trail past a junction with Dogwood Trail on the left.

3.5   White-Tail Trail junctions with Riverview and Backbone Trails. Veer right onto Riverview Trail, which is a wide, sandy two-track woods path.

3.7   Approach an open clearing and a junction with Powhatan Forks Trail. Continue on Riverview Trail, which bears right into the woods. A trail sign here notes that it is 1.27 miles to the end of Riverview at the York River. **Note:** The clearing is a former archeological dig site.

3.9   Bear right onto Powhatan Forks Trail at a Y-shaped junction. The trail here is a mowed path.

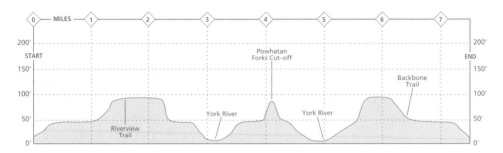

4.1 Powhatan Forks Trail splits left and right. Bear left on the North Branch Powhatan Forks Trail. The trail gradually descends to the York River through a forest lush with mountain laurel and American holly trees.

4.7 A wide spot on the North Branch Powhatan Forks Trail features views of the York River and a wood bench for resting. Follow the trail as it descends off the hillside to a boardwalk across a river marsh.

4.9 On the opposite side of the boardwalk, climb the stream bank to another overview of the York River and turn left onto the Majestic Oak Trail.

5.5 Bear right on Spurr Trail.

5.7 Turn left on Pamunkey Trail.

5.8 Turn right onto Backbone Trail.

6.7 Backbone Trail bends left to return to the park contact and fee station. Continue straight on Woodstock Pond Trail.

7.5 Ascend on Woodstock Pond Trail and follow a path as it bends left through the field and past the visitor center.

7.7 Arrive back at the state park contact and fee station.

Hike Information

Local Information

Williamsburg Area Destination Marketing Committee, (888) 882-4156, www.visit williamsburg.com

Local Events / Attractions

Estuaries Day, late Sept. Displays, demonstrations, boat tours, and other programs centered around Taskinas Creek. Contact the park for specific dates and times.

Ghost Trail Hayrides are held in the park in the fall.

Tours

Moonlight canoe trips are offered in the park May through Oct.

Organizations

Friends of York River State Park, Williamsburg, (757) 566-3036, www.friendsofyork riverstatepark.org

5 Belle Isle State Park

Since colonial times, farmers have tilled the fields of Belle Isle; parts of this state park are farmed even today. Bird watchers, hikers, horseback riders, and cyclists in the mood for wide-open spaces find this an ideal destination. Trails trace cornfields, cross tidal marshes, and wind through pine and hardwood filter strips—ribbons of woodland that separate fields from sensitive wetlands. Well-marked and easy to follow, trails feature interpretive boards explaining Chesapeake Bay ecology. Depending on the season, there's a better-than-average chance of spotting a bald eagle or two, flocks of wintering tundra swans, and in summer, maybe a dolphin cruising the wide Rappahannock.

Start: Mud Creek boat launch parking lot
Distance: 3.3 miles out and back
Hiking time: About 1 hour
Difficulty: Easy due to flat terrain, short distance, and well-marked trails
Trail surface: Gravel roads and dirt woodland paths through farmland, marsh, and swamp-fringe forest leading to river views
Land status: State park
Nearest town: Lancaster, VA
Other trail users: Cyclists and equestrians
Accessibility: Many of the park's trails are gravel, so wheelchairs may be able to use them with assistance. The 1,000-foot boardwalk, observation deck, and fishing pier are accessible.

Canine compatibility: Leashed dogs permitted (leashes no longer than 6 feet)
Trail contact: Belle Isle State Park, 1632 Belle Isle Rd., Lancaster; (804) 462-5030; www.dcr.virginia.gov/state_parks/bel.shtml. For camping and guesthouse reservations, call (800) 933-PARK or visit www.reserveamerica.com.
Schedule: Open year-round, sunrise to sunset. Campground open Mar 1 to the first Mon in Dec.
Fees/permits: Parking fee
Facilities/features: Boat ramp, canoe/kayak launch, and rentals for motorboats, canoes, kayaks, and bikes.
Map: USGS Lively

Finding the trailhead: From Lancaster Courthouse, take VA 3 west for 3 miles and turn left onto White Chapel Rd/VA 201 in the village of Lively. Drive 3.2 miles and turn right onto River Road/VA 354 at St. Mary's White Chapel. Head west for 3.2 miles and turn left onto Bell Isle Road/VA 683. The park office is 2 miles down the road. Turn right to the cartop launch parking area. The Mud Creek Trail starts on the wood's edge, behind a trail board. GPS: N37 46.931' / W76 36.203'. *DeLorme: Virginia Atlas & Gazetteer:* Page 60, B2.

The Hike

On a cold, moonless winter night, a boat circles in the black mist rising off the Rappahannock River. A bushel basket floats upside down in the water and underneath it, a light flickers. The pilot deftly navigates while two shadows operate a dredge. There's a sureness in their movements, though hardly a word passes between them.

Still, it's hard to stay hidden. Wind carries sounds ashore. A spotlight blasts through the fog, freezing the crew in its bright gaze. Momentarily stunned, the men snap to

The author reads an interpretive sign at Belle Isle State Park.

attention. Harsh words drift out of the darkness: "Cut your engines." Instead, the pilot revs his motor and swings toward deep water. Noise and wind drown out the *snap, snap, snap* of rifle shots. Nighttime swallows the poachers and their stash of oysters.

On land, the spotlight refocuses on the abandoned bushel basket; the wide beam also illuminates tall, skinny sticks marking an oyster bed. The light stays trained on this spot until dawn. A watchman, awake and alert, sits in a house on shore, rifle across his knee, ready for the next raider.

Starting after the Civil War, turning violent first in the 1880s and 1890s, and again in the 1940s and 1950s, the oyster wars of the Chesapeake Bay pitted Virginia and Maryland watermen against each other, vying for what was then the Chesapeake Bay's most sought-after resource. Along the Northern Neck and Eastern Shore, in alleys and saloons of tough water towns such as Crisfield, Maryland, and Colonial Beach, Virginia, Marylanders fought Virginians over the oyster. In the shallow waters of the Eastern Shore sounds, tongers—watermen who collected oysters using long-handled tongs—resisted dredgers, whose large scoops raped the bay bottom, and everyone, it seemed, fought the marine police, whose vigilance ebbed and flowed like the ocean tides—strict and trigger happy one moment, indifferent the next.

Belle Isle State Park, in Lancaster County on Virginia's Northern Neck, was—if not a hot spot in this war—a lukewarm spot, at least. On this spit of land, Thomas Powell staked out the original 500 acres for a farm and plantation in 1650. The period marked a population boom of sorts for the Northern Neck. In the 1650s settlers were gobbling up land on this northernmost of Virginia's peninsulas. Ancestors of three presidents—George Washington, James Monroe, and James Madison—settled farther up this strip during this period. Farms soon became plantations, modest homes turned into manor houses, and Belle Isle thrived as a tobacco-producing estate, with cotton, flax, wheat, and corn grown as well.

Yet Belle Isle's envious perch on the Rappahannock River could not be ignored. Native Americans called the Rappahannock the "quick-rising" river. Narrow and shallow, its brackish mix of salt water and freshwater extends upriver for miles, making it ideal for growing oysters—especially in tidal flats at the mouth of Mulberry and Deep Creeks, which create Belle Isle's distinctive landform.

Watermen jealously guarded these beds. For good reason, too. By one estimate, as many as 170 poachers operated in the Chesapeake Bay in the 1940s and 1950s. Worsening matters, after decades of overharvesting, oyster production was in decline. At a peak in 1880, watermen caught 125 million pounds of oysters. By 1958–59, a mere 4 million bushels were harvested. (There was a temporary rebound in the late 1970s, when the harvest jumped to 25 million pounds, but numbers dropped to 138,000 pounds by 1998.) Scarcity drove up price; suppliers paid $3.25 a bushel in 1958–59 (up from 60 cents a bushel in the 1880 heyday).

As overharvesting depleted natural oyster beds, seed beds like those off Belle Isle became a tempting target. To guard against poachers, watermen built shacks on elevated platforms overlooking tidal flats. Scattered along riverbanks and sounds of the Chesapeake Bay, the buildings-on-stilts formed a ragtag line of defense, akin to outposts on a distant frontier.

Across from Belle Isle State Park's offices, a wide, dirt and gravel trail passes by a field of corn to your right. Fields soon drop away and the trail enters a narrow strip of pine and hardwoods. Fringe forests like these act as a barrier between field runoff and fragile wetlands. Continuing on, the path crosses a neck of land bounded by tidal marshes. On your left you'll see where waterfowl flock to Porpoise Creek, and where its marsh grass segues into the deeper, blue waters of Deep Creek, look for wintering tundra swans in spectacular white groups numbering from ten to one hundred. (They arrive in December and leave in March.) Although a bit removed from the Atlantic Flyway—the north–south route for migrating birds that traces Virginia's Eastern Shore—migratory birds still flock to Belle Isle.

Potomac River shoreline at Belle Isle State Park.

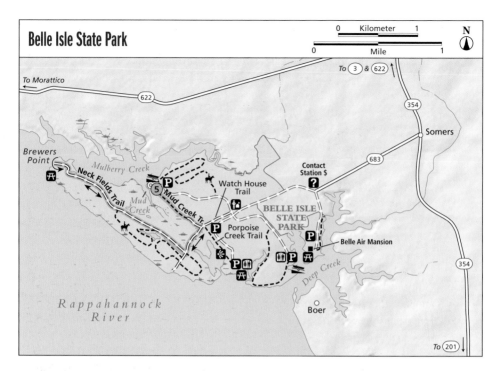

Belle Isle State Park

Finally, the trail meets the lapping shores of the Rappahannock River. Look closely around you for clues to a chapter in this plantation-turned-park's history. Overgrown with grass, decaying wood pilings and riprap mark the site of an old watch house. You've hiked only a short distance, but you've witnessed at least 350 years of history.

Miles and Directions

0.0   Start from the Mud Creek boat launch parking lot. Take Mud Creek Trail southeast, back toward the park office.

0.1   Mud Creek Trail passes between two thick-trunk oaks whose branches, high overhead, entwine to create a natural arbor.

0.2   Mud Creek Trail turns sharply left and emerges from the woods, then bears right to follow the edge of a cornfield. A red barn is visible across the field. As you emerge into the open, look for the round, spindly fruit of the sweet gum.

0.3   Mud Creek Trail ends at a T intersection with Watch House Trail, a wide gravel and dirt road that heads left and right. Turn right. **Note:** Turning left onto Watch House Trail will lead you to a picnic area and the park office, as well as a trailhead for horseback riders.

0.6   Arrive at a T intersection with Neck Fields Trail, another wide dirt and gravel road. Turn right onto Neck Fields Trail and continue your hike to Brewers Point.

1.5   The trail detours around a small pond hidden behind a tangle of small shrubs, vines, and trees. Peek through for a sighting of merganser and canvasback, two types of ducks that call Belle Isle home.

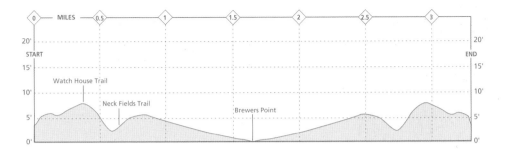

1.65 The trail ends at Brewers Point on the Rappahannock River. There is a picnic table here. Retrace your steps back to the boat launch parking lot.

3.3 Hike ends at the parking lot.

Hike Information

Local Information

The Northern Neck Tourism Council, Warsaw, (804) 333-1919, www.northern neck.org

Local Events/Attractions

Music by the River concerts are held in the park in the summer, and Haunted Evening programs take place in Oct.

Stratford Hall Plantation, Stratford, (804) 493-8038, www.stratfordhall.org. This is Robert E. Lee's ancestral home.

St. Mary's Whitechapel, Lancaster, (804) 462-5908, www.stmaryswhitechapel.org. George Washington's mother, Mary Ball Washington, was from Lancaster County, and many of her ancestors are buried in the churchyard.

Lodging

Lodging is available within the park at Bel Air House and Guesthouse and a full-service campground. For camping and guesthouse reservations, call (800) 933-PARK or visit www.reserveamerica.com.

Organizations

Friends of Belle Isle State Park, (804) 462-7055

6 Newport News Park

Newport News Park, an 8,000-acre preserve, is one of the largest municipal parks in America. The most heavily used parts surround Lee Hall Reservoir. Trails and dirt roads make possible a hike that at times feels remote, despite being set in the middle of a large city. The White Oak Trail Discovery Trail leads away from the visitor center and transports you across long stretches of marsh and past Civil War battle fortifications. Near the turnaround of this 5-mile hike, there is a detour into adjoining Yorktown Battlefield, where the last major battle of the Revolution secured American independence.

Start: Park Discovery Center
Distance: 5.0-mile loop
Hiking time: About 2.5 hours
Difficulty: Easy
Trail surface: Gravel road, dirt foot paths, and boardwalks
Land status: City park
Nearest town: Newport News, VA
Other trail users: Cyclists and joggers
Accessibility: There is a memorial plaza at the end of the Dam Bridge that is paved, and the bridge itself is accessible.
Canine compatibility: Pets are allowed on leash. Rabies certificate required to stay in campground.

Trail contact: Newport News Park, 13564 Jefferson Ave., Newport News; (757) 886-7912; www.nnparks.com/parks_nn.php. For reserved-site camping, call (757) 888-3333.
Schedule: Open daily year-round, sunrise to sunset
Fees/permits: None for day use
Facilities/features: Interpretive center, visitor center, bicycle rentals, picnic shelters, fishing, rentals (rowboat, paddleboat, canoe) on freshwater reservoir, full-service campground, 2 18-hole golf courses, disc golf, archery range
Maps: USGS Yorktown; free hand-drawn trail maps available at the park ranger contact station at the entrance and the Discovery Center

Finding the trailhead: From I-64 in Newport News, take exit 250B. Keep left to take the VA 143 West ramp toward VA 105. Turn left onto Jefferson Avenue/VA 143 and drive 0.4 mile to the park entrance on the right. Trailhead GPS: N37 10.905' / W76 32.236'. *DeLorme: Virginia Atlas & Gazetteer:* Page 50, C2.

The Hike

On April 16, 1862, Union forces under General George McClellan launched a military campaign from Fort Monroe in Hampton, Virginia. The goal was to push forward up The Peninsula, as the land between the James and York Rivers was called, all the way to Richmond, capital of the Confederacy.

A campaign planned as a quick thrust into the heart of the Confederacy faced its first test on the banks of the Warwick River in the vicinity of Lee's Mill, in what today is Newport News. There, Union forces met a Confederate army entrenched behind a series of earthen breastworks and trenches. Three times that day, Union forces rushed forward, only to be repelled by Confederate artillery. Soldiers from two

A multi-use trail at Newport News Park.

Vermont regiments suffered the heaviest loses: twenty-six dead and more than sixty wounded. It marked the start of a three-week siege that ultimately ended in a draw and a serious blow to McClellan's Richmond plans.

The ground that saw this long-ago action is now within Newport News Park. The Warwick River has been dammed to form Lee Hall Reservoir, a vast lake that is home to waterfowl and beloved for water sports like fishing and paddle boating. In the surrounding 8,000 acres, protected to ensure good water quality, hikers, joggers, and bike riders can access a huge outdoor playground of trails in one of Virginia's largest metro areas.

One mile into this hike, after turning onto Wynn's Mill Loop Trail, a hiker can see firsthand the remains of breastworks that protected Confederate and repelled Union soldiers. As you walk, notice a pronounced trend in the landscape that develops on each side of the trail: On the left, mounded dirt (now significantly overgrown with trees, but still visible in form) indicates breastworks, while on the right stand the swampy backwaters of a Lee Hall Reservoir tributary. Great blue herons are a common sighting here. Adult herons can stand chest-high to a person; to watch them stalk their fish and crab prey in the shallow edges of the swamp is a study in predator virtuosity as the heron spears a fish and quickly chokes it down the gullet.

Ducks in the reservoir at Newport News Park.

Waterside vegetation in this area indicates a freshwater source, a contrast to salt-tolerant habitats along the region's tidal creeks. Rather than salt marsh grasses, these watery guts are flush with lotus lily, arrow arum, pickerel weed, and cattails. The shrubby shorelines are thick with bayberry and groundsel tree. The latter is recognized easiest in fall, when seed pods open and white bristles emerge. A dense shoreline of groundsel tree (also called *silverling*) in autumn can appear to have received a light dusting of snow.

The habitat is dynamic in that zone where water and land meet and interact. Eastern box turtles and common musk turtles slide off the mud banks as you approach, their presence marked by a *kerplunk* and ripples on the water surface. Songbirds forage for food in the bayberry and holly trees. The cardinal is the flashiest, but there are some one hundred other songbird species on the park's bird list. On a hot, sunny day, stay alert for a northern black racer or rat snake sunning itself on an open stretch of trail. As you cross the many boardwalks and bridges, mallard ducks slip away and Canada geese *honk honk,* as if to warn you about getting too close.

Newport News Park is beloved by residents as an oasis amid their ever-growing city—a major interstate, I-64, is within ear shot of the park entrance. When you take time to delve farther into its substantial forest, you can truly appreciate its importance as both a nature refuge and a slice of American history.

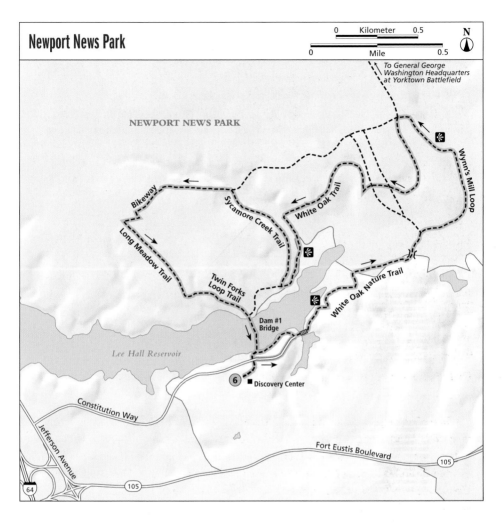

To General George
Washington Headquarters
at Yorktown Battlefield

NEWPORT NEWS PARK

Wynn's Mill Loop

Bikeway

Sycamore Creek Trail

White Oak Trail

Long Meadow Trail

Twin Forks
Loop Trail

White Oak Nature Trail

Dam #1
Bridge

Lee Hall Reservoir

6 ■ Discovery Center

Constitution Way

Jefferson Avenue

Fort Eustis Boulevard

105

64 105

Miles and Directions

0.0   Start at a trail board in front of the park Discovery Center. Look left for a wooden sign that reads Nature Trail and follow a boardwalk leading into the woods. Emerge from the woods to cross the paved park road, then turn right and follow a paved path that in about 20 feet becomes hard-packed rock and dirt.

0.3   Veer left at a fork in the trail and cross a boardwalk bridge. Trail signs indicate you are walking on the White Oak Nature Trail, not to be confused with the White Oak Trail that comprises a later portion of this route.

0.9   Cross Swamp Bridge. At the far side, turn right onto Wynn's Mill Loop. Look for Civil War-era breastworks, which are earthen berms that afforded soldiers protection during battle.

1.6   Turn left to continue on Wynn's Mill Loop. **Side trip:** Straight ahead in 2.1 miles is the site of George Washington's headquarters during the Yorktown battle. This side trip adds 4.2 miles to this loop hike.

2.2	Continue straight through a four-way junction with Swamp Fire Trail. Within a few feet, reach a second four-way junction and turn left on White Oak Trail.
3.0	Turn right on Sycamore Creek Trail, which is a wide, hard-packed dirt road.
3.5	Turn left on the park bikeway, a gravel road.
3.9	Turn left on Long Meadow Trail, a wide, grassy doubletrack.
4.3	Continue straight on Long Meadow Trail past a left turn (this is one leg of the Twin Forts Loop). In a few feet, turn left at a second junction. **Note:** A sign at this junction points the way to the Discovery Center.
4.6	Cross the Dam #1 Bridge. At the far side, walk through a small circular plaza area with a monument to the Battle of Lee's Mill, cross the park road, and enter the woods at a sign that reads Nature Trail.
5.0	Arrive back at the park Discovery Center.

Hike Information

Local Information

Newport News Tourism, (888) 493-7386, www.newport-news.org. The Newport News Visitor Center is located at the park entrance.

Local Events / Attractions

Newport News Fall Festival of Folklife takes place in the park the first weekend in Oct.

Celebration in Lights transforms the park into a magical drive-through light display, Thanksgiving through New Year's Day.

Lodging

The park's full-service campground has 188 sites. Call (757) 888-3333.

Honorable Mentions: Eastern Virginia

A. Great Dismal Swamp National Wildlife Refuge

Located on the Virginia/North Carolina border, 4.5 miles east of VA 32 in Suffolk. The 4.5-mile Washington Ditch Road leads to Lake Drummond, one of only two natural lakes in Virginia. Trails begin on Washington Ditch off VA 642 (White Marsh Road). Hike through a southern swamp forest of maple, tupelo, bald cypress, and pine. Spanish moss drips from the trees, and the distinctive knees of the cypress jut from inky swamp water. The swamp harbors species of migratory, song, and marsh birds. Day use only. (757) 986-3705; www.fws.gov/northeast/greatdismalswamp. GPS: N36 38.675' / W76 32.834'. *DeLorme: Virginia Atlas & Gazetteer:* Page 34, C2.

B. Sandy Bottom Nature Preserve

Located off the Hampton Roads Center Parkway in Hampton. From exit 261A off I-64, follow the parkway west to the nature preserve entrance, just past the intersection of Big Bethel Road on the right. There are eleven trails in the park. Trillium Trail is the longest at 3.3 miles. Old Crystal Trail, around a former sand pit turned lake, is 2.1 miles. Boardwalks cross wetland habitat, while graded dirt paths pass through hardwood forest. Fishing, recreational boating, and primitive camping are allowed. (757) 825-4657; www.hampton.gov/sandybottom. GPS: N37 03.713' / W76 25.998'. *DeLorme: Virginia Atlas & Gazetteer:* Page 50, D3.

C. Beaverdam Park

Located minutes from Gloucester Court House on Virginia's Middle Peninsula. From Business US 17 north, turn right onto VA 616/Roaring Springs Road. In 2.4 miles the road dead-ends at the park's main entrance at 8687 Roaring Springs Rd., Gloucester. There are 9.5 miles of multiuse trails for horses, mountain bikers, and hikers, as well as a 3-mile hiker-only trail. The main hiking trail passes along marshy fringes of the reservoir and through an upland hardwood forest. (804) 693-2107; www.gloucesterparks.org. GPS: N37 26.906' / W76 32.040'. *DeLorme: Virginia Atlas & Gazetteer:* Page 50, A2.

D. Hickory Hollow Natural Area Preserve

Located on the Northern Neck near Lancaster Courthouse, on VA 604, 0.3 mile east of VA 3. This is a special hike along the wooded bluffs overlooking Western Branch. Spur trails plunge off the hillside into the stream's marshy backwaters. Lancaster County once considered developing this 254-acre spot into an industrial park; bird watchers and nature lovers fought off the proposal with the aid of the Northern

Neck Audubon Society, which now owns it. (804) 225-2303; www.dcr.virginia.gov/natural_heritage/natural_area_preserves/hickory.shtml. GPS: N37 46.329' / W76 26.655'. *DeLorme: Virginia Atlas & Gazetteer:* Page 60, B3.

E. Caledon Natural Area State Park

Located in King George County at the top of Virginia's Northern Neck. From US 301, follow VA 206 to VA 218, then head east on VA 218 for 1.2 miles to the entrance. Created to provide nesting and roosting spots for bald eagles, Caledon has five short trails that lead to bird-watching spots along the Potomac River. Some trails may be temporarily closed to protect nesting birds. Sandy bluffs in the Horsehead Cliff area are imbedded with fossils. Day use only. Guided eagle tours are conducted mid-June through August. (540) 663-3861; www.dcr.virginia.gov/state_parks/cal.shtml. GPS: N38 20.032' / W77 08.594'. *DeLorme: Virginia Atlas & Gazetteer:* Page 71, B5.

Northern Virginia

What is Northern Virginia? Is it coastal or Piedmont? Urban or suburban? Could it even be rural? Northern Virginia is, in fact, all of these. First and foremost, it is a metropolis, with all the baggage this carries: highways, pollution, sprawl. Such conditions do not, however, negate quality outdoor experiences. This region—which encompasses the pastoral hills of Fauquier County, the ragged 90-foot cliffs at Great Falls, and the calm estuaries around Pohick Bay and Mason Neck—ranks as wildly diverse as any in the state. Absent the mountains of western regions, the region features streams that, over centuries, have carved out channels through granite, schist, and metagraywacke. Healthy forests of hardwoods crown river bluffs. Microcosms of Appalachian cove forest—with its stunning array of flowers, trees, mosses, and animals—pop up along quiet, secluded streams. Virginia's fall line bisects the region, creating picturesque waterfalls and cascades that transport you hundreds of miles away.

Northern Virginians work hard for these special environments. They work hard to find them, and they work hard to protect them. Preserved tracts of land on the Potomac, below Washington, DC, are recognized as top spots in the East for nesting and roosting bald eagles. Even land that has been logged, farmed, mined, and left to waste away—as was the case with Prince William Forest Park—has rebounded to a state of natural and scenic beauty. Years of preservation work in Northern Virginia have made possible just about every type of outdoor pursuit, from walking to rock climbing, bird watching to hunting.

Whatever natural wonders await the explorer in Northern Virginia, history makes doubly rewarding. More than a few chief executives have left their mark. Roosevelt Island, a vacation spot for Theodore Roosevelt, is prominent among them. James Madison fled a burning Washington, DC, during the War of 1812, stashing the Declaration of Independence in an old gristmill now preserved as a museum. Less prominent, but just as intriguing, are Civil War raiders who prowled eastern foothills of the Blue Ridge. Archeologists have unearthed the garbage heaps of prehistoric residents who encamped along the Potomac. And on the shores of America's river, the

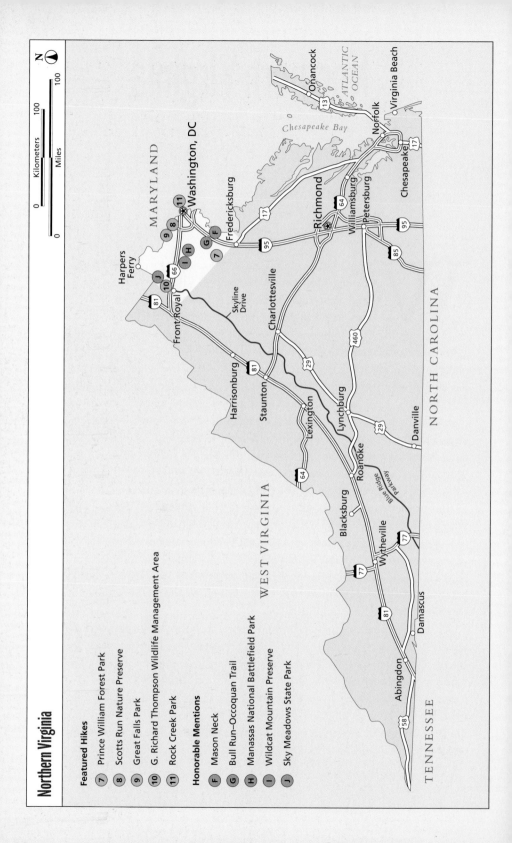

Northern Virginia

Featured Hikes

- (7) Prince William Forest Park
- (8) Scotts Run Nature Preserve
- (9) Great Falls Park
- (10) G. Richard Thompson Wildlife Management Area
- (11) Rock Creek Park

Honorable Mentions

- (F) Mason Neck
- (G) Bull Run–Occoquan Trail
- (H) Manassas National Battlefield Park
- (I) Wildcat Mountain Preserve
- (J) Sky Meadows State Park

Potomac, Chicocoan Indians watched Captain John Smith sail as far as the waterfalls at Georgetown during his legendary explorations of 1608.

The paths of our history are today the paths of hikers, bird watchers, and nature lovers. The stories behind place names and old buildings are as much a part of the outdoor experience in Northern Virginia as the flowers, birds, and trees.

The Hikes

7. Prince William Forest Park
8. Scotts Run Nature Preserve
9. Great Falls Park
10. G. Richard Thompson Wildlife Management Area
11. Rock Creek Park

Honorable Mentions

F. Mason Neck
G. Bull Run-Occoquan Trail
H. Manassas National Battlefield Park
I. Wildcat Mountain Preserve
J. Sky Meadows State Park.

7 Prince William Forest Park

Roughly 100 miles inland from Virginia's coast, a geologic boundary called the fall line marks a change in the landscape. Here the sandy soil of Virginia's coastal plain segues into the bedrock underlying the Piedmont. The effect is pronounced on rivers, where waterfalls and rapids form. Historically, these acted as barriers to ocean-faring vessels. Towns formed up and down the fall line to handle commerce between inland farmers and coastal traders. Prince William Forest Park, a small national park straddling the fall line in Prince William County, is tied to this history through the tobacco farmers and miners who used the nearby port town of Dumfries to ship their goods. Today the park still receives heavy use, but now hikers, cyclists, and nature lovers are drawn by the cascades, wildlife, rare plants, and historic ruins.

Start: Laurel Loop Trail map board behind Pine Grove picnic pavilion

Distance: 14.6-mile loop

Hiking time: About 5 hours

Difficulty: Moderate due to length, well-graded and clearly marked trails, and elevation change

Trail surface: A combination of dirt forest paths, dirt roads, and paved roads lead through hardwood forests and along streams to small cascades, rock outcrops, and waterfalls.

Land status: National park

Nearest town: Dumfries, VA

Other trail users: Joggers, cross-country skiers, and mountain bikers

Accessibility: The 0.4-mile Pine Grove Forest Trail is a paved loop with footbridges, boardwalks, and benches.

Kid Appeal: There are 30 orienteering courses in the park and free maps and extra compasses free at the park visitor center. You can even request a ranger-led program to learn how.

Canine compatibility: Dogs permitted

Trail contact: Prince William Forest Park, 18100 Park Headquarters Rd., Triangle; (703) 221-7181; www.nps.gov/prwi

Schedule: Park open daily, sunrise to sunset

Fees/permits: Entrance fee and camping fee; permit required for free backcountry camping

Facilities/features: Visitor center, cabins, and year-round 100-site campground for tents and RVs (no hookups). Chopawamsic Backcountry Area is a 1,500-acre area with 8 primitive campsites accessible from the 2-mile loop trail. There is no fee, but campers must obtain a permit at the park visitor center.

Maps: USGS Quantico, Joplin

Finding the trailhead: From I-95, take exit 150B and turn west onto VA 619/Joplin Road. Drive 1.7 miles and turn right into Prince William Forest Park. In 0.5 mile, turn left at a sign for Pine Grove Picnic Area. Immediately turn right into the long term parking area. Walk up the small knoll and locate the Laurel Loop Trail map board at the edge of the woods between the Pine Grove Picnic Area and the visitor center. Trailhead GPS: N38 33.644' /W77 20.943'. *DeLorme: Virginia Atlas & Gazetteer:* Page 76, D3.

Mountain Laurel are prolific in spring in Prince William Forest Park.

The Hike

There is plenty of rough, broken-up terrain along the Quantico Creek and South Fork Quantico Creek stream valleys. Mountain-laurel slicks coat steep hillsides. Stream water flows over bedrock slate, which, where exposed, creates small rapids and riffles. Quantico slate is super-resistant—water simply bounces over it and flows on its merry way. Here in Prince William Forest Park, it's a last hurrah of sorts. Within a mile or so, the small streams of Prince William Forest Park empty into Quantico Creek. The descent over Virginia's fall line is complete.

The fall line—a geologic formation that defines the bedrock boundary between the Piedmont and Coastal Plain regions—is one defining natural feature of this national park. Old fields that have reverted to meadows, young forest, beaver ponds and associated wetlands, and the 37 miles of hiking trail that span all of these are others. Climbing out of the South Fork stream valley, young trees of a third- and fourth-generation forest fall away, replaced by meadow. Tobacco was the cash crop of choice throughout colonial Virginia, and the men who tilled land along Quantico Creek were no different. These farmers had the added benefit of being close to Dumfries, Virginia's oldest continually chartered municipality, established in 1749. Town fathers drew up the boundaries and voted the town into creation a mere three hours before Alexandria, a few miles north. Unlike Alexandria, however, Dumfries's usefulness as a port declined soon after the Revolutionary War. Relentless tilling on land surrounding the town, including Prince William Forest Park, caused massive soil runoff. Dumfries's harbor filled with silt, and ocean ships could not sail into port.

The Taylor family was the last to farm inside the park proper. High Meadows Trail passes through their old lands between the South Valley Trail and Turkey Run Ridge. An off-trail detour leads to two tombstones in the family plot, surrounded by sun-dappled woodland. There are no marked trails, only vague animal paths. Dry leaves crackle underfoot. Hidden amid the leaf debris are small green stems. Somewhere, behind a shrub or camouflaged by other spring flowers, might grow a small whorled pogonia, an endangered species.

Since it's the commonwealth's most urban region, Northern Virginia seems the last place to look for a rare plant. Loudon, Fairfax, and Fauquier Counties, however, are among the fastest growing in the country. Development, then, is the biggest single threat to the small whorled pogonia. The US Fish & Wildlife Service lists it as threatened; Virginia ranks it as endangered.

This woodland orchid's bloom lasts a preciously short time. Within two weeks of the first yellow-green sepals, an entire colony will flower and lose its bloom. Following this, the flower reverts to a modest green-stemmed plant, with five or six slender leaves arranged in a whorl midway up the stem. There's a perplexing aspect to all this. The flower, when it reproduces, stores upwards of 1,000 seeds in a small capsule. Despite the potential, it's rare for a community to number more than twenty-five plants. Scientists can't say why.

Prince William Forest Park shelters not only the rare, but the common as well. A logbook at the visitor center lists sightings of deer, raccoon, turkey, and falcons, a diversity of wildlife that stands in sharp contrast from when the federal government took over the area. After the last farmer pulled up stakes here, and after a pyrite mine closed in the 1920s amid labor strife and strikes, the federal government took over as protector of the waters that flow into Quantico Creek. The area was first used as a demonstration site for land reclamation methods such as tree planting and erosion control. Gradually the emphasis shifted to recreation and protecting the Quantico Creek watershed.

The process of recovery is ongoing. The boundaries of old tobacco fields are still visible. Thistle and milkweed grow in them now. Ecologically, these weeds prove a better return for wildlife than tobacco ever did for humans. A threatened butterfly, the regal fritillary, prefers the thistle for food. Like the small whorled pogonia, this is a minor threatened species whose plight rarely receives notice. In Virginia, sightings have been recorded from Prince William Forest Park to mountainous regions of far southwest

A waterfall in Prince William Forest Park.

Virginia. There are, however, five or fewer confirmed population clusters of the regal fritillary in Virginia; biologists have had more success reintroducing this insect in Midwest states, where the tallgrass prairies make an ideal habitat. Pennsylvania is believed to have the only viable population of these orange and black butterflies in the East.

From a distance, the butterfly looks like a monarch. A female is distinguishable by the off-white circles on its rear, or hind, wings. A better way of identifying one is to watch mating rituals. A female regal fritillary signals her displeasure with a male suitor by flying straight up, as much as 100 feet, then entering a nosedive that scares away the unlucky male.

With such varied terrain and so much room to explore, it's easy to imagine seeing a regal fritillary, or a small whorled pogonia, as you hike about Prince William Forest Park. Finding either would be considered an accomplishment—they aren't endangered or threatened because they're plentiful. But half the fun is knowing they're there, somewhere. That, and appreciating the sanctuary that can harbor them.

Miles and Directions

0.0 Start from the Laurel Loop Trail map board behind the Pine Grove picnic pavilion. Do not enter the woods here, but rather turn left (north) and follow a narrow well-worn dirt path through a grassy area. You'll pass a playground and then enter a field at the far end of a paved parking lot. Walk down the right edge of the field, keeping the woods hard to your right. In the far northeast corner of the field, locate the yellow blazes for the alternate Laurel Loop trailhead, marked by a yellow blaze on a tulip poplar and a concrete trail post with a metal band that gives the trail's name and mileage to the next junction.

Prince William Forest Park

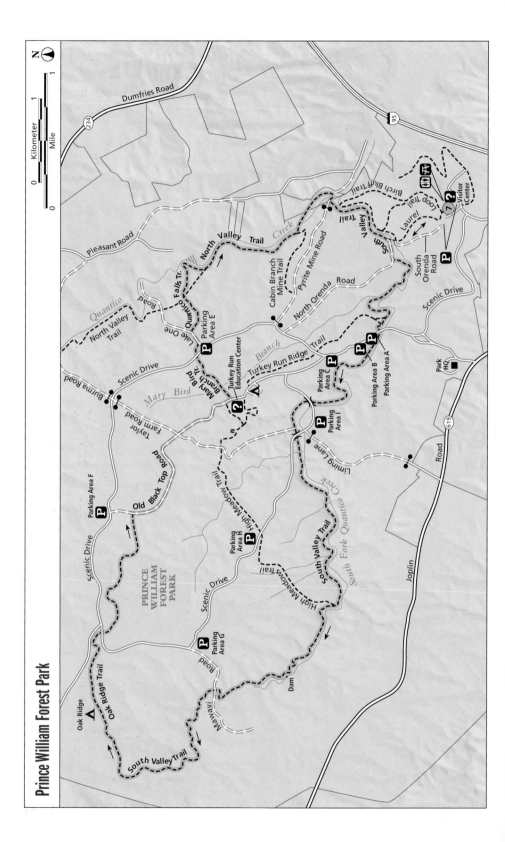

0.5 Turn left (west) and cross the South Fork Quantico Creek on a cable-supported bridge. On the opposite side, turn left (west) on a dirt road that is the combined South Valley Trail and North Orenda Road. **Bailout:** Don't cross the bridge; instead, bear right and follow a combination of Laurel Loop and Birch Bluff Trail to return to the Pine Grove picnic area for a quick 2-mile loop.

0.7 Turn left (south) on South Valley Trail as it splits off North Orenda Road.

1.4 Stay straight at a T junction with Turkey Run Ridge Trail. Ahead, South Valley Trail winds through bottomland forest formed by a bend in the stream and then turns north. **Note:** It is 1.4 miles on Turkey Run Trail to the Turkey Run Education Center, which has bathrooms and nature exhibits.

1.5 Bear left on South Valley Trail. **Note:** The trail straight becomes Turkey Run Ridge Trail where the cutoff from 1.4 miles merges on the right.

1.6 Cross over Scenic Drive.

2.1 Cross a footbridge over a small stream. Ahead, South Valley Trail climbs a hillside on switchbacks.

2.6 Cross beneath Scenic Drive via a boardwalk that hugs the concrete bridge abutment.

2.8 Stay straight on South Valley Trail at a junction with Taylor Farm Road on the right.

2.9 Cross over Scenic Drive and continue west on the South Valley Trail.

4.4 Turn left (west) and follow South Valley Trail downhill at this junction with High Meadow Trail, which continues straight uphill. **Bailout:** For a shorter 10.3-mile loop, hike uphill on High Meadow Trail and return to Pine Grove Picnic Area via High Meadow, Mary Bird Branch, Quantico Falls, North Valley, South Valley and Laurel Loop Trails.

5.2 Pass a dam across the South Fork. Above this, the creek spreads out to form a long, narrow lake.

6.0 Cross over gravel Mawavi Road and walk north on South Valley Trail up the stream valley.

6.4 Enter wetlands where, for the next 0.7 mile, the trail skirts an area of heavy beaver activity. This wet, wide-open ecosystem attracts waterfowl, songbirds, deer, raccoons, and foxes.

7.1 Begin a climb from the stream valley into dry upland forest of chestnut oak, yellow (tulip) poplar, and white oak that is in recovery from a 2006 wildfire that consumed 316 acres.

8.0 Turn right (east) on the yellow-blazed Oak Ridge Trail.

8.5 Cross straight over Scenic Drive.

9.2 After a level stretch of hiking through a young upland forest, descend into a small stream valley with a moist forest understory of fern and skunk cabbage.

9.5 Oak Ridge Trail ends at a T junction with Old Black Top Road. Turn right (south) and walk along the gravel road.

10.4 At a four-way junction with Taylor Farm Road, continue straight on Old Black Top Road.

10.9 Turn left (north) onto Mary Bird Branch Trail. There is a concrete trail post and a triple red blaze on a tree. Ahead, descend and cross Mary Bird Branch, a stream.

11.3 Cross straight over Scenic Drive and pass through the parking and Picnic Area E. Locate a white signboard for Quantico Falls Trail. Enter the woods on a footpath, following yellow blazes. **Note:** You'll periodically see brown trail blazes and trailside signs for the Geology Trail, which shares the trail from here to Quantico Creek.

11.4 Turn left onto a dirt road. Stay alert when, in less than 0.1 mile, Quantico Falls Trail branches right off the dirt road. Turn right here and follow the yellow-blazed trail through an upland deciduous forest of oak and hickory with an understory of beech, maple, and elm.

11.8 Cross over the North Valley Trail at a four-way trail junction.

12.0 A sharp descent ends at the edge of Quantico Creek. Turn right (south) and follow the stream valley. There are a scenic set of waterfalls off to the left.

12.2 Cross a footbridge over a small tributary and merge with the blue-blazed North Valley Trail. Veer left (south) and walk downstream. In summer and fall, the trail south of this junction offers good opportunities to rest and relax on exposed rock shelves in the river.

12.9 Pass interpretive signs for the Cabin Branch pyrite mine, which operated on Quantico Creek in the early 1900s.

13.0 Cross Quantico Creek on a bridge. On the opposite side, turn right to follow a footpath through river-bottom forest. **Side trip:** Before crossing the creek, walk straight ahead to another section of the pyrite mine in less than 0.1 mile.

13.2 A long boardwalk carries the trail over a wetland. Ahead, look for an overlook on the right that gives you a vantage point of the Cabin Branch mine across the stream.

13.5 After walking a short stretch on gravel road, turn right (west) and cross Quantico Creek on a bridge. On the opposite side, turn left (west) onto South Valley Trail.

14.1 Turn left (south) and cross South Fork Quantico Creek on a cable-supported bridge. After crossing, turn right onto red-blazed Laurel Loop Trail and ascend.

14.6 Arrive back at the Pine Grove picnic area.

Hike Information

Local Information

Prince William County/Manassas CVB, 10611 Balls Ford Rd., Ste. 110, Manassas; (703) 396-7130; www.visitpwc.com

Local Events/Attractions

The Prince William Forest Park Heritage Festival takes place in mid-Oct in the park.

Restaurants

Tim's Rivershore, 1510 Cherryhill Rd., Dumfries, (703) 441-1375, www.timsrivershore.com. Seafood on the shores of the Potomac.

Organizations

Friends of Prince William Forest Park, Woodbridge, (703) 791-2282, www.fpwfp.org

Capital Hiking Club, www.capitalhikingclub.org. Hikes and trips in Virginia, Maryland, and Pennsylvania.

Center Hiking Club, (301) 468-1896, www.centerhikingclub.org. Hikes and trips in Virginia, Maryland, and Pennsylvania.

Wanderbirds Hiking Club, www.wanderbirds.org. Hikes in Virginia, West Virginia, Maryland, and Pennsylvania.

Washington Women Outdoors, Germantown, MD, (301) 864-3070, www.washingtonwomenoutdoors.org. Outdoor adventures for women, including hiking, kayaking, rock climbing, and biking.

8 Scotts Run Nature Preserve

Scotts Run Nature Preserve offers Northern Virginians a relaxing way to spend some time in a deep-forest atmosphere of oak, beech, and tulip poplar. The small streams that spill off high river bluffs nourish carpets of ferns, grasses, and wildflowers. The most spectacular stream is, of course, Scotts Run, with its 30-foot multilevel waterfall that breaks just before the stream joins the Potomac River. Once known as the Burling Tract, named for one of its owners, this preserve is now linked with Riverside and Great Falls parks farther upstream as a link in the Potomac Gorge biological system, a complex of plants and animals—some globally rare and found no where else on earth—that eek out a life along the turbulent Potomac River.

Start: Parking lot off Georgetown Pike (VA 193) at Swinks Mill Road
Distance: 3.0-mile loop
Hiking time: About 2 hours
Difficulty: Easy due to wide, graded trails, with a few steep climbs between Potomac River bottomland and upland forests
Trail surface: Dirt footpaths and dirt roads wind through hardwood forest with some stands of eastern hemlock, tall river bluffs, wildflowers, rock outcroppings, riverine flats, and upland forests.
Land status: County park

Nearest town: McLean, VA
Other trail users: Joggers, cross-country skiers, dog walkers, and mountain bikers
Accessibility: None
Canine compatibility: Dogs permitted
Trail contact: Fairfax County Park Authority, River Bend Park, Great Falls; (703) 324-8702; www.fairfaxcounty.gov/parks
Schedule: Open year-round, sunrise to sunset
Fees/permits: None
Facilities/features: None other than parking
Map: USGS Falls Church

Finding the trailhead: From I-495, take exit 44. If traveling north on I-495, turn left off the exit onto Georgetown Pike (VA 193). In 0.7 mile, at the intersection of Swinks Mill Road (on the left), turn right into Scotts Run Nature Preserve parking area. GPS: N38 57.591' / W77 12.328'. *DeLorme: Virginia Atlas & Gazetteer:* Page 76, A4.

The Hike

You work up quite the appetite exploring Scotts Run Nature Preserve, what with negotiating steep hills, narrow billy goat–like paths, and a nest of trails through the upland forest. So I was half expecting the pronouncement, delivered in no uncertain terms, that my assistants—my niece and nephew—were hungry. They demanded food, and I, sensing their growing resolve, made an executive decision. Lunch all around, I muttered.

On a rocky point near Stubblefield Falls, where mayflies swarm heavy off the marshy shoreline, we found shelter from both insect and sun under a scrubby tree. Out came sandwiches, drinks, cheese-on-cheese crackers. I stifled a mutiny over mustard (no one

The author with her niece, Vanessa Kubick, re-hiking Scotts Run for the third edition.

told me they didn't like mustard) by pointing to a cryptic rock carving—some long phrase, partly weathered, carved in neat block letters, referencing trade imbalances, nature, and logic (clearly not ancient Native American writings, I told my disappointed niece and nephew). While they busied themselves, I scraped mustard off the white bread. My cell phone chirped and I took the call. Ahhh, nature.

That's when she screamed.

When a child screams, instinct kicks in. "Her mom's gonna kill me," I panicked. Out loud, I yelled, "What's wrong? Are you OK?" She screamed again.

I followed her pointing finger and at first saw nothing. Then a rock about 50 yards offshore moved. Or, the rock didn't, but the snakes did. Five—no, six, seven, eight—black, oily water snakes adjusted their sun tanning positions on a rock dam. The rock dam where they lay stretched far downstream, but these snakes felt uncomfortably close. Quietly, one slipped from off its perch and moved closer.

It's not unusual, in springtime, for the common variety water snakes—the dark brown–banded water snake and its lighter-shaded cousin, the northern water snake—to siesta on exposed rocks, bridge abutments, even dams. These are nonpoisonous, members of the colubrid family. They give birth to live young in the spring, and together the whole clan haunts rivers, lakes, and pond shorelines looking for food. Youngsters are skinny and harmless looking. Elders tend toward the heavy side, their thick heads, muscular jaws, and rows of sharp teeth conveying a slightly more sinister intent.

At this point, it should be established that I am, for better or for worse, a tree and rock guy. I get excited about rocks folded and broken by violent collisions of continental plates. I think it's cool that shale, subjected to extreme heat hundreds of millions of years ago, turned first to slate, then schist. And how schist, so hard it withstands the steady flowing drumbeat of the Potomac River, comprises the bedrock underfoot at Scotts Run Nature Preserve. I thrill at identifying an eastern hemlock along Scotts Run, at spying mountain laurel breaks on that same steep streamside hill. Wildflowers peaking through soggy ground rot in a cove forest make me downright giddy.

Hiking along the Potomac River in Scotts Run Nature Preserve.

All of which is a roundabout way of saying I am not a snake guy. Snakes make me shudder. That said, I understand leaders should wear a brave face. I regained some composure and made a mental checklist of snake facts and myths. Only about 10 percent of snake species worldwide are poisonous. One of them, unfortunately, is a water snake: the cottonmouth, or water moccasin. Fortunately, you'll find them no farther north than the Dismal Swamp in southeast Virginia, some 200 miles away. Even there, they're rare. Standing where I was, on the shore of the Potomac River, I reasoned I was relatively safe.

Snakes are nearly always smaller than you remember. Water snakes, in particular, average only about 3 feet in length. Naturally, the snakes I saw swimming against the current were 10 feet long. But maybe not.

Finally, snakes do not poison people with their breath. They can't charm prey to prevent flight. And snakes do not swallow little children whole. A water snake's diet consists of insects, crayfish, small fish, and, occasionally, small mammals.

That final thought jerked me back to reality and I quickly checked on my two small mammals. They weren't in immediate danger of being charmed, choked, breathed upon, coughed on, or sprayed (water snakes emit a foul, musky scent when handled), or—God forbid—swallowed whole, but I still played it safe. Saying a short prayer to St. Patrick, he who droveth the snakes from Ireland, I shepherded the kids off the rock. I may have even muttered "cool" once or twice to show I wasn't unhip.

I do recall declaring snake-viewing hour over. As I shoved lunch leftovers into a backpack, my nephew stated that a water snake would make a great pet. I tried distracting him.

"Look at this cool tree," I said. He ignored me. He'll probably grow up to be a snake guy.

Miles and Directions

0.0 Start at set of interpretive panels at the Scotts Run parking area at Swinks Mill Road. Follow a wide gravel road downstream (north) along Scotts Run. **Note:** Be prepared to cross Scotts Run three times before reaching the Potomac River.

0.4 Cross Scotts Run and follow a dirt road uphill. **Option:** An unmarked trail on the left as you begin climbing the dirt road is a bushwack route along Scotts Run. Like the dirt road you are climbing, it also leads to Scotts Run Falls and the Potomac River, but is considerably more rugged, cut into the steep-sided stream bank. There are many rock and tree hazards, and the trail is severely eroded in sections. The streamside trail is not a recommended route in wintertime, in times of inclement weather, or with young children.

0.5 An interpretive panel on the right side of the trail at the base of a set of wooden steps marks a side trip to ruins of a home belonging to the Burling family. The ruins consist of a chimney and house foundation.

0.6 Continue downhill past a junction with the blue-blazed Potomac Heritage Trail on the right to reach the scenic 30-foot waterfall that marks Scotts Run's confluence with the Potomac. From the falls, turn downstream (east) and follow an unmarked but well-worn dirt trail along the river's edge.

0.8 Continue straight at a junction where the blue-blazed Potomac Heritage Trail, which you passed en route to the falls, rejoins your path on the right. Your route is now a continuation of the blue-blazed Potomac Heritage Trail.

0.9 Turn right (south) and climb a steep hill alongside a small tributary of the Potomac. After a brief climb, veer left (east) to cross the tributary and climb the blue-blazed Potomac Heritage Trail up a set of stairs built into the hillside. **Note:** At the stream crossing, an unmarked path continues straight and uphill.

1.0 A hike along a cliff rim ends at a Potomac River overlook on the left. The panorama includes Stubblefield Falls directly in front and Turkey Island upstream left. Continue straight (east) along the blue-blazed Potomac Heritage Trail.

1.3 Merge right (south) and uphill with an old dirt road following the blue-blazed Potomac Heritage Trail.

1.5 Reach a four-way trail junction and turn right to visit another Potomac River overlook. The blue-blazed Potomac Heritage Trail turns left at this four-way junction. Trails from this point on are unmarked.

1.7 Reach the Potomac River overlook. Return and retrace your steps to the four-way junction with the Potomac Heritage Trail.

1.9 After returning to the four-way junction, turn right (south) and follow a dirt woodland path.

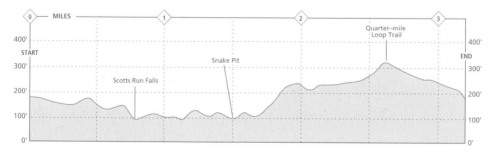

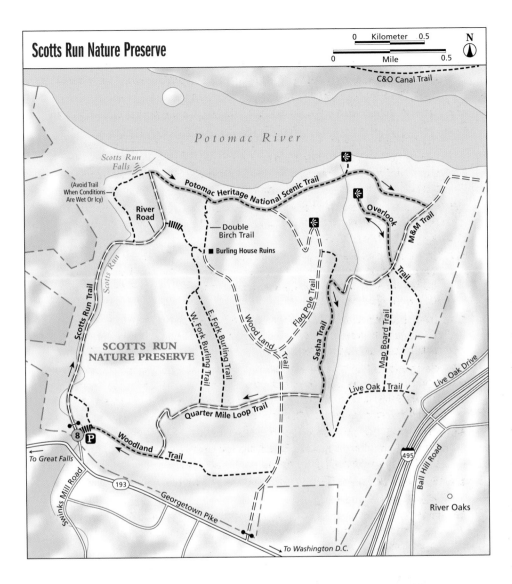

0   Kilometer   0.5

0   Mile   0.5

N

C&O Canal Trail

Potomac River

Scotts Run
Falls

(Avoid Trail
When Conditions
Are Wet Or Icy)

River
Road

Potomac Heritage National Scenic Trail

Overlook

M&M Trail

Double
Birch Trail

■ Burling House Ruins

Scotts Run Trail

Scotts Run

**SCOTTS RUN
NATURE PRESERVE**

W. Fork Burling Trail

E. Fork Burling Trail

Wood Land Trail

Flag Pole Trail

Sasha Trail

Map Board Trail

Trail

Live Oak Trail

Live Oak Drive

Quarter Mile Loop Trail

8 P

Woodland   Trail

To Great Falls

495

Ball Hill Road

Swinks Mill Road

193

Georgetown Pike

River Oaks

To Washington D.C.

2.0 At a fork in the trail, turn right (west). This dirt trail starts as a wide doubletrack but soon becomes a singletrack woods path and crosses a small stream.

2.1 Turn left (south) at a T junction. **Note:** Taking a right turn at this junction leads to another Potomac River overlook.

2.3 Turn right (west) at a T junction. Within 0.1 mile, cross straight through a four-way trail junction.

2.7 Follow the wide dirt footpath as it swings left (south) past a trail board for the Burling home ruins. **Note:** An unmarked path veers right here and leads to the ruins.

3.0 Arrive back at the Scotts Run parking area.

Hike Information

Local Information

Fairfax County Visitors Center, Tysons Corner, (703) 752-9500, www.fxva.com

Local Events / Attractions

Nearby Riverbend Park offers spring wildflower walks in Scotts Run. A Night Sky Festival in Feb and a Virginia Indian Festival in Sept take place at Riverbend.

Lodging

Arlington and Alexandria Bed & Breakfast Network, (703) 549-3415, www.aabbn .com. Assists with reservations for 30 area bed-and-breakfasts.

Restaurants

Old Brogue Irish Pub, Great Falls, (703) 759-3309, www.oldbrogue.com. Traditional Irish fare and live entertainment.

Deli Italiano, Great Falls, (703) 759-6782, www.deliitaliano.com. Grab a sandwich before heading into the park, or a slice of pizza afterward.

Serbian Crown, 1141 Walker Rd., Great Falls, (703) 759-4150, www.serbian crown.com. Fine Russian and French dining, with lighter fare at the piano bar.

Tavern at Great Falls, Great Falls, (703) 757-4770, www.greatfallstavern.com. Classic American cuisine and comfort food.

Organizations

Friends of Riverbend Park, www.forb.org

Capital Hiking Club, www.capitalhikingclub.org. Hikes and trips in Virginia, Maryland, and Pennsylvania.

Center Hiking Club, (301) 468-1896, www.centerhikingclub.org. Hikes and trips in Virginia, Maryland, and Pennsylvania.

Wanderbirds Hiking Club, www.wanderbirds.org. Hikes in the Washington, DC, area.

Washington Women Outdoors, Germantown, MD, (301) 864-3070, www .washingtonwomenoutdoors.org. Outdoor adventures for women, including hiking, kayaking, rock climbing, and biking in the Washington, DC, area.

Northern Virginia Hiking Club, Arlington, www.nvhc.com

Other Resources

Potomac Appalachian Trail Club (PATC), Vienna, (703) 242-0315, www.patc.net. Hikes in the Washington, DC, area. Contact for maps and book orders, cabin rentals, scheduled hikes, and membership. The PATC Map D covers Scotts Run, as does the PATC guidebook.

Public Transportation

Metro Bus, (202) 637-7000, www.wmata.com

9 Great Falls Park

Land and history are interwoven throughout Great Falls Park—the spot where George Washington championed a canal to skirt the Potomac River's 77-foot "great falls." This may be metropolitan DC, but beyond the crowds, you can find small reminders of a time when our nation's capital was a tidal backwater and our country's survival wasn't assured. Stones in a restored canal wall bear inscriptions unique to the masons who built it. Ruins of old chimneys and homes in Matildaville mark the boomtown that lived and died on hopes that the Patowmack Canal would succeed. For a time it did succeed, ferrying farm goods from western lands to eastern seaports. Then it went bankrupt, leaving us with canal ruins, inspired views over Mather Gorge, wildflowers that bloom spring through fall, and a moment of solitude.

Start: Park visitor center
Distance: 5.1-mile loop
Hiking time: 2–3 hours.
Difficulty: Easy; well-traveled trails with a few short, steep sections along the Potomac
Trail surface: Rocky cliff tops, dirt footpaths, dirt roads, riverside trails, hardwood forests, and marsh
Land status: National park
Nearest town: Great Falls, VA
Other trail users: Joggers, cross-country skiers, equestrians, mountain bikers, and rock climbers
Accessibility: Overlooks 2 and 3 are fully accessible, as is the Patowmack Canal Trail to the Holding Basin and the guard gate.
Canine compatibility: Leashed dogs permitted

Trail contact: Great Falls Park, Great Falls; (703) 285-2965; www.nps.gov/grfa (Great Falls is one park in a series under the umbrella of the George Washington Memorial Parkway. Other spots worth visiting are Turkey Run Park, Theodore Roosevelt Island, Arlington National Cemetery, and Dike Marsh Wildlife Preserve.)
Schedule: Open daily, 7 a.m. to sunset, except Christmas
Fees/permits: Entrance fee, good for 3 days and access to Maryland's C&O Canal National Historical Park. A state fishing license is required to fish in the park.
Facilities/features: Visitor center with museum and children's room, snack bar, restrooms, and picnic facilities
Maps: USGS Vienna, Falls Church

Finding the trailhead: From I-495, take exit 44 and turn left onto Georgetown Pike/VA 193. Go 4.4 miles and turn right onto Old Dominion Drive. Go 0.9 mile to the park. GPS: N38 59.820' / W77 15.277'. *DeLorme: Virginia Atlas & Gazetteer:* Page 76, A3.

The Hike

On a spring afternoon, an eagle soars above craggy Potomac river rocks below Great Falls, a 77-foot vertical drop of thunder, mist, and frothing water. The raptor dips and alights on the south wall of Mather Gorge. Upended boulders show distinct layers of compressed rock that built the gorge millions of years ago. Spleenwort ferns grow thick here, where the River Trail cuts dangerously close to the cliff edge. Lined with

An artist captures the powerful beauty of Great Falls of the Potomac.

pink spring beauties in May, this 1.5-mile route follows an up-and-down course, eventually reaching river level at the far southern end of the park. It gets heavy use, with side trails leading to gorgeous overlooks of the waterfalls. Beyond these points, however, foot traffic dwindles and the River Trail becomes a nice conduit to the less crowded areas in the park's southern reaches.

It should be expected that a park 20 miles from the nation's capital attracts a large number of visitors. Kayakers test their mettle in the surf below the falls. Rock climbers dangle off Birds Nest, one of the many mapped climbs on the cliffs of Mather Gorge. Joggers use the wide Matildaville Trail and Old Carriage Road. Painters set up easel and palette along Falls Overlook Trail. Picnickers lounge in grassy fields under shady red oaks.

All the activity makes the Swamp Trail—in the southern section of the park—that much more attractive. It's a hiker-only path that branches off the Ridge Trail. From a slight hill, it drops through a forest of tulip poplar and beech and reaches a swampy confluence of unnamed streams. Sluggish and meandering, the streams support a lush undergrowth of wood fern and wildflowers. Concave green trillium leaves spread across a widening forest floor. It's unusual to see this wildflower in such great numbers east of the Blue Ridge, but it thrives in these wet conditions nonetheless. In fact, on this brief stretch of trail, plant life approaches the variety typical of an Appalachian cove—a forest type defined by its wet, sheltered climate and diversity of trees and plants. Eastern hemlock, white basswood, tulip poplar—with a little sleuthing, you'll find representatives of each tree along the Swamp Trail.

▶ **Kid Appeal: Ages five and up can earn a Junior Ranger Badge. Pick up the booklet at the visitor center desk.**

The priceless scenery we enjoy today was viewed by James Rumsey as merely supplies. Rumsey came to Great Falls in 1785 as the overseer of construction on the Patowmack Canal, handpicked by George Washington and carrying tremendous expectations. From hophornbeam trees, Rumsey's workers fashioned tool handles. White oak trees fell to make planks for supply boats. Masons carved canal walls out of the bedrock. They inscribed finished blocks with a unique symbol to ensure they could document their work for pay.

Canal Cut, the final descent on the Great Falls skirting canal, drops 76 feet through solid rock in Mather Gorge. Considered an engineering marvel in its time, the canal—and especially this last passage—evolved painfully. Dynamite was a discovery some eighty years away, so workers on the Patowmack Canal hand-drilled boreholes, poured in black powder, and ignited the volatile mix. If dust particles exploded prematurely, few within range survived. Despite the difficulties in building the canal, George Washington believed the Potomac River, with its long reach from the coast into western farmlands, would serve as a great unifier for a young nation. He wasn't the first or the last to view the river as a means to an end. From the day Captain John Smith ventured up the Potomac to Little Falls (near present-day Georgetown), Americans have had their way with this river. Explorers, canal builders, farmers, miners, theme-park promoters—each has left a mark. Today various agencies, commissions, and nonprofits pursue watershed protection and monitor stream pollutants. Industries and farms situated in the Potomac's massive four-state, 15,000-square-mile river basin discharge pollutants into its tributaries daily. Along the southern shores of the middle Potomac, Northern Virginia continues to grow every year. Housing subdivisions gobble up land on such small tributaries as Bullneck Run, Pimmit Run, and Difficult Run.

But as Washington's Patowmack Canal illustrates all too well, the river has the final say. Despite Herculean efforts, seasonal fluctuations in water levels made the canal operable only a few months during the year. It declared bankruptcy in 1828.

For twenty-six years the Great Falls Canal moved thousands of pounds of flour, corn, livestock, and farm goods from western territories to eastern ports. Each boat that passed through finished its journey by dropping through Canal Cut. This same passage today bears little resemblance to its heyday. Trees cling to the hard-hewn cliff walls. Weeds grow everywhere. And beyond it all, the Potomac, America's river, keeps on rolling.

Miles and Directions

0.0 Start from the park visitor center. Walk around the building on a wide, graded path of dirt and crushed rock. Where the path splits, bear right (southeast). Once past the visitor center, turn left (east) onto Falls Overlook Trail, which leads past Overlooks 1, 2, and 3.

0.2 Bear left (southeast) onto blue-blazed River Trail. The route starts out as a wide dirt path, then narrows into a rocky footpath. **Note:** The trail straight from this junction is the Patow-mack Canal Trail and marks the return portion of this hike.

0.5 Turn left (east) at a four-way trail intersection and descend a set of stairs to the edge of the Potomac. When you're finished exploring, return to this junction and turn left (east) to resume hiking the River Trail.

0.8 Turn right (west) on a dirt footpath for a detour around Canal Cut. Cross two boardwalks, and then turn left (south). Within 0.1 mile, the route returns to follow the cliffs high above Mather Gorge.

1.2 Cross straight over a paved service road and reenter woods opposite. Stay alert over the next 0.1 mile when River Trail runs close and parallel to the Matildaville Trail on the right.

1.4 Look for remains of a redbrick fireplace off the left side of the trail. A few hundred yards beyond this, look downhill to the left, where a sandy beach is visible. The trail here crosses exposed rock, and footing is tough and technical as you come to Cow Hoof Rock. This promontory is your last chance to catch stellar views of the Potomac as it flows through Mather Gorge.

1.6 A steep climb ends at a T junction with Ridge Trail. Turn left (south) onto Ridge, which is a wide dirt road.

2.1 Stay straight at a left turn in Ridge Trail. A footpath dives off the hillside to reach Difficult Run near its confluence with the Potomac. This short, steep descent is a bushwhack on an unmarked trail. **Option:** For a route that bypasses this bushwhack, turn right (west) at 2.1 miles and follow Ridge Trail downhill to Difficult Run, then turn right (north). Resume mileage cues at 2.3 miles.

2.2 Emerge from the wooded hillside onto Difficult Run Trail, a wide road of hard-packed dirt and gravel. Turn right (north) and walk along the stream. Numerous side trails off to your left lead to overlooks onto Difficult Run and its many cascading falls.

2.3 Stay straight (north) as Ridge Trail intersects Difficult Run Trail. **Note:** If you opted for a right turn at 2.1 miles, resume mileage cues here.

2.8 Turn right (north) on an unmarked footpath that climbs steeply uphill. **Note:** This is a bushwhack on an established but unmarked trail. There are no trail signs or blazes at this junction. Prior to reaching it, look for a clearing on the right side of the trail that has the

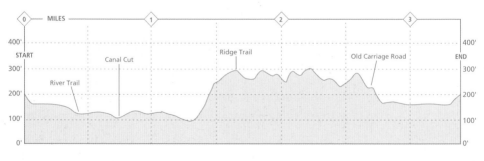

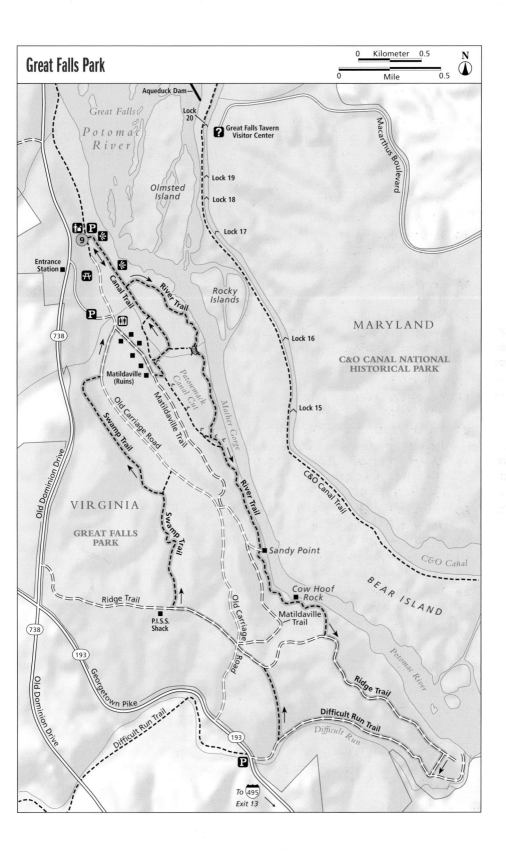

Great Falls Park

Kilometer 0.5

Mile 0.5

N

Aqueduck Dam

Lock 20

Great Falls
Potomac
River

? Great Falls Tavern
Visitor Center

Lock 19

Olmsted
Island

Lock 18

Lock 17

Entrance
Station

9

P

Canal Trail

River Trail

Rocky
Islands

Lock 16

Patowmack
Canal Cut

Matildaville
(Ruins)

Matildaville Trail

Mather Gorge

Lock 15

MARYLAND

C&O CANAL NATIONAL
HISTORICAL PARK

738

Old Carriage Road

Swamp Trail

VIRGINIA

GREAT FALLS
PARK

River Trail

C&O Canal Trail

Swamp Trail

Sandy Point

C&O Canal

Ridge Trail

Cow Hoof
Rock

BEAR ISLAND

P.I.S.S.
Shack

Matildaville
Trail

Old Carriage Road

Potomac River

738

193

Old Dominion Drive

Georgetown Pike

Ridge Trail

Difficult Run Trail

Difficult Run Trail

Difficult Run

193

P

To 495
Exit 13

Old Dominion Drive

Macarthus Boulevard

Remains of the historic Patowmack Canal at Great Falls Park.

appearance of an old quarry—or a severely eroded hillside. If you reach Georgetown Pike, you've gone too far; turn and retrace your steps.

3.0 Veer left (north) onto Ridge Trail and descend in 0.1 mile to a junction with Old Carriage Road. Cross straight over the road and climb.

3.2 Turn right (north) onto the Swamp Trail Connector.

3.5 Turn left (northwest) onto Swamp Trail. **Note:** This junction may not be marked, and the trail straight ahead (leading to Old Carriage Road) seems like the more obvious route. Swamp Trail is a singletrack woodland path, while the spur is a wide, grassy path elevated above the low, wet ground on a berm.

3.9 Turn left (north) onto Old Carriage Road.

4.1 Turn right (south) onto Matildaville Trail. There is a restroom a few feet north of this junction.

4.3 Veer left and downhill where Matildaville Trail branches right and enters the woods as a narrow footpath. Descend to a T junction with Patowmack Canal Trail. Turn right and follow the old canal route to Lock 1. After exploring the ruins, return to this junction and continue straight (north) on Patowmack Canal Trail. Look for side trails on the left that lead to ruins of the canal superintendent's home and other Matildaville homes.

4.6 Turn right at a fork in Patowmack Trail and cross the canal's holding basin. Within a few feet, a footbridge spanning a small creek was dug to control water levels in the holding basin. Beyond this footbridge, continue straight past a trail on the right that descends on a set of stairs to River Trail.

4.7 Stay straight as a leg of Patowmack Canal Trail merges on the right.

5.1 Arrive back at the visitor center.

Hike Information

Local Information

Fairfax County Visitors Center, Tysons Corner, (703) 752-9500, www.fxva.com

Local Events/Attractions

Reston Concerts on the Town, Sat evenings in June, July, and Aug, (703) 912-4062, www.restontowncenter.com. Sit back and enjoy a variety of musical entertainers under the stars.

Wolf Trap National Park for the Performing Arts, Vienna, (703) 255-1800, www.nps.gov/wotr. National park dedicated to performing arts. Three different facilities offer year-round performances. The Theater in the Woods is geared especially toward children.

Lodging

Arlington and Alexandria Bed & Breakfast Network, (703) 549-3415, www.aabbn.com. Assists with reservations for 30 area bed-and-breakfasts.

Restaurants

Old Brogue Irish Pub, Great Falls, (703) 759-3309, www.oldbrogue.com. Traditional Irish fare and live entertainment.

Deli Italiano, Great Falls, (703) 759-6782, www.deliitaliano.com. Grab a sandwich before heading into the park, or a slice of pizza afterward.

Serbian Crown, 1141 Walker Rd., Great Falls, (703) 759-4150, www.serbiancrown.com. Fine Russian and French dining, with lighter fare at the piano bar.

Tavern at Great Falls, Great Falls, (703) 757-4770, www.greatfallstavern.com. Classic American cuisine and comfort food.

Hike Tours

Park staff lead nature and historical tours throughout the year. See the schedule of events at www.nps.gov/grfa or call (703) 285-2965 for information.

Organizations

Fairfax Trails & Streams, www.fairfaxtrails.org. Champion of the Pimmit Run Trail and Fairfax Cross-County Trail, with links to other Northern Virginia hiking and preservation efforts.

Capital Hiking Club, www.capitalhikingclub.org. Hikes and trips in Virginia, Maryland, and Pennsylvania.

Center Hiking Club, (301) 468-1896, www.centerhikingclub.org. Hikes and trips in Virginia, Maryland, and Pennsylvania.

Wanderbirds Hiking Club, www.wanderbirds.org. Hikes in the Washington, DC, area.

Washington Women Outdoors, Germantown, MD, (301) 864-3070, www.washingtonwomenoutdoors.org. Outdoor adventures for women, including hiking, kayaking, rock climbing, and biking in the Washington, DC, area.

Northern Virginia Hiking Club, Arlington, www.nvhc.com

Other Resources

Chesapeake & Ohio Canal National Historical Park, Sharpsburg, MD, (301) 739-4200, www.nps.gov/choh. The C&O Canal along the Potomac River in Maryland succeeded where Washington's Patowmack Canal failed by linking farm markets west of the Appalachians to eastern seaports.

Potomac Appalachian Trail Club (PATC), Vienna, (703) 242-0315, www.patc.net. Contact for maps, book orders, cabin rentals, scheduled hikes, and membership. PATC Map D covers Great Falls and vicinity.

10 G. Richard Thompson Wildlife Management Area

Virginia's Department of Game & Inland Fisheries oversees thirty wildlife management areas around the state with the hunter and angler in mind. Fields are kept clear to attract grazing animals, and seed plots are sown to keep them plump and healthy. Streams and man-made lakes are stocked with trout and other fish. As the state makes these areas hiker-friendly as well, they'd do well to model the G. Richard Thompson Wildlife Management Area in Fauquier County, where hikers and naturalists stake as much a claim to the beautiful surroundings as outdoorsmen. The network of trails include a 7-mile section of the Appalachian Trail. There is an abundance of wildflowers—the area harbors one of the largest populations of large-flowered trillium in North America. Virginia's Native Plant Society lists the Thompson Wildlife Management Area on its register of important native plant sites.

Start: Stone Wall Loop: Parking Area 7; Ted Lake Loop: Upper Ted Lake Parking Area
Distance: Stone Wall Loop: 4.3 miles; Ted Lake Loop: 2.0 miles
Hiking time: 3–4 hours to do both loops
Difficulty: Easy along wide roads. Younger or inexperienced hikers may have difficulty with blowdowns on the unmaintained trail along the Stone Wall Loop to connect with the Appalachian Trail.
Trail surface: Dirt roads and woods paths wind through young second- and third-generation forests dominated by deciduous trees. This is the Blue Ridge, but the hills are more rolling than steep.
Land status: State wildlife management area
Nearest town: Linden, VA
Other trail users: Anglers, cyclists, equestrians, hunters (in season), and naturalists

Accessibility: Vehicle access and parking at Thompson Lake (Mile 2.0 in the Stone Wall Loop.)
Canine compatibility: Dogs permitted but must be leashed at all times outside of open hunting, chase, or training seasons
Trail contact: G. R. Thompson Wildlife Management Area, Sperryville; regional office (540) 899-4169; www.dgif.virginia.gov/wmas
Schedule: Open daily year-round, dawn to dusk. Hunting season for big and small game runs from Oct into Jan.
Fees/permits: Daily fee for those 17 and older. Fee is waived with a valid Virginia fishing, hunting, or trapping license. Visit www.dgif .virginia.gov/access-permit/ for daily permit information.
Facilities/features: None
Maps: USGS Linden, Upperville; good maps of trail network available at www.dgif.virginia .gov/wmas

Finding the trailhead: From I-66, take exit 13, turn left, and drive 0.2 mile south on VA 79. Turn left (east) on VA 55 and drive 1.3 miles to Linden. Turn left (north) on Freezeland Road (VA 638) and drive 3.5 miles to the Ted Lake Parking Area on the right. To reach Parking Area 7, continue 2.3 miles (the parking area is 0.1 mile after the road turns to gravel). GPS: Ted Lake Parking Area, N38 56.226' / W78 02.621'; Parking Area 7, N38 57.784' / W78 01.184'. *DeLorme: Virginia Atlas & Gazetteer:* Page 75, A5.

Hiking along the reservoir in the G. Richard Thompson Wildlife Management Area.

The Hike

It never received headlines the way taxes or elections seem to, but native plant lovers throughout Virginia still celebrated when the state declared purple loosestrife a "noxious weed." The very word *noxious* showed how seriously botanists view alien species. "Harmful to health, injurious, corrupting or unwholesome" are a few of the descriptors now legally associated with loosestrife, which is especially damaging to freshwater wetlands.

The battle against invasive alien species seems never-ending; they outcompete native plants and disrupt the web of life—in which native plants play an irreplaceable role. Kudzu was, for years, enemy Number One. Virginia's Department of Transportation planted it as groundcover along roadways. Much later, they watched this plant engulf entire stands of trees and shrubs. In Shenandoah National Park, rangers have watched as ailanthus (aka tree of heaven) replaces stands of oak killed by gypsy moth infestation. In coastal communities, the common reed spreads uncontrollably in wetland settings. The reed's root structure sinks 6 feet deep and deeper, making it impossible to extricate except through repeated burning and chemicals. Worse, this alien grass outcompetes the hays and cordgrasses that make a healthy marsh ecosystem.

If all this ever gets too much, Virginia's native plant lovers and wildflower aficionados—and anyone else for that matter—can find respite in the G. Richard Thompson Wildlife Management Area. Draped across the east side of the Blue Ridge Mountains, this small patch of land in far-western Fauquier County hosts an array of wildflowers. Most noticeable in April through June are the large-flowered trillium (1996 Wildflower of the Year in Virginia) that grow in large swatches on the slopes of this preserve.

Thompson Wildlife Management Area (WMA) is thought to have one of the largest concentrated populations of this wildflower anywhere in North America.

The Thompson WMA is not so much a destination as it is a place to wander. The easy 2-mile Ted Lake Loop leads through patches of mayapple, with blackberry bushes and sassafras filling the forest understory. Yellow poplar grows tall, as do the oaks that survived gypsy moth attacks in the mid-1980s. A tangle of wildflowers in a hedgerow alongside the trail sports delicate, white-petaled flowers with a sweet, apple-like fragrance. The return on the Appalachian Trail leads past an old home foundation and a heap of scrap metal. The white flowers that cover blackberry bushes in May hold promise of trailside snacking come July.

Several large birch trees stand out on the unblazed

Large-flowered trillium are common in the G. Richard Thompson Wildlife Management Area. US FISH & WILDLIFE SERVICE

path that leads back to the parking area. Where a large blowdown forces you to detour, the newly worn path leads not to brambles and frustration, but to large patches of trillium. Even when not in bloom, the flower is easily recognizable by its three broad leaves. Anyone familiar with the leaf appearance of garden-variety lilies will see the resemblance in trillium leaves. It's hard to imagine this flower is a cousin of the onion and asparagus, which are also members of the lily family.

The interaction between trillium and insects makes for a fascinating study of how various forms of life—plant, animal, and insect—rely on each other. The trillium's bright coloring attracts bees and butterflies, yet a nose-to-nose study of the flower proves it to have quite an offensive odor. That explains the presence of flies, which are the primary pollinators of trillium. In the matter of seed dispersal, plants generally rely heavily on birds ingesting then discharging seeds far afield. In the case of the trillium, its seeds excrete an oily substance that attracts ants, which come in droves and eat them.

If the Ted Lake Loop leaves you hungry for more hiking, follow a wide, grassy road leading out of Parking Area 7; it's the Stone Wall Loop. The old road ends at serene Lake Thompson, a man-made impound upon which ducks float and anglers cast their lines. There are plenty of distractions en route. A black snake slithers across the trail, and, a few minutes past it, rustling in the leaves leads to the discovery of a small, yellow-marked box turtle. Left unmolested, this reptile could live more than sixty years. If you're wondering how to tell its age, look at the shell. If it's 5 inches or smaller, the turtle is probably ten years old or younger.

Off either side of the trail, the surrounding forest shows signs of youth. The saplings are skinny and obstruct any clear view. The exception comes a half mile downhill from the parking area, where another overgrown road leads right, into the woods to a fire ring and a massive yellow poplar. Someone, a long time ago, had girdled the tree. A ring incised deep into the trunk would kill the tree slowly.

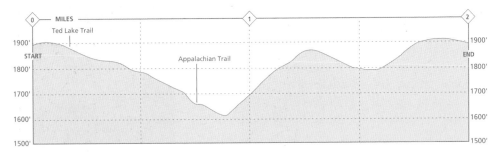

John Cahill, former president of the Nature Conservancy, once said: "Our society will be defined not only by what we create, but what we refuse to destroy." Staring at this old, grizzled tree, still standing despite repeated attacks to bring it down, brings that sentiment to mind. By saving small pockets of land like Thompson WMA, we acknowledge this is important. And every visit here makes us a community with others who have walked through the woods. As Shakespeare wrote: "One touch of nature makes the whole world kin."

Miles and Directions

Ted Lake Loop

0.0 Start at Ted Lake Parking Area where a dirt road, the Ted Lake Trail, heads downhill in a southeast direction. The road is wide and clear of obstacles. Blue blazes are few and far between. A hiker should ignore the double-yellow slash marks that appear on trees to the right of the road.

0.7 Turn left onto the white-blazed AT. The trail is a narrow footpath. In a few feet, a spur trail exits right to Manassas Gap Shelter. **Note:** There is a spring near the shelter. Treat any water before drinking it.

1.2 After a long, steady climb, the AT levels briefly, then undulates around rock outcrops. The forest consists of young eastern hornbeam, oak, and poplar. The large bushes alongside the trail are nannyberry, which flower in May and June. The small blue-black berries hanging off the red, drooping stalk are edible.

1.5 Turn left, as the AT intersects and runs concurrent with the Verlin Smith Trail.

1.6 At a three-way intersection, turn left and follow an unmarked road uphill in a southwest direction. Also at this intersection, the AT splits right and descends. The Verlin Smith Trail continues straight and reaches VA 638 at Parking Area 5 in 0.6 mile.

1.9 Emerge from the woods onto the Ted Lake Trail and turn right, uphill, to return to the parking area.

2.0 Arrive back at Ted Lake Parking Area.

Stone Wall Loop

0.0 Start from Parking Area 7. Hike down the chained-off road that drops off the left side of the parking lot. The road is gravel at first, then reverts to dirt and grass.

0.2 Walk straight past a junction with the Appalachian Trail (AT). **Side trip:** A right on the AT leads to Manassas Gap Shelter in 3 miles.

G. Richard Thompson Wildlife Management Area

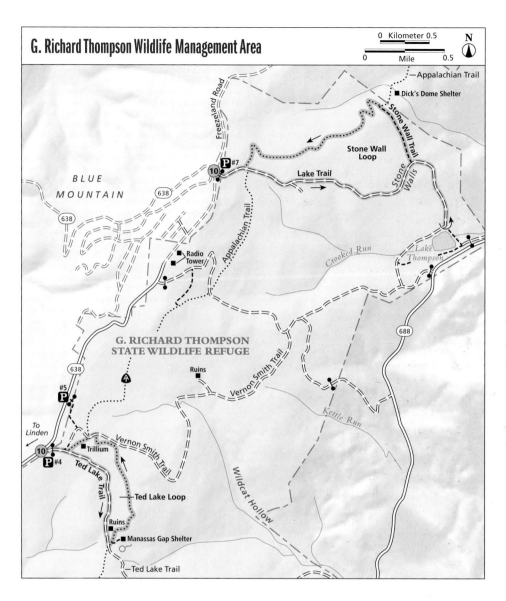

0.5 A grass road veers off to the right. Continue straight downhill on the main grass road.

0.6 Continue straight downhill past another grass road that turns right into a clearing. There is a fire ring in the clearing and a huge yellow poplar tree that survived a girdling many years ago.

1.3 The trail levels and on both sides, remnants of stone walls are visible. Within 0.1 mile, the trail passes a large black locust tree on the right. Continue toward the right on the grass road as an overgrown, unblazed footpath known as Stone Wall Trail branches off to the left.

1.8 The road emerges from the cover of trees. Ahead is a nice view across a valley to a farm on the opposite hill. The trail has the width of a road, but there is only a narrow footpath through waist-high grass.

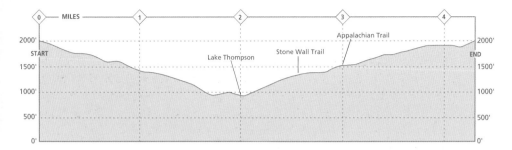

2.0 Reach Lake Thompson. Backtrack uphill. **Note:** Lake Thompson is stocked with rainbow trout and brown trout. White geese float on the small man-made impoundment. A multitude of butterflies flutter around milkweed. (Road access to the lake is via VA 688.)

2.6 Turn right onto an overgrown, unblazed footpath known as Stone Wall Trail. Within a few feet, you will cross a stone wall. As you climb from Lake Thompson, the black locust tree you passed at 1.3 miles makes a good landmark for where to make this right turn.

2.9 Pass by a set of large boulders in the woods to the left and climb steeply.

3.0 Emerge from the woods onto the AT. Walk straight ahead on the singletrack, white-blazed AT. **Side trip:** The AT downhill to the right reaches Dick's Dome Shelter in 0.3 mile.

4.1 Pass a huge oak tree on the left. In a few yards, the AT emerges onto a grass road. Turn right and head uphill to Parking Area 7.

4.3 Arrive back at Parking Area 7.

Hike Information

Local Information

Warrenton–Fauquier County Visitor Center, Warrenton, (540) 347-4414, www .fauquierchamber.org

Local Events / Attractions

Virginia & International Gold Cup Races, May and Oct, The Plains, (540) 347-2612, www.vagoldcup.com

Virginia Scottish Games & Festival, Sept, The Plains, www.vascottishgames.org

Linden Vineyards, Linden, (540) 364-1997, www.lindenvineyards.com

Organizations

Virginia Native Plant Society, Boyce, (540) 837-1600, www.vnps.org. Located at Blandy Experimental Farm in the Virginia State Arboretum.

Other Resources

Potomac Appalachian Trail Club (PATC), Vienna, (703) 242-0315, www.patc.net. Contact for maps and book orders, cabin rentals, scheduled hikes, and membership.

11 Rock Creek Park

As far back as 1866, people recognized Rock Creek's natural beauty and fought to protect it. It would be another quarter century before an actual park came into being. Long, narrow, and heavily wooded, this 10-mile-long park is a twisty green stripe through a sea of urbanism. It is also a magnet for hikers, joggers, horseback riders, and others. The spacious northern section of the park is big enough to hold them all. Here, it is hilly and wooded, with room to roam.

Start: Rock Creek Nature Center
Distance: 7.1-mile loop
Hiking time: 2-3 hours
Difficulty: Moderate due to distance and some confusing trail junctions
Trail surface: Paved paths, dirt woodland paths, and roads
Land status: National park
Nearest town: Washington, DC
Other trail users: Horseback riders, joggers, walkers, in-line skaters, and cyclists
Accessibility: The Edge of Wood Trail at the Nature Center is paved and has a rope guide for the visually impaired.
Canine compatibility: Leashed dogs permitted
Trail contact: Rock Creek Park, 3545 Williamsburg Lane NW, Washington, DC; (202) 895-6000, www.nps.gov/rocr
Schedule: The park is open daily during daylight hours. The Nature Center is open 9 a.m. to 5 p.m. Wed through Sat; closed Thanksgiving, Christmas, and New Year's Day.
Fees/permits: None, except for groups using the picnic area
Facilities/features: There are restrooms at the Nature Center and a chemical toilet at the Boundary Bridge parking area. The Nature Center features natural history displays and a planetarium. Throughout Rock Creek Park are historic buildings, tennis courts, a golf course, and an equestrian center.
Maps: USGS Washington West, DC, MD, VA; PATC Map N: Rock Creek Park Area
Special considerations: The park closes sections of Beach Drive to cars from 7 a.m. to 7 p.m. on weekends and federal holidays for recreational use by hikers, bicyclists, runners, and in-line skaters. Closed sections are: Beach Drive north from Broad Branch Road to Military Highway; from Picnic Area 10 to Wise Road; and West Beach Drive to the Boundary Bridge parking area. Bingham Drive and Sherrill Drive are also closed weekends and federal holidays.

In the south region of the park, the Rock Creek and Potomac Parkway traffic flow is altered for weekday rush-hour traffic. From Connecticut Avenue, it is one-way going south from 6:45 to 9:30 a.m., and one-way going north from 3:45 to 6:30 p.m. Also, access streets like Glover Road, Ross Drive, Bingham Drive, and Sherrill Drive are not maintained after heavy snowfall or in icy conditions.

Finding the trailhead: From Northern Virginia, cross the Potomac on I-66/US 50 (the Theodore Roosevelt Memorial Bridge). Take the Independence Avenue exit (right lane) and, after merging onto Independence, in quick succession turn right and merge onto Rock Creek and Potomac Parkway. In 0.7 mile, continue straight at an intersection with Virginia Avenue. As road signs indicate Connecticut Avenue approaching, stay right and follow signs for the National Zoo and Beach Drive. (**Note:** The Rock Creek and Potomac Parkway ends at Connecticut Avenue; Beach Drive becomes the main north-south route through Rock Creek Park.) Continue straight on Beach Drive at Klingle Avenue on the left and Piney Branch Parkway on the right. There is a traffic light at Beach Drive and Park Road/Tilden Street. In 0.3 mile past this, bear left at an intersection with Blagden Avenue. At 100 yards past this, turn left off Beach Drive onto Broad Branch Road. (**Note**: Beach Drive from this point north to Military Road is closed on weekends and holidays.) Cross Rock Creek and immediately turn right on Glover Road, following signs for the Rock Creek Nature Center. In less than 1 mile, fork left and uphill, avoiding Ross Drive, which forks right and downhill. In 0.8 mile past this fork, turn right into the Nature Center parking area.

From downtown Washington, DC, follow directions above from the intersection of the Rock Creek and Potomac Parkway and Virginia Avenue. Or, take New Hampshire Avenue north from DuPont Circle for 0.6 mile. Turn left onto 16th Street NW and in 3 miles, turn right onto a entrance ramp for Military Road. In 1 mile, turn left onto Glover Road. In 0.5 mile, turn left into the Nature Center parking area.

From Maryland and I-495/Capital Beltway, take exit 31B/Georgia Avenue, following signs for Georgia Avenue South and Silver Springs. Once on Georgia Avenue, stay in either of the two right lanes so that in 0.3 mile from I-495, you can exit right onto 16th Street. In 3.1 miles, turn right and merge onto Military Road. In 1 mile, turn left onto Glover Road. In 0.5 mile, turn left into the Nature Center parking area. Trailhead GPS: N38 57.594' / W77 03.103'. *DeLorme: Maryland/ Delaware Atlas & Gazetteer: Page 46, B3.*

The Hike

Rock Creek Park, at its broadest, is only a mile wide. It is a nearly 10-mile-long narrow stream valley park that passes as the long green swath of trees separating downtown Washington, DC, and Georgetown. But to look at it as a single homogenous unit is to miss the small details that make moving between the upland woods and streamside a joy.

Unmarked, but well used, are several angler's paths through floodplains along Rock Creek. If you're hiking the Valley Trail, you'll find one in a wide bend in the river north of Riley Spring Bridge; the other is between West Beach Drive and Boundary Bridge. They are the proverbial low road, alternatives to the higher, drier route of the official Valley Trail.

One advantage in following them is personal satisfaction. These unmarked paths bring you close to the creek. On a sandbar, a few tree logs that washed downstream in a high flood sit high and dry, perfect perches for a snack and relaxing. The stream is a melodious riffle, not so loud that you can't hear bird chatter. Rock Creek in calm water reflects back yellow and red leaves on overhanging trees, making a shimmering mirage of color.

In terms of plants, the floodplain just feels different from the upland. Here there is more smooth alder, but less holly, which is abundant in the understory of the drier forests that cover the stream valley's sloping hills. There is American hornbeam, a skinny tree whose ripply trunk and tight gray bark give the appearance of muscles. It's an apt comparison; this tough, heavy wood was preferred for making handles for axes and sledgehammers.

Rock Creek: The park's namesake stream.

Yellow poplar and American beech are two of the main trees you'll find in an upland forest, but in the floodplain, they're replaced by eastern black walnut. Donald Culross Peattie, in his book *A Natural History of Trees,* ranks black walnut second only behind pecan in usefulness. Indians chewed the bark to ease toothaches, and processed black walnut shells are "soft grit abrasives" and as such are perfect for "cleaning jet engines, electronic circuit boards, ships, and automobile gear systems."

The northern section of Rock Creek Park is the perfect spot to "converse" with both the upland woods and streamside floodplains. A long stretch of the West Ridge Trail, north from Bingham Drive to Beach Drive, covers hilly terrain. It is the largest chunk of unspoiled woodland in park, with only Wise Road bisecting it. This is the territory of the great horned owl and the screech owl.

A detour from this heavy upland forest down along Pinehurst Branch leads to other discoveries. By October, hackberry trees are in fruit along the Pinehurst

Bikers in Rock Creek Park.

Branch Trail, offering songbirds like the cedar waxwing valuable fuel. There are three shallow-water fords across the branch on our route; the last is a scramble up the stream bank to dry ground. The trail uphill is a narrow path that in summer almost disappears beneath the crowded shrub understory. In no time you're standing atop a knoll amid red oaks and tulip poplars. In this spot, in a park that records two million recreational visits annually, you can hear an acorn drop.

Miles and Directions

0.0   Start from the front entrance of the Rock Creek Nature Center. Follow a paved path west past the Edge of Woods Trail on the right. Where the path Ts, turn right (north) onto the green-blazed Western Ridge Trail, which here shares the route with a paved bike path. Walk downhill to four-lane Military Road and cross straight over.

0.2 Turn right at an interpretive sign for Fort De Russy. In the next 0.1 mile, you will veer left off the paved path as Western Ridge Trail becomes a wide dirt trail. Soon after this, make a right (north) turn at a double green blaze as Western Ridge Trail becomes a narrow woods trail. **Side trip:** The wide dirt path that continues straight from this double green blaze is a horse trail. In 200 yards or so, it passes the ruins of Fort De Russy, a Civil War–era defense. This is also the return leg of this hike.

0.5 Turn left at a double green blaze for Western Ridge Trail. **Note:** Straight ahead is Cross Trail 5 (CT 5), which descends to Millerhouse Ford on Rock Creek.

0.6 Emerge from the woods and trace a horse pasture fence on your right. At the end of the fence line, turn right (north) and walk between the pasture and a community garden on the right. The trail meets a paved road. Turn left (west) on the road, keeping a line of stubby wooden posts on your right.

0.7 Turn right onto a paved path marked by a wooden post with a green blaze for Western Ridge Trail. **Note:** This path is immediately past a gated road that will parallel the trail for a few hundred yards.

0.9 Cross Bingham Drive diagonal left. On the far side, Western Ridge Trail is still a paved path. Within a hundred yards, follow Western Ridge Trail as it forks left. Walk another 20 feet and turn right (north) on Western Ridge, which is now a path of dirt and crushed rock.

1.1 Stay straight on the green-blazed Western Ridge Trail at a junction with Cross Trail 3 (CT 3).

1.3 Western Ridge Trail veers right at a fork in the trail. Follow it a few feet downhill to a four-way trail junction. Turn right (east) onto Pinehurst Branch Trail and descend to cross the stream at a picturesque wading pool. This trail is for foot traffic only and is one of the most scenic in the park.

1.6 Cross Pinehurst Branch again at another scenic spot. The stream, now on your left side, makes a wide bend. At low water, exposed stream rocks are a perch to sit and soak in the scenery.

1.7 Pinehurst Branch Trail reaches a four-way trail junction. Turn left (east) and descend the stream bank to cross Pinehurst Branch. On the opposite side, turn left (north) and start to climb an unnamed, unmarked footpath. The route is steep on a narrow footpath that in summer is nearly overrun by shrubs and small trees.

1.8 At a T junction with another unnamed, unmarked trail, turn left (west).

2.1 Turn right (north) onto the green-blazed Western Ridge Trail.

2.2 Stay straight (north) on Western Ridge Trail at a junction with Cross Trail 2 (CT 2), which heads downhill to the right to Riley Spring Bridge on Rock Creek.

2.5 Cross Wise Road and reenter the woods on Western Ridge Trail, which here is a dirt footpath.

2.9 Western Ridge Trail ends at Beach Drive. Walk straight across the road, and reenter the woods at a wood trail sign that marks the trailhead for the blue-blazed Valley Trail. Briefly, this dirt footpath skirts the Boundary Bridge parking area on your left. **Note:** There is a chemical toilet at the parking area.

3.0 Turn right (north) and follow Valley Trail, now a wide, graded path of dirt and crushed rock, across Rock Creek on the Boundary Bridge. A few feet past the bridge, veer right (east) off Valley Trail onto a well-trod but unmarked angler's path. **Note:** The angler's path and Valley Trail are near West Beach Road. We prefer the angler's path—the low road, if you will— because it keeps us close to the creek and is good for bird sightings like great blue heron.

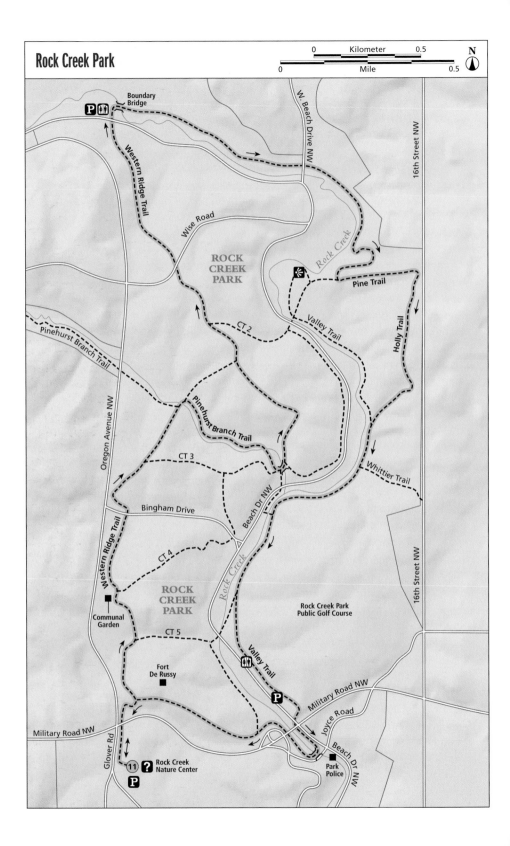

Rock Creek Park

0 Kilometer 0.5

0 Mile 0.5

N

Boundary Bridge

W. Beach Drive NW

16th Street NW

Western Ridge Trail

Wise Road

ROCK CREEK PARK

Rock Creek

Pine Trail

Pinehurst Branch Trail

CT 2

Valley Trail

Holly Trail

Oregon Avenue NW

Pinehurst Branch Trail

CT 3

Whittier Trail

Bingham Drive

Beach Dr NW

Western Ridge Trail

CT 4

Rock Creek

ROCK CREEK PARK

Rock Creek Park Public Golf Course

16th Street NW

Communal Garden

CT 5

Fort De Russy

Valley Trail

Military Road NW

Joyce Road

Military Road NW

Glover Rd

11

Rock Creek Nature Center

Beach Dr NW

Park Police

3.6   Merge with Valley Trail just before a bridge on West Beach Drive. Veer right onto the blue-blazed Valley Trail and pass beneath the bridge.

4.2   Climb Valley Trail to a junction with the yellow-blazed Pine Trail. Turn left (east) onto Pine Trail and begin climbing. **Side trip:** At this junction, turn right instead and walk 0.1 mile to an overlook onto Rock Creek. After enjoying the view, return to Pine Trail and resume this route.

4.4   Pine Trail levels at a junction with Holly Trail. Turn right (south) onto Holly Trail and immediately begin to descend on a narrow dirt footpath. You'll climb into and out of a seasonal stream in a steep-sided gully. **Note:** Straight uphill on Pine Trail leads to 16th Street.

5.0   After a steep descent on Holly Trail, reach a T junction with the blue-blazed Valley Trail. Turn left (south) onto Valley Trail. Soon after, the trail passes beneath Sherrill Drive Bridge. Keep an eye out for a blue blaze on the bridge abutment.

5.1   Stay straight (south) on Valley Trail as Whittier Trail branches left (east). For the next 1.5 miles, it is a wide, flat streamside dirt path.

5.6   Follow Valley Trail as it veers left (southeast) and uphill as a narrow, rocky footpath. **Note:** The streamside trail that continues straight from this junction is Cross Trail 5. It crosses Rock Creek at Milkhouse Ford.

5.8   Pass by a park service bathroom on the right side of Valley Trail.

6.0   A series of switchbacks carries the Valley Trail off the hillside and down to Beach Drive. Turn left (south) and walk along the road shoulder beneath the Military Road bridge. When you see the road shoulder getting pinched into a narrow strip of grass by the looming hillside on your left, cross Beach Road and continue south on the paved bike path.

6.2   Reach the intersection of Joyce Road and Beach Drive. Turn right (west) onto Joyce Road. Cross Rock Creek and immediately, on the other side, turn right (north) onto a paved bike path. Follow it as it passes beneath Military Road. Rock Creek is through the trees off to the right.

6.4   Turn right (north) onto an unnamed horse trail that crosses the bike path. Walk a few feet to where the horse trail forks. Here, bear left and begin an uphill climb. **Note:** The right fork trail goes north alongside Rock Creek to Cross Trail 5 and eventually Milkhouse Ford.

6.8   Pass the spur trail to Fort De Russy on the right. Within 200 yards, merge onto the green-blazed Western Ridge Trail by continuing to walk straight on the dirt trail. Avoid the green-blazed leg of Western Ridge Trail that heads right (north) at this merge. After walking a few hundred feet more, veer right onto a paved bike path, which shares the route with Western Ridge Trail.

6.9   Turn left (south) on the combined bike path/Western Ridge Trail. Walk downhill to Military Road and cross over. The path then climbs uphill alongside Glover Road.

7.0   Turn left at a sign for the Nature Center.

7.1   Arrive back at the Rock Creek Nature Center.

Hike Information

Local Information

Destination D.C., 901 Seventh St. NW, Fourth Floor, Washington, DC, (202) 789-7000, www.washington.org

Local Events/Attractions

Carter Barron Amphitheatre, Rock Creek Park, 3545 Williamsburg Lane NW, Washington, DC, (202) 426-0486, www.nps.gov/rocr/planyourvisit/cbarron.htm. Hosts summer entertainment from Shakespeare to jazz and reggae music.

Restaurants

Rock Creek Shopping Center on Grubb Road, Silver Springs, MD, features two local favorites: The Parkway Deli, (301) 587-2675, www.theparkwaydeli.com, and Red Dog Cafe, (301) 588-6300, www.reddogcafe.com.

Local Outdoor Store

Hudson Trail Outfitters, Tenley Circle, 4530 Wisconsin Ave. NW, Washington, DC, (202) 363-9810, www.hudsontrail.com

Tours

Ranger-led horseback tours are offered in the park. There are also a host of ranger and junior ranger programs led from the Nature Center.

Organizations

Potomac Appalachian Trail Club, 118 Park St. SE, Vienna, (703) 242-0315, www.potomacappalachian.org. Maintains the Valley Trail, the Western Ridge Trail, and the connecting trails.

Honorable Mentions: Northern Virginia

F. Mason Neck Wildlife Refuge/Mason Neck State Park

These two areas, nearly adjacent to one other on VA 242 (exit 163 off I-95), are known for bald eagles and trails that span freshwater marshes and shady woodland. Both the refuge and park have trails leading to marsh overlooks. Both are day use only. The state park offers picnicking and restrooms. National wildlife refuge, (703) 490-4979, www.fws.gov/masonneck. State park, (703) 339-2385, www.dcr.virginia .gov/state_parks/mas.shtml. GPS: N38 38.644' / W77 11.947'. *DeLorme: Virginia Atlas & Gazetteer:* Page 76, C4.

G. Bull Run–Occoquan Trail

A 17.5-mile point-to-point National Scenic Trail along the Bull Run River and Occoquan Reservoir. The southern trailhead is located in Fountainhead Regional Park off VA 123 near the town of Occoquan. The appreciable length of the trail, combined with stream crossings—some impassable after inclement weather—make this hike a real challenge. The northern trailhead is at Bull Run Regional Park off VA 28, south of I-66 near Manassas. Both county parks are open seasonally, mid-March through mid-November. (703) 352-5900. GPS: Fountainhead Regional Park, N38 43.502' / W77 19.828'; Bull Run Regional Park, N38 48.416' / W77 28.758'. *DeLorme: Virginia Atlas & Gazetteer:* Page 76, B2, C3.

H. Manassas National Battlefield Park

Located less than a mile from I-66; take exit 47 to VA 234. Park trails pass through the same fields where the North and South fought the first and second battles of Manassas during the Civil War. Scenery harkens back to nineteenth-century farmland. Open daily, dawn to dusk. Admission fee. (703) 361-1339; www.nps.gov/mana. GPS: N38 48.776' / W77 31.290'. *DeLorme: Virginia Atlas & Gazetteer:* Page 76, B1.

I. Wildcat Mountain Natural Area

A Nature Conservancy holding near Warrenton with more than 5 miles of trails through hills and stream valleys that mark the west side of Wildcat Mountain. The initial climb from the parking area is steep, but the trails that network through this old farm-turned-forest are graded and easy. Old stone walls marking field and property boundaries still stand, as does the Old Smith House, a tall two-story building with a fieldstone foundation. (434) 295-6106; www.nature.org. GPS: N38 47.516' / W77 51.342'. *DeLorme: Virginia Atlas & Gazetteer:* Page 75, B6.

J. Sky Meadows State Park

Located on US 17 in Fauquier County, just south of US 50. At Sky Meadows, the rolling Piedmont meets the Blue Ridge. This former farm has a historic house, hike-in primitive campsites, and wonderful views. (540) 592-3556; www.dcr.virginia.gov/state_parks/sky.shtml. GPS: N38 59.527' / W77 57.997'. *DeLorme: Virginia Atlas & Gazetteer:* Page 75, A5.

Central Virginia

A person traveling west from the Atlantic Coast would, after 100 miles or so, encounter a significant change in the landscape of Virginia. Around Richmond and Fredericksburg, the topography shifts from the flat lowland of the Coastal Plain to the soft hills of the Piedmont. Along rivers, impressive waterfalls mark this line of demarcation, the spot where resistant Piedmont bedrock gives way to sand and clay. A few miles downstream, the largest waterways cease acting as real rivers and instead become estuaries, filled with brackish water and ruled by the ebb and flow of the ocean's tide.

Upland from the fall line—which roughly traces I-95—Virginia's landscape begins a slow march to the Blue Ridge. The term *rolling Piedmont* borders on cliché, but remains the best description of the landscape, which dips and rises in ever-greater folds, until finally giving way to the mountains of western Virginia.

The landscape wasn't always so uniform. Piedmont bedrock shows signs of violent prehistoric mountain-building events. Large basins, some miles and miles in length and width, collected mud and silt that eroded from mountains to the west. This same material later, under intense heat and pressure, became Arvonian and Quantico slate, considered among the highest quality found worldwide. Today a thick mantle of clay and sediment covers most of the bedrock in the Piedmont.

The poverty of exposed rock makes outcrops visible along Holliday Creek in Appomattox-Buckingham State Forest a rewarding experience.

Evidence of Native Americans in Virginia dates from 10,000 years ago. In central Virginia, ancestors of the Monacan Indians traveled and camped along the major rivers. The rise of the powerful Indian confederacies, the Powhatan in Tidewater and the Monacans west of the Blue Ridge, left central Virginia as a buffer between them. Both tribes hunted and traveled in this area, but archeologists have yet to identify large permanent settlements on the scale that existed elsewhere in the state. Artifacts and stone piles near Willis Mountain point to the region possibly holding ritual or ceremonial significance for prehistoric Indians and their ancestors.

European contact in the 1600s brought the rise of the agricultural machine in central Piedmont. Planters grew tobacco. Bateaux laden with tobacco hogsheads,

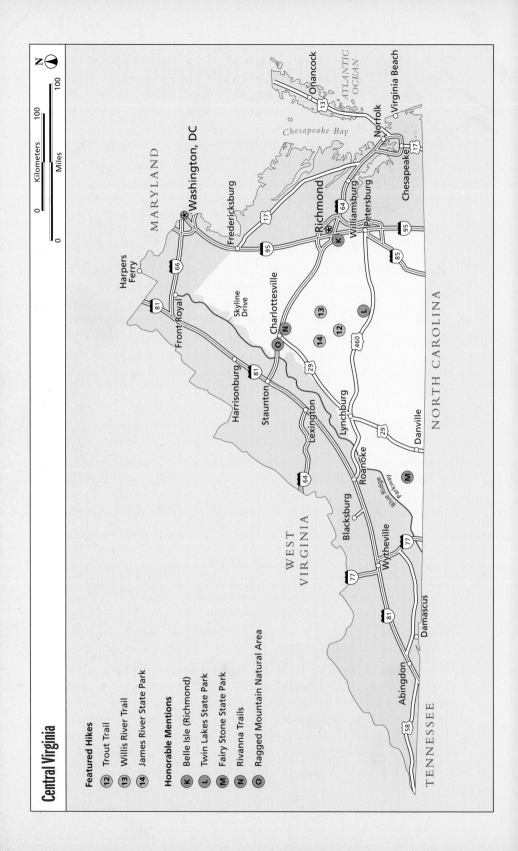

Central Virginia

Featured Hikes

- (12) Trout Trail
- (13) Willis River Trail
- (14) James River State Park

Honorable Mentions

- (K) Belle Isle (Richmond)
- (L) Twin Lakes State Park
- (M) Fairy Stone State Park
- (N) Rivanna Trails
- (O) Ragged Mountain Natural Area

livestock, and grains plied shallow streams such as the Willis and Slate Rivers. With advances in technology came the large-scale mining of gold, iron-ore, coal, slate, and other minerals.

Today those rivers that were the lifeblood of central Virginia commerce serve as natural hiking corridors. Grass and weed-choked floodplains give way to hillsides covered with mountain laurel. And where the landscape levels into fields, Virginia pine and black oaks dominate. Yet, due to this history of heavy farming, the overarching feature of central Virginia remains its wide-open landscape, a holdover from days when farmers planted acre after acre of tobacco until the soil failed, only to move west in search of fresh land. State forests created in the 1920s and 1930s have slowly rehabilitated depleted land by managing the growth of timber for commercial use. For people who enjoy the outdoors, this commercial-driven enterprise has a fortunate by-product: pockets of forest that offer quality recreation opportunities.

The Hikes

12. Trout Trail
13. Willis River Trail
14. James River State Park

Honorable Mentions

K. Belle Isle (Richmond)
L. Twin Lakes State Park
M. Fairy Stone State Park
N. Rivanna Trails
O. Ragged Mountain Natural Area

12 Trout Trail

Hikers are the latest folks to enjoy Holliday Creek in a line stretching back 8,000 years: Native Americans, gold miners, homesteaders, Confederate soldiers, scientists, foresters, and anglers—each found this beautiful stream suited their needs. Today, one of its greatest attributes—the scenery—enjoys protection within the largest of Virginia's state forests, the Appomattox-Buckingham. This prime Piedmont spot has mountain laurel bloom in spring, and the hills and a gorge near Holliday Lake dam defy anyone who equates Piedmont with pastoral. Throw in three unaided stream crossings and you've got an adventure that rivals any found in Virginia's mountains.

Start: Woolridge Wayside off VA 640
Distance: 7.4 miles point to point, with an option for an 11.5-mile loop
Hiking time: About 4 hours
Difficulty: Moderate due to 3 difficult stream crossings and occasional bushwhacks
Trail surface: Dirt forest roads and woodland paths lead hikers along grassy stream banks, a pristine river, and steep slopes, as well as through marshes and a gorge.
Land status: State forest and state park
Nearest town: Appomattox, VA
Other trail users: Anglers; open to foot traffic only
Accessibility: Trout Trail is not accessible; however, there are accessible facilities at Holiday Lake State Park.
Canine compatibility: Dogs permitted
Trail contacts: Appomattox-Buckingham State Forest, Dillwyn, (434) 983-2175, www.dof .virginia.gov/stforest/absf.htm; Holliday Lake State Park, Appomattox, (434) 248-6308, www.dcr.virginia.gov/state_parks/hol.shtml

Schedule: Park and forest open daily year-round, dawn to dusk. Hunting is permitted in the state forest (mid-Nov through the first weekend of Jan is the busiest season). Holliday Creek is stocked in the fall, winter, and early spring. Catch-and-release rules are in effect Oct through May (artificial lures only). Open harvest extends from June 1 to Sept 30.
Fees/permits: No state forest fee. State park parking fee and camping fee. A statewide fishing license is required, and a trout stamp is required when fishing June 1 to Sept 30. For fees and to purchase online, visit www.dgif .virginia.gov/fishing.
Facilities/features: The state park has camping, picnicking, swimming, and boating on a 150-acre lake.
Maps: USGS Holiday Lake. Hiking trail maps for all Virginia state park hiking trails can be found at www.virginiaoutdoors.com. A free map of the state forest and Trout Trail is available at the state forest headquarters located 1.1 miles north of the Woolridge Wayside on VA 636.

Finding the trailhead: From Appomattox Court House, drive 8.5 miles east on VA 24 from the intersection of US 460 and VA 24. Turn right onto VA 626 and in 3.4 miles turn left on VA 640 (Woolridge Road). In 0.3 mile after this intersection, pass the state park entrance road on the right. Continue straight another 1 mile on VA 640 to the Woolridge Wayside on the left side of the road. GPS: N37 25.585' / W78 39.447'. *DeLorme: Virginia Atlas & Gazetteer:* Page 45, A7.

Shuttle Point: From Woolridge Wayside, turn right and drive south on VA 640 for 1 mile. Turn left on VA 692/State Park Road and continue straight at an intersection with VA 614. In 3.8 miles, reach the ranger contact and fee station. Once inside the park, follow signs for the beach and picnic areas. The southern trailhead for the Lakeshore Trail is adjacent to picnic area #1. GPS: N37 23.712' / W78 38.336'. *DeLorme: Virginia Atlas & Gazetteer:* Page 45, A7.

The Hike

Virginia's Piedmont isn't exactly a hot spot for rocky gorges and deep stream valleys. Yet here you stand on the stream bank of Holliday Creek in Appomattox-Buckingham State Forest, watching water froth, twist, and turn through a narrow cleft between two steep hills. Stream boulders stir up rapids. Off one hillside, a small stream feeds the frenzy with spring runoff.

Watching the water tumble over a small cascade, you might consider how a prospector would view this scenery. The base of a waterfall, it turns out, is a great place to find gold.

Virginia settlers were first in the nation to mine gold. A lode deposit in Spotsylvania County triggered a rush that faltered only when California gold lured miners west in 1848–50. Around Buckingham County, gold ushered in some high times. Twenty or so mines operated, a few even into the 1900s. One near Dillwyn in Buckingham produced nuggets three pounds in weight, the largest found anywhere in the state. Up the road from Dillwyn, the name of the town Gold Hill speaks for itself—the precious metal was prospected here for a number of years.

Early miners focused on streams such as Holliday Creek, using a technique called placer (plas-ser) mining, whereby they panned up sandy streams for gold dust until the trail ran cold. Then they scouted surrounding hillsides, looking for the vein that produced the stream residue. If they found one, they sunk a shaft. Mine sizes varied. The Buckingham Mine in Dillwyn dug 183 feet. The Burnett Mine, also near Dillwyn, needed only 58 feet before hitting gold. After striking a vein, the difficult work of

Steps lead down to Holliday Lake.

Bridge across Holliday Lake.

extracting gold began. Workers at the Buckingham Mine crushed 20 tons of ore a day to produce 130 hundredweight (or 208,000 ounces) of gold per year.

Gold is just one mineral among many Virginia's Piedmont has yielded over the course of European settlement. Upstream from the confluence of the Appomattox River and Holliday Creek, the lake dam marks one end of a long, low ridge. Contained in the bedrock is another rock worth mining—Buckingham slate, considered in the slate industry to be among the highest quality produced in the United States today. Much of the activity centers around Arvonia, a village settled by immigrants of a Welsh town of the same name. Slate carving in Arvonia, Virginia, is an art. Eaves of some homes are trimmed in decorative slate. Tombstones in the cemetery, carved out of slate, are in the shape of household furniture, like beds, couches, and baby cribs.

Also in the vicinity of Holliday Lake stands the privately owned Willis Mountain, which is mined for kyanite, a mineral used in heat-absorbing products—like the white ceramic on a motor spark plug. Some people believe wearing a piece of this bluish-white mineral on a necklace or holding it in your hands induces a calm feeling during times of distress and aids meditation. (Kyanite also flakes and crumbles into tiny, sharp points and shards that may cause splinters. This, in turn, will produce a sensation quite opposite that of calm. So be careful if you handle it.)

If crystals aren't your thing, the clear waters of Holliday Lake produce a calming sensation as well. Works Progress Administration (WPA) workers dammed Holliday Creek and formed the 150-acre lake in 1938. Similar public works projects at Bear Creek Lake State Park in Cumberland County and Twin Lakes State Park in Prince Edward County served as a source of work for unemployed men during the Great Depression and a means of reclaiming overfarmed, barren land for recreational uses. Conspiracy buffs will enjoy the rumor circulating in Buckingham County about the size and location of Holliday Lake. Some will have you believe this long lake was built as a practice landing strip for amphibious aircraft pilots-in-training. This is undocumented, but still interesting. What's certain is that pike, pickerel, largemouth bass, and bluegill thrive in its water, and anglers are welcome to cast their lines here.

An archeological dig at the mouth of Holliday Creek has unearthed Native American arrowheads and pottery shards dating from 8,000 years ago. Signs of permanent settlement—domestication of plants and animals—date back 500 years. Anthropologists believe that prior to European colonization, the state was split between the Powhatans of eastern Virginia and the Monacans, who laid claim to land west of the James River headwaters. The region we call Central Virginia lay between them and acted as a kind of buffer zone between these sometimes-warring empires. Native Americans traveled regularly through the area, but did not settle the land. Instead, they treated it as a prehistoric preserve (or, in modern terms, a demilitarized zone) available to both for hunting and fishing. After 8,000 years and so many different uses, Holliday Creek has come full circle, enjoying status today as a preserve of the state.

Miles and Directions

0.0   Start at the Woolridge Wayside on VA 640. Exit the wayside by turning right (south) on VA 640 and walking downhill.

0.3   Cross Holliday Creek on VA 640 and immediately turn left (east) onto the Trout Trail, which is a faint road trace overgrown with grass. A wood gate blocks vehicle traffic. Follow this road trace downstream. Trout Trail is not blazed, but follows old roadbeds for all but a short stretch. **Note:** Late spring through summer, the trail is overgrown with thorny greenbrier and tall grass.

0.5   The trail ends at Holliday Creek. A steep-sided hill on the right forces a stream crossing. Passage during periods of low water is aided by a sandbar that divides the stream into two shallow channels.

0.8   A road enters the trail from the left. Continue straight on the Trout Trail.

1.2   The trail reverts to a narrow path as the hillside on your left steepens.

1.4   Cross a small tributary of Holliday Creek. There is a great swimming hole amid the shallow pools formed by the rocks and stream. **Note:** This is a rugged section of trail. Use caution.

1.7   Look closely at exposed rock on your left. It's shot through with small dikes of a white, crystal-like rock. The gray mass is felsic volcanic rock that oozed through crevices in the Piedmont landscape 800 million years ago. During ensuing periods of metamorphism, the white rock, called pegmatite, shot through the volcanic rock under incredible heat

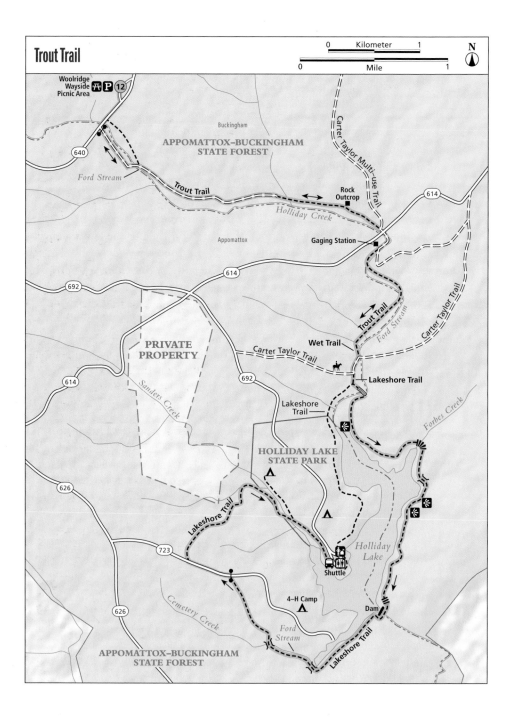

Trout Trail

Kilometer 0 — 1
Mile 0 — 1

N

Woolridge Wayside Picnic Area 🎪 🅿 12

640

Ford Stream

Buckingham

APPOMATTOX–BUCKINGHAM
STATE FOREST

Trout Trail

Holliday Creek

Rock Outcrop

Carter Taylor Multi-use Trail

614

Appomattox

Gaging Station

614

692

Ford Stream

Trout Trail

Wet Trail

Carter Taylor Trail

Carter Taylor Trail

PRIVATE
PROPERTY

Lakeshore Trail

614

Sanders Creek

692

Lakeshore Trail

Forbes Creek

HOLLIDAY LAKE
STATE PARK

Lakeshore Trail

626

Lakeshore Trail

723

Holliday Lake

Shuttle

626

Cemetery Creek

4–H Camp

Ford Stream

Dam

APPOMATTOX–BUCKINGHAM
STATE FOREST

Lakeshore Trail

and pressure. Geologists consider this outcrop one of the finer examples of this region's underlying rock strata.

1.9 Climb up a short hill to a junction with the Carter Taylor Multi-Use Trail. Turn right (east) and walk a few feet to paved VA 614/Walker Road. Turn right (south) again, walk down the road and cross the stream on the road bridge, then turn left down a gravel road. Near the stream bottom, avoid a short right-arching spur trail, which leads to a metal shed and a USGS water-quality testing facility.

2.0 The gravel road dead-ends at Holliday Creek, forcing another stream crossing. The water is deeper here and there are no sandbars to aid hikers. After crossing, walk up the stream bank and turn right on the combined Trout Trail/Carter Taylor Multi-Use Trail.

2.1 At a fork in the trail, veer right (south) and downhill toward the stream's edge. **Note:** The Carter Taylor Multi-Use Trail veers left at this junction.

2.4 Cross Holliday Creek and continue hiking the Trout Trail downstream.

2.9 Turn right (north) at a T-junction with the Carter Taylor Multi-Use Trail, following red blazes. **Note:** To the left at this junction is a stream crossing for horseback riders.

3.0 Veer left (west) on a footpath at a Y-junction. **Note:** The red-blazed Carter Taylor Multi-Use Trail veers right and uphill.

3.1 The Trout Trail ends at the Lakeshore Trail at a clearing with a picnic table. Turn left (east) onto Lakeshore Trail and cross Holliday Creek on a wooden footbridge, then turn right. **Note:** This junction requires some alert hiking, given that the Carter Taylor Multi-Use Trail passes close by. There are also trails to a fording spot for horses.

3.5 Pass by a nature observation deck on Holliday Lake.

4.1 Bear left and uphill at a wooden sign for an overlook. It is a 0.1-mile climb to the view. The overlook trail descends the opposite side of the hill and rejoins the Lakeshore Trail.

4.8 Come around the steep side of a hill and drop to the lake dam on a set of very, very steep stairs. **Note:** Look closely on exposed rock for fish-scale patterns. The dam is built on a fault where Holliday Creek, over millions of years, cut a path through Arvonian slate. This mica rock is softer than the volcanic rock known to exist in the hillsides around it. The effect is something like bookends. When the soft middle shifts, it creates the scale patterns.

5.3 Reach the southern tip of Holliday Lake. A fence marks the junction with a private trail leading to a 4-H Camp. Turn left and continue on the Lakeshore Trail and climb alongside Cemetery Creek into upland woods.

6.0 Reach VA 723 near the 4-H Camp gate. Walk straight across the road and reenter the woods. The trail parallels VA 723, which is on your left.

6.2 Turn right (north) onto a wide dirt and grass road.

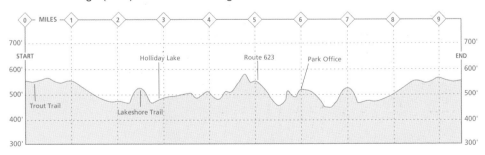

6.6 Turn left (north) off the dirt and grass road at a blazed junction. Enter the woods on Lakeshore Trail, which is a narrow dirt woodland path.

7.1 Cross Sanders Creek on a footbridge and turn left (downstream). There are picnic areas on the hillside slope on the left side of the trail.

7.3 Enter the beach area of Holliday Lake State Park. Cut across the grass parking area to reach picnic area #1.

7.4 Hike ends at picnic area #1 and the trailhead for Northridge Trail. **Option:** To extend this hike to 11.5 miles and make it a loop, continue north on the Northridge Trail to its junction with Lakeshore Trail, and continue thereon to Trout Trail and the trailhead at the Woolridge Wayside on VA 640.

Hike Information

Local Information

Appomattox Visitor Information Center, 214 Main St., Appomattox, (434) 352-8999, www.tourappomattox.com. Located in a historic train depot.

Local Events/Attractions

Historic Appomattox Railroad Festival, second weekend in Oct, Appomattox, (434) 352-2338, www.appomattoxfestivals.com/railroad. Food, music, crafts, a parade, and fireworks commemorate the donation of the Appomattox train depot to the town by Norfolk Southern Railroad.

Appomattox Court House National Historical Park, Appomattox, (434) 352-8987, www.nps.gov/apco. Park preserves the site where General Robert E. Lee surrendered to General Ulysses S. Grant, an act that formally ended the Civil War. Walking tours, interpreters, and special events commemorate this small village's big role in the war.

Hike Tours

Nature and history walks take place at Holliday Lake State Park. Call (434) 248-6308 or visit www.dcr.virginia.gov/state_parks/hol.shtml for dates and times.

Other Resources

Virginia Department of Game & Inland Fisheries, Farmville, (804) 367-1000, www.dgif.state.va.us. Information on fishing Holliday Creek and places to buy fishing stamps and licenses.

13 Willis River Trail

Cumberland State Forest is the second largest in the state forest system, and the Willis River Trail is the longest hiker-only trail in any of Virginia's state forests. From the flat land along the Willis River, the trail passes through oak and yellow poplar forest, under plantations of Virginia and loblolly pines, and past old farm sites. Beaver keep active in the swamps. There are also signs of turkey and fox in the sand along the river.

Start: Parking area at the dead end of Warner Fire Road, 0.5 mile off VA 608

Distance: 14.7 miles point to point

Hiking time: About 8 hours

Difficulty: Moderate due to length, frequent road crossings, eroded stream banks, frequent blowdowns that block the trail, and hard-to-follow stretches of trail along the Willis River

Trail surface: This route follows woodland paths, dirt forest roads, paved roads, small streams, and hilly terrain with little in the way of high peaks or deep valleys. The river flats are overgrown with grass and shrubs; the hillsides are shaded by hardwoods. Most hillcrests host plantations of loblolly and Virginia pines.

Land status: State forest

Nearest town: Cumberland Courthouse, VA

Other trail users: Hikers only

Accessibility: Facilities at Bear Creek Lake State Park, including the 0.16-mile Otter Trail

Canine compatibility: Dogs permitted

Trail contacts: Cumberland State Forest, Cumberland, (804) 492-4121, www.dof .virginia.gov/stforest/cumberland.htm. Forest headquarters provides maps of the Willis River Trail, plus information on other forest uses. It's recommended you at least inform forest staff of your itinerary, if merely to alert them to the presence of cars at either end of the trail. Bear Creek Lake State Park, (804) 492-4410, ww.dcr.virginia.gov/state_parks/bea.shtml.

Schedule: Open daily year-round, dawn to dusk. Hunting is permitted within the forest, and foresters report heaviest use from mid-Nov through the first weekend in Jan. Wear orange blaze during hunting seasons.

Fees/permits: No fees or permits required for hiking in the state forest. Bear Creek Lake State Park charges a parking fee and camping fees. There is also a pet fee at the park.

Facilities/features: None at the state forest; camping, restrooms, swimming, and boating at Bear Creek Lake State Park

Maps: USGS Whiteville, Gold Hill

Finding the trailhead: From Cumberland Courthouse, drive east on US 60 for 1.2 miles and turn left onto VA 622 (Trents Mill Road). Reach Bear Creek Market in 3.3 miles. Drive past the market and turn right onto VA 623, which turns from pavement to gravel. After 1.7 miles, turn left onto VA 624, a paved road, and drive 2.1 miles to the intersection of VA 608. Here you turn left onto VA 608 and look on the right for Warner Fire Road in 2.2 miles. Turn right onto the fire road, which is dirt, and drive 0.5 mile to a dead end. You'll recognize the trailhead by the swinging bridge over the Willis River. GPS: N37 37.191' / W78 12.803'. *DeLorme: Virginia Atlas & Gazetteer:* Page 56, D3.

Shuttle Point: From Cumberland Courthouse, drive east on US 60 for 1.2 miles and turn left onto VA 622 (Trents Mill Road). Reach Bear Creek Market in 3.4 miles and turn left onto VA 629.

The southern trailhead is located at Winston Lake on VA 629, 1.2 miles past Cumberland State Forest headquarters. (Bear Creek Market, on VA 622, or Bear Creek Lake State Park, on VA 629, offer convenient mid-trail parking.) GPS: N37 30.957' / W78 18.064'. *DeLorme: Virginia Atlas & Gazetteer:* Page 56, D3.

Bailout: Bear Creek State Park makes a convenient bailout for hikers who want to trim this hike to a 10-mile point-to-point. Easiest access is from the junction of VA 622 and VA 629 (mileage cue 9.1 in Miles and Directions) or from the junction of the blue-blazed Cumberland Multi-Use Trail with the Willis River Trail (mileage cue 9.9). GPS: N37 31.915' / W78 16.028'. *DeLorme: Virginia Atlas & Gazetteer:* Page 56, D3.

The Hike

The first thing you should know about the Willis River Trail is this: It's never looked as good it does today. Not in our lifetime, at least.

Sycamores, easily identified by their thick, white-splotched trunks, tower in open, grassy fields along the Willis River. On wooded slopes, oaks, yellow poplar, and beech lend old farmland a shady, deep forest feel. Along old dirt roads, pink-petal mallows peek out of roadside ditches. Taken together, it's land changing from farm to forest, a process that's been under way for seventy years and counting in Cumberland State Forest.

Abusive best describes how farmers once treated the soil here and elsewhere in central Virginia. By the Great Depression, the farm economy of Cumberland and neighboring counties bottomed out. A condition called *plow pan* typified the problem: White clay was compacted into a cement-like state that prevented plow blades from penetrating its surface. Rain couldn't nourish plant roots. Deprived of water, crops and trees shriveled, choked, and died.

When the US government paid pennies on the dollar for this land, it resembled the dust-bowl conditions of the nation's heartland. After Works Progress Administration (WPA) and Civilian Conservation Corps (CCC) workers built roads and dams, Virginia created state forests on the land. On the sides of roads, foresters planted farm and tree demonstration plots. Sleuthing by present-day rangers has revealed square, 1-acre stands of oak, poplar, and pines. The plots were used to show landowners not only what trees they could plant, but also how to manage forestland for a sustainable timber harvest. Restoration had begun.

The full benefits of seventy-plus years of restoration are best appreciated on the Willis River Trail. Beavers have laid claim to land along the first 2 miles of the trail. Notice the small channels that crisscross the landscape as it slopes toward the beaver swamp on the left side of the trail. As beavers range farther afield in search of their favorite food—hardwood saplings—they build canals for safe passage. That's one theory to explain the presence of these small drainages. A more likely explanation would be field furrows, planted and replanted so many times they've made indelible marks on the landscape.

Bear Creek Lake State Park is a nice base camp along the Willis River Trail.

Human handiwork is evident farther along the trail, where plantations of Virginia pine are visible through the forest understory of sassafras and holly. Foresters currently manage pine plots for about thirty-five years and then harvest. Hardwood stands, by contrast, can take seventy to one hundred years to reach maturity. In the case of both types, the lumber is used in state building projects.

Less evident along the Willis River Trail are signs of the river's busy past. At one time, flat-bottom riverboats (or bateaux) loaded with livestock and hogsheads of tobacco and/or flour congregated on this stream. The Willis River canal system, designed specifically for this shallow stream, worked most efficiently when four or five boats used a lock at once. Considered a pioneering form of navigation, the Willis River locks employed a wooden flash gate, which linked two stone jetties that stuck out into the river from either bank. Hinged at the bottom, this flash lock fell flat when opened. Boats coasted through the sluice and proceeded downstream. (Upriver navigation was a tad more difficult, relying on the brawn of bateau polers rather than gravity.) The locks made the Willis River navigable for up to 50 miles from its confluence with the James River. Gristmills and inspection warehouses occupied strategic points on the water route, often near locks. Names of local roads, such as Trents Mill, a few miles past Bear Creek Market on VA 622, reference these long-ago points of commerce.

For all the innovation, commercial use of the river was cyclical. When the channel filled with sediment or wooden flash locks rotted, traffic declined. It revived

Trail sign in Cumberland State Forest.

when local businessmen saw fit to pay for improvements—or petition the state to fund repairs. Yet even when the James River and Kanawha Canal—the main east–west commercial route in central Virginia to which the Willis River linked—was abandoned for railroads in 1880, Cumberland County farmers continued using parts of the Willis River to ship goods to railroad depots. Use declined only when the land could not sustain enough crops to make farming profitable.

Which brings us full circle, to land once misused, now protected and plentiful with trees and wildlife. Your footsteps can roust a turkey, partridge, or deer from protected feeding areas managed by another state agency, the Department of Game & Inland Fisheries. You can walk through forests used by scientists and researchers as laboratories for cultivating genetically improved versions of loblolly pine, white pine, and Virginia pine. Or you can engage in amateur research: Rock Quarry Natural Area, midway along the trail, is one of four natural areas in Cumberland left untouched by forest personnel. Here, nature manages growth. To a forester, it represents chaos, where less valuable hardwoods crowd valuable red and white oak and yellow poplar. For this hiker, it holds some of the wildest, most scenic portions of the Willis River Trail. You be the judge.

Miles and Directions

0.0 Start from a parking area at the dead end of Warner Forest Road. The white-blazed Willis River Trail heads south away from the river, entering the woods at the back of the parking area. The next 0.5 mile of trail runs up and down gentle bumps in the landscape and alongside a beaver swamp. **Note:** There is a scenic swing bridge that crosses the Willis River a few feet east of the parking area trailhead.

0.5 The trail begins a run on level ground amid loblolly pines. (Cumberland State Forest marks the farthest west this pine will grow in Virginia.) On this level stretch, you'll cross four drainages in succession, which makes for some wet walking in spring.

0.7 Reach VA 615 and turn left, following white blazes on the right side of the road. After crossing Reynolds Creek, turn right to reenter the woods. For the next 0.3 mile, the trail alternates between wet sections in the stream bottomland and short climbs over streamside hills. Sections of trail are often very narrow and eroded. Logs may block the path.

1.7 Cross Reynolds Creek. **Note:** Steep, eroded stream banks make this a difficult passage during periods of high water.

Willis River Trail

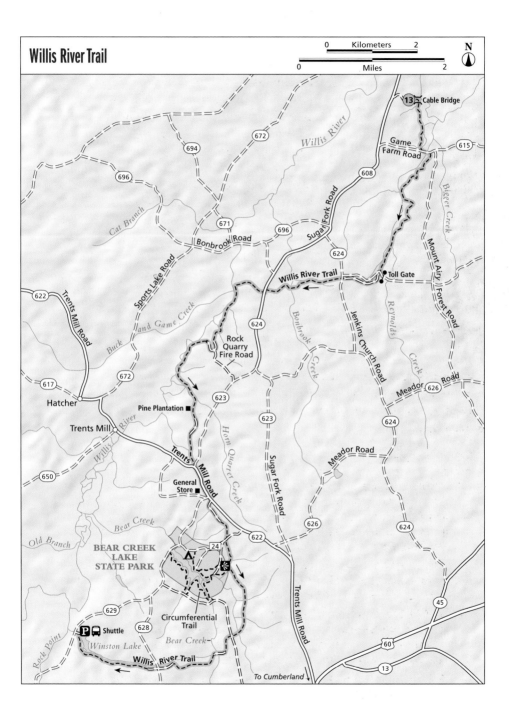

Kilometers 0 — 2

Miles 0 — 2

N

Cable Bridge

13

Willis River

Game Farm Road

672

694

696

615

608

Bigger Creek

Cat Branch

671

696

Sugar Fork Road

624

Mount Airy Forest Road

Bonbrook Road

Sports Lake Road

Willis River Trail

Toll Gate

622

Buck and Game Creek

Trents Mill Road

624

Bonbrook Creek

Jenkins Church Road

Reynolds Creek

Rock Quarry Fire Road

617

672

623

Meador Road

626

Hatcher

Pine Plantation

623

624

Willis River

Trents Mill

Horn Quarrer Creek

Sugar Fork Road

Meador Road

650

General Store

BEAR CREEK LAKE STATE PARK

Bear Creek

24

622

626

624

Old Branch

Trents Mill Road

45

Circumferential Trail

629

628

Shuttle

Rock Point

Winston Lake

Bear Creek

Willis River Trail

To Cumberland

60

13

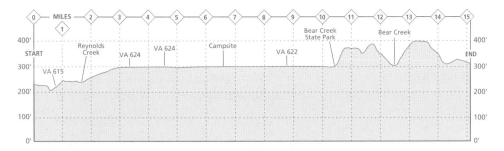

1.8 Crest a small hill amid a plantation of Virginia pine. The climb from the river is an ideal stretch to watch the forest transition from hardwoods (hornbeam, oak, and alder) at lower elevations to pines at the top. The trail then drops to the river.

2.5 After climbing over a small hill, descend to cross a small tributary of Reynolds Creek. The trail climbs again entering a pine plantation.

2.8 Reach a gate and turn right onto Toll Gate Forest Road. You'll pass a clear-cut on the right, moments before reaching VA 624.

3.5 Walk straight across VA 624 and reenter the woods. The forest boundary is somewhere between the blue house on the right and the trail, so don't stray too far. As you descend on a singletrack path, a small stream forms on the right, as the terrain on the left changes from field to wooded slope.

3.6 Cross a wet ditch and climb a small hill to avoid getting your feet wet where the stream cuts close to the base of the hill.

3.9 The trail turns sharply left, away from the stream. (Through the understory of sassafras and witch hazel, you'll make out the border of a pine plantation.) The trail almost reaches the pines, then turns to run parallel to the plantation in a narrow ditch.

4.2 Cross Bonbrook Creek. Look right for white blazes and follow the trail around the base of a hill as it climbs away from the creek.

4.5 Stay alert as the trail passes closely to the state forest boundary. Barbwire and yellow blazes on trees right of the trail mark this boundary. Through the woods on the right is a long white barn.

4.6 Walk straight across VA 624, turn left, and walk up the right side of the road. At a gated forest road with a stone apron, turn right onto a dirt road. In 0.1 mile, turn left and enter the shelter of the woods. Avoid following the forest road straight into a field.

5.0 The trail reaches the Willis River amid a field of tall grass and wildflowers. Here, the stream runs a wide, flat course. Its arrow-straight banks suggest it may have been straightened for commercial navigation. Cutting the bends out of the river allowed easier passage for bateaux, which measured 60 feet long and 8 feet wide.

5.2 Walk on the muddy bottomland along the Willis River. Keep a sharp eye out for the trail as it crosses wet ditches and passes through heavy vegetation. If you lose the trail, tend to the riverbank. You're on the mark if you see a large tree leaning out over the river.

5.4 A blue stripe on a tree marks the boundary of the Rock Quarry Natural Area, one of four in Cumberland State Forest. Natural areas are left wild and untouched. The trees here are larger, more mature species than you'll see elsewhere along the trail. The forest subcanopy is also overgrown, an appearance that results if the forest is not thinned.

6.0 Enter a clearing and turn left. This old road climbs through plantations of Virginia and loblolly pines.

6.2 Turn right onto Rock Quarry Fire Road. After a few paces, an old road goes left. Continue straight on Rock Quarry to where it dead-ends in a clearing. Here the trail bears left into the woods and takes a steep drop to the Willis River.

6.4 Reach the Willis River. The trail rides a ledge with a steep drop off the right side down to the river flats.

6.8 Descend onto the river floodplain.

7.0 Without the convenience of a double blaze, the trail takes a hard left and the trail widens. This is confusing because a wide path also continues straight ahead. If you miss the left turn, you'll know soon enough—the riverside path peters out in a blaze of vegetation.

7.3 Reach Horn Quarter Creek and turn left to follow it upstream along the left bank. This is a good spot for lunch or photos or just a quick swim.

7.5 Cross the stream and climb the opposite bank. The trail will soon convert to a wide dirt forest road and enter a pine plantation. **Note:** Where the land levels, look for signs of an old farm. There's a crater on the left side of the trail that's likely a collapsed well. In an overgrown field on the right side of the trail are piles of concrete blocks, indicating that a house or outbuilding once stood here. The stones are covered in vinca violets.

7.7 Stay straight on the forest road trail past a clearing on the right.

8.0 At a junction with a forest road, turn right (southwest). Within 0.1 mile, this road curves right. Instead, continue straight on the white-blazed trail.

8.3 Cross a small stream and turn left (south) into the woods. The trail starts climbing a short easy incline.

8.7 Emerge from the woods at a T intersection of VA 622 and VA 623. Walk straight across dirt VA 623 and continue walking up the left side of VA 622 in the corridor cut for the power lines.

9.1 At the intersection of VA 622 and VA 629, cross the road and enter the woods opposite Bear Creek Market. A wood post with a hiker icon and trail signs marks this trailhead for the southern leg of the Willis River Trail, which is marked by white squares. **Bailout:** Walk 1.2 miles down paved VA 629 to the Cumberland Multi-Use Trailhead (CMT) parking lot in Bear Creek State Park.

9.9 Cross the blue-blazed Cumberland Multi-Use Trail (CMT), which is a dirt forest road, and reenter the woods opposite as a singletrack footpath. **Bailout:** Turn right on the CMT and in 0.2 mile reach the CMT trailhead in Bear Creek State Park.

10.3 After descending through a young hardwood forest, turn left on an old road now overgrown with grass and weeds. In less than 0.1 mile, turn left again at a junction marked by a wood trail post and hike uphill on a singletrack woods path.

10.5 Begin a very scenic section of trail along Little Bear Creek where you ascend small hills that take you from stream level to lookouts some 50 feet above the stream. You'll see pawpaw (aka the "false banana" tree) on this stretch of trail. Its peanut-shaped fruit is a food staple for squirrels, raccoons, and birds.

10.9 Cross Little Bear Creek and climb the embankment. In 0.1 mile, cross the creek again. Begin a steep ascent.

11.2 A bend in the creek carves a steep-sided natural amphitheater in the hillside and the trail traces the edge high above stream level.

A DICKENS MYSTERY

THIS IS THE GRAVE of a little Child whom God in his goodness called to a Bright Eternity when he was very young. Hard as it is For Human Affection To reconcile itself To Death, In any shape (and most of all, perhaps at First In This) HIS PARENTS can even now believe That it will be a Consolation to them Throughout their lives, and when they shall have grown old and grey always to think of him as a Child IN HEAVEN "and Jesus Called a little Child unto him, and set him in the midst of them." He was the son of ANTHONY AND M.I. THORTON Called CHARLES IRVING. He was born on the 20th day of January 1841, and he died on the 12th day of March 1842. Having lived only 13 months and 19 days.

Charles Dickens wrote *Oliver Twist, David Copperfield,* and *A Tale of Two Cities*—all literary classics. But did you know he also wrote the tombstone epitaph above? It is located in the Thornton Family Cemetery within Cumberland State Forest.

The deceased was thirteen-month-old Charles Irving Thorton. Dickens was traveling in America at the time of the child's death. Why Dickens wrote the memorial is a mystery. Was he inspired by the death of such a young child? Or was he smitten with the child's mother, as Randolph W. Church speculated in a 1971 article in the *Virginia Cavalcade?* A less romantic and probably more likely theory suggests that Dickens's friend Washington Irving (of "Rip Van Winkle" fame) was close to the mother, and, perhaps, Dickens wrote the epitaph in consideration of this mutual friendship.

All that's known for certain is that the physician who attended the dying child requested that Dickens write the epitaph. Dickens mailed it back from Cincinnati, Ohio, where he was visiting. The marble headstone etched with Dickens's words is located in the state forest on the grounds of Oak Hill, the Thornton family's former homestead.

11.8 Cross Bear Creek Road at a parking area for the blue-blazed Cumberland Multi-Use Trail. Reenter the woods on the white-blazed Willis River Trail.

12.0 Cross Bear Creek. (WPA work crews dammed the stream to create popular Bear Creek Lake, one of seven lakes built in central Virginia between 1935 and 1937 for recreational use.) The trail on the opposite side climbs a hill and becomes an old road.

12.7 Turn left onto dirt Booker Forest Road.

12.9 As you approach VA 628, stay alert for a double blaze on the left side of the trail that marks a left turn. Follow a power-line easement paralleling the road. In less than 0.1 mile, turn right and cut through a strip of woods that separates the easement and the road. Cross VA 628 and reenter the woods on the opposite side.

13.3 The trail passes through a wet section with many springs and seeps that mark the headwaters of Winston Lake. From here the trail climbs to higher and drier hillsides and parallels the stream, which is downhill on the right.

13.9 Descend and cross the stream. Follow the trail along the stream's edge and cross it again in 0.1 mile. After the second crossing, begin your climb out of the lowlands of Winston Lake's backwater to walk along a hillside overlooking the south side of the lake. **Note:** Both stream crossings are scenic stops and a great place to sit and soak in the nature around the lake's headwaters.

14.7 Hike ends as you descend a set of stone stairs and cross a wood footbridge to reach a picnic shelter and parking area for Winston Lake.

Hike Information

Local Information

Commonwealth Regional Council, Farmville, (434) 392-6104, tourism.virginias heartland.org

Local Events/Attractions

Willis River 35K and 50K Trail Runs, mid-Jan; Richmond Road Runners, (804) 387-1526, www.rrrc.org

James River Bateau Festival, mid-June, James River: Lynchburg to Richmond; (434) 528-3950, www.vacanals.org. A weeklong celebration of a bygone era, with replicas of the bateaux that transported commerce up and down central Virginia rivers and canals in the 1800s travel from Lynchburg to Richmond, powered by volunteers in period costume.

Hike Tours & Resources

Old Dominion Appalachian Trail Club, http://olddominiontrailclub.onefireplace .org. This chapter of the Appalachian Trail Conference helped build the Willis River Trail in the early 1980s, and conducts maintenance and recreational hikes.

14 James River State Park

Set in bucolic Buckingham County, the 1,500-acre James River State Park perches on 3 miles of riverside property that has cultural roots reaching back to pre-Revolution and one of Virginia's most influential families. Trails range from flat paths along the James to pitchy routes through the young pine and hardwood forests on the valley hillsides. Equestrians are some of the park's heaviest users, but 15 miles of trails that span both river and forest habitats offer hikers a lesson in how a small park can still deliver big rewards.

Start: Grass parking area on the park road between the ranger contact station and nature center
Distance: 7.5-mile loop
Hiking time: About 3.5 hours.
Difficulty: Moderate due to length and pitchy terrain along woodland paths
Trail surface: Grass and dirt paths
Land status: State park
Nearest town: Bent Creek, VA
Other trail users: Equestrians and hunters (in season)
Accessibility: The 0.37-mile Green Hill Pond Loop is a paved trail with boardwalks over a scenic fishing pond.

Canine compatibility: Leashed dogs permitted
Trail contact: James River State Park, 104 Green Hill Dr., Gladstone; (434) 933-4355; www.dcr.virginia.gov/state_parks/jam.shtml
Schedule: Open daily, dawn to dusk. The park is closed for hunts for a few weeks in Nov and Dec.
Fees/permits: Day-use fee
Facilities/features: Canoe rentals, visitor center, and camping
Maps: USGS Shipman; hand-drawn map of trail system available at park

Finding the trailhead: From US 60 West in Buckingham County, turn right onto VA 605 (River Road). Travel 7 miles, then turn left onto VA 606 (Park Road) and immediately enter the park. GPS: N37 37.410' / W78 48.512'. *DeLorme: Virginia Atlas & Gazetteer:* Page 55, C5.

The Hike

A beautiful confluence of summertime sounds rises up from and around the James River as it sweeps around a lazy river bend. Water rushes over river rocks with a constant *shooshing*. Cicadas buzz and clatter in the tall riverside grass. Birdsong floats down from the broad sycamore and willow trees. It is a natural orchestra.

The mighty James River lends the park its name, but it is only one feature among many that make this a special place. Fields in the bottomland and forests on riverside slopes show a vigorous rebound from centuries of farming and logging. Skinny trunks amid the oaks and hickory and pine trees mark this as a young, growing forest. But they still provide welcome shade and the occasional wildlife sighting—a fox sighting along the Branch Trail wouldn't be surprising. Fields along the river's floodplain show telltale signs of old field succession, where pine saplings indicate a natural process that, if left untouched, would result in a mature hardwood forest. Other fields are kept mowed, while the high grass that lines trails through the river bottomland explodes with the bright yellows of golden ragwort and the purple of paintbrush.

Equal to the natural beauty is the impact of humans on the landscape. Ownership dates back to colonial Virginia and the Cabell family, who owned land throughout the Piedmont region. Land that is now state park was part of a larger estate called Green Hill, given in 1726 to Colonel John Cabell as a wedding present from his father. The original Green Hill estate is destroyed, its location near the new park visitor center on a hill overlooking Green Hill Pond.

Hiking amid fall wildflowers in James River State Park.

Farming was the subsidence of the Cabell family, but they also cast an eye out onto the James River and farther west. A farmer prospers when his goods can make it to market. For that purpose, the James served farmers well, but only seasonally. It could be too shallow to navigate in the hot summer and autumn months, and too volatile, subject to raging floods in winter and spring. Many believed the answer was a system of canals that would skirt the troublesome sections of the river and control its flow. Generations of Cabells threw themselves into developing the James River and Kanawha Canal system with the hope of linking eastern seaports with farms in the Ohio Valley and beyond. Started in 1785, it was only half completed to the Kanawha River by 1851. It ultimately stalled near Clifton Forge, Virginia, on the eve of the Civil War. That conflict and the rise of the "Iron Horse" locomotive doomed the concept of river-and-canal systems along the James.

The war also marked the end of the Cabell family's relationship to the land. In the 1870s this property was bought by the Dickens family, who owned it until purchase by the Commonwealth of Virginia in 1992—in total, nearly 300 years of ownership by only two families. The park opened in 1999.

The deep history is only one reason to appreciate a day spent hiking trails that span the river bottomland and wooded hills of James River State Park. Like old fields that grow to forest and rivers that flow to the sea, time marches on.

Miles and Directions

0.0 Start at a grass parking lot and trail board on the park road between the ranger contact station and nature center. Turn south, cross over the road, and enter woods opposite on the yellow-blazed Running Creek Trail. Within 20 feet, veer right at a fork, staying on the wide mowed path.

0.1 Stay straight and avoid a dirt path that splits left into the woods. Running Creek Trail is now a rocky footpath.

0.2 At a fork, veer left onto Running Creek Short Loop Connector Trail. The dirt footpath climbs through a young hardwood forest of oak, hickory, maple, and beech via switchbacks.

0.3 Cross paved Canoe Landing Road.

0.5 Reach a T junction and turn right on the yellow-blazed Running Creek Trail. **Note:** The trail on the left is the return portion of this loop hike.

1.0 As you descend off a hill toward a clearing, stay alert and veer right, cross two wooden footbridges, and emerge into the clearing at a trail board. Cross a dirt and gravel road and follow a grass trail downhill. The Canoe Livery is downhill on your left.

1.2 Stay straight and merge onto River Trail.

2.0 River Trail takes a hard right (east) to follow a jog around a small tributary before returning to the river's edge.

2.1 Take a moment to enjoy the James River: A footpath leads left to water's edge and a small sandbar perfect for a snack break.

2.6 The River Trail makes a sharp right and turns away from the river.

2.8 Veer left, cross a footbridge, and pass through a gate. Reach a gravel road and turn right, uphill, to access Cabell Trail. Within 0.1 mile, bear left onto Cabell Trail, which here is a mowed grass path.

3.1 Cross over the gravel Green Hill Pond access road and continue uphill on the orange-blazed Cabell Trail. At the crest of the hill, turn left and cross the park road. Cabell Trail climbs uphill as a wide dirt and gravel service road. **Note:** At this junction, there is a trail board with a map and several large sycamore trees that provide good shade for a midday break, as well as a park picnic area, restrooms, and a visitor center.

3.4 Continue straight past the Dixon Landing Overlook Trail on the left.

3.8 Turn left to access the Tye River Overlook. It is 0.1 mile to the wood platform with a view of the confluence of the Tye River into the James. Retrace your steps to the Cabell Trail and turn left to continue this route uphill.

4.2 Turn right and uphill as Cabell Trail leaves the service road and enters a pine forest as a woodland footpath.

4.4 Merge onto Branch Pond Connector Trail by staying straight at a trail junction where Cabell Trail turns right (east). Within 30 feet of this junction, swing left on an unmarked dirt path, avoiding a gravel road leading right, downhill, to a primitive camping area.

4.6 Wrap around the headwaters of Branch Pond, and at a junction soon after, turn right to follow the East Branch Pond Loop Trail.

5.0 Enter the Branch Pond Picnic Area. Stay alert and turn left on Branch Trail before you reach the gravel parking lot, restrooms, and picnic area.

James River State Park

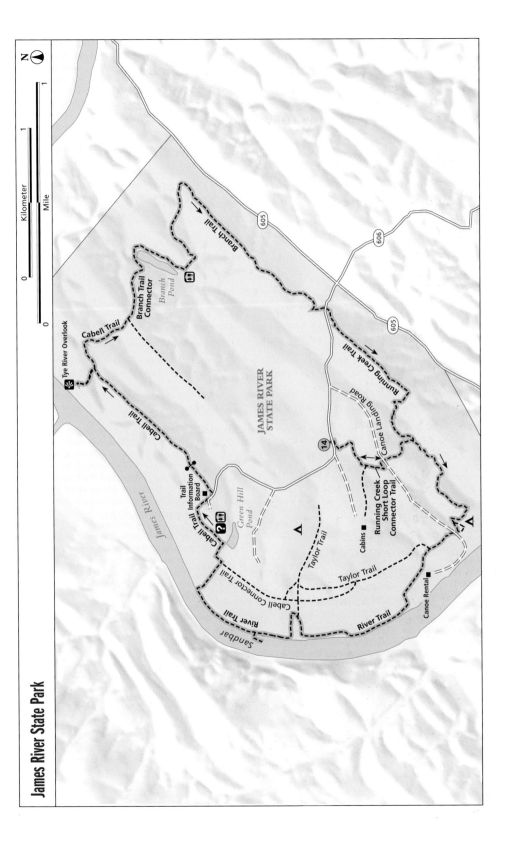

James River State Park

James River

Sandbar

River Trail

Canoe Rental

Cabell Connector Trail

Taylor Trail

Taylor Trail

Cabins

Running Creek Short Loop Connector Trail

Green Hill Pond

Cabell Trail Information Board

?

Cabell Trail

Canoe Landing Road

14

JAMES RIVER STATE PARK

Running Creek Trail

605

606

605

Branch Trail

Branch Pond

Branch Trail Connector

Cabell Trail

Tye River Overlook

Cabell Trail

N

Kilometer

Mile

0   1   1

0   1   1

6.2 Turn left and descend to the park road. The ranger contact station is visible uphill on the right. Cross and follow a short connecter to Running Creek Trail.

6.4 At a four-way junction, turn left onto Running Creek Trail, which is a wide mowed path blazed yellow.

7.1 Turn right onto Running Creek Short Loop Connector Trail.

7.2 Cross Canoe Landing Road.

7.3 Veer right onto Running Creek Trail.

7.5 Arrive back at the parking lot.

Hike Information

Local Information

Appomattox Visitor Information Center, 214 Main St., Appomattox, (434) 352-8999, www.tourappomattox.com

Local Events/Attractions

The James River Raft Race and Summer Festival takes place in the park each July.

Appomattox Court House National Historical Park, Appomattox, (434) 352-8987, www.nps.gov/apco. Park preserves the site where General Robert E. Lee surrendered to General Ulysses S. Grant, an act that formally ended the Civil War. Walking tours, interpreters, and special events commemorate this small village's big role in the war.

Lodging

The park features family lodges, cabins, a large full-service campground, horse camping, and primitive camping along the river. For reservations, call (800) 933-PARK or go to www.reserveamerica.com.

Restaurants

There is a country store at Bent Creek, about 7 miles from the park, but the nearest restaurants and grocery stores are in Appomattox (19 miles) and Amherst (22 miles).

Organizations

Friends of James River State Park, (434) 933-4355

An overlook above the confluence of the Tye and James rivers.

Honorable Mentions: Central Virginia

K. Belle Isle (Richmond)

This 54-acre island is part of the James River Park System, 450 acres of city-owned parks lining the James River, in the heart of downtown Richmond. From Main Street in downtown, follow signs for Belle Isle and the Valentine Museum. There is a parking lot on Tredegar Street past the museum. A footbridge crosses onto the island from the parking lot. A wide 2-mile loop runs past ruins of ironworks and a Civil War prison. More narrow trails explore the interior woodlands. Park closes at nighttime. (804) 646-8911; www.jamesriverpark.org. GPS: N37 32.053' / W77 27.044'. *DeLorme: Virginia Atlas & Gazetteer:* Page 58, D2.

L. Twin Lakes State Park

Located in the heart of Prince Edward–Gallion State Forest, Twin Lakes is accessed via VA 613 off US 360. The 6-mile loop hike around Prince Edward Lake leads from high, forested hills into the marshy flow of the Sandy River at the head of the lake. There are beaches and reserved-fee camping. (434) 392-3435; www.dcr.virginia.gov/state_parks/twi.shtml. GPS: N37 10.399' / W78 16.205'. *DeLorme: Virginia Atlas & Gazetteer:* Page 46, C2.

M. Fairy Stone State Park

Located in the foothills of the Blue Ridge Mountains northwest of Martinsville on Philpott Reservoir. The park entrance is 9 miles west of Bassett on VA 57. Whiskey Run Trail offers a wide view of the parkland and reservoir. Use it to form a 4.7-mile loop with Stuart's Knob Trail and Iron Mine Trail. There's a beach on Fairy Stone Lake, picnic facilities, and fee camping. (276) 930-2424; www.dcr.virginia.gov/state_parks/fai.shtml. GPS: N36 47.547' / W80 07.008'. *DeLorme: Virginia Atlas & Gazetteer:* Page 26, B2.

N. Rivanna Trails

This 20-mile greenbelt circles the entire city of Charlottesville, with numerous shorter loops possible. A good starting point is at Quarry Park. To get there, take exit 121 off I-64. Turn right onto Monticello Avenue, and take the first left onto Quarry Road. The park is on the left. The Rivanna Trails Foundation has maps and descriptions at www.rivannatrails.org. GPS: N38 0.915' / W78 28.696'. *DeLorme: Virginia Atlas & Gazetteer:* Page 68, D1.

O. Ragged Mountain Natural Area

This 900-acre nature preserve is a wonderful surprise just west of the Charlottesville city limits. The Ivy Creek Foundation—which also maintains the Ivy Creek Natural Area—manages the area. The 4-mile hiking trail circles Charlottesville Reservoir, rolling up and down the rugged and heavily forested Ragged Mountains. To reach the Ragged Mountain Natural Area, take exit 124 off I-64, then head north 0.5 mile on the VA 29 Bypass to the Fontaine Avenue exit. Turn away from Charlottesville onto Fontaine Avenue. After 0.25 mile, turn right onto Reservoir Road, which is a narrow, curvy gravel road. Use caution, as the road is popular with local joggers. The parking lot is on the right, approximately 2 miles down the road, just before the entrance to Camp Holiday Trails. Dogs are not permitted on the trails. www.ivycreekfoundation .org/raggedmountain.html. GPS: N38 01.584' / W78 33.345'. *DeLorme: Virginia Atlas & Gazetteer:* Page 67, D7.

Shenandoah National Park

In the 1920s, when the government proposed a national park along the spine of Virginia's Blue Ridge Mountains, wilderness purists scoffed. A century of farming and logging had left a legacy of barren soil and mountain slopes scarred with clear-cut. Wildlife had dwindled to near extinction. It irked some that so much time and effort would be spent on such a depleted landscape.

Oh, if the skeptics could see Shenandoah National Park today.

In a testament to nature's healing power, scars of the park's past have all but disappeared. Shenandoah is rightfully counted as one of the crown jewels in our country's national park system. Long and thin, it measures 75 miles from Front Royal in the north to Rockfish Gap in the south. Within its boundaries are some of Virginia's finest forests. From overlooks, on a clear day, views stretch east to Washington, DC, and west into West Virginia. You're as apt to see a bear or deer amble across Skyline Drive as you are another human. That's not incidental. Black bears are a park success story, having rebounded from near extirpation to several hundred in number.

On the mountaintops, a new generation of oaks and hickories has replaced the oak-chestnut forest that provided a livelihood for so many mountain dwellers. Waterfalls come in all shapes and sizes, from the reckless fury of a spring run on Big Devil Stairs to the free-form drops along popular day hikes like Whiteoak Canyon.

Above all are the mountains. Approached from the east, the Blue Ridge sweeps skyward underlaid with granite that formed more than one billion years ago—before recorded life on earth—making the Blue Ridge one of the oldest Mountain ranges on earth. Basalt lava flows and metamorphic catoctin greensonte indicate a violent prehistoric past when, deep in the bowels of the earth, heat and pressure formed new rocks from old, then thrust them upwards to form the mountains we see today. So large a barrier did these mountains post to colonists in Virginia that is bred two distinct cultures: a land-owning aristocracy on eastern Piedmont and Coastal Plains, and a Scots-Irish farm culture in the western valleys and ridges. Today, the only restriction to travel is your imagination and leg power. Hundreds of miles of trails spread through the park and its 93,000 acres of designated wilderness. Each trail invites the traveler to step from the car and explore what lies beyond what the eyes can see.

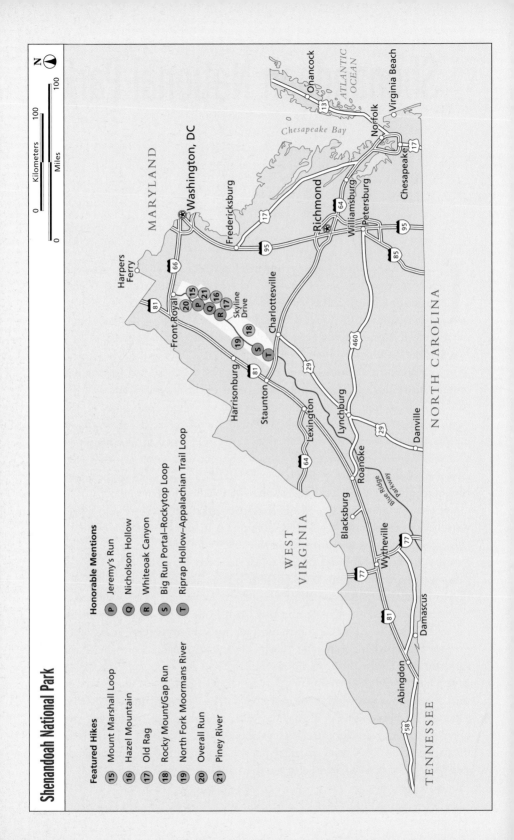

Shenandoah National Park

Featured Hikes

- (15) Mount Marshall Loop
- (16) Hazel Mountain
- (17) Old Rag
- (18) Rocky Mount/Gap Run
- (19) North Fork Moormans River
- (20) Overall Run
- (21) Piney River

Honorable Mentions

- (P) Jeremy's Run
- (Q) Nicholson Hollow
- (R) Whiteoak Canyon
- (S) Big Run Portal–Rockytop Loop
- (T) Riprap Hollow–Appalachian Trail Loop

MARYLAND

WEST VIRGINIA

VIRGINIA

NORTH CAROLINA

TENNESSEE

ATLANTIC OCEAN

Chesapeake Bay

Washington, DC

Harpers Ferry

Front Royal

Skyline Drive

Charlottesville

Fredericksburg

Richmond

Williamsburg

Petersburg

Norfolk

Virginia Beach

Chesapeake

Onancock

Harrisonburg

Staunton

Lexington

Lynchburg

Danville

Roanoke

Blacksburg

Wytheville

Blue Ridge Parkway

Damascus

Abingdon

N

The Hikes

15. Mount Marshall Loop
16. Hazel Mountain
17. Old Rag
18. Rocky Mount/Gap Run
19. North Fork Moormans River
20. Overall Run
21. Piney River

Honorable Mentions

P. Jeremy's Run
Q. Nicholson Hollow
R. Whiteoak Canyon
S. Big Run Portal–Rockytop Loop
T. Riprap Hollow–Appalachian Trail Loop

15 Mount Marshall Loop

The dual peaks of Mount Marshall loom large over Shenandoah's northern district. With summits above 3,000 feet and open rock cliff-tops, North and South Marshall offer inspired views west over the Shenandoah Valley as you trek along the Appalachian Trail. Their counterpoint is an equally inspired view eastward from the craggy boulders that punctuate aptly named The Peak, accessed via the Bluff Trail. This steep-sided mountain, crowned with billion-year-old granite, measures just under 3,000 feet in elevation. The rugged ascent—1,000 feet in just over 0.5 mile, on a trail no longer maintained by the park service—makes it one of Shenandoah's lesser known, but more-demanding, climbs. This 16-mile hike links these peaks and the breathtaking gorge carved by Big Devil Stairs, capturing what makes Shenandoah National Park so popular: great views, waterfalls, and woodland trails.

Start: Jenkins Gap parking area on Skyline Drive

Distance: 15.8-mile loop

Hiking time: 8 hours

Difficulty: Difficult due to distance and an optional side trip on a steep, unmarked path up The Peak

Trail surface: Hike mountain slopes on single-track woodland paths, old forest roads, and a bushwhack to breathtaking views from The Peak.

Land status: National park

Nearest town: Front Royal, VA

Other trail users: Cross-country skiers

Accessibility: This trail is not accessible to people with disabilities; however, most of the facilities within the park are. Check out the accessible 1.3-mile Limberlost Trail (Mile 43).

Canine compatibility: Leashed dogs permitted (leashes no longer than 6 feet)

Trail contact: Shenandoah National Park, 3655 US 211 East, Luray; (540) 999-3500; www.nps.gov/shen

Schedule: Open year-round. Skyline Drive may close without advance warning due to inclement weather. Portions of this road may be closed at night from early Nov to early Jan to discourage poaching. All facilities open mid-May through Oct; limited services rest of year.

Fees/permits: Entrance fee required, valid for 7 days, or annual pass. Free backcountry camping permits, available at ranger stations and visitor centers between sunrise and 1 hour before sunset, are required. Campfires prohibited except in established fireplaces. Before visiting, review backcountry regulations, which cover such issues as group size, where to camp, and waste disposal. Call (540) 999-3500 for regulations. To fish in Shenandoah National Park (SNP), Virginia residents age 16 or older must have a Virginia state fishing license. Five-day nonresident licenses are available at Big Meadows Wayside and local sporting goods stores. Nonresidents age 12 or older must have a Virginia license.

Facilities/features: The park offers a wide variety of lodging, camping and dining.

Maps: USGS Chester Gap; PATC #9: Shenandoah National Park Northern District

Finding the trailhead: From Front Royal, travel south on US 340 from the intersection of VA 55 and US 340 in downtown Front Royal. In 0.3 mile, turn left onto Skyline Drive. In 0.5 mile, pass the park entrance booths. Drive south on Skyline Drive to the Jenkins Gap parking area between mileposts 12 and 13, on the right (west) side of the road. There is parking for 20 cars. GPS: N38 48.433' / W78 10.862'. *DeLorme: Virginia Atlas & Gazetteer:* Page 74, B3.

An AT shelter on the Bluff Trail.

The Hike

Springtime in the Blue Ridge Mountains begins not with green leaves, but with flowering trees. Lavender, white, pink, and yellow buds overflow their small calyx and coat charcoal-shaded branches with color. Tree buds appear first on warmer, southwest-facing hills and in moist creases in the mountain slopes. As April turns to May, the days lengthen and temperatures warm. The ornamental redbud—a tree preferred by George Washington over even Virginia's official tree, the flowering dogwood—strikes a note by filling its moist soil habitat with a mix of lavender, purple, and pink buds. Dogwoods, habitual to dry slopes, follow with showy white petals, cloven and red-tinged. Later in May, white and pink cups burst from the dark evergreen of mountain laurel. By June, this spring symphony will drop into anonymity. Sunlight-gobbling oaks, elms, and poplars will leaf out and overshadow all else. In these still-cold days of April and early May, though, the small trees shine as stars of the landscape.

The Bluff Trail along the east flank of Mount Marshall is hardly the only place in Shenandoah National Park to catch spring's colorful performance. The trail does, however, offer a side bonus in spring—great views down the Blue Ridge onto the small farms and crossroads of the mountain's eastern foothills. The narrow and sometimes uneven route rises to three distinct overlooks with vistas onto a wide, pastoral valley. Each view only whets the appetite for what lies ahead on top of The Peak (2,959 feet).

Hiker Jodi Urban on the Mount Marshall Trail.

The Peak stands alone, separate from the main trunk of the Blue Ridge Mountains. The path to the summit fell off the park's list of maintained trails about a decade ago. USGS topographic maps still show the route, and a sharp-eyed hiker will find the trailhead at the junction of Mount Marshall and Jordan River Trails. Just minutes into your climb up The Peak and the challenges are evident: First a steep pitch, without benefit of switchbacks, then fallen trees and overgrown trail; finally, poor or nonexistent trail markers. Locals nicknamed this mountain Little Bastard. From first glimpse to final weary steps, the name fits. The exposed rock at the summit is charnockite, a billion-year-old granite found the world over. Joseph Charnock, the Englishman for whom the rock is named, founded the city of Calcutta, India. His tombstone is a charnockite rock. Legend says the explorer died from injuries when he tripped over a large chunk of this rock and struck his head. True or not, it serves as a timely reminder as you pick your way over the rough, exposed charnockite boulders descending The Peak. Watch your step!

The Peak once belonged to a family, the Millers, who owned it as part of their 6,000-acre mountain estate. For a time, they worked the tanbark trade. Workers stripped bark off chestnut trees and, using the roads we hike on today, drove mule-pulled carts across Mount Marshall to a tannery in Browntown. The process of turning animal hides into leather required the tannin found in the bark of chestnut and oak trees (also found, in smaller doses, in acorns, coffee, and tea). Tanning was a smelly, dirty job. After grinding the chestnut bark, a tanner mixed bark with water and submerged animal hides in the concoction. Over a period of months, the tannic mixture cured the hide, making it leather. Until the blight of the early 1900s, the American chestnut was preferred for this process because of its high tannic content.

The road that runs along The Peak's south flank is a remnant of the tanbark trade, but today it's hard to imagine anything but foot traffic on it. Fallen trees impede progress at every turn. Thickets of mountain laurel grow off the steep-sided slopes and grass has overgrown the wheel ruts. As you climb through brush, violet pinwheeled periwinkle pokes through last fall's leaf debris, its roots spreading across the dry slope. Closer to the summit, bloodroot, great chickweed, and liverwort splotch the woods with white blossoms. The chickweed practically begs for attention, growing in large tufts that make it attractive to the butterflies that flock to its red-tipped stamens.

There are no chestnut trees left in Shenandoah National Park, or none that could produce bark in the quantity it once did. The chestnut blight stifles tree growth, and young chestnuts die before they can grow more than head-high. There are, however, plenty of oak trees. Hickory has replaced chestnut as a companion tree. Mountain laurel is ever-present in the understory. There are dogwoods, witch hazel, and spicebush as well. Witch hazel deserves mention, if only for how it reproduces. When the shrub's seedpods dry, they burst and release two seeds that can fly outward 30 feet. This not only explains why witch hazel seems omnipresent, but also confounds an old saying about seeds not falling far from the tree. Less reliable are claims that a forked witch hazel branch functions as a divining rod, leading a person to underground water sources. If by chance it does, credit luck, not witchcraft. The shrub takes its name from the Old English word *wych,* meaning "flexible."

The vistas off Bluff Trail spread east over the Blue Ridge foothills and Piedmont. Four mountains fill the horizon: Keyser, Jenkins, Wolf, and The Peak. Their presence illustrates just how complicated Blue Ridge geology can be. Here, within a few miles, stand mountains with marked differences in shape, not to mention rock. Mount Marshall is young—its bedrock is basalt lava, formed by a series of lava flows that oozed from the earth's crust about 550 million years ago. The Peak and its neighbors are old, weathered stubs of resistant granite that date from a billion years ago. The valley between them is more than the route of some picturesque stream. Beneath its crust lies a geologic fault. Faults, by their very nature, slip. That movement breaks rocks, and, over a period of millions of years, the land overlying them collapses. Water, seeking the easiest route downhill, finds the groove and contributes to further erosion. A crease becomes a valley. What's left? Mount Marshall and The Peak, standing like two prizefighters on either side of an imaginary line.

Gravel Springs Hut has a one-night minimum stay for hikers who are out for three days or longer. There is a spring, privy, and fireplace here. Tenters can use the four marked primitive tent sites uphill behind the privy; these have none of the restrictions associated with the hut. However, all park backcountry camping regulations do apply.

Miles and Directions

0.0 Start from the Jenkins Gap parking area on Skyline Drive. Exit the parking lot by turning right (south) on Skyline Drive and walking alongside the road shoulder. **Note:** The return leg of this loop enters Jenkins Gap parking area to the right as you exit.

0.4 Turn left (east) off Skyline Drive onto the yellow-blazed Mount Marshall Trail, which is a forest road lined with mountain laurel. The trail follows folds and contours along Mount Marshall's east slope as you descend.

1.7 Cross Waterfall Branch. There is a series of small waterfalls downstream from this crossing, and a flat area alongside the creek makes a good primitive camp.

2.6 Cross Sprucepine Branch which is shaded by tall, straight-trunked yellow (tulip) poplars.

3.7 Cross an unnamed stream, one of several that form the headwaters of Jordan River.

3.9 Reach a T junction with the Bluff Trail on the right. Continue straight on Mount Marshall Trail. **Option:** To eliminate The Peak and shave 2.3 miles off this hike, turn right (south) on Bluff Trail and follow mileage cues below starting at mile 6.1.

4.3 Reach a T junction with Jordon River Trail on the left. From this junction, follow a distinct footpath that leads into the woods in a southeast direction. The trail is blazed intermittently with light blue paint slashes. **Note:** It is a 1,000-foot ascent in 0.7 mile to the top of The Peak.

4.6 After a steep uphill, the footpath intersects the faint trace of an overgrown road. Turn right, walk 10 to 15 feet, and look for the trail continuing uphill on the left. The trail from here to the top is a steep pitch with large boulders and outcrops. **Note:** The road trace continues at a more level pace around The Peak and to a saddleback that allows a more moderate approach but adds 0.6 mile to this hike.

5.0 Reach The Peak with its open rock summit and views southeast over the Rush River valley and the town of Washington. Turn and retrace steps downhill.

5.7 Emerge from the bushwack path and turn right (north) on Mount Marshall Trail to ascend to the junction with Bluff Trail.

6.1 Turn left (west) on Bluff Trail. The trail ascends through a boulder field on a singletrack woodland path. For the next 2.5 miles, the trail follows the contours of Mount Marshall with brief inclines and several wet areas where mountain streams begin forming in the creases of the hillside.

8.4 At a junction with the trail to Big Devil Stairs, continue straight on Bluff Trail. **Side trip:** Turn left to explore Big Devil Stairs, a deep gorge carved into Mount Marshall with nice falls overlooks. There are trailside clearings for one or two primitive campsites within 0.1 mile of this side trip. The first falls overlook is in 0.4 mile, followed by a steep descent to two more overlooks. The trail to stream level near the park boundary is a 2-mile side trip.

9.3 Views open up on the left side of the trail overlooking Harris Hollow.

9.8 Turn right on Bluff Trail at a junction with Harris Hollow Trail. For the next 0.1 mile, Bluff and Harris Hollow Trails share the pathway.

9.9 After a switchback in the trail, continue straight on Bluff Trail as Harris Hollow Trail branches right and uphill.

10.0 Enter a clearing and bear left (west) toward Gravel Springs Hut. Avoid a light-duty dirt road that ascends from the clearing on the right. Near a freshwater spring adjacent to the hut, ascend a blue-blazed path that climbs the hill behind Gravel Springs. There is a spring, privy, and fireplace here.

Mount Marshall Loop

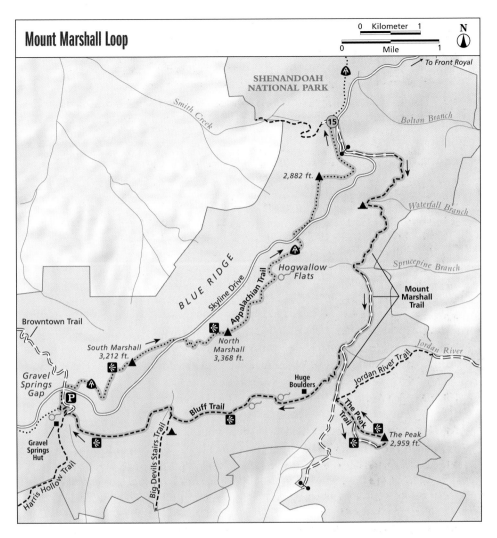

10.3 Turn right (north) onto the white-blazed Appalachian Trail.

10.5 Pass through Gravel Springs parking area. Cross Skyline Drive and walk past a gate. Immediately past the gate, turn right on the white-blazed Appalachian Trail.

11.5 Summit the 3,212-foot peak of South Marshall, with clear views to the west and north.

12.0 Cross Skyline Drive to the east side and begin an ascent of North Marshall on a series of switchbacks.

12.6 Cross the summit of North Marshall (3,368 feet).

13.6 An unmarked trail on the right leads 30 feet to a spring. Continue a descent through Hogwallow Flats.

14.2 Cross Skyline Drive to the left (west) side of the highway and begin an easy ascent.

15.8 Hike ends by turning right on yellow-blazed Jenkins Gap Trail and walking 150 feet to the Jenkins Gap parking area.

Hike Information

Local Information

Front Royal–Warren County Visitors Center, Front Royal, (800) 338-2576, www .visitfrontroyal.com

Local Events/Attractions

Wildflower Weekend, May, Shenandoah National Park, Luray, (540) 999-3500, www .nps.gov/shen. Guided hikes and programs throughout the park.

ARAMARK, the park's concessioner, offers a variety of activities. Visit the calendar at www.visitshenandoah.com/events.aspx.

Lodging

Park lodges at Skyland (Mile 41.7) and Big Meadows (Mile 51) and cabins at Lewis Mountain (Mile 57.5) are seasonal. Skyland is open late Mar through Oct; Big Meadows opens in mid-May and closes in Oct. Call (888) 896-3833 or go to www.visit shenandoah.com for reservations.

Reserved campsites are located at Matthews Arm (Mile 22.1), Big Meadows (Mile 51), Lewis Mountain (Mile 57.5), and Loft Mountain (Mile 79.5). For campground reservations, call (877) 444-6777 or visit www.recreation.gov.

Backcountry trail huts (7) and cabins (6) are operated by the PATC. For reservations, call (703) 242-0315 or visit www.patc.net for availability.

Restaurants

ARAMARK, the park's concessionaire, operates full-service restaurants at Big Meadows Lodge (Mile 51.2) and Skyland (Mile 41.7), and seasonal Wayside Food Stops at Elkwallow Wayside (Mile 24.1), Big Meadows Wayside (Mile 51.2), and Loft Mountain Wayside (Mile 79.5). Call (888) 896-3833 or go to www.visitshenandoah.com for information.

Hike Tours

Ranger-guided programs are offered spring, summer, and fall.

For commercial tour operators that are permitted in the park, visit www.nps.gov/ shen/planyourvisit/permitted-business-services.htm.

Other Resources

Potomac Appalachian Trail Club (PATC), Vienna, (703) 242-0315, www.patc.net. Publishes maps and guides and sponsors hikes in the park.

Shenandoah National Park Association, Luray, (540) 999-3582, www.snpbooks .org. A nonprofit partner that sells guidebooks, maps, brochures, and CDs on the history, flora, and fauna of Shenandoah National Park, to benefit park activities.

16 Hazel Mountain

Hazel Mountain and Sams Ridge once offered a sizable mountain community all the tools and products for a decent living. Today it draws people for its natural beauty. At Hazel River Falls, the stream drops 30 feet into a pool ringed by tall cliffs in the shape of a natural amphitheater. From here a trail climbs to the heights of White Rocks before dropping back to the river and more scenic cascades. Throughout the area a sharp-eyed hiker will spy evidence of mountain settlers. Trails follow old roads used to transport farm products, and old fields, apple orchards, and home foundations are visible.

Start: Trailhead at the Meadow Springs parking lot

Distance: 10.8-mile lollipop

Hiking time: About 5 hours

Difficulty: Moderate due to steep climbs along White Rocks and unaided stream crossings of the Hazel River

Trail surface: Dirt footpaths and old wagon roads lead to waterfalls and rock overhangs at Hazel Falls, views off White Rocks, streamside trails along the Hazel River, and an old home-site on Sams Ridge.

Land status: National park

Nearest town: Luray, VA

Other trail users: Hikers only

Accessibility: This trail is not accessible to people with disabilities; however, most of the facilities within the park are. Check out the accessible 1.3-mile Limberlost Trail (Mile 43).

Canine compatibility: Leashed dogs permitted (leash no longer than 6 feet)

Trail contact: Shenandoah National Park, 3655 US 211 East, Luray; (540) 999-3500; www.nps.gov/shen

Schedule: Open year-round. Skyline Drive may close without advance warning due to inclement weather. Portions of this road may be closed at night from early Nov to early Jan to discourage poaching. All facilities open mid-May through Oct; limited services rest of year.

Fees/permits: Entrance fee required, valid for 7 days, or annual pass. Free backcountry camping permits, available at ranger stations and visitor centers between sunrise and 1 hour before sunset, are required. Campfires prohibited except in established fireplaces. Before visiting, review backcountry regulations, which cover such issues as group size, where to camp, and waste disposal. Call (540) 999-3500 for regulations. To fish in Shenandoah National Park (SNP), Virginia residents age 16 or older must have a Virginia state fishing license. Five-day nonresident licenses are available at Big Meadows Wayside and local sporting goods stores. Nonresidents age 12 or older must have a Virginia license.

Facilities/features: The park offers a variety of services, including camping, dining, and lodging.

Maps: USGS Thornton Gap, Old Rag Mountain; PATC #10: Shenandoah National Park Central District

Finding the trailhead: From Luray, drive east on US 211 for 8.8 miles. Turn left onto the Skyline Drive access road at the Thornton Gap entrance station. Proceed south on Skyline Drive. Park at the Meadow Springs parking area on the left (east) side of Skyline Drive between mileposts 33 and 34. A concrete post at the back of the parking lot marks the start of Hazel Mountain Trail. GPS: N38 38.298' / W78 18.820'. *DeLorme: Virginia Atlas & Gazetteer:* Page 74, C2.

To my considerable disappointment, Mr. Bear didn't stick around to answer questions about life on Sams Ridge. He saw me before I saw him, and my view constituted his posterior ambling into the brush. A bear in the wild ranks as one of Mother Nature's more fleeting encounters (gaping at the bear from your car on Skyline Drive does not count). But what adrenaline! My imagination worked overtime. Would the bear circle back and track us to our tent? Did bear reinforcements lie in waiting nearby? Mentally, I prepared myself for a late night banging pots around a bonfire.

Then I tripped. Rocks in the trail are a definite hazard if you're daydreaming. Abandoning the trail, I followed Mary past small shrubs and creeper vines toward a patch of uneven ground. An iron stove and a blue-and-white-specked pail lay partly buried. Faint markings of an old home foundation were visible. Of all the homesites scattered around Hazel Mountain, this spot surely qualified as prime real estate. Views carried east across the Hazel River to White Rocks's four distinct peaks. A thick mat of green broad-leafed plants crowded a nearby spring. Hazel Mountain Road, a main route across the Blue Ridge in the 1800s, passed just a half mile up the trail.

A hike around Hazel Mountain (you never actually climb this 2,880-foot mountain) runs with ghosts of mountain settlers from beginning to end. The initial descent to the Hazel River passes by hidden ruins of settler homes, and patches of apple trees indicate old orchards. As recently as 1900, the trail itself was a busy thoroughfare through Thornton Gap; a church and school stood at the junction of Sams Ridge and Hazel Mountain Trails. White Rocks Trail and Sams Ridge Trail were old roads as well. On White Rocks Trail—where it arcs right around a boulder field—the landscape to the right side looks suspiciously like an overgrown field. On Sams Ridge, where we found a home foundation, there also stood a fruit tree, a twisted piece of metal stove, and a pile of rocks—each a ghostly sighting of a past life in the mountains.

Hazel Mountain trail marker.

In the black-and-white photos of that period, mountain settlers rarely smile. But to say theirs was a hardship is misleading. Certainly by our modern standards it was hard. Fireplaces provided the only heat during cold winter months. One personal recounting of a season spent on the Blue Ridge describes how blankets froze where the sleeper's breath touched it. Otherwise, life revolved around subsistence farming. Warmer months found men and women outdoors, working fields, cutting wood, planting garden plots. Kids attended school in between chores. Small garden plots supplied most of a family's organic food; larger fields were sown with corn, rye, or oats to be sold in town. Through the 1800s Thornton Gap was a busy thoroughfare. A mill complex on the east side of the mountain ground corn and cut lumber. A blacksmith was located here, and a distillery, too. On the western flank of the Blue Ridge, leading to Luray, a tannery operated.

This was the age of the chestnut tree. Once the dominant tree of the Southern Appalachians, the American chestnut supplied wood for homes, nuts for eating, and bark for tanning. As the nuts ripened, kids would stand under the trees throwing rocks into the branches, trying to shake loose the round, burry fruit. Tea from the leaves, mixed with honey, made a natural cough syrup. In fall, dry leaves were gathered and stuffed in

The author and friend Jodi descend the Hazel Mountain Trail.

mattresses (they called these "talking beds" for the noise they made). The tree bark proved most profitable. Tanners chopped, ground, and mixed bark with water to form a thick, watery, acrid-smelling stew. Animal hides were layered in vats filled with this liquid. Over the course of a year or so, tannic acid—a harsh, bitter, yellowish substance plentiful in the chestnut tree bark—leached into the animal hide and cured it. As you climb through the gap between Hazel and Catlett Mountains on the Sams Ridge Trail, it's hardly a stretch to imagine a wagon loaded with sheets of chestnut tree bark en route to the tannery near Luray, driver perched atop the running board.

Coincidence is sometimes unsettling. In 1900 plants imported from Japan to a New York City zoo contained a blight that would destroy the mature American chestnut population within forty years. In 1925 President Hoover proposed a national park along the Blue Ridge south of Front Royal. In the fall and winter of 1931–32, the two events—the chestnut blight and construction of a national park—converged on the upper slopes of Hazel Mountain, Catlett Mountain, and other peaks in the northern Blue Ridge. For months, standing dead chestnuts shimmered ghostly, their bark stripped, the wood bleached white. At a time when mountain residents were facing displacement and relocation for a new national park, the tree that had provided sustenance in so many ways was dying as well.

Seventy-plus years later, Shenandoah National Park faces another tree crisis. This time, it's the eastern hemlocks, a mighty tree visible near the junction of White Rocks and Hazel Mountain Trails. Exposure to years of air pollution and the droughts of the late 1980s have weakened hemlocks. This makes them vulnerable to blight, specifically to the hemlock woolly adelgid. The microscopic organism coats the underside of hemlock needles with millions of white sacs. Defoliation results, and, from that point, the tree's death is assured within a year or two. Rangers at Shenandoah predict that without a deterrent, large stands of old-growth hemlock will be a thing of the past within several years.

I don't believe in specters, but I had to agree with Mary as we climbed back to Skyline Drive: There was an unsettling feeling in the air on Sams Ridge, in the vicinity of old homesteads, and along the Hazel River, where we stared at the old hemlocks. The ghosts of people and trees—not the haunting kind—just silent reminders of how time marches on.

Miles and Directions

0.0 Start at the concrete post labeled Hazel Mountain Road. Walk downhill and bear right past the trailhead for the blue-blazed Buck Hollow Trail, which branches off left. Continue straight on the yellow-blazed Hazel Mountain Trail, which is an old dirt road.

0.4 Buck Ridge Trail, marked by a concrete post, enters from the left. About 50 paces past here is an unmarked campsite on the right of Hazel Mountain Trail.

1.3 Hazel Mountain Trail begins paralleling the Hazel River, which is audible to your right. **Note:** This is not an open-harvest stream, and all fish caught must be released.

1.6 Turn left (north) onto the yellow-blazed White Rocks Trail. **Note:** Straight on Hazel Mountain Trail is the return leg of this loop.

1.7 White Rocks Trail begins a long curve right, skirting a spot that shows evidence of an old settlement or field. Trees are sparse or young growth. Shrubs and vines run riot here and

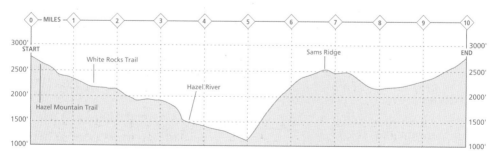

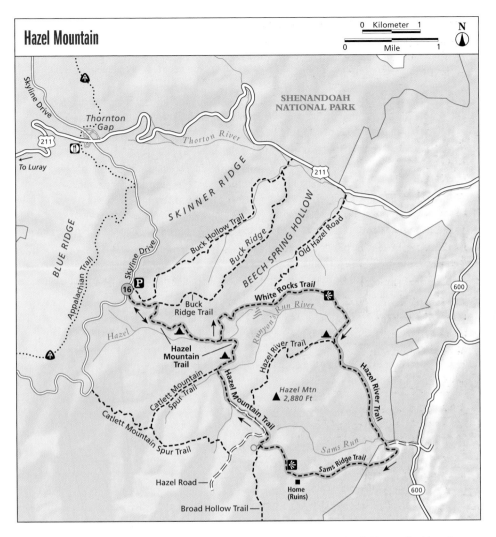

Hazel Mountain

0 Kilometer 1

0 Mile 1

N

SHENANDOAH
NATIONAL PARK

Skyline Drive

Thornton
Gap

211

To Luray

Thorton River

SKINNER RIDGE

211

BLUE RIDGE

Appalachian Trail

Skyline Drive

Buck Hollow Trail

Buck Ridge

BEECH SPRING HOLLOW

Old Hazel Road

600

P
16

Buck
Ridge Trail

White Rocks Trail

Runyon's Run River

Hazel

**Hazel
Mountain
Trail**

Hazel River Trail

Hazel River Trail

*Catlett Mountain
Spur Trail*

Hazel Mountain Trail

Hazel Mtn
▲ 2,880 Ft

Catlett Mountain Spur Trail

Sams Run

Sams Ridge Trail

Hazel Road —

Home
(Ruins)

600

Broad Hollow Trail —

dominate the understory. It was common for settlers, when clearing fields, to pile the rocks or make stone fences. Remnants of both are visible.

2.5 Enter a "four-corners" trail junction. Turn right and descend 0.15 mile down a steep, narrow footpath to the Hazel River. At the stream, turn right and hike upstream a few feet to a 30-foot waterfall. (Birds nest in the rock overhangs, and the common blue violet peeks out from thin patches of soil amid the rock boulders.) To return to White Rocks Trail, follow the route you descended.

2.8 Back at the "four corners" trail junction, turn right to continue on White Rocks Trail. The trail climbs to the four knobs whose exposed white rocks give this ridge its name. To the southeast, the lush Hazel River valley unfolds. Look left for a nice view of the remaining White Rock knobs.

4.2 After a long descent, reach the Hazel River. Cross and bear left, walking downstream along the river. This is a good camping spot, with several established sites marked by fire rings.

4.4 Reach a T intersection with the Hazel River Trail. Turn left and follow the Hazel River Trail to the park boundary. **Bailout:** Turn right on Hazel River Trail and climb over Hazel Mountain. Reach Hazel Mountain Trail in 2.0 miles, turn right, and follow mileage cues below starting at 8.0 miles. This shaves 1.5 miles off the route, but avoids a steep ascent up Sams Ridge.

5.7 Turn right onto the blue-blazed Sams Ridge Trail, begin a steep ascent, and exit the park. **Option:** An alternate starting point for this hike is straight ahead on the Hazel River Trail, which empties onto VA 600.

6.2 Reenter the park. Boundaries are marked by red slashes on the trees.

7.0 The trail levels as you near the top of Sams Ridge. Around you, the vegetation changes from the hardwood-dominated ridge flanks to a lush mix of evergreens and scrub hardwoods. The woods thin and again you're entering an old settlement area. Metal stoves, pots, stone walls, and piles of rock all testify to the previous inhabitants, displaced when the federal government seized land to create this park. Spend some time and explore, but don't disturb the remains.

7.6 Broad Hollow Trail exits on the left to access trails around Catlett Mountain and Nicholson Hollow. Continue straight on the blue-blazed Sams Ridge Trail. There is a spring just around the bend from this junction.

7.8 Turn left onto Hazel Mountain Trail, marked by a concrete trail mark post.

8.0 Continue straight past a junction with Hazel River Trail on the right. **Note:** If you opted for the bailout at 4.4 miles, continue with mileage cues from this point.

8.2 Pass an established primitive campsite off the left side of the trail. The trail is now a wide, old dirt road.

8.7 Cross a small tributary stream and bear right on Hazel Mountain Trail at a junction with Catlett Spur Trail on the left. **Note:** Catlett Spur Trail follows Runyon's Run upstream 1.2 miles to Catlett Mountain Trail.

9.3 Pass the trailhead for White Rocks Trail and continue straight.

10.8 Arrive back at the Meadow Springs parking lot.

Hike Information

Local Information

Luray–Page County Chamber of Commerce, Luray, (888) 743-3915, www.luray page.com

Local Events/Attractions

Christmas Bird Counts, Shenandoah Audubon Society, Dec and Feb, Winchester, www.audubon-nsvas.org

Wildflower Weekend, May, Shenandoah National Park, Luray, (540) 999-3500, www.nps.gov/shen. Guided hikes and programs throughout the park.

ARAMARK, the park's concessioner, offers a variety of activities. Visit the calendar at www.visitshenandoah.com/events.aspx.

Lodging

Park lodges at Skyland (Mile 41.7) and Big Meadows (Mile 51) and cabins at Lewis Mountain (Mile 57.5) are seasonal. Skyland is open late Mar through Oct; Big Meadows opens in mid-May and closes in Oct. Call (888) 896-3833 or go to www.visit shenandoah.com for reservations.

Reserved campsites are located at Matthews Arm (Mile 22.1), Big Meadows (Mile 51), Lewis Mountain (Mile 57.5), and Loft Mountain (Mile 79.5). For campground reservations, call (877) 444-6777 or visit www.recreation.gov.

Backcountry trail huts (7) and cabins (6) are operated by the PATC. For reservations, call (703) 242-0315 or visit www.patc.net for availability.

Restaurants

ARAMARK, the park's concessionaire, operates full-service restaurants at Big Meadows Lodge (Mile 51.2) and Skyland (Mile 41.7), and seasonal Wayside Food Stops at Elkwallow Wayside (Mile 24.1), Big Meadows Wayside (Mile 51.2), and Loft Mountain Wayside (Mile 79.5). Call (888) 896-3833 or go to www.visitshenandoah.com for information.

Hike Tours

Ranger-guided programs are offered spring, summer, and fall.

For commercial tour operators that are permitted in the park, visit www.nps.gov/shen/planyourvisit/permitted-business-services.htm.

Other Resources

Potomac Appalachian Trail Club (PATC), Vienna, (703) 242-0315, www.patc.net. Publishes maps and guides and sponsors hikes in the park.

Shenandoah National Park Association, Luray, (540) 999-3582, www.snpbooks .org. A nonprofit partners that sells guidebooks, maps, brochures, and CDs on the history, flora, and fauna of Shenandoah National Park, to benefit park activities.

17 Old Rag

Old Rag is so popular, the park has special rules for recreational use. There's a fee to park and use the trails on certain weekends and holidays during summer and fall. What's the attraction? Old Rag is a quick drive from Northern Virginia and offers day-trippers a craggy knob with eye-popping views. Beating the crowds on Old Rag means hiking in the off-season. Mountain laurel decorates the Saddle Trail with white and pink blossoms during spring. In fall, views from Old Rag across Weakley Hollow are filled with autumn colors. Whatever the season, carry a warm overshirt or jacket; wind and no tree cover can make Old Rag's summit feel positively alpine.

Start: Parking lot at the end of VA 600, 1.3 miles west of Nethers. There is also an overflow parking lot on VA 600, 1.2 miles before the trailhead.

Distance: 7.4-mile loop

Hiking time: 7–8 hours

Difficulty: Difficult due to the route's length and strenuous climbs

Trail surface: Dirt roads and dirt trails meander through mixed hardwood forest on lower slopes and along the trout stream at the foot of the mountain; the path is mostly exposed rock face along the cliffs and through the narrow passages between house-size boulders around the peak.

Land status: National park

Nearest town: Syria, VA

Other trail users: Hikers only

Accessibility: None

Canine compatibility: Dogs not permitted for their own safety

Trail contact: Shenandoah National Park, 3655 US 211 East, Luray; (540) 999-3500; www.nps.gov/shen

Schedule: Open year-round. Skyline Drive may close without advance warning due to inclement weather. Portions of this road may be closed at night from early Nov to early Jan to discourage poaching. All facilities open mid-May through Oct; limited services rest of year. The Old Rag trailhead is outside the park boundary, so you do not have to use Skyline Drive.

Fees/permits: Even though the trailhead is outside the park, you must pay a park entrance fee to a ranger if present, or self-pay at the Old Rag Fee Station. Overnight camping is limited and prohibited above 2,800 feet. You must obtain a free backcountry permit from a ranger station. Campfires prohibited except in established fireplaces. Call (540) 999-3500 for regulations.

Facilities/features: Porta-johns at the registration station, and 2 shelters on the trail for day use only

Maps: USGS Old Rag; PATC #10: Shenandoah National Park Central District

Finding the trailhead: From Sperryville, drive south on US 522 and in 0.8 mile, turn right onto VA 231. In 8 miles, turn right onto VA 601 and follow signs to the parking area, about 3 miles; the road number changes from VA 601 to VA 707 and finally VA 600. It is a 0.8-mile walk to the trailhead. Parking at the trailhead and along the roadside is prohibited. GPS: N38 34.215' / W78 18.050'. *DeLorme: Virginia Atlas & Gazetteer:* Page 74, B3.

A rock formation on Old Rag.

The Hike

The climb up Old Rag leads from mountain slopes thick with oak and tulip poplar to a rugged, exposed landscape of rock and straggly table-mountain pine. The forest floor, littered with dead leaves along Hughes Run near the trailhead, sports a thick mat of pine needles at higher elevations. Where you had once seen witch hazel growing in the forest subcanopy, now mountain laurel sinks its tenacious roots into thin, rocky soil. For the hiker, this is a noticeable change with a subtle, less noticeable effect on the mountain. Near the summit, those pine needles collect in puddles of water on open rock. Nitrates released from the needles mix with billion-year-old granite rock, and the erosion process begins. Bowl-shaped depressions form in rock boulders. And just like that, another piece of Old Rag wears away.

As sturdy a mountain as the Blue Ridge ever produced, Old Rag is nonetheless a still-evolving mountain. Still evolving is a curious description for a peak of such stature that, by park estimates, 100,000 people climb it annually. But it explains both how Old Rag's signature summit came to exist and how it continues to change. Millions of years of weathering led to the exposure of granite boulders at the summit. More recently, rain-triggered rock slides reshaped the mountain's east slope (which is well known to only the most experienced bushwhackers and rock climbers). The exposed rock in the recent slides has triggered new interest in Old Rag among geologists. Carbon dating of rocks in the last few years debunked a long-held belief that Old Rag granite is the oldest rock in America's oldest mountain range. Samples of rock

The view from Old Rag.

taken near Mary's Rock on Skyline Drive date a few hundred million years earlier. This new information doesn't diminish or change Old Rag; it merely adds to a story that is being written in small ways every day.

Climbing the last mile on the Ridge Trail demands strength and balance. At one point, a narrow rock ledge is all that separates you from a long fall onto a pile of loose rocks. At another point, you may need a boost from behind to climb over a boulder. The trail negotiates steps made of Catoctin greenstone, rock pillars and boulders as large as a house, and short tunnels between the first false summit (where the trail emerges from the forest) and the true summit at 3,268 feet. The difficulty of the last mile, coupled with the crowds that flock here from June to October, will cause climbing delays.

Approaching Old Rag on the Saddle Trail is less popular, but it recommends itself for exactly that reason: Few people hike it. Hiking on Weakley Hollow Road, views open in the forest canopy and stretch all the way to the mountain. If you bushwhack off Weakley Hollow Road, it's possible to find relics of Old Rag village. In the 1780s there was a post office, school, church, and homes. (The post office stood at the junction of the Saddle Trail with Old Rag Road.) Local mountain men were employed by Skyland Resort to carry packs for the visitors climbing and camping out on Old Rag. Byrds Nest Shelter No. 1, a mountaintop picnic spot just shy of the peak, was donated by another well-heeled Old Rag climber: Virginia governor and senator Henry Flood Byrd Sr. climbed the mountain every year on his birthday.

Land at the foot of Old Rag was once one of the most populated and developed areas of Shenandoah National Park. Archeologists estimate 460 people lived in a network of hollows and coves, including Weakley Hollow. Recent surveys have identified nearly ninety sites that were once homes, gristmills, churches, or schools. It is from Weakley Hollow—and the communities in neighboring Nicholson and Corbin Hollows—that the image of Appalachian mountain folk as barefooted, moonshine-swilling hillbillies emerged. A 1933 sociological study called "Hollow Folk" described residents of the Blue Ridge as "unlettered folk, sheltered in tiny mud-plastered log cabins and supported by a primitive agriculture." That description went a long way in swaying public and political opinion to evict residents in favor of building Shenandoah National Park.

> Byrds Nest No. 1 and Old Rag Shelters are day-use only. If you're hiking on the weekend, arrive early to beat the crowds.

Seventy years later, archeologists with the Colonial Williamsburg Foundation are revisiting these hollows and rewriting the history. Material recently collected, from calendars and watches to medicine bottles and music, paints a picture of inhabitants not as primitive people who lived hand to mouth. Rather, they were rural people who faced and overcame weather, soil, and social conditions that might have—and probably did—humbled people of lesser character. Testament to the power of catalog marketing, the Sears Roebuck Company probably did more to bring the outside world to hollow folk as any technological advancement.

Climbing away from the remains of Old Rag village, the Saddle Trail passes by thick patches of blackberries. A shredded log shows where a bear ripped away soft, rotted wood hunting for grubs. Unlike deer, which were reintroduced to the park in 1935, bears returned to the park on their own. They now number between 250 and 300 (deer number in the thousands).

On a quiet day, the staccato of a woodpecker echoes through the woods. In winter, the source of sound may well be a yellow-bellied sapsucker, a bird species that extracts sap from tulip poplars. Nestled below a rock outcrop at lower elevations along Saddle Trail, dusk wraps around the mountain. Wind buffets the peak and drifts downslope. It whistles outside the tent. One gets the sense that the mountain is alive.

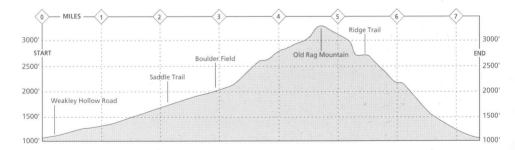

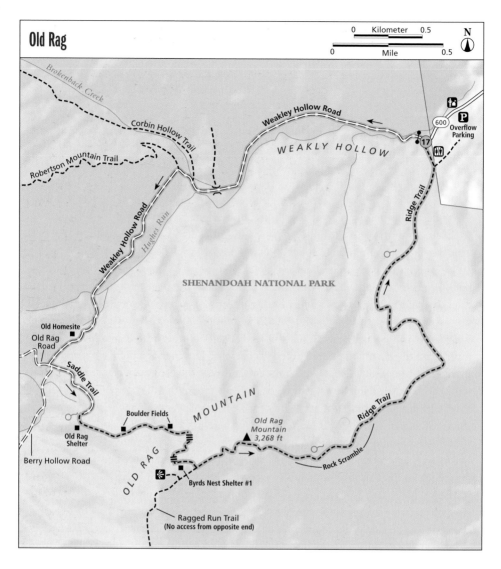

Miles and Directions

0.0 Start from the parking lot at the end of VA 600 (Weakley Hollow Road). In the southwest corner of the parking lot, a yellow chain blocks vehicle traffic from passing. Follow the road as it drops to Hughes Run, crosses on a metal bridge, and begins a long, steady climb.

1.1 Continue straight on Weakley Hollow Road as Corbin Hollow Trail enters on the right. **Note:** Corbin Hollow Trail leads up Brokenback Creek and intersects with Old Rag Road in just more than 2 miles.

1.2 Continue straight on Weakley Hollow Road as Robertson Mountain Trail enters on the right. **Note:** Robertson Mountain Trail leads across the top of Robertson Mountain and intersects with Old Rag Road in 2.4 miles.

2.1 Turn left onto Old Rag Road. In a few feet, turn left again onto the blue-blazed Saddle Trail, an old road overgrown with grass. The signboard has information on park fees and the "leave no trace" ethic.

2.5 Pass the Old Rag Shelter and a spring on the right side of the Saddle Trail. **Note:** The shelter is for day-use only. The spring is marked by a concrete post with yellow striping. If you drink water from the spring, make sure you treat it first.

2.8 Saddle Trail narrows and crosses a boulder field.

3.1 Pass around a boulder the size of a small house. Steps lead uphill to a switchback in the trail.

3.5 Reach Byrds Nest Shelter No. 1. **Note:** An unmarked and unnamed footpath leads past the day-use-only shelter to a perch overlooking Weakley Hollow. Use caution when walking on exposed rock or near cliff edges. The views are beautiful, but they're not worth dying for. Another unmarked trail descends down the east slope of Old Rag. This trail is abandoned and ends at private property with no public access.

3.7 Saddle Trail forks. Bear right and switchback to continue ascent of Old Rag.

4.0 Reach the top of Old Rag. A concrete post marks the end of the Saddle Trail and beginning of the Ridge Trail. **Note:** For views, turn left at the concrete post and climb the rocks. To descend on the Ridge Trail, return to the concrete post and turn left.

4.5 Begin rock scrambling beneath boulders wedged in crevices. The next 0.5 mile brings steep drop-offs and tricky passages around and over the rocks.

4.7 Pass over the "false summit" of Old Rag. A look back up the trail nets a nice photo op of the Old Rag summit.

5.1 The Ridge Trail leaves Old Rag's exposed granite and reenters the woods under a canopy of oak and yellow poplar.

7.4 Arrive back at the parking lot.

Hike Information

Local Information

Rappahannock County Tourism, Visitor Center, 3 Library St., Washington, (540) 675-3153, www.visitrappahannockva.com

Local Events/Attractions

Prince Michel Winery, Leon, (540) 547-3707, www.princemichel.com

Lodging

Just minutes from the trailhead, Old Rag Cottage can accommodate groups of up to 6 people. 3504 Weakley Hollow Rd., Syria, (540) 672-2421, www.oldragcottage.com

Graves Mountain Lodge is also near the base of the mountain, offering affordable lodging with meals included. (540) 923-4231; www.gravesmountain.com

Park lodges at Skyland (Mile 41.7) and Big Meadows (Mile 51) and cabins at Lewis Mountain (Mile 57.5) are seasonal. Skyland is open late Mar through Oct; Big Meadows opens in mid-May and closes in Oct. Call (888) 896-3833 or go to www.visitshenandoah.com for reservations.

Reserved campsites are located at Matthews Arm (Mile 22.1), Big Meadows (Mile 51), Lewis Mountain (Mile 57.5), and Loft Mountain (Mile 79.5). For campground reservations, call (877) 444-6777 or visit www.recreation.gov.

Backcountry trail huts (7) and cabins (6) are operated by the PATC. For reservations, call (703) 242-0315 or visit www.patc.net for availability.

Restaurants

ARAMARK, the park's concessionaire, operates full-service restaurants at Big Meadows Lodge (Mile 51.2) and Skyland (Mile 41.7), and seasonal Wayside Food Stops at Elkwallow Wayside (Mile 24.1), Big Meadows Wayside (Mile 51.2), and Loft Mountain Wayside (Mile 79.5). Call (888) 896-3833 or go to www.visitshenandoah.com for information.

The town of Madison, about 14 miles away, has several good restaurants, as does Sperryville, about 19 miles.

Hike Tours

For commercial tour operators that are permitted in the park, visit www.nps.gov/shen/planyourvisit/permitted-business-services.htm.

Other Resources

Potomac Appalachian Trail Club (PATC), Vienna, (703) 242-0315, www.patc.net

Old Rag Master Naturalists, www.oldragmasternaturalists.org

18 Rocky Mount/Gap Run

Rocky Mount's western flank is a demanding climb of 850 feet in just over 1 mile. If you're not breathless at the top, the view will steal what breath is left. A series of ridges and peaks intersect and rise in succession to the limitless horizon. A return hike on Gap Run Trail takes you from soaring heights into shaded forest. It's said trails in the south district of Shenandoah National Park get less use than other areas of the park. The Rocky Mount/Gap Run loop is proof of this. As a day hike, it is a strenuous full-day trip. Overnighters will find that a quiet tent site along Gap Run allows time to tarry and enjoy the deep-woods scenery.

Start: Concrete post on the west, or southbound, side of Skyline Drive, 0.1 mile north of Twomile Run Overlook

Distance: 10.1-mile lollipop

Hiking time: About 7 hours

Difficulty: Moderate due to a steep climb up Rocky Mount

Trail surface: Make your way along dirt and grass footpaths, rock slides, high-water washes, old streambeds, and rock outcrops on Rocky Mount to the old-growth chestnut oak forests and the dark, sheltered stream valley.

Land status: National park

Nearest city: Elkton, VA

Other trail users: Hikers only

Accessibility: This trail is not accessible to people with disabilities; however, most of the facilities within the park are. Check out the accessible 1.3-mile Limberlost Trail (Mile 43).

Canine compatibility: Leashed dogs permitted (leash no longer than 6 feet)

Trail contact: Shenandoah National Park, 3655 US 211 East, Luray; (540) 999-3500; www.nps.gov/shen

Schedule: Open year-round. Skyline Drive may close without advance warning due to inclement weather. Portions of this road may be closed at night from early Nov to early Jan to discourage poaching. All facilities open mid-May through Oct; limited services rest of year.

Fees/permits: Entrance fee required, valid for 7 days, or annual pass. Free backcountry camping permits, available at ranger stations and visitor centers between sunrise and 1 hour before sunset, are required. Campfires prohibited except in established fireplaces. Before visiting, review backcountry regulations, which cover such issues as group size, where to camp, and waste disposal. Call (540) 999-3500 for regulations. To fish in Shenandoah National Park (SNP), Virginia residents age 16 or older must have a Virginia state fishing license. Five-day nonresident licenses are available at Big Meadows Wayside and local sporting goods stores. Nonresidents age 12 or older must have a Virginia license.

Facilities/features: The park offers visitor centers, wayside pull-offs, dining, and lodging.

Maps: USGS McGaheysville; PATC #11: Shenandoah National Park South District

Finding the trailhead: From the south, take exit 99 off I-64 and proceed north on Skyline Drive for 28 miles. Twomile Overlook is at Mile 76.2, on the west side of Skyline Drive. From the north, access Skyline Drive from US 33 in Swift Gap. Drive south on Skyline Drive for 11 miles to reach Twomile Overlook on the right side of the highway. From the overlook, walk 0.1 mile north along the west shoulder of Skyline Drive to reach the Rocky Gap Trailhead, marked by a concrete post. GPS: N38 17.944' / W78 38.826'. *DeLorme: Virginia Atlas & Gazetteer:* Page 67, B6.

Gap Run can be a monster. That much was clear from tree limbs and other forest debris scattered across its floodplain. Rocks larger than a human head lay piled around the base of larger trees, some 20 feet removed from the actual stream bank. Thinking of the torrent that moved them made me reconsider the small, puddling, barely moving flow that trickled past my campsite. You see, in late July, Gap Run is anything but a monster: a puddle here and a puddle there, and not much else.

A few feet upstream, my nephew, Matthias, took advantage of summer's low-water conditions to scramble over streambed rocks in search of a crayfish or salamander. I had gone over with him proper streambed hunting techniques: Squat or hunch down on a rock, I said, and just stare at one spot in the stream. Then slowly, with two fingers, lift one stone at a time. Give the silt time to settle, then, if you don't see what you're looking for, replace the stone where you found it. A lot of critters call this stream their home, I said. And no one likes to come home and find his house rearranged.

These are the good times, I thought as I watched him explore. A few hours earlier, it was all about adjusting packs, lightening loads, tending to blisters and hot spots, and helping a struggling seven-year-old come to terms with carrying his food, water, and clothing for miles on end, all so we could sit in the woods, eat prepackaged food, and sleep on hard ground.

Rocky Mount trail marker.

Leadership training, whether for business or wilderness adventure, preaches the importance of monitoring your group's morale. A happy camper interacts better with others and is more willing to help the group. With children, this is especially true. There usually comes a time, a critical moment—almost always after a difficult stretch of trail—when an uncomfortable thought settles in: This, they state plainly, is too much like work.

Our group—Mary, myself, and our niece and nephew, Sarah and Matthias—began the hike off Skyline Drive on Rocky Mount Trail. It started nicely on a dirt footpath that posed little risk of injury, on a gentle slope with sporadic views southwest to Twomile Ridge. When the trail steepened and curved around the east side of a small knob, legs weakened. Complaints started drifting back my way and I heard someone say they were dizzy. All indicators pointed to a much-needed rest. The opportunity presented itself once the trail reentered the shade of forest.

Every leader needs a bag of tricks and the next 2 miles exhausted my personal stash. We played "Trail-Wheel of Fortune." We set group challenges to hike a certain distance in a certain period of time. We sang songs. Every time a view opened on the trail, I used it as a topographic lesson by pointing out where we stood. We juggled loads, adjusted shoulder straps, medicated sore feet, and, before long, we hit a nice campsite on the Gap Run Trail. Three miles in six hours—the pace left a little to be desired, but a successful first day by all other measures.

Sigurd Olson, author of *Campfires,* wrote "anyone who has traveled in the wilds knows how much he looks forward to the time of day when he can lay down his burden and make camp." I'm not sure Olson ever hiked with children, because for them, camp means one thing: Work. Unpack your backpack. Help set up tents. Prep dinner. Get firewood. Get water. Then a chorus of don'ts: Don't go in the tent with shoes. Don't throw dirt at your sister. Don't touch that plant. Don't eat that bug . . .

At this delicate point, when commands are flying fast, it pays to remember: The poor kids have already completed a Herculean task just getting here. More importantly, if their needs aren't met, they can hardly be expected to meet someone else's.

With imagination, jobs can be fun. Matthias and I drew water duty, which led us to search Gap Run for some running water, which in turn led to not getting water at all. Instead, we moved up and down the dry wash, checking out small pools for aqua-critters. A *snap-crackle* brought us to the shoreline where, in dry oak leaves, a turtle the size of a half-dollar pumped tiny legs in a vain attempt to escape detection. We tracked it for ten minutes or so, until I remembered that without water, we wouldn't eat. We filtered and headed back to camp.

Anticipation motivates. Over breakfast the next morning, Mary and I announced the day hike would be without packs. That prospect sent Matthias and Sarah up the trail like shots. When we caught up, their flushed faces and panting told the story: It's hard to keep an excited kid down, but it's also difficult to run up Rocky Mount. As we approached the white outcrops of the summit, I told the kids to be on the watch. The Erwinian quartzite is pocked with small fossil wormholes that date from a period

A rock outcrop on Rocky Mount.

when this incredibly hard rock was the beach of a prehistoric ocean. As amazing as that sounds, I witnessed something even more mind-boggling: two kids running uphill the last tenth of a mile, each trying to be the first to the summit.

Atop Rocky Mount, we stared across to Rocky Mountain and Twomile Ridge, each of us alone in our thoughts. Turkey vultures rode air currents, wings shifting to-and-fro as they held a tricky balance of speed and direction. "This," said eleven-year-old Sarah, "is the most awesome thing I've ever seen in my entire life."

Miles and Directions

0.0   Start at the Rocky Mount trailhead 0.1 mile north of Twomile Run Overlook on Skyline Drive.

0.6   The trail climbs briefly, then drops to an easy stretch along a footpath. **Note:** The trail shows signs of once being a road. In fact, this route once served as a fire road up from Berrytown, a town at the foot of the Blue Ridge west of Rocky Mount. Occasional views open west to Twomile Ridge and east into the Hawksbill Creek valley and Weaver Mountain.

1.0   Hike along an exposed stretch of trail as you make a brief, 200-foot climb up over a small knob. The trail reenters the woods as it descends the northwest side of this hill.

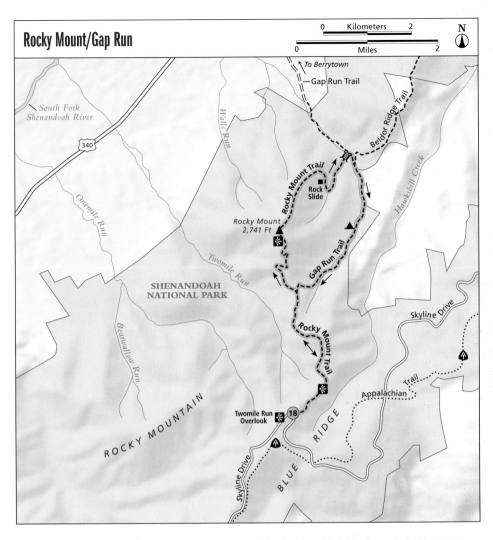

2.2 Come to the intersection of Gap Run Trail and Rocky Mount Trail. Continue straight to climb Rocky Mount. **Note:** Gap Run Trail heads off to the right and descends past the headwaters of Gap Run. It junctions with the opposite end of Rocky Mount Trail in 2.2 miles.

2.5 Begin a steep climb up Rocky Mount. Views of Twomile Ridge open up when the trail switches back to the right.

2.9 Exposed chunks of chalky rock become more frequent. Close examination reveals fossilized wormholes in this Erwin quartzite.

3.2 About 40 yards shy of the wooded peak on Rocky Mount are cliffs with views of Twomile Ridge, and six ridges rising in succession beyond. **Note:** There is rocktripe lichen on the rocks at this summit. It appears brown, with folded-up edges, and is brittle to the touch. *The Audubon* field guide describes this lichen as "rarely seen," so take a minute to enjoy.

3.8 A large slab of rock becomes increasingly visible on the left side of the trail as you descend. Old-growth chestnut oaks line the trail on your right, and the forest understory

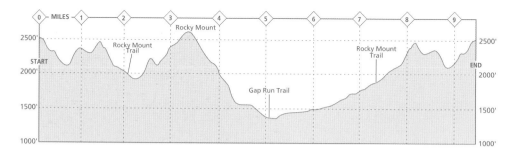

is a mix of blueberries, sassafras, and scrub oak. (The sassafras has quite a history. Explorers and colonists treated it as a cure-all. It shrinks less than any southern hardwood, thus was favored in building fences and boats, but its odor supposedly drove away bedbugs, which made it a favored wood for building a bed frame. It was once used widely as a flavor agent. Lately, scientists have found that safrole, a clear oil found in the roots of sassafras, is a cancer-causing agent. Its use in food and drinks is forbidden in the United States.)

4.7 Cross the first of several rock slides that have covered the mountain below and above the trail with boulders. (Be careful when crossing the rock slides. There is no danger of further slippage, but footing is tricky.) After this the trail descends via switchbacks to a small tributary of Gap Run.

5.1 Cross a small stream and follow the right bank downhill. Within several hundred yards, you'll hop back across the stream and follow the left bank. The trail is clear; stream crossings are well marked.

5.5 Cross Gap Run and reach a T intersection where Rocky Mount Trail meets Gap Run Trail. Turn right onto Gap Run Trail. **Note:** To the left, Gap Run departs the park in 0.8 mile and reaches VA 630 near Berrytown in 1.7 miles.

5.7 An open area to the right of the trail marks an established primitive camp site.

6.2 Gap Run Trail, which has followed the footprint of an old dirt road, becomes a footpath as it crosses a washed-out section of Gap Run. The stream forks into many small rivulets and the trail crosses them as it winds up the wide stream valley. In 0.1 mile, the trail reverts back to a wide, graded path.

6.4 Veer right and continue walking upstream on a woodsy footpath. **Note:** The old road veers left and uphill. Red paint slashes on the trees mark the national park boundary.

6.6 Cross Gap Run. As you climb up the stream valley for the next mile, you will cross the stream two more times.

7.6 Cross Gap Run for the final time and begin a steep ascent to a saddle and the junction with Rocky Mount Trail.

7.9 Gap Run Trail ends at Rocky Mount Trail. Turn left to return to Skyline Drive.

10.1 Hike ends at Skyline Drive. Turn right and head downhill 0.1 mile to parking at Twomile Run Overlook.

Hike Information

Local Information

Greene County Tourism, Ruckersville, (434) 985-6663, www.gatewaytocharlottesville
.com

Local Events/Attractions

The Town of Stanardsville has specialty shops, lodging, and dining.

Lodging

Park lodges at Skyland (Mile 41.7) and Big Meadows (Mile 51) and cabins at Lewis
Mountain (Mile 57.5) are seasonal. Skyland is open late Mar through Oct; Big Meadows opens in mid-May and closes in Oct. Call (888) 896-3833 or go to www.visit
shenandoah.com for reservations.

Reserved campsites are located at Matthews Arm (Mile 22.1), Big Meadows (Mile
51), Lewis Mountain (Mile 57.5), and Loft Mountain (Mile 79.5). For campground
reservations, call (877) 444-6777 or visit www.recreation.gov.

Backcountry trail huts (7) and cabins (6) are operated by the PATC. For reservations, call (703) 242-0315 or visit www.patc.net for availability.

Hike Tours

Ranger-guided programs are offered spring, summer, and fall.

For commercial tour operators that are permitted in the park, visit www.nps.gov/
shen/planyourvisit/permitted-business-services.htm.

Other Resources

Potomac Appalachian Trail Club (PATC), Vienna, (703) 242-0315, www.patc.net.
Publishes maps and guides and sponsors hikes in the park.

Shenandoah National Park Association, Luray, (540) 999-3582, www.snpbooks
.org. A nonprofit partners that sells guidebooks, maps, brochures, and CDs on the history, flora, and fauna of Shenandoah National Park, to benefit park activities.

19 North Fork Moormans River

North Fork Moormans River runs a modest path down the foothills of the Blue Ridge along Shenandoah National Park's east boundary. Fly fishers work the stocked waters. Hikers push upstream toward the waterfalls on picturesque mountain streams that feed the North Fork. Beyond the most popular day hikes lies rugged Shenandoah backcountry. From Sugar Hollow Reservoir deep into the park, the landscape shows scars of a 1995 flood that swelled the river and tributaries with water, rocks, trees, and mud. This is not only a great day hike, but also a firsthand account of earth-shaping events, and the process of recovery that follows.

Start: National park boundary north of the Sugar Hollow Reservoir on VA 614 at the parking area for the North Fork Moormans River Trail

Distance: 3.2 miles out and back

Hiking time: About 3 hours

Difficulty: Easy due to short distance and level terrain. There are dangerous passages across rock slides and undercut stream banks, however.

Trail surface: Mostly dirt roads and occasional streambeds wind through an expansive stream valley hewn by floodwaters and fed by numerous small mountain streams. One tributary, Big Branch, drops 50 feet off barefaced rock into a deep pool.

Land status: National park

Nearest town: White Hall, VA

Other trail users: Mountain bikers and cross-country skiers

Accessibility: The Paths to Happiness and the John Kostanecki Memorial Trail provide access to Moormans River for anglers with mobility impairments.

Canine compatibility: Leashed dogs permitted (leash no longer than 6 feet)

Trail contact: Shenandoah National Park, 3655 US 211 East, Luray; (540) 999-3500; www.nps.gov/shen

Schedule: Open year-round. Skyline Drive may close without advance warning due to inclement weather. Portions of this road may be closed at night from early Nov to early Jan to discourage poaching. All facilities open mid-May through Oct; limited services rest of year.

Fees/permits: Since you enter from outside the park you do no need to pay the entrance fee. Free backcountry camping permits, available at ranger stations and visitor centers between sunrise and 1 hour before sunset, are required. Campfires prohibited except in established fireplaces. Before visiting, review backcountry regulations, which cover such issues as group size, where to camp, and waste disposal. Call (540) 999-3500 for regulations. To fish in Shenandoah National Park (SNP), Virginia residents age 16 or older must have a Virginia state fishing license. Five-day nonresident licenses are available at Big Meadows Wayside and local sporting goods stores. Nonresidents age 12 or older must have a Virginia license.

Facilities/features: No facilities. There are numerous swimming holes as you hike up the river bottom.

Maps: USGS Browns Cove, Crimora; PATC #11: Shenandoah National Park South District

Finding the trailhead: From White Hall, drive 5.6 miles west on VA 614 to Sugar Hollow Reservoir. Past the reservoir dam, the road turns to gravel. At 5.6 miles, enter a turnaround area and bear right (north) on a rutted road. Follow it 0.1 mile to a parking area that marks the end of vehicle access. There is parking for five cars. Parking spaces fill quickly on weekends. If the lot is full, return to the turnaround and park there, then walk the rutted road to the trailhead. GPS: N38 08.641' / W78 44.912'. *DeLorme: Virginia Atlas & Gazetteer:* Page 67, C6.

An example of the destructive force of the river.

The Hike

Geologists study materials that form the earth, and the elements that work on those materials, like wind, water, heat, and pressure. They work with history, but on a scale so much larger and longer than the human time frame, it's often difficult to fathom.

Not all geologic activity is ancient history, however. On the North Fork Moormans River, it appears uncomfortably recent. Stream banks look like a rogue bulldozer blew out banks 20 feet high. Trees, their exposed roots bleached by sun, lay mixed in with piles of rock rubble. Vines drape over unstable stream banks underlain by a mud-clay-rock conglomerate. Loose boulders show a fresh, rough aspect, a marked difference from smooth, rounded shapes expected along streambeds. From uprooted logs to piles of boulders waist-high, all signs point to a great force that swept down the river valley.

The cataclysmic event that caused this began on June 22, 1995. Rain fell throughout Shenandoah National Park for six days. On June 27 an intense storm pocket formed over the North Fork. Nine hours of hard rain followed. In a two-hour period, the dam manager at Sugar Hollow Reservoir, which is fed by the North Fork,

The author cools off in a pond near the end of the trail.

recorded 11.5 inches of water. A USGS report by geologists Benjamin Morgan and Gerald F. Wieczorek offers a chilling account of how quickly water rose.

> *At 7 p.m., Virginia Power had received reports of power failure in Sugar Hollow from residents below the dam. At 9–9:30 p.m., a lineman rearming a safety device on a pole near White Hall, Virginia, found that water had suddenly risen up to his knees within a few minutes. Rapidly rising water to chest level flooded his truck before he could drive to higher ground.*

White Hall is 6 miles downstream from the reservoir. Above the lake, no one witnessed what occurred along the North Fork Moormans River. If they did, there is no saying they'd be alive to describe it.

Trouble started on the steep slopes rising out of the stream valley. In this area of Shenandoah National Park, a thick coating of saprolite overlays the Blue Ridge rock complex of billion-year-old granite, greenstone, and Chilhowee sandstone. Saprolite has a claylike consistency that, under proper conditions, can loosen and shift. When this happens, other surface elements—topsoil, block fields, and loose rocks—will join the flow and create a landslide. In June 1995, all elements coalesced in a single spot—the North Fork Moormans River. What followed is described as a once-a-millennium geologic event.

Geologists documented more than one hundred landslides in a 5-mile area upstream from Sugar Hollow Reservoir. Soil slips and debris flows turned hillsides into liquid, muddy concoctions that ripped trees from their roots and moved boulders by the ton. Transported downstream, this material pummeled stream banks. Evidence of its power is visible a mile and a half upstream from the reservoir, on the right bank, where water cut a stream bank 20 feet high.

Up on mountain slopes west of the river, small streams became channels 100 to 200 feet wide. Big Branch, a stream that discharges into the North Fork at a spectacular waterfall, experienced an estimated water flow rate of 6,200 cubic feet per second. Amazingly, this means flow down Big Branch equaled, for a time, the rate of water flowing over Great Falls on the Potomac River (when the Potomac's water level is at the low level of 3.5 feet above median). The National Park Service calls any flow rate a "guess," given that there are no gauges on the river. Even so, their rough estimates exceeded the 500-year magnitude flood estimate by 155 percent.

As far as recreation use of the North Fork goes, little has changed since the flood. The trail is an old fire road that follows a gently ascending route into the folds of the Blue Ridge. Streams drop off the hillsides, often in small waterfalls. Great slabs of rock attract sunbathers and shutterbugs to the picture-perfect pool at the base of Big Branch. Hikers unload packs and climb Pasture Fence Mountain to pitch a tent, legalities be damned. Veteran fly fishers practice their timing upstream. Their protégés stand knee-high in the stream, entangled in yards of fishing line while brook and brown trout swim around them.

The flood did turn a hike that has been, for most people, a convenient excuse to skip class or work, into a showcase of geologic activity. Rock slides that crossed the trail display stones of banded gneiss with its alternating bands of light and dark streaks. Near Big Branch, the old road narrows to a footpath and crosses rock and debris flows halted by logjams. The trail here makes a short climb, then drops back to water level amid blown-down trees on the right and rubble on the left. Farther up the hillside, bare spots are just beginning to show signs of recovery. In dry streambeds, small trees sprout up through stone rubble. Wild ginseng has returned, and naturalists have spotted the rare wildflower, white monkshood. The brook and brown trout, temporarily flushed from the basin by the flood, have returned. A fish survey two weeks before the storm counted thirteen different species in the stream, including thirty brook trout; a survey after the storm netted six fish—total.

Not all areas are so quick to recover. Before the flood, trees, ferns, and other riverside plants crowded the mouth of Big Branch. Now it is bare rock. Quieter geologic processes have begun. Over hundreds of years, soil and weathered rock will build up. Small plants first, then trees, will sink roots. Someday, the flood of 1995 will be ancient history—which makes this chance to see its bare effects today all the more special.

North Fork Moormans River

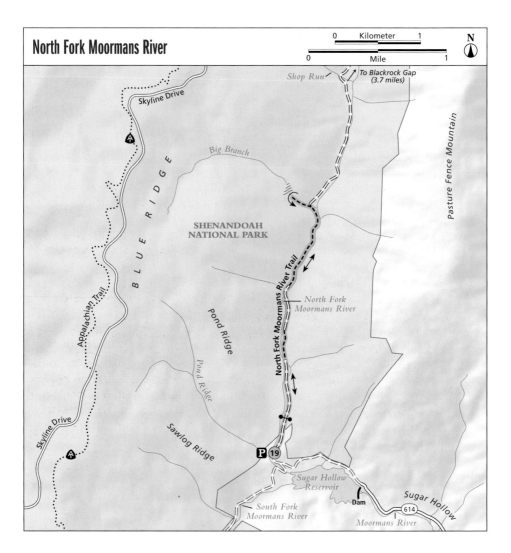

Miles and Directions

0.0   Start from the parking area for the North Fork Moormans River Trail. A small sign details park backcountry rules and regulations. Walk straight (north) on the North Fork Trail, a dirt road. Yellow blazes are infrequent. In the first 0.1 mile, you will pass a concrete trail marker giving mileage to Big Branch Falls and the Appalachian Trail at Blackrock Gap, as well as a park interpretive sign detailing the 1995 storm that forever changed the North Fork Moormans River valley.

0.3   Cross the North Fork Moormans River. All crossings are by fording, no bridges. **Note:** Upstream right, the river undercuts a rock face that offers a close-up view of the Catoctin formation, which underlies the east side of the stream. This geologic formation is made up of metabasalts, or ancient lava flows, that oozed from the earth and hardened.

0.4 Cross the river again. **Note:** There is a nice swimming hole upstream from this crossing. Also, at low water, the streambed itself is hikeable by rock hopping for those seeking variety on this short hike.

1.0 Cross the river again. As you hike upstream, scan the opposite bank for evidence of the 1995 flood, here illustrated by sheer banks up to 50 feet high that were carved by the debris flow that moved through this stream valley.

1.3 Pass through an area of widespread destruction caused by the 1995 flood. Landslides moved the trees and rocks seen here, a force strong enough to snap tree trunks. On the left, uphill, a washout illustrates how wide an area these landslides affected.

1.6 Descend to the river's edge. Turn left and climb to the falls on Big Branch, a few yards uphill. Turn back and return to the parking area on the North Fork Trail. (Take time to explore Big Branch. Once a small stream, it has been forever altered by the storm. The lower falls, especially, show signs of being blown out by massive floods of water pouring off the slope.) **Side trip:** North Fork Trail continues past Big Branch to reach Blackrock Gap on Skyline Drive in 3.7 miles. A section of this route upstream leaves the national park for 1.2 miles, then reenters the park to climb steeply up a stream hollow to Skyline Drive.

3.2 Arrive back at the parking area.

Hike Information

Local Information

Visit Charlottesville, (877) 386-1103, www.visitcharlottesville.org

Local Events / Attractions

Crozet Arts and Crafts Festival, May and Oct, Crozet, (434) 823-2211, www.crozet festival.com

White Hall Vineyards, White Hall, (434) 823-8615, www.whitehallvineyards.com

Monticello, Charlottesville, (434) 984-9822, www.monticello.org. Thomas Jefferson's home, featuring a restored orchard, vineyard, and gardens. Open every day except Christmas.

Lodging

Montfair Resort Farm, (434) 823-5202, www.montfairresortfarm.com. An eco- and pet-friendly retreat 3.5 miles north of White Hall.

Inn At Sugar Hollow Farm, Charlottesville, (434) 823-7086, www.sugarhollow .com. Located on VA 614 west of Charlottesville.

Park lodges at Skyland (Mile 41.7) and Big Meadows (Mile 51) and cabins at Lewis Mountain (Mile 57.5) are seasonal. Skyland is open late Mar through Oct; Big Meadows opens in mid-May and closes in Oct. Call (888) 896-3833 or go to www .visitshenandoah.com for reservations.

Reserved campsites are located at Matthews Arm (Mile 22.1), Big Meadows (Mile 51), Lewis Mountain (Mile 57.5), and Loft Mountain (Mile 79.5). For campground reservations, call (877) 444-6777 or visit www.recreation.gov.

Backcountry trail huts (7) and cabins (6) are operated by the PATC. For reservations, call (703) 242-0315 or visit www.patc.net for availability.

Restaurants

Crozet Pizza, 5794 Three Notch'd Rd., Crozet, VA 22932, (434) 823-2132, www .crozetpizza.net. Famous for its hand-tossed pies.

Numerous restaurants in Charlottesville provide ample dining opportunities after a long hike.

ARAMARK, the park's concessionaire, operates full-service restaurants at Big Meadows Lodge (Mile 51.2) and Skyland (Mile 41.7), and seasonal Wayside Food Stops at Elkwallow Wayside (Mile 24.1), Big Meadows Wayside (Mile 51.2), and Loft Mountain Wayside (Mile 79.5). Call (888) 896-3833 or go to www.visitshenandoah .com for information.

Hike Tours

Ranger-guided programs are offered spring, summer, and fall.

For commercial tour operators that are permitted in the park, visit www.nps.gov/ shen/planyourvisit/permitted-business-services.htm.

Other Resources

Therapeutic Adventures, (434) 981-5834, www.TAonline.org. Offers adaptive adventure programs in the Charlottesville area.

Potomac Appalachian Trail Club (PATC), Vienna, (703) 242-0315, www.patc.net. Publishes maps and guides and sponsors hikes in the park.

Shenandoah National Park Association, Luray, (540) 999-3582, www.snpbooks .org. A nonprofit partner that sells guidebooks, maps, brochures, and CDs on the history, flora, and fauna of Shenandoah National Park, to benefit park activities.

20 Overall Run

Peaks and waterfalls surely rank as one of the prime motivators—and rewards—for a day spent hiking, and doubly so if you work hard to get there. There are no shortages of waterfalls in Shenandoah National Park, from the wildly popular Whiteoak Canyon to the Rose River Falls, where multiple cascades flow off bare-faced rock after heavy rains. But there's only one "tallest": 93 feet to be exact, and it's found on the western slope of the Blue Ridge at Overall Run. From the staggering falls, the mountainous panorama unfolds westward over Massanutten's double ridges, and farther off on the hazy horizon looms Great North Mountain.

Start: Thompson Hollow Trail parking area on VA 630, 2.5 miles south of Bentonville, VA
Distance: 6.0 miles out and back, with an option for an 11.5-mile loop hike
Hiking time: About 4 hours
Difficulty: Moderate due to unaided stream crossings and a vigorous climb to the top of the Overall Run headwall
Trail surface: A brief stint on paved and gravel road leads to the park boundary. From there on, it's singletrack woodland paths interrupted by 3 stream crossings and an opportunity to rock scramble near the lip of the Overall Run falls.
Land status: National park
Nearest town: Front Royal
Other trail users: Hikers only
Accessibility: None

Canine compatibility: Leashed dogs permitted
Trail contact: Shenandoah National Park, 3655 US 211 East, Luray; (540) 999-3500; www.nps.gov/shen
Schedule: Park open 24 hours; headquarters open Mon through Fri, 8 a.m. to 4:30 p.m.
Fees/permits: Park entrance fee; none if accessing trail from outside the park
Facilities/features: None at this access point
Maps: USGS Bentonville; PATC #9: Shenandoah National Park Northern District
Special considerations: Winter is a spectacular time to visit, with huge ice sheets forming on the cliff. During the coldest snaps, the falls may even be frozen solid. But be extremely careful on slippery rocks and keep your distance from the edge: It's 93 feet straight down.

Finding the trailhead: From Front Royal, drive south on US 340 for 9 miles. In Bentonville, turn left (east) onto VA 613. After 0.5 mile, turn right (south) on VA 630 and drive 2 miles to the Thompson Hollow Trail parking area, a widened shoulder on the right side of the road. Trailhead GPS: N38 48.105' / W78 18.888'. *DeLorme: Virginia Atlas & Gazetteer:* Page 74, B2.

The Hike

On the western slope of the Blue Ridge, downhill from Hogback Mountain, in a crease where Beecher Ridge and Mathews Arm meet, a small spring gives rise to a stream. Its course for about a mile is that of a merry brook bouncing over river rocks, dropping a foot or so off small ledges and slipping under logs.

Then, with drama befitting a western panorama, comes the free fall.

The authors atop Overall Run.

Overall Run's 93-foot drop into a steep-sided box canyon ranks as the highest in Shenandoah National Park. Views from the lip of the falls stretch west to Massanutten Mountain and Great North Mountain beyond.

It's not the size of the river that impresses. It's the drop into a canyon that has few rivals in the park. Archeological research has found evidence of prehistoric Indians who used the canyon as a place to drive into and slaughter mastodons.

▶ **April and May is the time to catch the drama of Overall Run. By summer Overall Run flow is a trickle, and it has all but gone into hiding come September. Winter brings hints of a new flow, as ice and snow form small ledges over the stream.**

This hike starts outside the park boundaries, leading into Shenandoah through one of its many "backdoors." As you drop down off Thompson Hollow Trail, Overall Run itself is audible long before you reach it. The landscape north of the trail is gently sloping, betraying none of the drama that will unfold a mile or so up the trail.

The falls of Overall Run have the highest vertical drop in Shenandoah National Park.

As you hike toward the falls, the river's bottomland forest spreads out. In summertime, the grass can be as high as your waist in some places, lending the trail a remote sense. Piles of small stones are visible off trail, possible indications of field-clearing activity from the eighteenth- and nineteenth-century residents. A stream on the left side leads to a springhouse some distance off the trail, where there is evidence of a building foundation as well.

The last 0.75 mile of the trail scales Mathews Arm as it rises to the headwall of the canyon. In the imagination, a band of Paleo-Indians might be pressing their prey into the canyon's narrow confines. It is only 5 miles north, near Limeton, where archaeologists in the 1970s unearthed one of the East Coast's most influential prehistoric Indian settlements. Thunderbird, as it's known, dates back to 10,000 BC, with evidence in the form of points, tools, and weapons that indicate sites of a quarry, a base camp, and a bog where animals were driven for the kill.

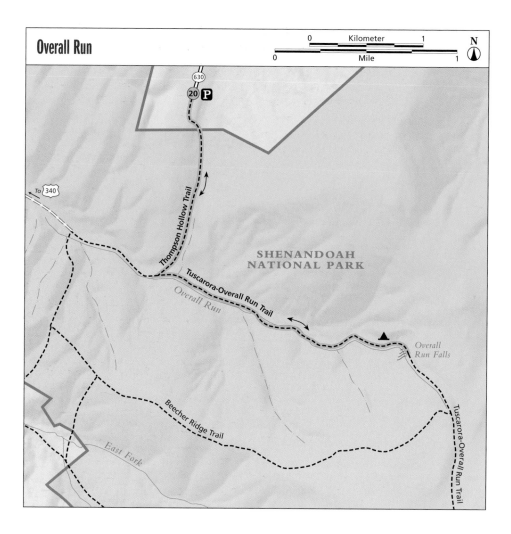

0   Kilometer   1   **N**

0   Mile   1

SHENANDOAH
NATIONAL PARK

*Overall
Run Falls*

Overall Run

Tuscarora-Overall Run Trail

Thompson Hollow Trail

Beecher Ridge Trail

East Fork

Tuscarora-Overall Run Trail

Miles and Directions

0.0   Start from the Thompson Hollow Trail parking area on VA 630. Walk south along the paved road past a gated road on the right. The road dips into and out of a streambed. After this, bear right onto a dirt path through the grass.

0.3   Enter Shenandoah National Park on Thompson Hollow Trail at a trailhead marked by a concrete post.

0.7   Stay straight as the blue-blazed Tuscarora Trail merges with Thompson Hollow Trail from the right.

1.0   The sound of rushing water cues you to the approach of Overall Run Trail. Descend to the T junction and turn left on a singletrack dirt trail that follows the stream's bottomland forest.

1.5   Cross Overall Run.

2.0   Cross Overall Run.

2.3	Begin a 1-mile steep climb up the headwall of Overall Run.
2.5	Take a break at a small campsite that overlooks the falls and canyon.
2.8	A steady climb relents. Follow the trail right to the lip of the falls.
3.0	Reach top of Overall Run waterfall. Return to the trailhead by retracing steps down Overall Run Trail. **Option:** continue beyond the falls on Overall Run Trail for a strenuous 11.5-mile loop via Beecher Ridge Trail.
5.0	Turn right onto Thompson Hollow Trail.
6.0	Arrive back at the Thompson Hollow Trail parking area.

Hike Information

Local Information

Front Royal Visitor Center, 414 E. Main St., Front Royal, (540) 635-5788, www .frontroyalva.com

Restaurants

Melting Pot Pizza, 138 W. 14th St., Front Royal, (540) 636-6146. Locals and visitors alike get their pizza fix at the place that's been serving it for more than 30 years.

Hike Tours

Shenandoah Mountain Guides, 8848 Indian Springs Rd., Frederick, MD, (866) 455-8672, www.shenandoahmountainguides.org

Potomac Appalachian Trail Club (PATC), Vienna, (703) 242-0693, www.potomac appalachian.org

21 Piney River

Heavily settled prior to Shenandoah National Park's formation, the woods tucked between Piney River and Keyser Run today hold clues both obvious and obscure, from family cemeteries to low stone field walls long overgrown by a resurgent forest. Above all, it is a sanctuary of rushing water and steep cliffs. Those who like to save the best for last will appreciate our twist on conventional wisdom: Most people like to climb *up* Little Devil Stairs, but we save this knee-knocking route along Keyser Run for a finishing act.

Start: Parking area and park registration booth on VA 614/Keyser Run Road
Distance: 7.4-mile loop
Hiking time: About 5 hours
Difficulty: Moderate due to several unaided stream crossings and a moderate elevation, with one strenuous segment through Little Devil Stairs due to steep, rough terrain and numerous unaided stream crossings
Trail surface: A gravel forest fire road gives way to centuries-old roads that have reverted to singletrack paths. A majority of this hike is along streams, and in sections exposed rocks and roots make for uneven terrain. The last segment of this route is over exposed rocks, some as big as cars, and steep drop-downs. In spring, sections of trail may be washed out.
Land status: National park
Nearest town: Sperryville

Other trail users: Equestrians permitted on Hull School Trail between the Bowers Family Cemetery and Piney Branch Trail
Accessibility: None
Canine compatibility: Leashed dogs permitted
Trail contacts: Shenandoah National Park, 3655 US 211 East, Luray; (540) 999-3500; www.nps.gov/shen
Schedule: Open year-round
Fees/permits: Entrance fee, payable at a self-serve fee station at the trailhead. If camping, obtain a free backcountry permit at a park ranger station. Virginia residents need a state fishing license if age 16 or older (5-day permits are available at Big Meadows and Loft Mountain, on Skyline Drive). For non-resident anglers, age 12 and older, a Virginia license is required.
Facilities/features: None
Maps: USGS Thornton Gap; PATC #9: Shenandoah National Park Northern District

Finding the trailhead: From Sperryville, follow the combined US 211/522 east. In 2.1 miles, turn left (north) on VA 622/Gid Brown Hollow Road. Drive 2 miles and turn left onto VA 614/Keyser Run Road. Stay straight on Keyser Run Road as first VA 672 and then VA 623 branch off left and right, respectively. In 5 miles from the highway, enter a trailhead parking area with room for ten or more cars. Trailhead GPS: N38 43.831' / W78 15.517'. *DeLorme: Virginia Atlas & Gazetteer:* Page 74 C2.

The Hike

The woods that descend to Piney River are a beautiful place on a sunny morning, especially so after a strong spring rainstorm. Birdsong floats down from the tree

Piney River with early spring color.

canopy, and sunlight dapples the leaves and ground. Dry streambeds are flush with runoff. Deer poke about the forest understory, chewing on twigs. On the trailside, lush green plants grow in a seep from the rocks. Lettuce saxifrage and Solomon's seal are telltale plants that mark the spot of many natural springs.

Ephemeral streams emerge after a heavy rain. As you descend Hull School Trail toward Piney River, a run of small plate-size rocks may be visible off the left side of the trail. First instinct is to call it a boulder-strewn spring or streambed. Further exploration shows it's more likely a stone stream; while water runs down it after heavy rain, it is dry other times. Skinny-trunked maples grow from the rock bed, indicating soil stability not found in a consistently running stream. Crusty lichen, another indication of stability, appears on rocks near the edges of the stone stream.

Piney River, reached at the junction of Hull School and Piney Branch Trails, gushes downstream with force. Stream crossings without the aid of a footbridge force a search upstream and downstream for a fallen log or rocks suitable for hopping. In the forest near the stream's edge, small rivulets form on both sides of the Piney Branch Trail, marking points of minor flooding.

Where the Piney River passes through a steep gorge, the trail steepens as well, climbing the hillside on switchbacks. Where it briefly levels, the river can be heard, but not seen. A small window through the forest canopy does offer a glimpse to the solid cliff wall on the opposite side. Just the spot, perhaps, a denning bear or mountain lion might prefer.

The presence of mountain lions—also referred to as cougars, pumas, panthers, and catamounts—is subject to debate. Officially, the last eastern subspecies of mountain lion, *Felis concolor cougar,* was documented in Virginia in 1882. But sightings, if not actual documentation, are commonplace. A national park resource management newsletter in 1997 stated that reliable reports of mountain lion sightings had been made in the park since 1932. Whether the population is a resurgence of the native eastern cougar, a wanderer from another region (Florida currently has the only population of cougars in the East, the highly endangered Florida panther, *Felis concolor coryi*), or an escaped or released pet is unknown.

Any thought of a lurking predator is dispelled as you climb away from the Piney River gorge along Pole Bridge Link Trail. In spring, the grassy fringes of the trail here are a spectacle of wildflowers, whether the ephemeral spring beauties, the white petals of giant chickweed, delicate purple wild geraniums, or common violets and buttercups. Dry, grassy spots host a profusion of common lousewort, a red-and-yellow blossom that seems more at home in a cow pasture than these woodlands.

The descent through Little Devil Stairs offers what Piney Branch Trail only hinted at: up-close interaction with rugged nature. There are at least eight stream crossings, and after a heavy rain, probably more. At one point the cliffs on either side close in so tightly, you're forced to walk down a small island that conveniently emerges from the stream.

A rock talus marking the halfway point of the descent through Little Devil Stairs highlights the geologic dynamism of the park. A "river" of its own sort, the talus covers the hillside with rocks and boulders, most of them tire-size or smaller. *Talus creep* describes the slow downslope movement of this rock slope toward the valley bottom. In a geologic time frame, this slope is considered dynamic and moving. The slope and the quartzite rock itself show no signs of the stability (lichen or vegetation) that was evident on the stone stream alongside the Hull School Trail.

Miles and Directions

0.0 Start from the Little Devil Stairs parking lot. Follow a gravel road uphill from the west end of the lot.

0.2 Swing right (north) on the fire road and walk past signs marking the boundary of Shenandoah National Park.

1.1 After a steady climb, enter a clearing that is the junction of Keyser Run Fire Road and Hull School Trail. The Bolan family cemetery is off to the right. After exploring, depart the clearing on the left, following yellow-blazed Hull School Trail, which descends as a narrow woodland footpath.

1.7 A small stream cuts across the trail. Ahead, in 0.2 mile, cross another stream and then swing left as the trail continues a gradual descent to Piney River.

1.8 Turn right on Piney Branch Trail at a T junction and hike upstream on the blue-blazed trail. Just before reaching this junction, study the woods off the trail on the right. Rock piles amid a young forest indicate possible field-clearing activity dating from when this park was settled. Careful exploration of the rock piles yields the presence of a freshwater spring at the base of a pile of rocks.

1.9 Pass a primitive campsite off the trail on the left. Soon after, cross Piney River. **Note:** After a heavy rain, you may have to explore up- or downstream for a suitable place to cross.

2.3 Continue straight (north) on Piney Branch Trail past a junction with Piney Ridge Trail on the left.

2.5 After a short stretch of trail that runs close to the stream, begin a climb from river-bottom forest up the side of a river gorge.

3.0 A vigorous climb levels briefly and the forest canopy opens to views of the imposing cliff face on the opposite stream bank. In the next 0.1 mile of trail, look for unmarked paths leading off-trail right to the river's edge.

3.3 Cross Piney River on stream rocks and start a steady uphill climb on Piney Branch Trail. The stream is now on your left side.

3.5 The trail levels briefly, and off the trail to the left is a primitive campsite.

4.2 Detour off the trail to the left to explore the cliff line that gives visual proof to the elevation you've gained in the last 1.2 miles.

4.6 Turn right (east) on Pole Link Bridge Trail. Level terrain off both sides indicates you are traversing across the flat top of a ridge.

4.7 Pass a primitive campsite off the-trail to the right.

4.9 Stay straight on Pole Bridge Link Trail at a junction with Sugarloaf Trail on the left.

5.4 Reach Fourway, a junction with Keyser Run Fire Road and Little Devil Stairs. Cross the fire road diagonal left and reenter woods on Little Devil Stairs Trail. The trailhead is marked by a concrete trail marker.

5.7 Begin a series of five switchbacks that carry you down a steep slope into Little Devil Stairs Canyon.

5.8 Cross Keyser Run, the first of four unaided stream crossings over the next 0.3 mile. **Note:** The next 1.1 miles descend *extremely* technical terrain as you scurry across, squeeze through, drop down off, and hop across rocks and boulders that litter this stream gorge.

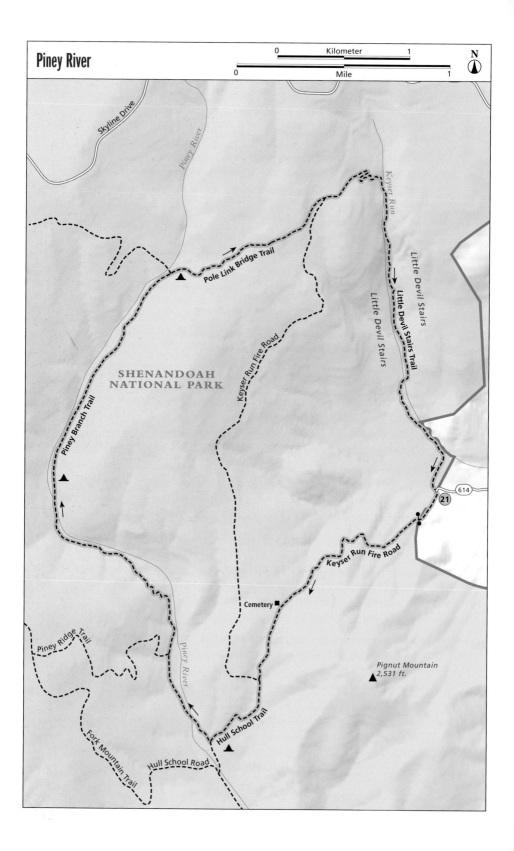

6.0 Cross Keyser Run for the fourth time and pass beneath a 20-story-high cliff line that forms the right stream bank of the canyon. A talus in this area is littered with tire-size rocks, and the trail footbed is loose rubble.

6.1 Two quick stream crossings put you back on the right stream bank. Ahead, Keyser Run is squeezed by cliffs and the trail takes a middle course down an island formed by a split in the stream. Watch for blue blazes on trees for guidance. **Note:** In spring or after heavy rainfalls, this section may be washed out, requiring you ford downstream as you follow the blue trail blazes.

6.3 Cross Keyser Run from the right to left stream bank. This is the first of four stream crossings as the trail emerges from the gorge into a wider stream valley.

6.7 Cross from the left to right stream bank, the last in this dizzying descent. Ahead, the trail separates from the streamside and crosses a small knoll.

7.2 Begin a long stretch of hiking across flat bottomland forest. Just before reaching the trailhead parking lot, cross a stream.

7.4 Arrive back at the parking lot.

Hike Information

Local Information

Rappahannock County Visitor Center, 3 Library Road, Washington, VA 22747, (540) 675-5330, www.visitrappahannockva.com

Local Events/Attractions

Wilderness Weekend is held each Oct at the park's Byrd Visitor Center, mile 51 on Skyline Drive, near Big Meadows.

Restaurants

Thornton River Grille, 3710 Sperryville Pike, Sperryville, (540) 987-8790, www.thorntonrivergrille.com

Local Outdoor Store

Blue Ridge Mountain Sports, 251 W. Lee Hwy., Warrenton, (540) 428-3136, www.brmsstore.com

Hike Tours

Park rangers lead a variety of nature, wildflower, and geology hikes Apr through Labor Day.

Organizations

Potomac Appalachian Trail Club (PATC), Vienna VA, (703) 242-0693, www.potomac appalachian.org

Honorable Mentions: Shenandoah National Park

P. Jeremy's Run

At nearly 14 miles, this is one of the longer hikes in the park. Begin at Elkwallow Picnic Area, milepost 24 on Skyline Drive in the park's northern district. The descent is steep and stream crossings are difficult, but the rewards of hiking along this beautiful, cascading stream far outweigh the challenges. Consider making it an overnighter, camping at one of the established primitive campsites in Jeremy's Run Drainage. (540) 999-3500. GPS: N38 44.46' / W78 18.713'. *DeLorme: Virginia Atlas & Gazetteer:* Page 74, C2.

Q. Nicholson Hollow

Park at Stony Man Overlook at milepost 38.6 on Skyline Drive in the park's central district. Nicholson Hollow was once a populated area of 400 families. Old home foundations and other evidence of past lives are visible along this 5.8-mile one-way trail. Use Corbin Hollow Trail and Indian Run Trail to make an extended backcountry loop, with primitive campsites and swimming holes. (540) 999-3500. GPS: N38 36.769' / W78 21.632'. *DeLorme: Virginia Atlas & Gazetteer:* Page 74, D2.

R. Whiteoak Canyon

Parking for the Whiteoak Canyon Trail is at milepost 42.6 on Skyline Drive in the park's central district. The steep gorge that features waterfalls, giant boulders, and quiet pools make this one of the most popular and beautiful places in the park. There are old-growth hemlocks along the connecting Limberlost Trail, which is accessible for people with disabilities. The park notes that the trail is overcrowded for camping on weekends, so consider camping midweek. (540) 999-3500. GPS: N38 35.174' / W78 22.972'. *DeLorme: Virginia Atlas & Gazetteer:* Page 74, D2.

S. Big Run Portal-Rockytop Loop

Begin this hike at Big Run Overlook at milepost 81.2 on Skyline Drive in the park's southern district. A classic Shenandoah hike: all downhill to the park boundary, followed by a steep climb back to Skyline Drive. In total, a strenuous 14.6-mile loop. (540) 999-3500. GPS: N38 15.229' / W78 41.046'. *DeLorme: Virginia Atlas & Gazetteer:* Page 67, C6.

T. Riprap Hollow-Appalachian Trail Loop

The parking area for this 10-mile hike is at milepost 90 on Skyline Drive in the park's southern district. Chimney Rock, Calvary Rock, and a swimming hole are highlights on this trip. So are the springtime mountain laurel blooms along Riprap Trail as it descends through Cold Spring Hollow. (540) 999-3500. GPS: N38 10.649' / W78 45.896'. *DeLorme: Virginia Atlas & Gazetteer:* Page 67, C5.

Valley & Ridge

I am now in the very midst of that great congregation of hills, comprising all the spurs, branches, knobs and peaks of the great chain which has been called, with a happy attitude, the backbone of America.

James Kirk Paulding wrote this during his Virginia travels in 1816. Any person might think as much when venturing into the Allegheny Mountains today. Bringing order to this landscape is hopeless. The hills are long, straight ridges tending in a northeast–southwest direction, divided by deep, narrow valleys, like waves and troughs of the earth's crust folded and faulted by gigantic continental collisions millions of centuries ago.

Little is consistent about the Valley & Ridge region. Shoulder spurs shoot off in all sorts of directions, appearing as broad buttresses for the many rocky balds and tree-covered knobs. An otherwise straight ridge will warp with S turns, alluding to the powerful, earth-shaping forces that create mountains. Streams cut deep grooves in the mountain slopes, and a trove of plants and trees soak up life from these veins of moisture, giving rise to the Appalachian cove forest, one of Earth's most diverse ecosystems. Rock slides inhibit forward progress in one direction, while in the other, a sharp-rising ridge presents a seemingly insurmountable obstacle.

The Appalachian Mountains, which include the Allegheny chain of Virginia and West Virginia, are among the oldest mountains on the planet. The Southern Appalachians as a whole are considered a biological wonderland. Virginia's Valley & Ridge region supports that claim with vigor. In Laurel Fork, elements of northern boreal forest inhabit the high-altitude knobs and stream valleys, while miles away, dry forests on lower ridges display the classic oak-hickory forest type. So it is that the hiker passes from dank, moist streambeds to high, exposed cliff-lines to laurel-shrouded mountain slopes in a single day.

Anyone who travels the mountains of Virginia with any regularity is bound, sooner or later, to come upon a spot so special, so utterly beautiful at that moment in time, it brings them to pause. It could be a soaring view, a mist-shrouded wilderness pond or a mountain stream, a swath of pink and white–blooming mountain laurel or

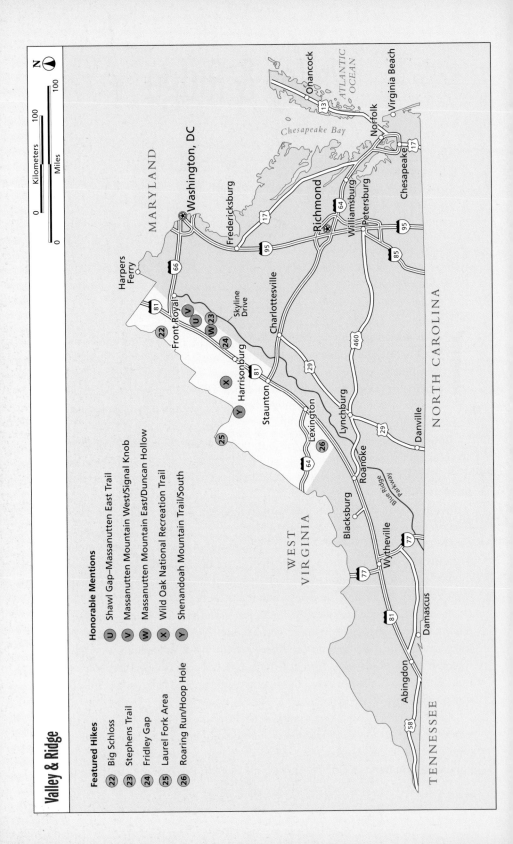

Valley & Ridge

Featured Hikes

- 22 Big Schloss
- 23 Stephens Trail
- 24 Fridley Gap
- 25 Laurel Fork Area
- 26 Roaring Run/Hoop Hole

Honorable Mentions

- U Shawl Gap–Massanutten East Trail
- V Massanutten Mountain West/Signal Knob
- W Massanutten Mountain East/Duncan Hollow
- X Wild Oak National Recreation Trail
- Y Shenandoah Mountain Trail/South

N

Kilometers
0   100

Miles
0   100

a sun-dappled cove cooled by the shade of old-growth hemlock. Wherever, whenever, this spot remains an abiding image long after the hike ends. That is the gift of Virginia's mountains.

The Hikes

22. Big Schloss
23. Stephens Trail
24. Fridley Gap
25. Laurel Fork Area
26. Roaring Run/Hoop Hole

Honorable Mentions

U. Shawl Gap–Massanutten East Trail
V. Massanutten Mountain West/Signal Knob
W. Massanutten Mountain East/Duncan Hollow
X. Wild Oak National Recreation Trail
Y. Shenandoah Mountain Trail/South

22 Big Schloss

In German, *schloss* means "castle." In Virginia, schloss can only refer to one geologic wonder, a towering outcrop of sandstone on Mill Mountain. Big Schloss is a popular day trip from Wolf Gap Recreation Area, a primitive camping site 2 miles south. A more strenuous trip begins far to the north, in a quiet river valley better known by hunters than hikers. The hike begins at Wilson Cove Wildlife Management Area, a 5,200-acre piece of the national forest designated for muzzle-loader buck hunting only, in late November and early December. Along Pond Run, old-growth hemlocks stand out from the smaller trees growing thick along this stream. Rock slides, steep inclines, overlooks, and quiet views off Mill Mountain follow in succession.

Start: Bridge over Waites Run on Waites Run Road (WV 5/WV 1).
Distance: 19.5-mile lollipop
Hiking time: About 12 hours
Difficulty: Moderate due to length, sections of rocky and uneven trail, and steep climbs
Trail surface: Dirt forest paths and old logging roads lead through rock formations and cove forests along Pond Run and Little Stony Creek.
Land status: National forest
Nearest town: Wardensville, WV
Other trail users: Mountain bikers, cross-country skiers, and hunters (in season)
Accessibility: None

Canine compatibility: Dogs permitted
Trail contact: Lee Ranger District, Edinburg; (540) 984-4101; www.fs.usda.gov/gwj
Schedule: Open year-round. Hunting is permitted in national forests. Wilson Cove Wildlife Management Area hosts a special muzzle-loading season in Dec. Deer season lasts from Nov to early Jan.
Fees/permits: None
Facilities/features: No facilities. There are primitive campsites along the trail and camping facilities at nearby Wolf Gap Recreation Area.
Maps: USGS Wardensville, Woodstock, Wolf Gap

Finding the trailhead: From Strasburg, follow VA 55 (also called Wardensville Pike) west for 20 miles, crossing into West Virginia en route. In Wardensville, bear left at the VA 55/VA 259 junction. In 0.5 mile, turn left onto Carpenters Avenue, at the 7-Eleven store. In 0.8 mile, turn right onto Waites Run Road (WV 5/WV 1). Pass a community park on the left. Enter George Washington National Forest in 1.3 miles. In 5.3 miles, reach a concrete bridge spanning Waites Run. Across the bridge a sign indicates the boundary of Wilson Cove Wildlife Management Area (WMA). There are pull-offs for cars on either side of the stream and campsites for late-day arrivals. GPS: N39 00.951' / W78 36.324'. *DeLorme: Virginia Atlas & Gazetteer:* Page 73, A6.

The Hike

The Native American phrase for *Appalachia* translates roughly as "endless mountain." That seems an apt description standing atop one of Mill Mountain's many outcrops. The view west is of one mountain rippling onto another and another, each one dissected by a narrow, wooded valley. Trees drape the entire landscape—a rare scene in these otherwise well-developed hills.

Mill Mountain attracts hikers just for these kinds of panoramas. The trail is well marked and the views easy to find. It's hard to imagine that this same trip, if undertaken 300 years ago, would be considered folly. On the whole, early settlers avoided steep uphill routes across mountains. Huge oaks and chestnut trees made passage difficult; a frustrating undergrowth of laurel, creeper, and shrubs reduced their pace to a crawl. Instead, settlers stuck to roads through the valleys, routes first blazed by Native Americans. The most famous, the Great Warriors Path, became the Great Wagon Road as settlers replaced indigenous populations. So numerous were the Scotch-Irish, German, and English migrants moving south on the Great Wagon Road from Pennsylvania, it has been said travelers numbered in the tens of thousands up to the Revolutionary War.

Stunning rock outcrops typify Big Schloss.

Before settlers, Iroquois Indians had used the north–south route for hundreds of years. Virginia Governor Alexander Spotswood and his companion explorers found the route when they reached the shores of the Shenandoah River. Marked by hatchet notches in trees, the Great Warriors Path aided Iroquois travel from Canada into southern regions for war and trade. It was on one such trip that a band of Iroquois stayed south and settled in villages on the Neuse and Pamlico Rivers in northeastern North Carolina, which is where European traders and explorers encountered these "mild" and "gentle" people. Their name, from the Iroquoian word for "hemp gatherers," was Tuscarora.

Whatever the English's first impression, relations between the Tuscaroras and settlers turned ugly. Broken treaties and a rash of kidnappings of Indian children contributed to a Tuscarora-led massacre in 1711, at New Bern in North Carolina. (English settlers had built New Bern on the site of a Native American town, Chattoka.) The killings were unusually brutal. Women were pinned to the floor and staked through, children killed, and homes burned. A two-year war ensued. By 1713 the Tuscaroras were defeated. Chieftains sent word north along the Great Warrior Path to the League of Five Nations, in upstate New York, asking for help. In 1714 the Tuscaroras began migrating up the Appalachians into Virginia, Maryland, Pennsylvania, and, finally, New York. A Virginian settler in the 1750s and 1760s might see groups of these Indians, their worldly possessions piled on horseback, traveling in small bands, sometimes settling in an area for years, then moving north again. Officially, the Tuscaroras were accepted into the League of Five Nations (now Six Nations) in 1722. Their migration lasted at least another half century beyond this date. Today their tribe numbers 600 people on reservation land near Niagara Falls.

In name and spirit, the Tuscaroras remain in Virginia to this day. At Waites Run, a hiker who steps onto Tuscarora Trail enters a forest world of mountain streams and hemlock groves. The wide-trunked evergreens show black, gnarled roots, some reaching into Pond Run, soaking in the water. Along this stream, Tuscarora Trail shares the path with Pond Run Trail. In a gap between Half Moon and Mill Mountains, Tuscarora Trail branches east. Uphill from a good spring at the headwaters of Half Moon Run, the blue-blazed route plunges left into heavy woods. The grade steepens. Boulders and small rocks make walking difficult. The fractured gray rock underfoot shows a quartz-pebble conglomerate. In these stones, the Tuscarora name crops up again as Tuscarora sandstone, a type found at the core of mountains from Virginia to Pennsylvania. (Admittedly, the term *sandstone* gives reason to pause. This is, after all, one of the most erosion-resistant rocks in the Appalachians, a fact at odds with the idea of sand, which is easily eroded. The key here is metamorphism—a change in which a rock, subjected to intense, volcano-like heat and pressure, changes and becomes a new rock. So the chief ingredient of sandstone is recrystallized sand—sand subjected to so much heat and pressure it turned to quartzite, which is one of the most resistant rocks around.)

The hiker and Tuscarora Trail part on Mill Mountain, where the latter turns east and heads for the Shenandoah National Park while the Mill Mountain Trail follows the ridgeline south. From Waites Run, the trail has climbed 1,500 feet; the next 4 miles undulate more gently on a slope leading south to Big Schloss. It's a dry hike. Except for water at Sandstone Spring, there are no reliable sources on the ridge. There are, however, views. Short branch trails end at rough-textured rocks that will skin knees and elbows if you scramble up for a view. Finally, there is Big Schloss (German for "castle") visible above tree line, accessible by boardwalks over crevices and steep rock faces. Free-fall views surround the high point on this rock formation—there's nothing but blue sky east-west-north-south and straight up.

From the high-and-dry altitude of Mill Mountain, Big Schloss Cut-off Trail descends through a sea of mountain laurel (peak blooms in June) to reach Little Stony Creek. Where the trail on Mill Mountain is bedded with sand and stone flints, the route up Stony Creek Trail is muddy, lined with ferns, and full of chirping birds. There are red-eyed vireos, Acadian flycatchers, and ovenbirds rustling about the brush. Scarlet tanagers roost on treetops, then swoop in a flash of red to feed on insects in the brush. Also present are warblers, although hardly in numbers they once were. This songbird's decline in the Southern Appalachians is an alarm for naturalists. The decline rate varies by species, but as a whole, nearly three-quarters of the fifty warbler species known to inhabit the southern forests are in decline. For an explanation, look no further than the burned and clear-cut forest along Little Stony Creek below FR 92. Habitat loss and fragmentation, whether caused by logging, development, or natural events, has impacted warblers to a degree that has made it an issue of study by the Forest Service.

Past Sugar Knob Cabin, Stony Creek Trail intersects the Tuscarora Trail and the return to Waites Run begins. Just when it feels the hike won't end, reach the gap between Half Moon and Mill Mountains. The route downhill along Pond Run leads to the trailhead, but consider shedding the pack here for one final viewpoint. Follow white blazes out of the campground to a rock outcrop on the edge of the mountain. The view from here is endless. The Indians had an apt description for this kind of view: Appalachian.

Miles and Directions

0.0 Start from a signboard for the Pond Run Trail (also known as the Tuscarora Trail). Standing on the concrete bridge spanning Waites Run, looking upstream, the signboard is on the right stream bank. From it, a blue-blazed dirt footpath climbs over a small hill and drops back to water and follows Waites Run upstream.

0.4 Veer right to follow the trail up Pond Run. Prior to this, there are campsites under hemlocks on your left. **Note:** Green paint slashes on trees alongside the trail designate the wildlife management area, not the trail.

0.5 Make the first of eight stream crossings on Pond Run as you walk up a cove past fine specimens of old-growth hemlock.

1.4 After crossing Pond Run once again, the trail passes a thick-trunked hemlock and climbs a rocky route up the right hillside. Berry bushes crop up in the understory, signaling passage from the moist environment of the stream to drier slope environs.

2.2 A glade of waist-high ferns heralds the approaching gap in Great North Mountain between Mill Mountain and Half Moon Mountain.

2.4 Reach a grassy junction. Turn left and immediately pass a campsite on the right. An unmarked footpath, marked with white "i" blazes, descends from this campsite to a rock outcrop with a beautiful view of unspoiled forest land. **Note:** One-tenth of a mile past the campsite is a spring, the last reliable water source for 3 miles.

2.7 Bear left onto a narrow, rocky, blue-blazed footpath. Avoid the old road that climbs the hill to the right. The footpath is a leg of the Tuscarora Trail and covers some rugged ground as it bends around Mill Mountain to a bluff overlooking Wilson Cove and Paddy Mountain, before cutting southeast to meet Mill Mountain Trail.

3.9 Tuscarora Trail empties into a grassy clearing. Walk straight through the clearing and onto Mill Mountain Trail, a dirt road overgrown with grass. **Note:** A right turn leads along a now-abandoned section of Tuscarora/Big Blue. A left turn is the return trail from Sugar Knob Shelter.

4.3 A trail branches off to the right to a now-destroyed airway beacon site and a metal shed. (The trail to the old airway beacon is crowded with huckleberry, which bloom in early June.) Past this junction, the trail threads a set of concrete posts and reverts to a single-track woods path.

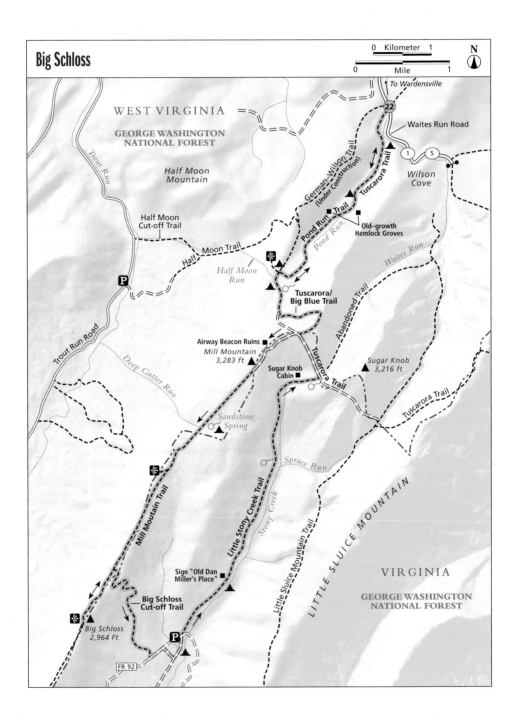

Big Schloss

0 Kilometer 1

0 Mile 1

N

To Wardensville

22

Waites Run Road

WEST VIRGINIA

GEORGE WASHINGTON
NATIONAL FOREST

Half Moon
Mountain

Trout Run

Half Moon
Cut-off Trail

German–Wilson Trail
(Under Construction)

Tuscarora Trail

1 5

Wilson
Cove

Pond Run Trail

Pond Run

Old–growth
Hemlock Groves

Waites Run

Half Moon Trail

Half Moon
Run

Tuscarora/
Big Blue Trail

Abandoned Trail

P

Trout Run Road

Deep Gutter Run

Airway Beacon Ruins

Mill Mountain
3,283 ft

Sugar Knob
Cabin

Tuscarora Trail

Sugar Knob
3,216 ft

Tuscarora Trail

Sandstone
Spring

Spruce Run

Little Stony Creek Trail

Stony Creek

Little Sluice Mountain Trail

LITTLE SLUICE MOUNTAIN

VIRGINIA

GEORGE WASHINGTON
NATIONAL FOREST

Mill Mountain Trail

Sign "Old Dan
Miller's Place"

Big Schloss
Cut-off Trail

Big Schloss
2,964 Ft

P

FR 92

5.4   After a steep, rocky decline, reach Sandstone Spring, shaded by hemlocks. This is a good water source and campsite.

6.0   An unmarked trail to the right reaches an overlook west to Long Mountain. From here, you also get a nice view south along the spine of Great North Mountain, a range once called Devil's Backbone.

6.7   Reach the Big Schloss Connector Trail branching left off Mill Mountain Trail. From here, the Big Schloss rock formation is 1.2 miles straight ahead on Mill Mountain Trail. Continue straight.

7.9   Reach Big Schloss. Views span 360 degrees east across the Great Valley and west into West Virginia. To continue this loop hike, return to Mill Mountain Trail and the Big Schloss Cut-off.

9.1   Back at the junction of Mill Mountain Trail and Big Schloss Cut-off Trail, descend the east slope of Mill Mountain on the Cut-off Trail on steep switchbacks amid slicks of mountain laurel.

10.8 Pass a signboard inviting hikers to join the Stonewall Brigade, a trail maintenance group. The trail drops to FR 92. Turn left and follow the gravel road downhill.

11.1 An unmarked logging road drops off the right side of FR 92. This marks a bushwhack to Little Stony Creek that takes you through landscape scarred by clear-cutting and fire. After descending on the logging road and passing through a clearing, find any one of a number of animal paths through the entanglement of vines and briars. Past this thick undergrowth is a dirt logging road. At this point, Little Stony Creek is audible, but obscured by a fringe of woods. Turn left and follow the logging road. There are several large blowdowns that force detours into the brush, but this logging road remains the main trail to FR 92.

11.5 Pass a dirt road leading to campsites on Little Stony Creek. Two more roads leading to Little Stony and good campsites follow in quick succession.

11.7 Reach FR 92. Cross the gravel road and reenter the woods. Little Stony Creek Trail is a narrow yellow-blazed path that follows the stream, crosses several times, then climbs with alternating steep pitches and level stretches.

15.2 Reach Sugar Knob Cabin, a PATC-sponsored hut. There is a spring in the vicinity and several fire rings. **Note:** The PATC cabin is locked and for use through reservation only. Call (703) 242-0693.

15.3 Turn left onto the Tuscarora/Big Blue Trail, a wide road overgrown with grass. As you climb, look off to the sides for knee-high ant mounds.

15.9 Turn right at the junction with Mill Mountain Trail. This spot completes the Mill Mountain/ Little Stony Creek loop.

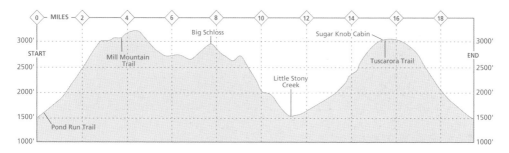

17.1 Turn right onto Pond Run Trail and head down the shaded mountain stream valley. Take time as you descend to notice how different the trees and terrain seem. You climbed this trail at the start of the hike, but it seems a different trail altogether as you descend.

19.5 Arrive back at Waites Run Road.

Hike Information

Local Information

Shenandoah Valley Travel Association, New Market, (877) VISIT-SV, www.visit shenandoah.org

Local Attractions

Route 11 Chips, Mount Jackson, (800) 294-7783, www.rt11.com. Watch Virginia's own potato chips being made.

North Mountain Vineyard & Winery, Maurentown, (540) 436-9463, www.north mountainvineyard.com. Secluded winery with a pet-friendly touch.

Lodging

Hotel Strasburg, Strasburg, (800) 348-8327, www.hotelstrasburg.com. Small pets allowed.

Restaurants

Kac-Ka-Pon Restaurant, Wardensville, WV, (304) 874-3232. Country home cooking open for breakfast, lunch, and dinner.

Organizations

Potomac Appalachian Trail Club (PATC), Vienna, (703) 242-0315, www.patc.net

23 Stephens Trail

Camp Roosevelt opened in 1933 as America's first Civilian Conservation Corps camp. Living in tents and earning $30 a week, unemployed men built the roads, campgrounds, picnic shelters, and fire towers we still use today. Their handiwork included a limestone block tower and shelter on Kennedy Peak. Its squat, low-rising design often surprises hikers expecting a tall lookout, but it's still high enough to give commanding views off the 2,600-foot Kennedy Peak. Eastward lies Page Valley and, to the west, Shenandoah Valley, both outlined with patchwork farms, towns, and forests.

Start: Camp Roosevelt Recreation Area
Distance: 8.5-mile loop
Hiking time: About 5 hours
Difficulty: Easy, with a few climbs and most of the trail following old logging roads
Trail surface: Dirt footpaths and dirt forest roads lead to ridgetops, forest coves, and the craggy Kennedy Peak, with views of the Blue Ridge and Allegheny Mountains.
Land status: National forest
Nearest town: Edinburg, VA
Other trail users: Mountain bikers, equestrians, cross-country skiers, and hunters (in season)

Accessibility: The 0.5-mile Lions Tale Accessible Trail is just a few miles south of Camp Roosevelt on FR 274 (Crisman Hollow Road).
Canine compatibility: Dogs permitted
Trail contact: Lee Ranger District, Edinburg; (540) 984-4101; www.fs.usda.gov/gwj
Schedule: Open year-round. Camp Roosevelt is open May through Oct. Hunting is permitted in national forests, with the busiest season Nov to early Jan.
Fees/permits: Camping fee
Facilities/features: Camp Roosevelt has flush toilets, drinking water, and campsites.
Maps: USGS Hamburg, Luray, Rileyville, Edinburg

Finding the trailhead: The Forest Service website gives these directions, from Edinburg: From I-81, take exit 279. Turn east on VA 675. At the intersection of US 11 and VA 675 in the center of Edinburg, turn left onto US 11. Make another right turn back onto VA 675 at the north end of Edinburg. Follow VA 675 for 5.9 miles over Massanutten Mountain to a stop sign at Kings Crossing. Turn right and continue on VA 675 for 3.4 miles to an X intersection of VA 675, FR 274, and VA 730. Turn left, still on VA 675. Camp entrance is 0.3 mile up, on the left side of the road. GPS: N38 43.883' / W78 31.024'. *DeLorme: Virginia Atlas & Gazetteer:* Page 73, C7; Page 74, B1.

The Hike

Spotted wintergreen's tolerance of poor soil makes this exotic-looking plant stand out amid the otherwise drab mountain slope leading to Kennedy Peak. From the flower's telltale green-and-white leaves rises a single, top-heavy stem crowned by five white petals that arc backwards. To see the green plug-like pistil and pale yellow stamens, gently lift the flower and peek beneath.

Dry forest conditions breed more than curious-looking wildflowers. They breed forest fires, the threat of which prompted Jack Stephens to walk from his home in Fort

Camp Roosevelt was the site of the first Civilian Conservation Corps Camp, built in 1933.

Valley to Kennedy Peak on a regular basis. Stephens's route up Kennedy Peak varied little. From Fort Valley, he climbed on switchbacks to a small saddleback between what is now called Stephens Pass. Turning right, he walked atop the narrow Massanutten Ridge, then made his way up the steep, rocky hill to the fire tower.

Stephens's route is now engraved into the slope of Massanutten Mountain by a generation of hikers and horseback riders. Blueberries and scrub oak crowd the forest understory, a monotone landscape highlighted in places by very colorful spotted wintergreen. Grouse and turkeys and deer inhabit this woodland, too. In the saddlebacks between small knobs, grass grows waist-high. Trees are spaced and signs of old orchards and stone walls are visible.

The advantages of a tower on Kennedy Peak are clear from the moment you ascend. Massanutten Mountain stretches 55 miles from Front Royal to Harrisonburg, and along its entire length there are few if any steep or dramatic interruptions. Kennedy Peak is the exception, sticking up 200 feet from the main trunk just before the ridge descends to a small gap. The knob, barren of trees, affords unblocked views in all directions. If you could peer back in time from here as well, you would witness a time when local wardens received $5 a year to monitor fire activity in a newly created national forest. The period was World War I, and two forest units existed in northern Virginia, the Massanutten and Potomac Districts. To build pride and win over suspicious locals, the forest supervisor fostered a rivalry between them. For three years—1913 to 1916—wardens from each side met for a tug-of-war at the Shenandoah County Fair. The winner took home bragging rights and a wooden Forest

Service shield. The rivalry ended in 1917 when the two districts merged. (For the record, Massanutten District won the tug-of-war twice, Potomac once. Both regions fall within the present-day Lee Ranger District.)

Where Stephens Trail retraces the footsteps of one man, a different route to Kennedy Peak, on the Massanutten East Trail out of Camp Roosevelt, follows the steps of hundreds of men. The first Civilian Conservation Corps camp opened at Camp Roosevelt in 1933, and for nearly a decade following, unemployed men and World War I veterans spread across what was then Shenandoah National Forest (the name was later changed to George Washington National Forest to avoid confusion with Shenandoah National Park). Nicknamed Roosevelt's Tree Army, these men planted trees to replace the acres clear-cut for charcoal and timber. To build the Kennedy Peak fire tower, they carried limestone blocks quarried from the mountains.

Limestone proved a valuable commodity for others, too: Early American blast furnaces required limestone to make pig iron. Along Stephens Trail, hikers can see clearly the red cake-like rocks, some the size of bricks, that iron-ore producers craved. These stones are hematite-laden; the red color ensured prospectors that the rocks would produce good-quality iron. They were carted off to local blast furnaces, where molten pig iron flowed out of the bottom of the furnace into molds for pots and kettles and tools.

During the Civil War, blast furnaces shifted production. Out of mountain iron-works such as Elizabeth Furnace and Catherine Furnace came the bullets, cannons, and guns that supplied Confederate troops. General Stonewall Jackson stated, "If the Valley is lost, Virginia is lost," and embarked on the Valley Campaign of 1862 to ensure that wouldn't happen. Battles at Kernstown, McDowell, Cross Keys, and Front Royal kept the Valley in Confederate hands until 1864, when Northern general Philip Sheridan began sweeping through the Shenandoah Valley, burning homes, looting supplies, and slaughtering livestock.

The best view from Kennedy Peak lies west, across the northern Shenandoah Valley. This is the valley traveled by Quakers and Scots-Irish from Pennsylvania and Maryland in the early 1700s. With their arrival, two Virginias evolved. In coastal regions, a few wealthy landowners controlled land and an economy based on tobacco and slave labor. Mountain Virginia reflected the religious fervor of German and Scots-Irish immigrants. Wheat fared better here than tobacco, due in part to limestone-rich soil. Nicknames for these two Virginians developed: Easterners were Tuckahoes, a term derived from the arum root that grows around marshes; western Virginians were Cohees, slang derived from "Quothe he," a reflection of the settlers' strong religious backgrounds.

From the Cohees' valley towns, Massanutten Mountain appears as a single, continuous ridge. At its northern reach, the bedrock divides into two ridges separated by a bowl-like depression called Fort Valley. In the 1700s, English colonists built a fort here for trading and protection against the French and Native Americans. The boast "Washington Slept Here" rings true in Fort Valley and neighboring towns such as

Winchester and Front Royal. These mountains and valley were a proving ground for the young George Washington, who first visited as a surveyor for Lord Fairfax, and then as an officer in the Virginia militia.

The views off Kennedy Peak show that a century of human progress has erased physical signs of the destruction of the past. The whole of Massanutten Mountain appears separate from the valley that unfolds at its feet. In reality, it is just the opposite. You cannot remove the mountain from the valley. Nor would it seem right to do so.

Miles and Directions

0.0 Start at the entrance of Camp Roosevelt. Turn left and walk up VA 675 to a white forest gate on the left in 0.1 mile. **Note:** On the right side of the road is a trailhead for Duncan Hollow Trail. It leads south to New Market Gap.

0.1 Turn left onto the orange-blazed Massanutten East Trail. It climbs uphill past the white forest gate.

0.2 Enter a clearing, turn right, and climb on the Massanutten East Trail. The trail passes under a set of power lines several times and narrows from a dirt road into a footpath. **Note:** There is a locked equipment shed in the clearing. The trail that leads straight past the shed is Stephens Trail.

0.8 The trail reaches VA 675. Turn left and walk 50 yards up the left side of the road, reentering the woods on a forest road. There is an impressive view over Fort Valley on the side of VA 675.

1.9 Massanutten East Trail branches right from the dirt road to circumvent a knob. In 0.2 mile, the trail repeats this pattern. There are nice views here, across Fort Valley to Massanutten Mountain's west ridge.

2.2 Pass a campsite on the right side of the trail. Kennedy Peak is visible at this point.

2.4 The trail switchbacks northwest amid a rock slide.

2.6 Where the trail bends right around the side of Kennedy Peak, there are good views west over Fort Valley. At shoulder height on your right side, thick slabs of sedimentized rock stick out of the hillside at a 45-degree angle. A lone mountain laurel grows from between two slabs.

3.2 Reach the spur trail to Kennedy Peak. Turn right and make the short, 0.2-mile uphill trek to a stone shelter/lookout tower constructed by the Civilian Conservation Corps stationed at Camp Roosevelt in the 1930s. Return to the Massanutten East Trail and hike north atop the ridge.

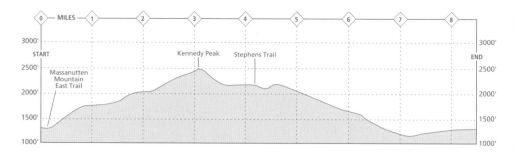

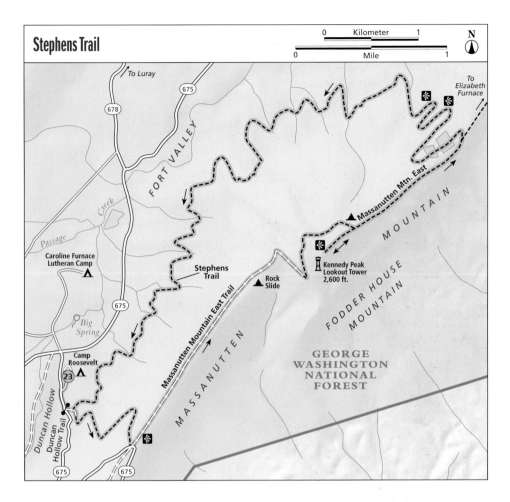

Stephens Trail

0 Kilometer 1

0 Mile 1

N

4.0 Where the trail drops briefly off the right side of a knob, look for exposed sections of rock that show the layered sandstone rock formations. This is Massanutten sandstone, light gray and highly resistant rock found only in the Massanutten Range.

4.2 Stephens Trail branches left while Massanutten East Trail continues a northward route to Elizabeth Furnace. Turn left onto Stephens Trail and make a beeline through open hardwood forest. Where the downslope pitch steepens, the trail switches back to descend along the northwest flank of Massanutten Mountain. Watch for red flinty rocks underfoot, indicative of the iron-ore deposits found in the mountain bedrock.

5.3 As you wrap around a shoulder ridge and begin a lateral descent on the wavy course of Stephens Trail, there are good views over Fort Valley west. For 2 miles, the trail will alternate between moist coves and exposed hillsides as it crosses the many unnamed tributaries of Passage Creek, which flows through Fort Valley, a basin formed by the east and west ridges of Massanutten Mountain.

8.3 Enter a clearing and hike straight past a junction with the Massanutten East Trail. The brown equipment shed is on your right.

8.4   Reach VA 675. Turn right and walk downhill to Camp Roosevelt.

8.5   Arrive back at Camp Roosevelt.

Hike Information

Local Information

Shenandoah Valley Travel Association, New Market, (877) VISIT-SV, www.visit shenandoah.org

Local Events/Attractions

Edinburg Ole' Time Festival, held in Sept, (540) 984-7272, http://edinburgoletime festival.org

    Luray Caverns, Luray, (540) 743-6551, www.luraycaverns.com. One of several commercial caves in the Shenandoah Valley. Guided tours available.

Lodging

The Widow Kips, Mount Jackson, (540) 477-2400, www.widowkips.com. Pets welcome in their guest cottages.

Restaurants

The Spring House Tavern, Woodstock, (540) 459-4755, www.springhousetavern.net. Casual eatery with great food.

Organizations

Potomac Appalachian Trail Club (PATC), Vienna, (703) 242-0315, www.patc.net
Civilian Conservation Corps Legacy, www.ccclegacy.org

24 Fridley Gap

Some days, you can hike for miles and feel like you never left the parking lot. Other times, it can feel like you walked through four different worlds in a single afternoon. Thankfully, you'll find Fridley Gap fits the latter experience. Squeezed together accordion-like, the long, parallel ridges of First, Second, Third, and Fourth Mountains concentrate an awful lot of up-and-downs into a day of hiking, and, consequently, a number of different habitats. At the lower elevations, stream valleys attract deer to the water's edge. Skinny rays of sunlight filter down to the forest floor through hemlock. A half mile away stands another world: the dry, barren ridgetops. With no tree cover, views stretch for miles. Two different worlds, one hike.

Start: Gate across FR 65
Distance: 9.4-mile lollipop
Hiking time: About 5 hours
Difficulty: Moderate, with steep climbs up Third and Fourth Mountains
Trail surface: Dirt paths, old logging roads, and gravel forest roads wind through a hemlock grove along Fridley Run and rock outcrops along Fourth Mountain, and lead to a waterfall and swimming hole on Mountain Run.
Land status: National forest
Nearest town: Shenandoah, VA

Other trail users: Equestrians, mountain bikers, cross-country skiers, and hunters (in season)
Canine compatibility: Dogs permitted
Trail contact: Lee Ranger District, Edinburg; (540) 984-4101; www.fs.usda.gov/gwj
Schedule: Open year-round. Hunting is permitted in national forests, with deer season the busiest from Nov to early Jan.
Fees/permits: None
Facilities/features: None
Maps: USGS Elkton West, Tenth Legion

Finding the trailhead: From Elkton, from the junction of Business 13 and VA 635 (River Road), drive north 3.3 miles on VA 635 and turn left on VA 602 (East Point Road). At 4.4 miles, turn right onto VA 636 (Runkles Gap Road). In 2.2 miles, enter the George Washington National Forest. In 0.1 mile past the forest boundary, VA 636 ends, although the gravel road straight ahead continues as gated FR 65 (Cub Run Road). Pass a small parking area and go through a forest gate (park here if it is locked). In 0.2 mile, find the trailhead off the left side of the road. There is minimal parking here. GPS: N38 27.245' / W78 41.825'. *DeLorme: Virginia Atlas & Gazetteer:* Page 67, A6.

The Hike

Oak trees have always fascinated people. Pagan worshipers likened the tree's physical traits—tall, sturdy, and long-lived—with the most powerful gods. Zeus, the Greek god of thunder and lightning, considered the oak sacred. This, in turn, may have informed the old English saying "Beware the oak; it draws the stroke," a reference to just how often oaks get struck by lightning.

Reverence for the oak seems justifiable given its usefulness. Ancient people treated it like a department superstore, a complete package, able to provide all the stuff for

A view of Massanutten Mountain taken from Skyline Drive in Shenandoah National Park.

living. Acorns not only made food (acorn cakes), but also attracted the deer, bear, and small game that became food. Homes and furniture were built of oak boards. Oak logs provided fuel for heating and cooking. And while it's true that Europeans looked down their noses at the North America white oak sent to them, the wood proved durable enough to construct the first ships for the US Navy.

Oaks, in their natural setting, define the forest type between southern New England and Georgia. Their presence sets the tone for how large or widespread other trees grow. Additionally, more than 200 known species live off the oak, from the squirrels that survive on its acorns to the mushrooms growing on its trunk. Elevation and soil conditions matter little; there's a type of oak for every location. In the mountains, white oaks grow in stream valleys and on moist hillsides. Chinquapin and bear oak are found as thickets in the young second- or third-generation forests. Red oaks mix with the whites, the beeches, and the maples at low elevations, but emerge in pure stands at higher elevations. Chestnut oaks, so named for the leaf's resemblance to that of the much-diminished American chestnut, take root on rocky hillsides and dry ridges.

Changes in elevation and moisture occur quickly over short distances in the Massanutten Mountain chain. This 55-mile-long grouping of ridges and knobs rises from the floor of the Shenandoah Valley in the shape of a needle, with forks of the Shenandoah River flowing along either flank. At its southern end—the point of the needle—stand the highest points, Lairds Knob (3,282 feet) and Massanutten Peak (2,922 feet). Here also stands Third Mountain, as well as its neighbors First, Second, and Fourth Mountains, all of them long, parallel ridges squeezed together like the folds of an accordion. For every wrinkle in this mountain landscape, there's an oak tree to tell hikers about the soil conditions, climate, and annual rainfall. Leaf litter along the Massanutten South Trail shows telltale signs of white oak. Along this same trail, a mile past Boone Run, red oaks replace white as the dominant tree along the descending ridge of Fourth Mountain. (Hikers should be able to distinguish between the two most abundant oaks—red and white. The leaf of a white oak has rounded tips between the deep lobes; a red oak leaf has pointed or bristly tips.)

Oak trees aside, little about the terrain on the southern portion of Massanutten Mountain is consistent. Boone Run and Fridley Run illustrate how a small geographic area can hold such contrasting habitats within close proximity. The streams flow off in opposite directions: Boone Run south to the South Fork Shenandoah River, Fridley Run north to Mountain Run. Third Mountain separates these two streams, and the Massanutten South Trail follows alongside both.

As you climb to a gap in Third Mountain and pass the headwaters of Boone Run, the forest canopy disappears, and the ground is a flinty stone or sand. This is in sharp contrast to the sun-dappled pleasures of Fridley Run, which runs at the base of Third Mountain's northwest slope. Along Fridley Run, hemlocks loom over the stream bank. Green moss blankets wet rocks. The river flows for a short distance, then spills

The author and Coco take a break at Boone Run Shelter on Massanutten.

over a ledge and collects in a pool, repeating this pattern again and again as it moves downhill. It is a scene as lush and beautiful and sheltered as the top of Third Mountain is dry, exposed, and nondescript.

The red oaks don't look healthy on Fourth Mountain. There are signs of gypsy moth infestation, a blight to which oaks are particularly vulnerable. Damage from the gypsy moth is not limited to eating the leaves off the tree; acorn production declines in their wake. Animals migrate in search of a more reliable food source. A thinning of the forest canopy lets light reach the forest floor. Fast-growing trees and shrubs replace oaks. A pattern of forest succession begins. It will take hundreds of years before the climax forest returns, too long for one human to witness. We can take simple comfort in knowing how it ends, though. The oaks will return.

Miles and Directions

0.0 Start at a gate across FR 65 at the end of gravel VA 636. Walk past this gate up the left side of the road. Boone Run flows in the gully on the left.

0.2 Descend left off the FR 65 road embankment, following orange blazes of the Massanutten South Trail. The trail immediately crosses a stream. The trail is as wide as an old road, narrows into a footpath, then widens again. Watch for orange blazes. Faint traces of old roads branch into the woods.

0.7 Hillsides close in and Massanutten South Trail narrows to become a footpath. Boone Run cuts through some impressive exposed rock that shows the uplifting that created the series of First, Second, and Third Mountains.

1.0 Hike past a blue-blazed trail on the left. In a few feet, a white-blazed trail goes left to a shelter in 0.1 mile. **Note:** The blue-blazed trail leads to Kaylor Knob.

1.9 The trail steepens. Boone Run, once a bubbling stream, is a dry, sandy groove in the hillside.

2.2 Follow the Massanutten South Trail as it enters a clearing and turns left at a four-corners trail junction. **Note:** The trail straight ahead is Fridley Gap Trail, which is the return leg of this loop hike.

3.1 Massanutten South Trail, as it descends Third Mountain, narrows and enters a dark hemlock cove on Fridley Run. There is a campsite here with signs of hunter use.

3.5 The trail wraps around Fourth Mountain and steepens.

4.0 Begin a descent off Fourth Mountain.

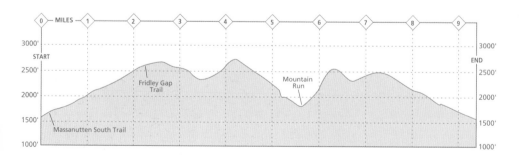

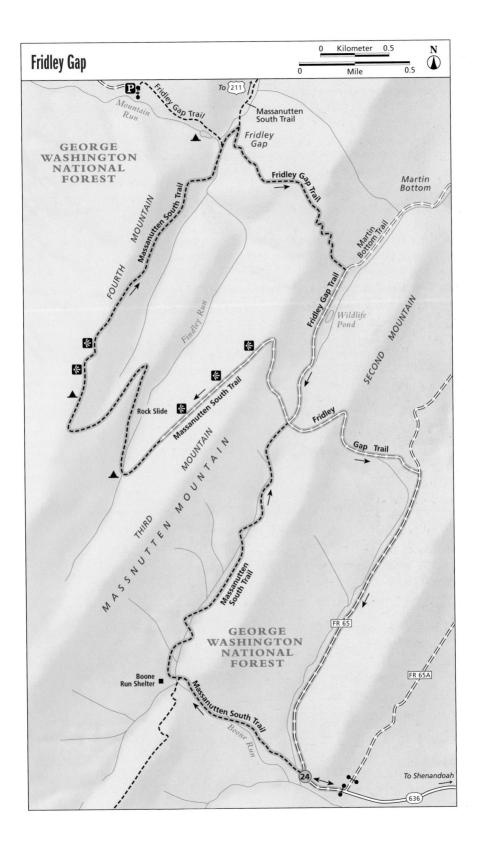

Fridley Gap

To 211

**GEORGE
WASHINGTON
NATIONAL
FOREST**

Mountain
Run

Fridley Gap Trail

Massanutten
South Trail

Fridley
Gap

Fridley Gap Trail

Martin
Bottom

FOURTH MOUNTAIN

Massanutten South Trail

Martin
Bottom Trail

Fridley
Run

Fridley Gap Trail

Wildlife
Pond

SECOND MOUNTAIN

Rock Slide

Massanutten South Trail

Fridley

Gap   Trail

THIRD   MOUNTAIN

MASSANUTTEN MOUNTAIN

Massanutten
South Trail

FR 65

FR 65A

**GEORGE
WASHINGTON
NATIONAL
FOREST**

Boone
Run Shelter

Massanutten South Trail

Boone
Run

24

To Shenandoah

636

4.2 Pass a campsite on the left. There is a rock outcrop and views behind the campsite. The next 0.5 mile brings more excellent views on similarly marked trails on the left.

5.4 Massanutten South Trail crosses Fridley Run just above the stream's junction with Mountain Run. There is a waterfall and deep swimming hole near here. This spot gets heavy use from day-trippers, with FR 722 just 0.5 mile downstream.

5.5 Turn left and hike uphill. In a few feet, turn right onto purple-blazed Fridley Gap Trail. **Note:** At the junction with Fridley Gap Trail, the Massanutten South Trail goes straight, eventually reaching the national forest visitor center at New Market Gap.

6.3 After a very steep climb, cross the wooded crest of Third Mountain.

6.6 Exit the woods onto a dirt road. Turn right and follow Fridley Gap Trail uphill. **Note:** The road on the left is the Martin Bottom Trail.

7.2 Enter a clearing at a four-way trail junction and turn left to continue on Fridley Gap Trail as it climbs Second Mountain. The trail climbs through an area scarred by a wildfire caused by a lightning strike.

7.6 Crest Second Mountain and begin a descent along a rough, rocky trail.

8.1 Reach Fire Road 65A and turn right (south) to follow the dirt and gravel road downhill.

9.4 Arrive back at the gate across FR 65.

Hike Information

Local Information

Harrisonburg is the closest city with amenities of all kinds, being a college town. Harrisonburg Tourism, (540) 432-8935, www.harrisonburgtourism.com

Shenandoah Valley Visitor Center, New Market Gap, (877) 847-4878, www.visit shenandoah.org

Lodging

Stonewall Jackson Inn Bed & Breakfast, (800) 445-5330, www.stonewalljacksoninn .com. B&B in a 1885 restored mansion close to downtown Harrisonburg.

Massanutten, (540) 289-9441, www.massresort.com. A four-season resort even closer to the trailhead, being east of the city of Harrisonburg. Golf, spa, ski, or play in the indoor water park.

Restaurants

Billy Jack's Wing & Draft Shack, 92 S. Main St., Harrisonburg, (540) 433-1793, www .billyjacksshack.com

Earth & Tea, 120 S. Main St., Harrisonburg, (540) 432-8280. An eclectic, Asian-inspired international eatery with warm, cozy booths and free Wi-Fi.

25 Laurel Fork Area

Laurel Fork once ranked as a top site in Virginia for wilderness protection, but strong opposition from inholders—families who own private property inside national forest boundaries—beat this proposal back. The desire to keep this place forever wild is understandable. There's a whiff of spruce in the air. Songbirds trill and peep in the bushes. Pine needles pile thick on the forest floor. Streams wriggle around and over the deadfall and boulders strewn in their path by storms and hurricanes. Native trout swim the Laurel Fork. It has been a long seventy years since loggers cleared the red spruce and fir trees. Nature has reclaimed Laurel Fork fully, and for this, we're all better off.

Start: Locust Springs Picnic Area
Distance: 11.2-mile double loop
Hiking time: About 6 hours
Difficulty: Moderate due to numerous stream crossings and steep trails up Middle Mountain that merge with streambeds. Because of its elevation, Laurel Fork receives heavy snowfall in winter.
Trail surface: Dirt footpaths and old forest roads wind through high-altitude red spruce forests and stream coves.
Land status: National forest
Nearest town: Monterey, VA

Other trail users: Mountain bikers, equestrians, and hunters (in season)
Canine compatibility: Dogs permitted
Trail contact: Warm Springs Ranger District, Hot Springs; (540) 839-2521; www.fs.usda .gov/gwj
Schedule: Open year-round. Hunting is permitted in national forests, with deer season running from Nov through early Jan.
Fees/permits: None.
Facilities/features: The Locust Springs Day Use Area has a vault toilet, but no drinking water.
Maps: USGS Thornwood, Snowy Mountain

Finding the trailhead: From Monterey, drive west on US 250. In 22 miles, turn right onto VA 28 and drive north for 6.7 miles. Turn right onto FR 60/FR 106, following signs for Locust Springs Picnic Area. In 0.3 mile, bear left onto FR 60. At a second intersection in 0.3 mile, bear right and uphill, following signs for Locust Springs Picnic Area. The picnic area is on the right on FR 142 in 0.4 mile. GPS: N38 35.129' / W79 38.527'. *DeLorme: Virginia Atlas & Gazetteer:* Page 64 (inset), A1.

The Hike

Laurel Fork is a classic mountain stream, appreciation of which requires little effort. A big boulder helps. Sit on the rock and stare. In early morning hours a haze wraps around overhanging branches. Spray tossed up by the water sparkles. And just like that, an entire day watching birds flit from branch to branch seems a reasonable proposition.

It would, however, preclude exploration of the 10,000 acres in Laurel Fork Special Management Area. The steep west slope of Middle Mountain beckons. Up Christian

A pond formed by beavers along the Buck Run Trail in Laurel Fork Area.

Run or Cold Spring Run, the narrow footpaths are overrun with rhododendron. Trails and creeks intermingle without regard. The moss is spongy. There's a dank smell of moist, decomposing leaves. When the trails widen, the earth buckles and ripples where railroad ties were once embedded. Laurel Fork was privately owned until 1922. Railroads chugged up and down the mountain slopes carrying workers in and logs out. Today's trail network follows these grades, and rusted cast-iron remains of old railroad engine parts lie near the junction of Bearwallow Trail and Laurel Fork Trail.

Loggers were after the red spruce that gives Laurel Fork a unique aura. Much of it went to pulp mills. The highest quality boards, craftsmen used in musical instruments; they preferred spruce to other woods because of its consistent growth patterns. Consider that a felled tree exhibits growth rings of varying size. Thick rings indicate the salad years, when sunlight and water were plentiful. Narrow rings reflect leaner times. Spruce somehow avoids these highs and lows; its growth rings are almost always the same size and compact, two qualities favorable for musical instruments. (Another interesting aside: The older the instrument, the better it sounds—but that's only if it's played, not left under glass to age. Wood becomes elastic with vibration, so an old wood instrument can sound as poor as one made of "green" wood if left untouched.)

For a hiker whose exposure to needle-leaf trees extends from jack pine to hemlock, a spruce forest can seem like an altered state. Technically, Laurel Fork is an "Appalachian extension of a northern boreal forest." Nontechnically speaking, it's cold, snows like crazy in winter, and harbors animals normally found farther north. If you're lucky, a snowshoe hare might hop across the trail. The distribution map for this animal shows a shaded area over all of Canada and parts of Minnesota, Wisconsin, and New York. The map also shows fingerlike extensions reaching down the chain of Appalachian Mountains as far south as the Great Smoky Mountains in Tennessee. This sums up nicely the whole boreal forest effect. Glaciers never reached as far south as Virginia (as indicated by the dearth of natural lakes). But even if the ice never made it, the northern species of trees and animals suited for that environment did.

Buck Run Trail is a good introduction to the habitat. From Locust Springs Picnic Area the trail leads first past beaver dams. In the backwaters of all the major drainages—Buck Run, Slabcamp Run, and Bearwallow Run—you'll find sizable beaver populations. Their handiwork is not confined to dams. Springtime finds logs felled across trails; the gnawed pointed trunk gives away the culprit. The shallow ponds created by the dams are thick with salamanders and frogs and the shrill of spring peepers.

One of the northern trees you'll see along with the red spruce is the Fraser fir. In 1784 the tree's namesake, John Fraser, a Scotsman, sailed into Charleston hoping to follow in the footsteps of his contemporaries, William Bartram and Andre Michaux, botanists who made names for themselves studying the flora and fauna of the Southern Appalachians. Fraser was an amateur, primarily concerned with making a fortune (why he chose botany as a career is a mystery). He roamed the Southern Appalachians collecting specimens for the highest bidder. His short list at times included the king of England, Catherine the Great of Russia, and her successor, Czar Paul. For a brief period, Fraser and Michaux traveled together, but their competing interest (Michaux was sending samples to Louis XVI of France) soon caused them to part company. Michaux let Fraser travel ahead, and, as a result, Fraser had the good fortune of being the first to discover the tree that now bears his name.

Nature is an exact science, down to the arrangement of needles on a red spruce branch. Clusters of needles minimize heat loss and keep the tree branch warm through the winter. The interlocking branches weave a canopy that blocks out sun and lends everything below a gloomy aspect. Thick piles of fallen needles mat the forest floor. Moist green sphagnum moss covers roots and rocks. Besides moss, little else grows under a mature spruce-fir forest canopy. It's a vicious little circle, whereby needles and moss give the soil a high acid content, and the acid soil in turn slows decomposition. The moss, especially, thrives by coating dead logs and whatever else will host it.

The red spruce that dominate in Laurel Fork are well suited for life here. The soil is thin, a product of years of logging and erosion. The tree spreads wide, shallow roots into this soil. Porcupines like to nibble on the sweet bark of these trees, while red squirrels seem adept at extracting seeds from cones. Berry shrubs sprout and survive to feed a host of birds and small rodents through the lean winter months. Bearberry and prickly gooseberry mingle with the more readily identified high- and low-bush blueberries.

When West Virginia seceded from Virginia after the outbreak of the Civil War, it took with it some of the roughest natural terrain on the East Coast. Virginia's valleys and ridges seem downright pastoral when compared to the jumble of peaks, cliffs,

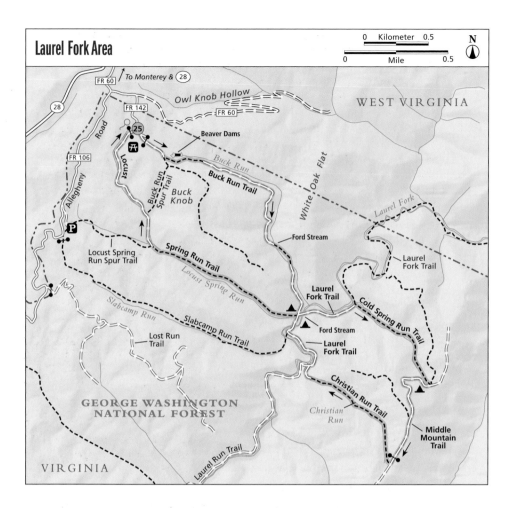

Laurel Fork Area

0   Kilometer   0.5

0   Mile   0.5

N

To Monterey & 28

Owl Knob Hollow

WEST VIRGINIA

FR 60

FR 142

FR 60

28

25

FR 106

Beaver Dams

Locust

Buck Run

White Oak Flat

Laurel Fork

Buck Run Trail

Buck Run Spur Trail

Buck Knob

Allegheny Road

P

Ford Stream

Spring Run Trail

Locust Spring Run Spur Trail

Locust Spring Run

Laurel Fork Trail

Laurel Fork Trail

Cold Spring Run Trail

Slabcamp Run

Slabcamp Run Trail

Ford Stream

Lost Run Trail

Laurel Fork Trail

GEORGE WASHINGTON NATIONAL FOREST

Christian Run Trail

Christian Run

Middle Mountain Trail

VIRGINIA

Laurel Run Trail

and ridges that form the Allegheny Mountains in West Virginia. Virginia can at least take some comfort in having kept this corner of Highland County and the Laurel Fork watershed.

Miles and Directions

0.0   Start at the Locust Springs Picnic Area. Walk up a dirt road at the east end of the picnic area. Almost immediately, look for a gated forest road on the right, marked with blue blazes and a hiker sign. This is the Buck Run trailhead. Turn right, pass by the gate, and follow the road, which is overgrown with grass.

0.4   Turn left off the grass road. Pass through a stand of red spruce. The ground is flat and the trail is now a dirt singletrack. There are several beaver dams in this area. **Note:** Buck Run Spur Trail is straight ahead on the grass road.

1.3   The trail descends off the side of Buck Knob and switchbacks five times as it drops to Buck Run.

1.6 A rock cairn marks the crossing of Buck Run on a bridge constructed of three skinny logs. Cross and walk downstream following the left bank. In 0.1 mile, re-cross Buck Run to the right stream bank. **Note:** From now until the junction with Laurel Fork Trail, note how the slopes on either stream bank host starkly different plants: The left slope is covered with rhododendron, while the right supports more hardwoods, and sparse at that. Many exposed rock formations on this leg make it a geologist's delight, amateur or otherwise.

3.0 Buck Run Trail ends at a junction with the Laurel Fork Trail. Turn left onto Laurel Fork Trail and cross the stream. After crossing, turn left and hike downstream. (In the river floodplain, yellow sundrops may be in bloom. Pink lady slippers and the white bell-shaped flowers of Solomon seal grow near the edge of the forest. Red elderberry displays its fruit in August.) **Note:** From the end of Buck Run Trail, Laurel Fork Trail also leads straight upstream and intersects Locust Springs Run Trail, Slabcamp Run Trail, and Christian Run Trail.

3.7 Turn right and ascend on the blue-blazed Cold Spring Run Trail. The trail joins the stream for a short stretch, then widens to show signs of an old railroad bed.

4.7 The ground levels on both sides of the trail as it enters a grassy meadow. **Note:** The fields on Meadow Mountain were cleared for grazing when the mountain was privately owned. Today, The Stamp, an in-holding farther south on the mountain, remains the last piece of private property in the special management area.

4.9 Turn right onto Middle Mountain Trail, following blue blazes.

6.0 Pass a hunters' camp on the left, by a Forest Service gate. A large field opens up on your left. Turn right and walk through a meadow. Blue arrows on trees on the right fringe of the field will guide you to where the Christian Run Trail enters the woods.

6.7 The trail narrows and runs close to Christian Run. It crosses three times.

7.0 Christian Run Trail junctions with Laurel Fork Trail. Turn right and walk along the right stream bank.

7.4 Where Slabcamp Run Trail branches left and crosses Laurel Run, continue straight on Laurel Fork Trail. There are several good campsites on this stretch of trail, including one, just prior to crossing Laurel Fork, that overlooks a swimming hole.

7.6 Cross Laurel Fork and hike along the left stream bank.

7.8 Turn left onto Locust Spring Run Trail. The next 1.5 miles brings numerous stream crossings. In places, the stream and trail merge for some messy hiking.

9.9 Bear right and away from a left-branching trail, which is Locust Spring Run Spur Trail. It leads to FR 106.

11.2 Hike ends at the Locust Spring Picnic Area.

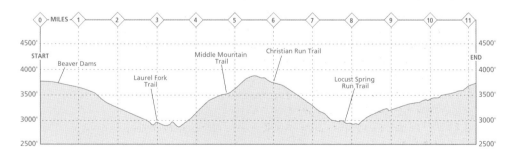

Hike Information

Local Information

Highland County Chamber of Commerce, Monterey, (540) 468-2550, www.high landcounty.org

Local Events / Attractions

The Highland Maple Festival, held in Mar, Monterey, (540) 468-2550, www.high landcounty.org/maplefestival.html. Celebrates the opening of the trees with a festival and camp tours.

Lodging

Highland Inn, (888) 466-4682, www.highland-inn.com. Monterey's historic hotel right on Main Street.

Restaurants

Highs Restaurant, Main Street, Monterey, (540) 468-1700. Serves breakfast, lunch and dinner 7 days a week.

26 Roaring Run/Hoop Hole

In an inconspicuous corner of Botetourt County, seven peaks converge to form a backcountry nook where bears just may outnumber human visitors. The region's namesake, Roaring Run, pulses through a break in Rich Patch Mountain with force enough to have powered a blast iron furnace for half a century. Ruins of that furnace mark the beginning of a loop hike that takes you along the high, dry top of Pine Mountain, then down to headwaters of three small streams. Between ridgetop and riverbed spreads a forest that is as secluded as it is satisfying.

Start: Trail board next to the restrooms at Roaring Run Furnace National Recreation Area
Distance: 10.0-mile lollipop
Hiking time: About 5 hours
Difficulty: Moderate due to long climbs and length. The bushwhack up Pine Mountain requires skills in across-country hiking, including the ability to use a compass.
Trail surface: Dirt footpaths and old dirt roads lead along dry ridges, through extended fields of heath, boulder fields, and stream headwaters.

Land status: National forest
Nearest town: Clifton Forge, VA
Other trail users: Hikers only
Canine compatibility: Dogs permitted
Trail contact: Eastern Divide Ranger District, Blacksburg; (540) 552-4641; www.fs.usda .gov/gwj
Schedule: Open year-round
Fees/permits: None
Facilities/features: Vault toilets and streamside picnic sites
Map: USGS Strom

Finding the trailhead: From Clifton Forge, drive west on I-64 to the Low Moor exit. Drive south on VA 696 and, in 0.1 mile, turn left onto VA 616. Drive 5.7 miles, then turn left onto VA 621 at Rich Patch Union Church. In 3.3 miles, turn right into the Roaring Run National Recreation Area. GPS: N37 42.400' / W79 53.594'. *DeLorme: Virginia Atlas & Gazetteer:* Page 52, C3.

The Hike

In 1804 William Clark, a man whose name would become synonymous with exploration, left the small town of Fincastle in Botetourt County, Virginia, for the unknown of the American frontier. He and friend Meriwether Lewis would lead the Corps of Discovery through the void of middle America to the Pacific Ocean, and back. Three years later, Clark returned to Fincastle a national hero. He settled and married the daughter of wealthy landowner George Hancock. Clark's journals from the Corps of Discovery expedition were stored and edited in Fincastle, in Hancock's home. In 1810 President Thomas Jefferson appointed him governor of the Missouri Territory, thus ending his Virginia residency. Clark departed for St. Louis and left behind a legend proudly guarded by Fincastlians, who are known to claim their town as the real point-of-embarkation for the Lewis and Clark expedition.

Roaring Run iron ore furnace.

Fincastle, a town of roughly 300 souls, is as fitting a beginning for Clark's journey as any spot. For a brief period before the Revolutionary War, this town sat on the edge of the great unknown. The boundaries of Botetourt County, of which Fincastle was the county seat, stretched as far as the Mississippi and contained parts of seven present-day states. Standing atop Pine Mountain on a clear fall or winter day, you get a small sense of that vast landholding, where views stretch into West Virginia and the imagination, if prodded, farther. And as is the case for all good explorations, getting to this secluded vista on Pine Mountain is as much a reason for going as the payoff.

The journey begins at Roaring Run Furnace, a national recreation area south of Clifton Forge in Botetourt County. The Iron Ore Trail climbs from the ruins of a blast furnace on old dirt roads and abandoned railroad grades. In a saddle between Shoemaker Knob and Iron Ore Knob, the trail turns and skirts the slope of Pine Mountain as a footpath. If a hiker sticks to the blazed trails, the route eventually leads to a forested saddle of the Pine Mountain ridge. But there's an alternate route up Pine Mountain, a short, steep path—more a detour than a true bushwhack. Look for this route as you climb Hoop Hole Trail, less than 0.5 mile uphill from the T intersection with Iron Ore Trail. In a world of well-blazed, clearly defined paths, this side trail is a gift. Marked by infrequent plastic squares the size of a quarter, following it still requires hunt-and-peck skills. These are times a hiker falls back on basic skills: orientating, identifying telltale plants, determining whether they are typical of a certain elevation or slope, and wondering who, or more precisely what, has walked here before you. (Lewis and Clark would be so proud.)

The last question is answered atop Pine Mountain. Amid the outcrops of sandstone, logs show signs of being clawed and shredded by black bears looking for larva and insects. By-products of their munching, scat piles, lay in clumps here and there. With a range up to 15 miles, a number of bears have made the Pine Mountain/Rich Patch Mountain slopes home turf.

From Pine Mountain's first knob, a sight line carries southwest along the 3,000-foot-high ridge to a point where Pine Mountain buttresses against Rich Patch Mountain. Patches of stunted vegetation grow in shale soil on the upper slopes of the ridge. Berry bushes thrive here, where the larger, moisture-loving witch hazel will not. Wild grasses propagate in gaps of forest created by fire. Among the berry bushes, poverty oat grass grows in gray-green mats. Another grass, yellow sedge, is found on more gently graded slopes. Both grasses are present in early stages of forest recovery and may be indicators of a recent fire. The shoots need only a thin soil cover and seem adaptable to the acidic, nutrient-deficient soil typical of dry, fire-ravaged areas.

So thick is the undergrowth at points, Hoop Hole Trail can become difficult to follow. At these times, it pays to watch for the red stone flakes that litter the trail; this color indicates the mineral hematite. Hematite is a principal iron-ore mineral and its presence, embedded in sandstone deposits formed 400 million years ago, helped catapult this region into a leading producer of iron ore during the second half of the nineteenth century.

Roaring Run Furnace, where this described loop begins, operated as a blast furnace for only thirty years. That's a short time in a region famous for iron production. The furnace's obscurity may explain, in a backhanded way, how it survived intact through the years. During the Civil War, Tredegar Iron Works leased Roaring Run as an insurance policy against losing its larger furnaces located in the Great Valley. Union forces eventually destroyed three of Tredegar's mines in an effort to disrupt the Confederate's supply of bullets, cannons, and gun parts. Tredegar, especially, held significance. From its Virginia furnaces, it produced the cannons at Fort Sumter, South Carolina, site of the first battle between North and South. And even Grace Furnace, an iron-ore furnace 5 miles west of Roaring Run, fell to Union forces. It all points to a conclusion that Roaring Run survived because it wasn't producing iron ore. Tredegar's records show it blasted the furnace once, in 1865, just before the war ended. This inactivity made it an impractical target for Union forces.

Evidence of mining activity around Roaring Run Furnace is visible in the large depressions cut from the mountainside. In other spots, talus (rock piles) lay beneath gouged out chunks of hillside. For some unknown reason, the minerals around Roaring Run were never exploited to the extent they were elsewhere in Virginia. By 1870, Virginia iron furnaces were switching to a more efficient, coke-based fuel source. Charcoal-burning furnaces such as Roaring Run faded into obscurity. Given that a furnace consumed on average 750 bushels of charcoal in a single day—the equivalent of an acre of woodland—the furnace's inactivity once again held an unintended benefit. This time, it saved a beautiful corner of the forest from mining and logging—a benefit hikers can certainly appreciate.

0.0 Start from a trail board next to the restrooms at Roaring Run Furnace. Follow the wide, orange-blazed Iron Ore Trail under hemlocks and table mountain pines.

0.2 At a fork in the trail, bear left and climb on the Iron Ore Trail. Soon, the falls on Roaring Run are audible downhill on the right.

0.4 Pass under power lines.

0.7 At a T junction, turn left and follow the orange-blazed Iron Ore Trail, which is still a dirt road. **Note:** Avoid the road that leads straight from this intersection. It is marked with yellow blazes.

0.8 Pass a road that splits right and uphill away from Iron Ore Trail. In another 20 yards, Iron Ore Trail forks right onto a narrow trail leading uphill; bear right at this fork and follow the Iron Ore Trail uphill. It breaks from the woods to pass under power lines, then reenters the woods.

1.0 Switchback up the northeast slope of Iron Ore Mountain. Iron Ore Trail climbs steadily to a gap between Iron Ore (2,117 feet) and Shoemaker Knob (2,429 feet). Iron Ore Trail is wide and well-graded in sections where it follows old roads or railroad that date from a time in the nineteenth century when the blast furnace at Roaring Run was in operation.

1.7 At a double blaze, turn left and cross the dry creek bed of Deisher Branch.

2.0 Pass a campsite nicely situated in a large, flat clearing on the left side of Iron Ore Trail.

2.3 At a T intersection, turn right onto the yellow-blazed Hoop Hole Trail. **Note:** A left onto Hoop Hole leads along the lower elevations of Pine Mountain. It is the return leg of this loop hike.

2.5 Turn right on an overgrown path that leads sharply uphill. The route is marked with plastic yellow diamonds, about the size of a quarter, nailed into trees. Be alert: The trail is over-grown and hard to follow. Markers are small and infrequent. This route is a steep, 0.3-mile ascent of Pine Mountain's first knob (2,789 feet). In fall and winter, this peak provides the best views off the mountain into West Virginia. **Option:** The climb up Pine Mountain's first knob, while blazed, is difficult. A hiker can avoid it by continuing straight on the Hoop Hole Trail. A half mile from this junction, Hoop Hole Trail enters a clearing in a saddle between Pine Mountain's first and second knob. In this clearing, the route from Pine Mountain's first knob rejoins Hoop Hole Trail.

2.8 At the top of Pine Mountain's first knob, turn left onto an overgrown trail marked with faint yellow paint slashes. The trail descends. **Note:** This route description applies to hikers who followed the detour to Pine Mountain's first knob. Otherwise, see mileage cue 3.0.

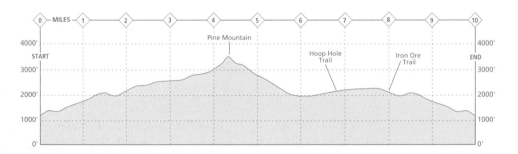

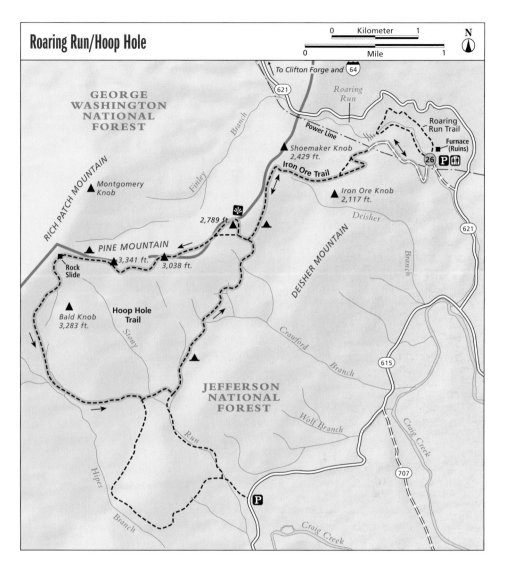

3.0 Rejoin the Hoop Hole Trail in a saddle between Pine Mountain's first and second knobs. Hike straight on the Hoop Hole Trail along the top of the ridge as it climbs toward Pine Mountain's second knob.

3.5 Shale rock outcrops on the right mark the approach of Pine Mountain's second knob (3,038 feet). This stretch of trail is enveloped in waist-high berry bushes and mountain laurel.

3.8 Climb out of the gap between Pine Mountain's second and third knobs. Hoop Hole Trail stays left of the ridgetop.

4.1 Climb on Hoop Hole Trail to the spine of Pine Mountain. In a few hundred yards, reach a campsite. From this spot, Hoop Hole Trail drops gradually off the left side of Pine Mountain. **Note:** Another unmarked trail leads from this campsite up the spine of Pine Mountain and tops out on Rich Patch Mountain.

4.4 A mass of boulders marks the rocky joint of the Pine Mountain ridge and Rich Patch Mountain. Follow Hoop Hole Trail as it turns left and threads a gap between Rich Patch Mountain and Bald Knob.

5.7 Cross the headwaters of Hipes Branch.

6.4 Turn left at a T junction and follow Hoop Hole Trail. **Note:** A right turn at this T junction leads to parking on VA 615.

6.7 At a fork in the trail, bear left onto the yellow-blazed Hoop Hole Trail. **Note:** Bearing right at this fork leads to parking on VA 615.

8.0 Turn right onto Iron Ore Trail.

9.1 After descending along a section of trail with steep banks and a trough-like appearance, Iron Ore Trail bears right. Look straight into the woods for an ill-defined footpath marked with faint yellow-painted blazes. It descends to a power line cut in 0.1 mile. Follow the power line easement downhill to a T junction with a dirt road. Turn left onto this dirt road and, in 0.1 mile, turn left onto the Iron Ore Trail.

10.0 Hike ends at the trail board near the restrooms at Roaring Run Furnace.

Hike Information

Local Information

Roanoke is the closest largest city, with lots of visitor amenities. Roanoke Valley Convention & Visitors Bureau, (540) 342-6025, www.visitroanokeva.com

Clifton Forge is a quaint small town, close to the trail. (540) 862-2000, www .cliftonforgemainstreet.org

Local Events / Attractions

Clifton Forge Farmer's Market, every Fri spring through fall, (540) 862-2000, www .cliftonforgefarmersmarket.com

Lodging

Firmstone Manor in Irondale, was, appropriately for this hike, built by the ironmaster of the Irondale Furnace Company. (800) 474-9882, www.firmstonemanor.com

Restaurants

Club Car Shop & Deli, Clifton Forge, (540) 862-0777, www.clubcarva.com

Honorable Mentions: Valley & Ridge

U. Shawl Gap-Massanutten East Trail

Start at Elizabeth Furnace on VA 678. This 12.4-mile loop uses the Botts Trail and Sherman Gap Trail, with a return along Massanutten East Trail. Elizabeth Furnace, an antebellum iron-ore blast furnace, is the start and end point, with camping facilities available. (540) 984-4101. GPS: N38 55.461' / W78 19.898'. *DeLorme: Virginia Atlas & Gazetteer:* Page 74, A2.

V. Massanutten Mountain West/Signal Knob

From Strasburg, drive east on VA 55 and then south on VA 678 to the Signal Knob Trail parking area on the right. This 17-mile hike climbs Signal Knob, then swings south down the western ridge of Massanutten and provides great views overlooking the Shenandoah Valley. Hike it as an out-and-back, or a point-to-point with a shuttle on VA 653 east of the village of Toms Brook. (540) 984-4101. GPS: N38 56.119' / 78 19.197'. *DeLorme: Virginia Atlas & Gazetteer:* Page 74, A2.

W. Massanutten Mountain East/Duncan Hollow

Begin at Camp Roosevelt on VA 675. (See "Finding the trailhead" for Hike 23: Stephens Trail.) Duncan Hollow is a lesser-used portion of the Massanutten East Trail with great loop options using Peach Orchard Gap and Scothorn Gap. (540) 984-4101. GPS: N38 43.819' / W78 31.073'. *DeLorme: Virginia Atlas & Gazetteer:* Page 73, C7.

X. Wild Oak National Recreation Trail

This 25.4-mile loop trail begins near the North River Gorge area north of Churchville, off FR 95, 1 mile north of Stokesville. There are views off Little Bald Knob and difficult terrain past Camp Todd, a full-service national forest recreation area with a lake, campsite, and picnic area. The Wild Oak Loop intersects with trails leading into Ramsey's Draft Wilderness. (540) 828-2591. GPS: N38 20.361' / W79 12.446'. *DeLorme: Virginia Atlas & Gazetteer:* Page 66, B2.

Y. Shenandoah Mountain Trail/South

A 22-mile point-to-point hike that begins at the Confederate breastworks on VA 250, 17 miles west of Churchville. The southern end is on VA 627 (Scotchtown Draft Road), off VA 629. This difficult, high-ridge hike along the spine of Shenandoah Mountain is best done as a two-day trip. (540) 885-8028. GPS: N38 18.675' / W79 23.053'. *DeLorme: Virginia Atlas & Gazetteer:* Page 65, B7.

Blue Ridge Parkway

Climb the mountains and get their good tidings. Nature's peace will flow into you as sunshine flows into trees. The winds will blow their freshness into you, and the storms their energy, while cares will drop off like autumn leaves.
John Muir, Our National Parks, *1901.*

Designer Stanley Abbot envisioned a roadway that "lay easy on the land," a route devoid of commercial traffic carrying motorists along six mountain ranges of the Appalachian chain, dropping into gaps and gracefully regaining the top of the Blue Ridge. Pull-offs link with more than 100 walking and hiking trails, from half-mile leg-stretchers, to the great Georgia-to-Maine Appalachian Trail. The scene through the car window ranges from rolling pastures dotted with grazing cattle to dramatic granite domes.

One of the three Peaks of Otter, Sharp Top (milepost 83) was long revered as the state's highest peak at 3,875 feet. Its stone was used in DC's Washington Monument, which is inscribed: "From Otter's summit, Virginia's loftiest peak. To crown a monument to Virginia's noblest son."

When geologists later measured Mount Rogers in southwest Virginia, they declared that 5,729-foot peak tallest. But mere numbers do little to diminish inspiring views from atop Sharp Top (unrivalled even by Mount Rogers', whose summit is tree-covered). A short, lung-busting climb ends at panoramic views of the surrounding peaks and valleys. Far below, dense forest is interrupted only by the Peaks of Otter Lodge on tranquil Abbott Lake, named for the Parkway's designer.

Sharp Top is a monument in itself, memorializing the sweat and talent of immigrant stoneworkers who fashioned elaborate steps to its peak. Out-of-work masons were given the task during the Depression. Their beautiful arched bridges, tunnels, retaining walls and paths, all using native stone, can be seen throughout the park.

Many other Parkway hikes are "top-down." Rock Castle Gorge (milepost 169) epitomizes this, beginning along the parkway in quiet pastures and dropping into the deep, quiet world of an Appalachian cove forest. You can spend the night in one of the

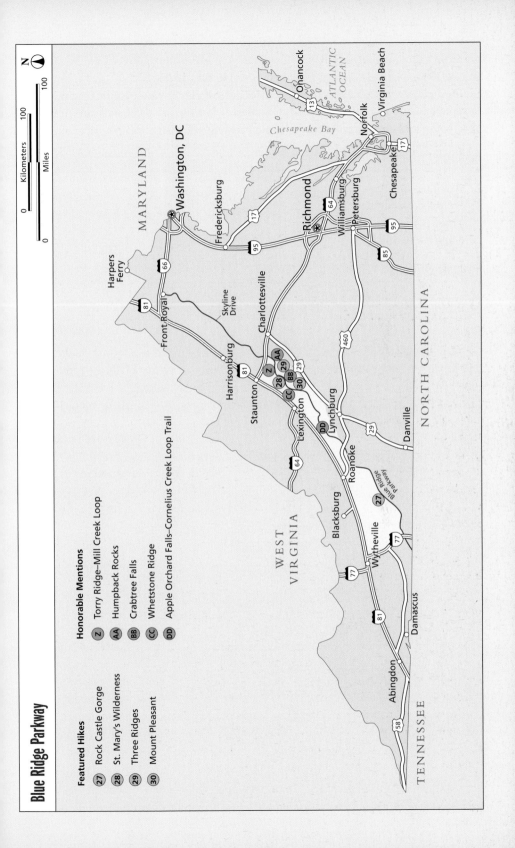

Blue Ridge Parkway

Featured Hikes

- (27) Rock Castle Gorge
- (28) St. Mary's Wilderness
- (29) Three Ridges
- (30) Mount Pleasant

Honorable Mentions

- (Z) Torry Ridge–Mill Creek Loop
- (AA) Humpback Rocks
- (BB) Crabtree Falls
- (CC) Whetstone Ridge
- (DD) Apple Orchard Falls–Cornelius Creek Loop Trail

primitive campsite alongside Rock Castle Creek, a stream that powered six sawmills around 1910, when upwards of 70 families lived in this "holler."

Grazing cattle are still a common sight along the Parkway, with pastures leased out to approximately 500 families. There's intentionally a sense of "no boundaries" to the park, with farmland instead of fences at the Parkway's outskirts.

The Hikes

27. Rock Castle Gorge
28. St. Mary's Wilderness
29. Three Ridges
30. Mount Pleasant

Honorable Mentions

Z. Torry Ridge–Mill Creek Loop
AA. Humpback Rocks
BB. Crabtree Falls
CC. Whetstone Ridge
DD. Apple Orchard Falls–Cornelius Creek Loop Trail

27 Rock Castle Gorge

This strenuous loop begins innocently enough: in the cow pasture and mountain balds that flank the Blue Ridge Parkway. Its true nature soon reveals itself as you descend some 1,800 feet in just 3 miles to the edge of bubbling, rock-strewn Rock Castle Creek. The hillsides and stream valley of this national recreation area harbored a sizable community of mountain settlers leading up to the Great Depression; evidence of their homes—vine-encased foundations, clearings, and fruit trees—are visible throughout the trip. After a walk along the lush streambed, the return to the Parkway will be sure to prompt that age-old hiker question: Which is more difficult, hiking uphill or downhill?

Start: Rocky Knob Campground, milepost 167.1 on the Blue Ridge Parkway
Distance: 10.6-mile loop
Hiking time: About 7 hours, with option of an overnight
Difficulty: Strenuous due to steep grades
Trail surface: Dirt footpaths, old fire roads, and streamside paths
Land status: National recreation area
Nearest town: Floyd, VA
Other trail users: Anglers and hunters (in season)
Accessibility: None
Canine compatibility: Leashed dogs allowed, but make sure they are in good shape for the steep and rocky portions.
Trail contacts: Blue Ridge Parkway Headquarters, (828) 271-4779, www.nps.gov/blri; info

line: (828) 298-0398; Rocky Knob Visitors Center, (540) 745-9661
Schedule: The Blue Ridge Parkway and trails are open year-round, but may close in inclement weather. The Rocky Knob Visitors Center is open late May through Oct.
Fees/permits: No entrance fee. A free permit (available at Rocky Knob Visitors Center) is required to use the backcountry campsite along Rock Castle Creek.
Facilities/features: None on the trail. Rocky Knob Visitors Center has a gift shop and restrooms.
Maps: USGS Woolvine; "Rocky Knob Trails," a hand-drawn brochure published by the National Park Service

Finding the trailhead: From Floyd, drive south on VA 8 for 5.8 miles. Turn left onto the southbound entrance of the Blue Ridge Parkway and go 1.8 miles to the entrance of the Rocky Knob Campground. Park along the roadside near the entrance to the campground. Alternate parking is available at Saddle Overlook, on the northbound side of the Parkway 0.9 mile south of the campground entrance. A leg of the Rock Castle Gorge Trail links Saddle Overlook with the trailhead described in this hike. Trailhead GPS: N36 49.878' / W80 20.658'. *DeLorme: Virginia Atlas & Gazetteer:* Page 25, B7.

The Hike

Coves are some of the most sheltered, protected pockets of the Appalachian forests, found on steep mountain terrain and infused with rich flora. While famous for its

The author with Sasha on Rock Castle Gorge Trail.

profusion of spring wildflowers, by late summer the gorge's mesic habitat sports a single color—green—albeit with many subtle variations to be found between club moss, ferns, laurel, trees, and grass.

Add to this thick vegetation rain-dripping mistiness, and a journey up Rock Castle Gorge can take on a near Middle Earth quality. Combine this with the pastoral beauty of its mountain bald meadows, and you get the sense that the 10.6-mile loop has all the ingredients for a classic Blue Ridge adventure.

The hike off the ridge begins gently enough, but soon demands full attention. The slope to the left drops off with cliff-like severity and the trail narrows into a billy goat path. Tree roots became steps and handholds that prevented our tripping down.

When it's over, treat yourself to a good, foot-numbing soak in Rock Castle Creek. Measuring about 15 feet wide, this stream in late summer doesn't show the strong flow that once enabled it to power six sawmills in the gorge. Around 1910, upwards of seventy families lived here along the creek or in smaller hollows up in the hills.

A locally published memoir, *Little Boy Blue,* recounts Robert Blue's years growing up in this gorge, or "hollow," as locals referred to it (the term *gorge* was tacked on by the US Park Service. Blue's family grew fruit trees on the hillside and sold the harvest in the surrounding towns. While lore and legend play up the famous Appalachian lawlessness of moonshiners and their ilk, I like Blue's stereotype-busting image of a hard-working family. Judging by the ruins we found, homes in the gorge were small, basically a place to sleep and eat, with time in between spent scraping out a living, or in the case of the young boy Blue, exploring nature in a beautiful hollow.

The gorge is a perfect place to spend a day with a good book, lying in a hammock slung up by the creek. Camping is limited to this one spot along the river, which

A foggy day hiking amongst cattle on Rock Castle Gorge Trail.

leaves two-night campers a whole day for exploring hillsides for specimens of the stream's namesake—quartzite rock formations that early settlers thought resembled rock castles. Rock Castle is a catch-and-release trout stream as well; two fly fisherman passed by camp and gave good reports from the small pools higher up.

The hike out of the gorge is all uphill. *Euphoria* wouldn't be too strong a description of how it feels to pass out of the cove environment into cow pastures that flank the Blue Ridge Parkway. The scene is reminiscent of the famous mountain balds along this same parkway in North Carolina's high country.

The final climb up Rocky Knob (elevation 3,572 feet) is a fitting ending to hike, offering a majestic view of the gorge you've journeyed through. Rock Castle Gorge viewed from this height looks like a deep gash in the mountain, wrapped in clouds of mystery.

Miles and Directions

0.0 Start from the Rocky Knob Campground (milepost 167.1). Cross the Blue Ridge Parkway and pass through a fence stile. Turn left and follow signs for the green-blazed Rock Castle Gorge Trail. **Note:** If you are starting from alternate Saddle Overlook parking area (milepost 168), it is 0.7-mile hike north to this start point.

2.3 After a long descent, begin paralleling Little Rock Castle Creek.

3.0 Your 1,800-foot descent off the Blue Ridge Parkway ends at Rock Castle Creek. Turn right on the green-blazed Rock Castle Gorge Trail, which now follows an old fire road up the stream valley.

3.2 Pass a backcountry camp on the right. **Note:** A permit is required to camp here. See "Fees/permits" in the hike specs.

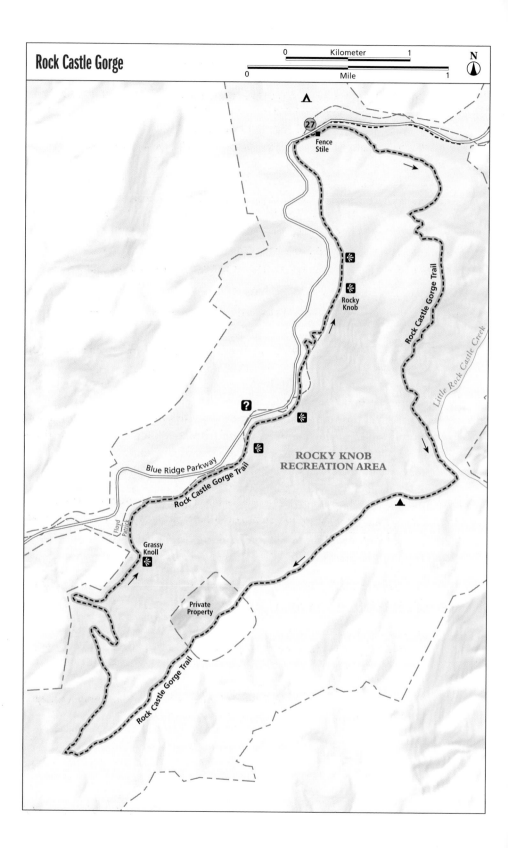

Rock Castle Gorge

Kilometer

0 — 1

Mile

0 — 1

N

27
Fence
Stile

Rocky
Knob

Rock Castle Gorge Trail

Little Rock Castle Creek

Blue Ridge Parkway

Rock Castle Gorge Trail

ROCKY KNOB
RECREATION AREA

Floyd
Patrick

Grassy
Knoll

Private
Property

Rock Castle Gorge Trail

4.5	Pass through a private inholding in the Rocky Knob Recreation Area. This is the site of an abandoned but well-cared-for two-story home.
5.6	Veer right off the fire road and descend a singletrack woods path to the water's edge. Cross Rock Castle Gorge Creek and begin a long ascent to the Parkway.
5.8	Pass through a boulder field of large, house-size rocks.
7.0	Pass through a fence and enter a cow pasture. The trail here is marked by posts with arrows.
8.7	Continue straight at a junction with the blue-blazed Black Ridge Trail on the left.
9.3	Veer right and follow green blazes as you begin climbing Rocky Knob. **Note:** The trail straight ahead at this junction returns to the Saddle Overlook parking area in 0.5 mile.
9.8	Reach the summit of Rocky Knob.
10.1	Pass the Saddle Overlook on the left.
10.6	Arrive back at the fence stile across from the entrance to Rocky Knob Campground.

Hike Information

Local Information

The great little town of Floyd has a general store that doubles as a bluegrass venue, the Floyd Hotel, and cute shops. (540) 745-4407, www.visitfloyd.org

Local Events/Attractions

The picturesque and historic Mabry Mill is a working gristmill with adjacent blacksmith shop and cabin, picnic area, and visitor center, just 9 miles north at milepost 176.

Lodging

Rocky Knob Campground, milepost 167, has tent and RV sites, restrooms, and a picnic area. Open May through Oct, winter camping is weather permitting. Reservations: (877) 444-6777, www.recreation.gov

Restaurants

Floyd Country Store, 206 Locus St., Floyd, (540) 745-4563, www.floydcountrystore .com. Offers homemade, healthy, no-nonsense cooking.

Organizations

Friends of Blue Ridge Parkway, (800) 228-7275, http://friendsbrp.org

Other Resources

Hiker registration and maps are available at Rocky Knob Visitors Center, milepost 169, (540) 745-9660.

28 St. Mary's Wilderness

There are two types of Virginia hikers: those who have visited St. Mary's Wilderness and those who soon will; more people visit this 10,000-acre plot of protected wild land on the western slope of the Blue Ridge than any other Virginia wilderness. Easy access to the premier attraction, St. Mary's Falls, ensures this won't change any time soon. And a beauty this waterfall is—a wide, 15-foot drop into a deep, narrow gorge replete with massive river boulders and mountain laurel. Beauty of a subtler nature lies deeper into the wilderness. Take the time to explore a bit farther.

Start: Gravel parking lot opposite Fork Mountain Overlook, milepost 23 on the Blue Ridge Parkway
Distance: 10.6-mile loop
Hiking time: About 7 hours
Difficulty: Moderate due to the hike length and the steep grades along Mine Bank Creek
Trail surface: Dirt roads and footpaths traverse steep mountain slopes, upland meadows, and waterfalls.
Land status: National forest and wilderness area

Nearest town: Steeles Tavern, VA
Other trail users: Cross-country skiers and hunters (in season)
Accessibility: None
Canine compatibility: Dogs permitted
Trail contact: Glenwood-Pedlar Ranger District, Natural Bridge Station; (540) 291-2188; www.fs.usda.gov/gwj
Schedule: Open year-round
Fees/permits: None
Facilities/features: None
Maps: USGS Vesuvius, Big Levels

Finding the trailhead: From Steeles Tavern, drive east on VA 56. In the town of Vesuvius, the road turns left, crosses railroad tracks, and continues east. After a long stretch of winding road and switchbacks, VA 56 junctions with the Blue Ridge Parkway 5.6 miles from Steeles Tavern. Proceed north on the Blue Ridge Parkway for 3.8 miles. At the Fork Mountain Overlook (milepost 23), turn left into a gravel parking lot. There is room for eight to ten cars. GPS: N37 54.682' / W79 05.202'. *DeLorme: Virginia Atlas & Gazetteer:* Page 54, A2.

The Hike

People visit St. Mary's Wilderness for one overriding reason: waterfalls. The largest, on St. Mary's River, impresses not so much with height as with width and power. Farther upstream, smaller cascades await in the mountain gullies that feed the river. In these sheltered coves, rock and water interact in more subtle ways, as on Mine Bank Branch, where the stream glistens and shines as it tumbles down step-falls. It's a small reminder why the path less-traveled can sometimes be the most rewarding.

The hunt for waterfalls leads farther up into the wilderness. Small streams run off Mine Bank Mountain, Bald Knob, Big Levels, and Cellar Mountain. On them, cascades of varying shapes and sizes spill water en route to St. Mary's River. There are 20-foot drops into small pools on Sugartree Branch. On Mine Branch, water rolls down like a slinky down the streambed. Small as they appear, each stream contributes

A creek bed dry in summer's heat.

Green Pond completely dried up into a meadow in the summer.

volumes of water to St. Mary's River, which changes from a meandering stream near its headwaters into the frothing, churning powerhouse at St. Mary's Falls.

In late spring, the rash of mountain laurel blossoms along Mine Bank Branch serves as a timely reminder that waterfalls aren't the only attraction here. For a few days, the landscape looks as if a late-season snowstorm hit. The dusting of pink and white fills folds and faults where the stream cuts steeply through bedrock, as if Tinkerbell had brushed hills with a pixie dust. This is the Appalachian wake-up call that marks the end of spring blooms; mountain laurel is the last to flower, after the redbuds, apple blossoms, and dogwoods have shown their stuff.

The sheer volume of mountain laurel makes one consider how this tree reproduces. Stamen on the flower act like a spring. When triggered by bees, the pod-like fruit opens, the anther is released, and oblong pollen beads shake out. Leave the laurel's honey to the bees, though; if ingested, it'll cause cramps and chills—even vomiting in extreme cases.

Not to be outdone by the rush of pink and white laurel, June-blooming rhododendron adds its color a month later. Along the fire road that links Green Pond to the Bald Mountain Trail, pink blossoms are abundant. Lore has it that rhododendron hid the moonshiner's still. Growth is so dense, so high, and seemingly impenetrable, it's quite possible to pass within a yard or so of someone—or something—and never know it. The tree's spindly hardwood trunk is unyielding. Not surprisingly, rhododendron and laurel wood have never amounted to much commercially, outside of use in making briar pipes, a tobacco pipe shaped from the root burls, or knots, of heath plants. Manufacturers favored the burl—the hard, dense knots found on roots of these trees—for shaping the bowl of the pipes because it burned slowly.

In late July, mountain laurel and rhododendron flowers give way to the blueberry—the über-berry of its class. Trapped inside these little blue bombers are enough cancer-fighting antioxidants to rank the small blueberry number one among fruits and vegetables in this category. Health benefits don't stop there, either. Anthocyanin, a chemical that gives berries their blue color, is said to ease eyestrain and improve circulation. Other studies suggest blueberries may even slow the aging process, reason enough to toss another handful into your mouth.

Health is an appropriate subject to consider in light of the threats that face St. Mary's Wilderness. Here, direct human activity has only the slightest impact. Even scars from mining activity as recently as the 1950s fade as grass and trees overgrow the old railroad grades and mine camps. More insidious is acid rain, which has raised pH levels in St. Mary's River to a point where native trout are suffering—to say nothing of such small aquatic life-forms as salamanders and frogs. The issue put the Forest Service in a quandary: Wilderness areas, by their very definition, are exempt from the tinkering of forest rangers and land managers. This area is intended to return to nature in whatever form that takes. There is an exception to this rule, however. In cases of fire, insect infestation, or disease, the Forest Service can intervene, as it has since done in St. Mary's. If one considers acid precipitation a disease, then the possibility of liming the river (lime is a natural base that counterbalances the acid) is justified. Barring this, recovery hinges on the long-term reduction of pollutants as required by the Clean Air Act.

Miles and Directions

0.0 Start from a trail sign for the Mine Bank Trail on the wooded side of the gravel parking lot. A few feet after starting the hike, turn left and follow the orange blazes of Mine Bank Trail. The Bald Mountain Trail that turns right at this junction is the return portion of this hike.

0.3 The trail switches back several times as it drops down the side of Mine Bank Mountain. The trail surface is loose pebbles. In fall, the views soar across the river valley below to Cellar Mountain.

0.5 After a steep descent, reach the headwaters of Mine Bank Branch. The trail bears left and descends with the stream to the right. Mountain laurel and rhododendron are plentiful here. A few hemlocks grow alongside the streambed.

1.0 Cross the stream to the right bank. As you cross, the stream drops 20 feet or so on a series of steps cut into the bedrock. The trail descends steeply with the stream on the left.

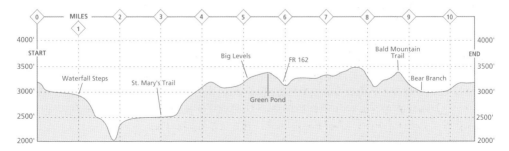

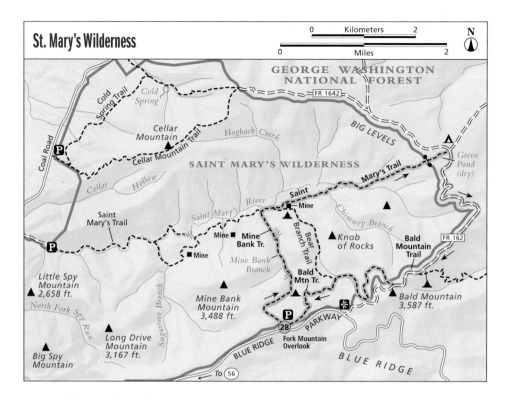

St. Mary's Wilderness

GEORGE WASHINGTON NATIONAL FOREST

SAINT MARY'S WILDERNESS

1.3 Cross back to the left stream bank. The trail continues to descend past rock outcrops on the left hillside. Take time to cut through the woods on the right for wonderful photo-ops of the stream's many small waterfalls.

2.1 Mine Bank Branch takes the first of two steep plunges off the mountain slope. The trail, which has descended at a moderate rate, steepens at each waterfall.

2.6 The trail and stream part ways, with Mine Bank Trail arcing left through the oak-hardwood forest. **Note:** In spring, this is a muddy stretch of trail.

3.0 Turn right onto blue-blazed St. Mary's Trail. Follow St. Mary's River upstream. **Side trip:** St. Mary's Trail to the left leads 2.3 miles to the St. Mary's Falls Trail. The trail passes first through an old mine operation and, farther downstream, rugged Sugar Hollow. St. Mary's Falls Trail is a 0.5-mile hike to the 15-foot St. Mary's Falls. This detour adds 5.6 miles and several hours to this loop hike.

3.2 Cross Bear Branch as it enters from the right. Follow St. Mary's Trail upstream. **Option:** To shorten your trip, you can turn right onto the unmarked Bear Branch Trail as it follows Bear Branch for a return to the Bald Mountain Trail. This bushwhack requires you to follow the Bear Branch stream bank for about a mile, after which an old road leads another mile to Bald Mountain Trail.

3.3 Signs of old iron-ore mining operations are visible off the trail. Dirt mounds cover rusted buckets, and an inspection of the tall grassy areas reveal twisted pieces of metal and concrete footings. The trail passes through some shallow mining pits and reenters the woods.

4.0 After crossing a much diminished St. Mary's River several times, the trail begins climbing on an old road. Several times, it dips into the woods for switchbacks to aid the steep ascent.

5.1 Enter Big Levels, a mountain plateau. Continue straight on St. Mary's Trail.

5.6 Reach Green Pond. Pass to the left of the pond. The trail leaves the wilderness area for 0.3 mile.

5.9 Turn right onto FR 162. This wide dirt and gravel road with no markings climbs Bald Knob on switchbacks.

7.1 FR 162 levels as it crosses Flint Mountain.

7.4 Views open on the left side of the trail. Torry Ridge is visible to the north. To the east, Three Ridges looms beyond the Blue Ridge Parkway. The trail arcs southwest and climbs at a more gradual pace.

8.8 Turn right onto the yellow-blazed Bald Mountain Trail. Look for a wilderness boundary sign on the right as a guide mark. The trail drops down the slope through a young hardwood forest. Where it crosses small hillside drainages, hemlocks are present.

9.3 Continue straight past an unmarked road that descends downhill on the right. This is the upper end of the Bear Branch bushwhack.

9.6 Cross a small stream on a three-log bridge amid heavy growth of hemlock, mountain laurel, and rhododendron.

9.8 The trail arcs left and the climb, which has been gradual the last half mile, steepens.

10.2 Cross several earthen embankments intended to block vehicle traffic on the trail, which is now an old roadway. There are campsites in this area.

10.5 Turn right onto a narrow footpath and walk several hundred yards to a junction with Mine Bank Trail.

10.6 Turn left onto Mine Bank Trail and arrive back at the gravel parking lot.

Hike Information

Local Information
Staunton Convention & Visitors Bureau, Staunton, (540) 332-3865, www.visit staunton.com

Local Events/Attractions
Woodrow Wilson Birthplace & Museum, 24 N. Coalter St., Staunton, (540) 885-0897, www.woodrowwilson.org

The Cyrus McCormick Farm & Workshop, Raphine, (540) 377-2255, www.arec .vaes.vt.edu/shenandoah-valley. Site where McCormick invented the first mechanical reaper, with a blacksmith shop, gristmill, and museum. Admission is free.

Organizations
Tidewater Appalachian Trail Club, Norfolk, www.tidewateratc.com. Maintains several trails in the St. Mary's Wilderness.

29 Three Ridges

The term *wilderness* conjures visions of craggy peaks and untamed woodland far from the beaten track. Virginia's newest designated wilderness area, Three Ridges and The Priest region, isn't quite that. And that's not necessarily a bad thing. The Appalachian Trail (AT) traverses both peaks and the two AT shelters on either side of Three Ridges suits an overnight hike perfectly. The link between them, the Mau-Har Trail, follows Campbell Creek past a 40-foot waterfall and numerous smaller cascades. The treacherous terrain, soaring views, and sheer elevation gain makes this one of the most strenuous and dramatic hikes in Virginia.

Start: Swinging bridge over the Tye River, 0.1 mile downhill from VA 56
Distance: 13.8-mile lollipop
Hiking time: About 10 hours
Difficulty: Difficult due to the steep climb up Three Ridges via Chimney Rock, and rocky, eroded trail conditions along Campbell Creek
Trail surface: Dirt footpaths and old dirt forest roads run through steep mountain ridges, high-elevation rock outcrops, stream gorges, and sloping hardwood forests.
Land status: National forest and wilderness area

Nearest town: Lovingston, VA
Other trail users: Hunters (in season)
Accessibility: None
Canine compatibility: Dogs not permitted
Trail contact: Glenwood-Pedlar Ranger District, Natural Bridge Station; (540) 291-2188; www.fs.usda.gov/gwj
Schedule: Open year-round
Fees/permits: None
Facilities/features: None
Maps: USGS Massies Mill, Horseshoe Mountain, Sherando, Big Levels

Finding the trailhead: From Lovingston, drive south on combined US 29/VA 56. In 4.6 miles, follow VA 56 west as it branches right, off US 29. In 4.9 miles, VA 56 merges with VA 151. Turn right and follow the combined VA 56/VA 151 north. In 2.7 miles, follow VA 56 west as it branches left off VA 151. Drive 6 miles on VA 56 as it crosses back and forth over the Tye River. Pass through the small communities of Massie Mill and Tyro. In 6 miles from the split from VA 151, turn left into a dirt parking area. GPS: N37 50.299' / W79 01.370'. *DeLorme: Virginia Atlas & Gazetteer:* Page 54, B4.

The Hike

The region surrounding the mountains of Three Ridges and The Priest packs gorgeous scenery and rugged terrain into a small area. Situated in Virginia's Blue Ridge Mountains and spread over 10 square miles, the two peaks boast an elevation gain of 3,000 feet and rank among the hardest climbs in Virginia. Approaching Three Ridges from the Tye River, the mountain soars 2,973 feet in 6 miles to an elevation of 3,970 feet. The Priest, visible from Three Ridges' southern cliffs and rock outcrops, offers an almost identical elevation gain. Standing at Harpers Creek and staring up

The authors in Three Ridges Wilderness.

the seemingly vertical ascent up Three Ridges leaves you with a feeling not often encountered in Virginia—that is, a feeling of being completely dwarfed by the land.

Hikes that start with this kind of bang are prone to ending with a whimper. The return along Campbell Creek on the Mau-Har Trail happily defies this notion. (The odd-sounding name *Mau-Har* is derived from the features it links: Maupin Field Shelter and Harpers Creek.) The trail downhill from Maupin Field Shelter is a narrow footpath etched into the steep-sided stream banks traversing loose rocks. Footing in some areas is as dangerous as the ascent of Three Ridges is difficult.

In 2000 President Clinton signed a bill designating 11,000 acres in The Priest and Three Ridges area as Virginia's seventeenth wilderness area. The Forest Service and Appalachian Trail Conference (ATC) have, since 1993, treated the area as wilderness in anticipation of this move. (Which includes, by the way, volunteers maintaining the AT by nonmechanical means. The ATC has held workshops on Three Ridges on the proper use of crosscut saws to fell trees 3 feet in diameter.) When the wilderness designation went to Washington, DC, in 2000, Nelson County residents and wilderness advocacy groups cited development pressures as a reason for protection. The land itself is too rugged for timber management, but it protects headwaters of three rivers: the Tye, Piney, and Rockfish Rivers. Two other streams, Campbell and Harpers Creeks, source from the slopes of Three Ridges itself. (Lest anyone think designating wilderness is a regular occurrence, the Three Ridges–The Priest Wilderness was the first for Virginia in thirteen years.)

Another view of why Three Ridges deserved wilderness protection comes on Chimney Rock, a well-placed rest and overlook on the AT along the south tip of the mountain. From this elevation of 3,204 feet, the rugged aspect of Virginia's Blue Ridge fills the horizon. Absent are long, parallel ridgelines that define Virginia's mountains to the west. Here, it appears a force punched the earth's crust from below, randomly pushing up steep-sided mountains etched with deep V-shaped gorges down their slopes. It's as clear a picture a hiker will receive of Virginia's dual mountain systems. The Blue Ridge Mountains originated in prehistoric volcanic activity. The Allegheny Mountains to the west, by contrast, evolved into long ridges and valleys during extensive folding and faulting of layered rock.

The ruggedness of Three Ridges has given rise to an unusual variation on old-growth trees. You won't find the enormous trunks and towering heights normally associated with centuries-old stands of oaks, hemlocks, and other ancient hardwoods here. Instead, it's small oaks—called Virginia orchard oaks—that qualify as old growth. They occupy the highest portions of Three Ridges, a factor that shaped both their appearance and their preservation. Why were they spared? They were simply too difficult to get to and remove.

Designation of Three Ridges as a wilderness completes a triumvirate of specially protected lands in the central Blue Ridge of Virginia that includes St. Mary's Wilderness and the special management area at Mount Pleasant. Special protection doesn't necessarily mean solitude, however. The 20-foot waterfall on Campbell Creek, 3 miles from VA 56 on the Mau-Har Trail will likely ensure Three Ridges remains a popular destination for day-trippers. St. Mary's remains the most heavily used of all Virginia's wilderness areas—reports of hikers carrying coolers up to the falls on St. Mary's River persist. Thankfully, the ascent from Harpers Creek Shelter to the highest point on Three Ridges is so severe, a backpack is all the weight that can be safely transported. And that's the way it should be.

Miles and Directions

0.0 Start at a parking area on the south side of VA 56. Cross the highway and descend 0.1 mile to a hand-built cable suspension bridge (reconstructed in 1992 by AT club members). Walk across the bridge and follow the white-blazed AT as it climbs on switchbacks through a forest of mixed hardwoods.

0.3 The AT levels out atop a small knob. It eases across the knob and in 0.1 mile begins another steep climb through an oak forest. During the climb, the slope downhill to the right segues into a field and apple orchard.

1.7 Turn right and follow the AT at a junction of the AT and Mau-Har Trail. The next mile is a descent to Harpers Creek.

Three Ridges

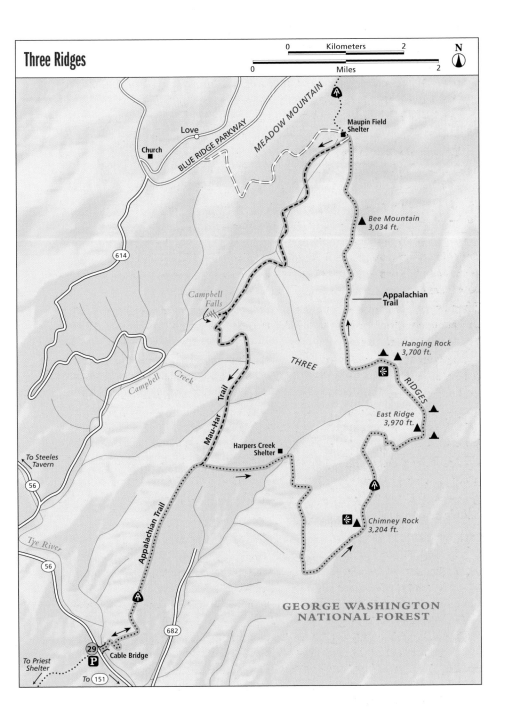

Kilometers 0 — 2
Miles 0 — 2

N

Love

Church

BLUE RIDGE PARKWAY

MEADOW MOUNTAIN

Maupin Field Shelter

Bee Mountain
3,034 ft.

614

Campbell Falls

Appalachian Trail

THREE

Hanging Rock
3,700 ft.

RIDGES

East Ridge
3,970 ft.

Campbell Creek

Mau-Har Trail

Harpers Creek Shelter

To Steeles Tavern

56

Chimney Rock
3,204 ft.

Tye River

56

Appalachian Trail

GEORGE WASHINGTON
NATIONAL FOREST

682

29

To Priest Shelter

P

Cable Bridge

To 151

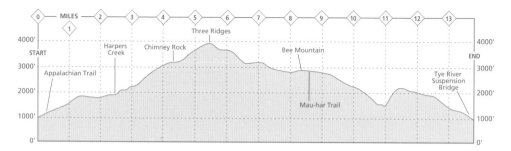

2.5 Cross Harpers Creek and hike upstream with the brook on your left. In 0.1 mile, turn right as the AT switches back and begins a steep ascent. **Note:** At this turn, a faded dirt road leads straight to the Harpers Creek Shelter in about 400 yards. The shelter sleeps six and there is room to pitch tents around it.

4.4 Pass Chimney Rock off the left side of the AT. This overlook, along with Hanging Rock on the north side of Three Ridges, offers the best views off Three Ridges. (The term *chimney* refers to the rock formation of solid, uniform blocks of granite beneath your feet.)

5.8 Begin a traverse of the highest point on Three Ridges. The landscape is flat. The grassy forest floor and widely spaced maple and oak trees give this summit approach the appearance of a wooded meadow.

6.1 Turn left at a double white blaze and follow the AT over the top of Three Ridges. **Note:** There are some well-used campsites in this area. Farther up, off the right side of the trail, are more secluded spots with access to small rock outcrops with views north to the Blue Ridge Parkway.

6.8 The dirt AT turns to open rock face as the trail crosses Hanging Rock. Views to the south take in The Priest and the Harpers Creek stream valley. The view makes this one of the most coveted tenting spots on this stretch of trail.

8.4 Cross Bee Mountain. After this 3,034-foot knob, the AT continues its descent on a narrow, rocky footpath. In 0.3 mile, it widens and turns grassy.

8.8 Reach Maupin Field Shelter and turn left onto a wide road. Cross the headwaters of Campbell Creek at the shelter and, in 300 yards, turn right and descend on the blue-blazed Mau-Har Trail along Campbell Creek.

9.3 Cross Campbell Creek twice in the next 0.3 mile. **Note:** Use caution on this narrow section of trail; portions are eroded.

10.0 The trail climbs into and out of a gorge where a stream, tumbling off Three Ridges' steep slope, empties into Campbell Creek.

10.5 Mau-Har Trail bears left and uphill, departing the stream valley for a return to the AT. (There is a swimming hole here.) Downstream 0.1 mile is Campbell Falls, a 40-foot waterfall.

12.1 Turn right onto the AT for a return to VA 56 and the Tye River.

13.7 Cross the Tye River on the suspended bridge.

13.8 Hike ends at parking lot on VA 56. (Author recommendation: Ditch the pack, return to stream, and soak yourself in the icy cool of the Tye River.)

Standing on Chimney Rock on the AT overlooking the Harpers Creek Valley.

Hike Information

Local Information

Nelson County Convention & Visitors Bureau, Lovingston, (800) 282-8223, www .nelsoncounty.com

Local Events/Attractions

Waltons Mountain Museum, Schuyler, (434) 831-2000, www.waltonmuseum.org. The school attended by Earl Hammer Jr., creator of *The Waltons,* preserves sets from this classic '70s television series. Open first Sun in Mar until first Sun in Nov.

Spring Wildflower Symposium, Wintergreen, held in May, (434) 325-7451

Lodging

Wintergreen Resort, Wintergreen, (800) 266-2444, www.wintergreenresort.com. Lodging in ridgetop condos, a nature foundation, a wilderness school, and 30 miles of its own hiking trails.

Organizations

Tidewater Appalachian Trail Club, Norfolk, www.tidewateratc.com. Maintains the Mau-Har Trail.

30 Mount Pleasant

Mount Pleasant must rank as one of Virginia's most aptly named peaks. Few hikes, if any, offer so much for so little work. For the price of a small elevation gain, hikers can climb two of the Blue Ridge's highest peaks on a loop trail that is, for lack of a better phrase, quite pleasant. Steep, rocky climbs along the final miles to Mount Pleasant will appease the gung ho hiker. Otherwise, it's easy hiking on wide paths and old roads through thick masses of rhododendron and mountain laurel; forests of oak, hickory, and beech; and small pockets of high-grass open forest.

Start: Parking area on FR 48, 0.3 mile past a forest gate at Hog Camp Gap

Distance: 4.8-mile loop

Hiking time: About 4 hours

Difficulty: Moderate due to a long uphill approach along the Henry Lanum Loop Trail and a single, steep climb on Mount Pleasant Spur Trail

Trail surface: Dirt roads and forest footpaths lead through open rock formations, fields, open peaks, mountain meadows, remnant chestnut forests, steep cliffs, and along streams.

Land status: National forest special management area

Nearest town: Buena Vista, VA

Other trail users: Hunters (in season)

Accessibility: None

Canine compatibility: Dogs permitted

Trail contact: Glenwood-Pedlar Ranger District, Natural Bridge Station; (540) 291-2188; www.fs.usda.gov/gwj

Schedule: Open year-round

Fees/permits: None

Facilities/features: None

Maps: USGS Montebello, Forks of Buffalo

Finding the trailhead: From Buena Vista, drive east on US 60 for 8 miles to the town of Oronoco. Turn left onto VA 634 (Coffey Town Road) at a small general store. In 1.7 miles, turn right onto VA 755 (Wiggins Spring Road), which turns into a rough gravel FR 48 and veers right in 1.4 miles. Continue on FR 48 across the Appalachian Trail (AT) in 1.4 miles. Come to a fork and sign for Mount Pleasant in 0.2 mile. Turn right and go 0.2 mile to the parking area. GPS: N37 45.553' / W79 11.338'. *DeLorme: Virginia Atlas & Gazetteer:* Page 54, B2.

The Hike

The wind—you notice it first, and it never really goes away. Long gusts wrap around Mount Pleasant's highest point, a 4,090-foot exposed rock face with views in all directions. It chaffs cheeks and hands as you stare out to the low-lying Piedmont rolling east from the mountain. Falcons or some other raptor too far off to distinguish with certainty circle on the upward-spiraling currents. A blurry rush fills your ears, and soon after it chills your bones.

You descend off the peak, but the wind isn't done yet. In an under-grown forest gap below the Mount Pleasant summit, streaks of air rustle a thin forest canopy.

The view from the top of Mount Pleasant National Scenic Area, one of only seven such designations in the county.

Sunlight leaks through a patchwork of young oak and poplar, playing crazy angles with pole-size tree trunks. As the day lengthens, the wind picks up strength. Streaks of light and shadows interlace across the woodland. Grass bristles in the breeze. Here, a circle of light stretches halfway up a tree trunk. There, the setting sun alights on branch tips of an oak. In the darkness that drops suddenly, the wind remains, wrapping around you as it races through the trees.

Wind generates some of the Virginia mountain's most severe storms. As systems of high and low pressure move eastward across the mountains, the haphazard arrangement of steep-sided mountains and deep valleys creates small tempests. Under proper conditions, a storm pocket will wreak sizable damage. Far more common, however, are isolated windthrows (aka downbursts or microbursts), where a sudden, fierce storm has torn down, snapped, or uprooted a few acres of trees. These are the seemingly out-of-place gaps in an otherwise solid forest that appear suddenly as you approach Mount Pleasant from the southwest. These gaps lack the clear, defined lines of a meadow. A rash of subcanopy vegetation, plants such as Virginia creeper or poison ivy, blur the line between forest and open space. Grasses that normally perish in the shadows of a forest canopy lend the subforest a pastoral look. To a bone-weary hiker, they appear as a perfectly peaceful spot to camp. Closer inspection, however, shows mounded soil where trees came uprooted, indicating a violent episode sometime in the past.

Disturbances, whether natural or man-made, have long been a part of the Mount Pleasant landscape. Meadows atop Cole Mountain, in the southern portion of the 7,580-acre Mount Pleasant Special Management Area, date from a time when private landowners grazed livestock (indicated by place names such as Cow Camp Gap and Hog Camp Gap). Maintaining the open fields through prescribed burns and timber management kept Mount Pleasant from being named a federal wilderness. Instead, in 1994 it was designated a special management area, a status that allows forest rangers to keep the fields open and clear. Although much smaller, the fields inevitably invite comparisons to the high-country meadows of Mount Rogers National Recreation Area.

The southern slope of Cole Mountain drops into the North Fork Buffalo River, and from this stream rises Chestnut Ridge, a long ascending buttress that leads to Mount Pleasant's peak. Unfortunately, the ridge's name only reminds us of when the American chestnut tree blanketed the Appalachian forest. Here's a reminder that ecological disturbances come in many forms, not just wind. Consider as you descend along the trail that a forest canopy once rose 100 feet and higher overhead, that tree trunks measured 10 feet in diameter. "No greater catastrophe has ever befallen a tree in our time," Roger Tory Peterson wrote of the chestnut blight. That may well be an understatement. Imported from Asia, the blight—a fungus that appears as a black canker on the tree trunk—spread virulently down the Appalachian chain, destroying, in a span of twenty years, an estimated 3.5 million trees. (Look for signs of chestnut blight beyond Pompey Mountain as you hike the Henry Lanum Loop Trail away from Mount Pleasant.) It also deprived today's hiker the opportunity to see this once strong tree grow past head-height—the size at which, today, the blight destroys chestnut trees. This is a humbling status for a tree once considered North America's most productive.

Hope, however, is not lost. Biologists believe they now have an American chestnut that is 95 percent resistant to the blight. Here in Virginia, the American Chestnut Cooperator's Foundation is experimenting with grafting techniques in the Warm Springs Ranger District of the George Washington National Forest. This technique takes young American chestnuts with no signs of blight and grafts resistant chestnut stems onto them. The hope is that the tree will produce nuts with blight-resistant genetics. In the Lesane State Forest, located in Virginia's mountain region, three American chestnuts were grafted in a similar manner in 1980. Cankers appeared, but botanists injected them with a hypovirulence—essentially a virus that attacked the blight that was attacking the tree. Presently, the three trees survive, while around them untreated specimens die off. A reason, perhaps, to hope.

Mount Pleasant

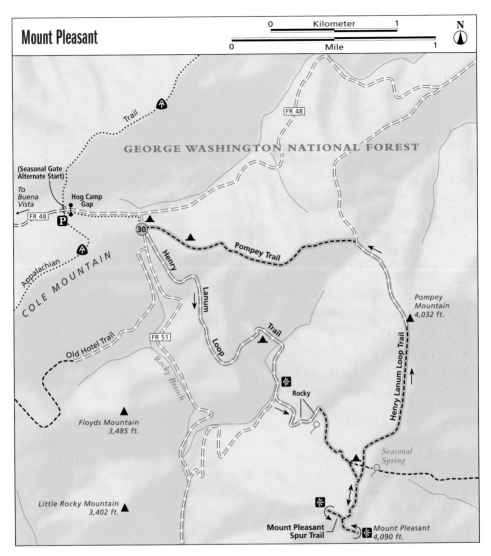

Miles and Directions

0.0 Start from a trail board in the parking area on FR 51. Walk straight past the trail board and follow the blue-blazed Henry Lanum Loop Trail as it descends gently on a dirt road. **Note:** The Pompey Trail, which is the return leg of this loop hike, departs from this parking area. It climbs left from the trail board on a dirt road.

0.8 Cross two seasonal streams. The trail slowly arcs right and continues to descend.

1.5 Turn left at a double blaze and climb. The trail, a bit rockier, crosses a stream. A mature hardwood forest covers the slopes, replacing the fields and gaps at lower elevations.

1.7 Turn right at another junction with an unmarked forest road. The trail is now a footpath and crosses several seasonal drainages. **Note:** Do not count on water from these sources during summer or fall.

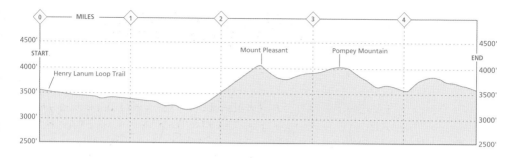

1.9 A relentless climb marks the approach to Mount Pleasant. The trail switches back several times. Large boulders along the trail make for convenient rest points.

2.3 Turn right onto the Mount Pleasant Trail and begin a final ascent of Mount Pleasant.

2.6 Reach the open rock face of Mount Pleasant's 4,090-foot summit. To return to the Henry Lanum Loop Trail, turn and descend 0.3 mile on the Mount Pleasant Trail. Before doing so, however, take time to soak in the views that encircle the mountain. Far eastward rolls the Piedmont. To the north is Pompey Mountain. Chestnut Ridge approaches the mountain from the south. Through the valley south of the mountain runs the Buffalo River.

2.9 Intersect the Henry Lanum Loop Trail and hike straight ahead. As you descend off the mountain, continue straight ahead. **Note:** A sign points to a spring right of the trail. It is a steep drop to the water source, which turns out to be hardly reliable.

3.0 The blue-blazed trail crosses a saddle between Mount Pleasant and Pompey Mountain. Several gaps in the forest open up as you walk through a grassy landscape.

3.2 The trail passes just to the left of Pompey Mountain. (Although only a few feet shorter than Mount Pleasant, Pompey Mountain is wooded with no views.) After passing the summit, the trail drops hard down the north slope.

3.6 Turn left onto a narrow footpath that wends its way through a spare forest notable for the waist-high grass. The trail climbs and reenters forest land, where rhododendron form a brief tunnel. There are campsites off either side of the trail along this section.

4.1 Cross a small knob and begin a descent to the parking area.

4.8 Hike ends at the parking area on FR 51.

Hike Information

Local Information

Lexington Visitor Center, Lexington, (877) 453-9822, www.lexingtonvirginia.com

Local Events / Attractions

Theater at Lime Kiln, (540) 463-5375, www.theateratlimekiln.org

Honorable Mentions: Blue Ridge Parkway

Z. Torry Ridge-Mill Creek Loop

A long trek that departs from White Oak Campground at Sherando Lake. Reach the lake via the Blue Ridge Parkway, milepost 16. This Blue Ridge hike has it all: mountains and streams, blueberries, rhododendron, and the convenience of a base camp with showers and flush toilets. (540) 291-2188. GPS: N37 55.226' / W79 00.382'. *DeLorme: Virginia Atlas & Gazetteer:* Page 54, A3.

AA. Humpback Rocks

A challenging day hike off the Blue Ridge Parkway 6 miles south of Rockfish Gap and I-64. Trailhead located at milepost 6. Humpback Rocks is a 3,080-foot outcrop of greenstone with wide views west to the Shenandoah Valley. The hike to the rocks is 1 mile on the Appalachian Trail. Humpback Mountain and more views await another mile down the trail. (540) 291-2188. GPS: N37 58.101' / W78 53.781'. *DeLorme: Virginia Atlas & Gazetteer:* Page 55, A5.

BB. Crabtree Falls

Trailhead is 17 miles northeast of Buena Vista on VA 56. This 3-mile trail runs along a creek that has five major cascades, overlooks, and ends at a parking lot on VA 828. The cumulative 1,200-foot drop in elevation along Crabtree Creek makes this one of the highest waterfalls east of the Mississippi. The Forest Service has built steps and installed railings along the trail to aid with hiking over treacherous terrain. (540) 291-2188. GPS: N37 51.071' / W79 04.749'. *DeLorme: Virginia Atlas & Gazetteer:* Page 54, B3.

CC. Whetstone Ridge

A point-to-point hike with the northern trailhead on the Blue Ridge Parkway, milepost 29, and southern access on VA 603, northeast of Buena Vista. This is the longest trail in the Glenwood-Pedlar Ranger District of the George Washington–Jefferson National Forest. Notable for views of Three Ridges, The Priest, and Adams Peak. (540) 291-2188. GPS: N37 52.179' / W79 08.867'. *DeLorme: Virginia Atlas & Gazetteer:* Page 54, B2.

DD. Apple Orchard Falls-Cornelius Creek Loop Trail

Begin at Sunset Field Overlook near milepost 78 on the Blue Ridge Parkway for this 7.5-mile loop. Two-hundred-foot waterfalls and old-growth forest are the highlights of this special management area. (540) 291-2188. GPS: N37 30.458' / W79 31.420'. *DeLorme: Virginia Atlas & Gazetteer:* Page 53, D6.

Southwest Highlands

Southwest Highlands cover two distinct geological regions of the state: a southwest portion of the Valley & Ridge province, and the Appalachian Plateau of far southwest Virginia. This is the land of timber, iron ore, and coal—and more recently, natural gas production. The rugged terrain, coupled with its distance from metropolitan centers on the East Coast, gives the area a remoteness that adds to its allure as a destination.

Rivers shape and define this region as much as the mountains. The New River, the oldest flowing body of water on the North American continent, flows northwest out of the North Carolina hills. Moving in the opposite direction is the Roanoke River. Farther south, the Clinch and Powell Rivers flow along deep troughs between tall mountain ridges, their supply feeding the Tennessee River. Most spectacular of all is Russell Fork, viewed from atop the 1,000-foot cliff walls where it passes over the Virginia-Kentucky border.

The forces that wrought southwest Virginia's mountains are inseparable from those elsewhere in the state: volcanic activity along the Blue Ridge, sedimentary rock in the valley and ridge region, then periods of heat, pressure, folding, and faulting. Amid this, one area stands apart. Pine Mountain, along the Virginia-Kentucky border, is a stellar example of thrust plate movement, where one piece of the earth's crust ramped up onto another. North from Pound Gap, the edge of the mountain drops steeply into Kentucky, while to the east, the terrain rolls downhill.

For generations, southwest Virginia remained an isolated region, both from the state and the country as a whole. Even after timber and coal barons brought riches in the form of logging and mining, pockets of poverty persisted. The booms in economic and cultural life were grand times. Big Stone Gap lured vacationers from New York City and royalty from abroad. When busts hit, they hit hard. Throughout the twentieth century, quality of life hinged on the price of coal. Since the 1970s, demand and price for Virginia coal has declined. That has forced leaders to find other economic stimuli, chief among them is outdoor recreation. Given the natural beauty of the region, this is a happy development for hikers and mountain bike riders alike.

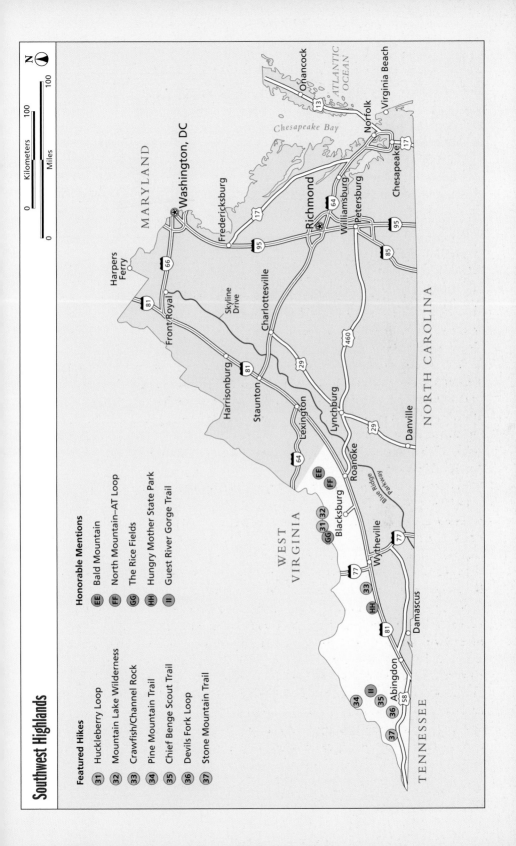

Southwest Highlands

Featured Hikes

31 Huckleberry Loop
32 Mountain Lake Wilderness
33 Crawfish/Channel Rock
34 Pine Mountain Trail
35 Chief Benge Scout Trail
36 Devils Fork Loop
37 Stone Mountain Trail

Honorable Mentions

EE Bald Mountain
FF North Mountain–AT Loop
GG The Rice Fields
HH Hungry Mother State Park
II Guest River Gorge Trail

The Hikes

31. Huckleberry Loop
32. Mountain Lake Wilderness
33. Crawfish/Channel Rock
34. Pine Mountain Trail
35. Chief Benge Scout Trail
36. Devils Fork Loop
37. Stone Mountain Trail

Honorable Mentions

EE. Bald Mountain
FF. North Mountain–AT Loop
GG. The Rice Fields
HH. Hungry Mother State Park
II. Guest River Gorge Trail

31 Huckleberry Loop

Two of Virginia's long trails, the Appalachian Trail and the Allegheny Trail, pass through Peters Mountain Wilderness, a patch of forestland on the steep ridge that constitutes the Virginia–West Virginia border. But neither well-traveled trail quite captures what it means for a forest to turn wild as well as the Huckleberry Loop. The trail down Dismal Creek on the eastern slope of Peters Mountain is as rough as they come, overrun with rhododendron, blocked by blowdowns, and often lost altogether in the streambed. There are car-size boulders en route, and rotted logs litter the creek bed. This trail sums up everything a wilderness should be: beautiful, difficult, and, in the end, extremely satisfying.

Start: Dirt road off VA 722/Glen Alton Drive
Distance: 8.0-mile loop
Hiking time: About 4 hours
Difficulty: Moderate due to easy hiking on clearly marked, well-graded trails, with one very difficult stretch down Dismal Creek
Trail surface: Dirt woods paths and dirt roads lead through hardwood forest slopes, fields, a river valley, and streambed.
Land status: National forest
Nearest town: Pembroke, VA

Other trail users: Hunters (in season)
Accessibility: None
Canine compatibility: Dogs permitted
Trail contact: Eastern Divide Ranger District, Blacksburg; (540) 552-4641
Schedule: Open year-round. Hunting is permitted in national forests, with Nov through Jan the busiest season.
Fees/permits: None
Facilities/features: None
Map: USGS Interior

Finding the trailhead: From Pembroke, drive north on US 460 for 2 miles and turn right onto VA 635. There is good signage for White Rocks NRA and Glen Alton. After 5.6 miles, follow VA 635 as it turns left and crosses Stony Creek. Drive another 8.1 miles and turn left onto gravel VA 722/ Glen Alton Drive. Immediately cross Stony Creek and, in 0.2 mile, turn left onto Kelly Flats Road. In 0.1 mile, there will be a forest gate that may only be open during hunting season. If closed, park here (do not block road) and walk 0.4 mile to the trailhead. GPS: N37 25.597' / W80 33.331'. *DeLorme: Virginia Atlas & Gazetteer:* Page 41, A5.

The Hike

Dismal Branch runs a noisy route for 3 miles down the slope of Peters Mountain. In a gully between Pine Swamp Ridge and Huckleberry Ridge, a series of obstacles force stream and hiker to detour. A blown-down tree too big to either crawl over or under sends the hiker through rhododendron so dense it requires pushing back thickets with both arms. At this point, Dismal Creek disappears underground beneath a rock slide. Five paces downhill, this unsinkable stream spurts from beneath the rocks and runs around a huge boulder. The stream disappears beneath rocks once more, then returns to the surface to spill off a small rock cleft into a pool. So calm is this pool, so

A cable assists a stream crossing on the Huckleberry Loop Trail.

calm is the water, it's almost as if the stream is making a statement: "See, that wasn't so hard, was it?"

Huckleberry Loop, an 8-mile trail through Peters Mountain Wilderness and pastoral Kelly Flats, cannot be judged by one difficult stretch of trail. But it's a fact: Memories of Dismal Creek will stay with a hiker long after sweet-smelling hemlocks along Dixon Creek and the quiet solitude of the North Fork fade. The reason is simple. Dismal Creek captures the essence of wilderness in Virginia, a place where plants and land are free to take whatever shape nature deems appropriate.

Virginia's forestland is, by and large, comprised of second- and third-generation trees. Axes, crosscut saws, plows, shovels, dynamite, fire, even the hands of the herb and mushroom collector—all have reshaped the land, plants, and trees. Clear-cutting of Virginia forests reached a peak between 1890 and 1920, when nearly every usable tree was cut and shipped to the sawmill. There's a rusted railroad car wheel lying in the brush alongside the North Fork, evidence of this area's logging past. The wide, flat terrain along the stream was the grade on which railroad cars ran, loaded with wood. Few areas escaped the clear-cutting. Where old-growth timber stands, it's as much thanks to chance as any intent to preserve the trees.

Despite all this, forests are adaptable. Left unchecked, climax species will return on land clear-cut for lumber. On Peters Mountain, oak and hickory will someday stand tall. (Efforts are ongoing, but it's debatable whether chestnut, once a dominant tree of the Southern Appalachians, will ever return. A blight, *Cryphonectria parasitica*, attacks the chestnut in its infancy. The tree, which once towered 100 feet high, may grow head-height before succumbing.) At lower elevations, nature has a head start on 40 acres near Dixon Branch. Here you'll find a stand of old-growth eastern hemlocks, a climax tree that normally requires generations to reach its peak growth. It took hundreds of years to reach the breadth of those that stand along Dixon Branch—a staggering thought, given the timber industry's penchant to shear mountaintops of all usable lumber.

Forest recovery begins in the forest understory, where competition for sunlight and water is stiff among the many small trees and shrubs. Hardly the stars of any forest, spicebush, witch hazel, black haw, and maple leaf viburnum fill an important niche.

The author about to enter a dense rhododendron grove on the Huckleberry Loop Trail.

Fox, grouse, and pheasant eat the fruit, bark, and leaves of these trees. White-tailed deer will tug on clusters of blackish-blue berries on the black haw, or nibble the bark off a mountain maple sapling. Huckleberry Ridge and neighboring Peters Mountain are home to a population of black bear, and the blueberry and huckleberry patches that cover higher slopes are a primary food source for this animal. Heath-type shrubs, especially, are dynamos. A huckleberry (a bit darker in the bark than the blueberry and peppered with telltale yellow resin spots on the leaves) has ten seeds per berry. Its cousin, the blueberry, has more than one hundred seeds in each blue ball.

A half mile into this loop, where the trail turns off a gravel road and rises on a gentle shoulder of Locust Knob, shrubby plants gobble up the dry, leafy forest real estate. It stands in stark contrast to the shaded, moist terrain along Dixon Branch and, especially, Dismal Branch, both of which lie ahead. On these dry slopes, mountain laurel and rhododendron are conspicuously absent. You'll see young chestnut oak and maple trees, flowering dogwood with its characteristic white blossom in springtime, and sassafras, a curious tree with three distinctly different leaves. Along Dixon and Dismal Branches, by comparison, the moist ground supports a habitat marked by slicks of rhododendron, mosses, and ferns. Taller still are the hemlock, tulip poplar, sweet buckeye, and, most beautiful in spring, mountain silverbell. As different as these two environments appear, both are less than one hundred years recovered from logging.

Sassafras is one clue to a forest's ongoing recovery, and the small tree is plentiful in this area. Sassafras's three leaves are distinct: one oblong, one shaped like a mitten, the other lobed in the center. During spring and summer, a hiker is likely to brush past one without a second notice. In fall, however, the tree's brilliant red foliage catches your attention; sassafras is one of the more showy autumn plants in southern forests. Safrole, a clear oil extracted from the bark, has long been used to flavor root beer, teas, and stews. (Recently, safrole has been shown to cause cancer in laboratory experiments. The FDA bans use of the oil in foodstuffs.) I can't help but pass along, however, that boiling the leaves and twigs for tea produces an intense buzz. I now know that it's sassafras roots—not twigs and leaves—that have for years flavored teas and root beer. But when you've forgotten your edible plant book and you're feeling adventurous, strange things happen.

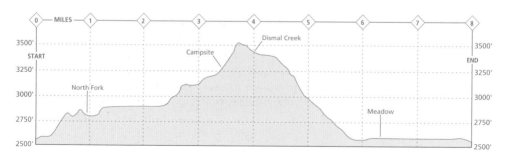

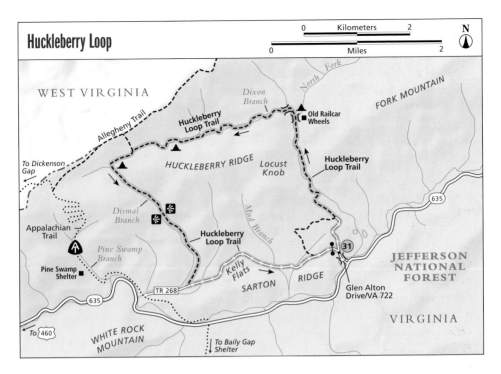

Miles and Directions

0.0   Start at the red Forest Service gate on VA 722. The Huckleberry Loop Trail follows VA 722 for 0.4 mile and is blazed with single yellow triangles nailed on trees on the left side of the road.

0.4   Turn right off the gravel road onto a well-blazed narrow woods path through chestnut oak and maple. A small yellow and brown sign with a hiker symbol marks this turnoff.

0.9   Thick stands of rhododendron line the descent to the North Fork, where you'll turn left and hike upstream, climb a short hill, then drop to the river's edge to cross.

1.1   Cross the North Fork and hike up the right side of the stream on a flat, narrow woods path. Small hemlocks and rhododendron separate the trail and stream. Up the slope to the right of the trail is a young hardwood forest. Mayapple grows along the path, and rotting logs and trees host a variety of coral and trumpet mushrooms. **Note:** This trail used to be called Flat Peter—a hybrid of Kelly Flats and Peters Mountain—and some brochures and books still refer to it by that name.

1.9   Pass by an unblazed trail that branches right off Huckleberry Loop Trail. In a few yards, pass rusted pieces of a railcar in the underbrush on the right side of the trail.

2.0   Pass over the North Fork on a wooden footbridge. There is a nice streamside campsite on the opposite bank. Bear left out of the campsite, follow Dixon Branch upstream a few feet and cross it on three moss-coated logs. The trail now follows Dixon Branch up the north side of Huckleberry Ridge to a saddle between the ridge and Peters Mountain. The route is lined with hemlocks and rhododendron. Numerous stream crossings make for a wet hike during the spring.

3.4   Reach a campsite on Dixon Branch just before your seventh stream crossing. On the other side, trail conditions deteriorate steadily. Logs block the trail and stretches of the path are very rocky. The next half mile brings four more stream crossings.

4.0   As the trail approaches the headwaters of Dismal Branch, it passes through a fern glade and a tall canopy forest dominated by tulip poplar. After a stretch of trail overgrown with mountain laurel and berry bushes, you'll reach Dismal Branch and turn southeast to travel downstream past a nice campsite with a fire ring.

4.7   A massive blowdown forces you off the trail and into the creek bed. Here, the stream runs through narrow channels formed by car-size boulders, then under a rock slide. It's audible, but you can't see it. The next 0.5 mile brings numerous stream crossings. At points, the trail and stream run the same course.

5.9   Exit Peters Mountain Wilderness. The trail, which has slowly changed from torturous, rocky streambed to wide, grassy road, turns left to return through the fields of Kelly Flats, a series of old fields flanked by Huckleberry and Sarton Ridges.

6.3   Enter a clearing bordered by plantations of white pines and wide-open fields of grass, milkweed, and other weeds. The trail follows a rutted road along the upper edges of the meadow.

8.0   Reach a forest gate, pass through, and turn left onto a gravel road. The parking area is a few short feet uphill.

Hike Information

Local Information

Giles County Administration, Pearisburg, (540) 921-2525, www.gilescounty.org

Local Events/Attractions

Glen Alton, in Giles County, is a 304-acre farm purchased by the national forest in 1999. Besides farm buildings, there are ponds, canals, dams, and orchards. Call the USFS at (540) 552-4641 in Blacksburg for more information, or visit http://giles county.org/glenalton.html.

Lodging

Nesselrod on the New, Radford, (540) 731-4970, www.nesselrod.com. A B&B on the cliffs overlooking the New River.

White Rocks National Recreation Area Campground, Giles County, (540) 552-4641

Claytor Lake State Park, Montgomery County, (540) 643-2500, www.dcr.virginia .gov/state_parks/cla.shtml. Cabins and camping are available.

32 Mountain Lake Wilderness

Hear a name like Mountain Lake Wilderness, and thoughts of Caribbean-blue lakes and tall peaks might pop into mind. In fact, Virginia's only true mountain lake sits outside this, the largest of all Virginia wilderness areas. And most of your climbing is done in the car getting here. Which is just fine, really, because this saves your breath for exploring upland bogs on Lone Pine Peak, slabs of Tuscarora sandstone on Salt Pond Mountain, and a red spruce glade on Potts Mountain. Trails through Mountain Lake Wilderness are well marked and maintained (the Appalachian Trail is the most-traveled route).

Start: Parking lot for the War Spur Loop on the right side of VA 613
Distance: 10.2-mile loop
Hiking time: About 6 hours
Difficulty: Moderate due to distance, steep climbs, and poor trail markings on Potts Mountain
Trail surface: Narrow dirt woodland paths lead through fern glades, mountaintop swamps, and steep rock outcrops.
Land status: National forest wilderness
Nearest town: Blacksburg, VA

Other trail users: Hikers only
Accessibility: None
Canine compatibility: Dogs permitted
Trail contact: Eastern Divide Ranger District, Blacksburg; (540) 552-4641
Schedule: Open year-round. Hunting is permitted on national forest property, with Nov through Jan the busiest season.
Fees/permits: None
Facilities/features: None
Maps: USGS Waiteville, Interior

Finding the trailhead: From Blacksburg, drive north on US 460 for 10 miles and turn right onto VA 700. In 6.8 miles, pass through Mountain Lake Resort. Here, VA 700 changes to VA 613 and wraps around the west side of Mountain Lake. The road turns to gravel 0.7 mile past the hotel. After another 0.9 mile the road forks; bear left. The parking area for the War Spur–Chestnut Loop is 3.5 miles past the resort. **Option:** If using a shuttle, drive a second car 2.1 miles up VA 613 to a parking area for Wind Rock and the Appalachian Trail (AT). GPS: N37 23.445' / W80 30.481'. *DeLorme: Virginia Atlas & Gazetteer:* Page 41, A5.

The Hike

Admit it. Hiking is an obsession. The gear, the trail, the miles—all of it has consumed your life. The new grill in the backyard stands idle while you sprint from work on Friday to meet that mountaintop on Saturday. The lawn needs mowing, but you've got no time for such frivolity. On the trail, your mantra is *Farther, Faster.*

Suddenly, after a long, sweaty day in pursuit of the almighty loop, you encounter the unusual. Maybe it's a great view. Maybe it's a morning mist rising off a wildlife pond, or a stream's song as it cuts through crowded woodland. Whatever form it takes, these are as unexpected and pleasant as a breeze on a hot day. They stir something

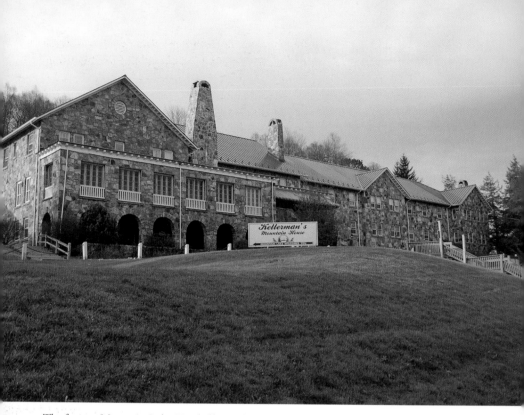

The famous Mountain Lake Hotel, filming location for "Dirty Dancing," is on the edge of the Mountain Lake Wilderness.

deep within. The mellow you, the one who tugs at your conscience, says, *Hey, hold up. Stay here a while.*

Because the experience is both unusual and infrequent, coming across an upland bog ranks as that type of special moment. The observant hiker finds upland bogs in small depressions on a flat mountaintop or in broad gaps. They often form the headwaters of streams—even when the stream doesn't appear to be in the immediate area. Steeped in water year-round, an upland bog hosts plants that wouldn't survive 10 feet away in dry, gray-brown soil of the deciduous forest. Animals converge on it as if it were a desert oasis, both to eat and sometimes to be eaten.

Salt Pond Mountain in Mountain Lake Wilderness holds the right ingredients for an upland bog. The highest point is a flat pan of forest stretching a half mile in a northwest direction. The forest is mostly skinny hardwoods—oak, beech, poplar. As War Spur Connector Trail approaches a downhill stretch that will end at the Appalachian Trail (AT), trees on the left give way to a grassy patch. It looks at first glance like a nice campsite. One step into the clearing, the ground turns soft and wet. Perhaps, you think as you pull a foot from the mire, this is why there are no fire rings. Walking the perimeter of the bog, you see Indian pipe stem and Virginia chain fern. Unseen to the eye, the fern spreads long, thin rhizomes beneath the soil. New ferns grow off this rhizome while roots sink deep into the bog, with its layered leaf rot. Bogs hold water like a sponge, ensuring lush conditions even in drought.

After you've climbed to the summit of Lone Pine Peak, you'll notice another upland opening on the right side of the AT on Lone Pine Peak. Here, the ground is drier. Laurel and winterberry add a shrubby, dense appearance to the forest understory encircling the bog. Camouflaged and positioned carefully, you might see a deer pick its way through mountain maple and scrub oak, nibbling on the grass or ferns covering the wet, spongy earth. In August or September, the red or gray fox might approach a mountain winterberry for a mouthful of red fruit. Long-stalked holly, similar in appearance to the winterberry, grows exclusively in the moist conditions of upland bogs. The chief difference between these two deciduous shrubs is the flowers: Long-stalked holly's flowers are a yellow-green color; the flower of a mountain winterberry has white petals.

Wind Rock on the Potts Mountain Trail.

Sit next to either bog for a spell and the sound of busy birds calling and singing fills your ears. If it's early spring, it's a male songbird who has arrived early from southern environs to prepare a nest. You might hear black and white wrens, a solitary vireo, and robins. You might see a tufted titmouse flit from thin branch to ground for a quick forage among the leaf litter. But whether you can tell the song of an eastern wood-pewee (*pee-ah-wee*) from a white-breasted nuthatch's call (a rapid *wer-wer-wer*) isn't really the point. Purse your lips and make up your own song, then see what kind of bird comes to investigate.

The best of Mountain Lake Wilderness's bogs comes last. In the Southern Appalachians, where you find red spruce, you'll find Fraser fir (like a married couple, they're always together, thus giving rise to the nicknames: he-balsam for spruce and she-balsam for fir). Not so on Potts Mountain, a long, high ridge that forms the state border of Virginia and West Virginia. Potts Mountain lost its oak, chestnut, and red spruce in the first decade of the twentieth century—all, that is, except for small patches now protected by federal wilderness. A red spruce bog grows in the headwaters of Stony Creek on Potts Mountain's south-facing slope; there are strong ecological ties between this spot and the highland wilderness of Mount Rogers. Despite a difference in elevation of about 1,000 feet, both Little Wilson Creek Wilderness at Mount Rogers National Recreation Area (NRA) and Mountain Lake Wilderness Areas protect old-growth red spruce. It's worth pondering, as you sit next to this rarest of upland bogs, why the red spruce, the most common of the native spruce trees in the East and a mainstay of northern forests, is relegated to isolated spots here in Virginia. No matter what answer you arrive at, their rarity makes listening to that inner voice—the one that tells you *Stay here a while*—a lot easier.

Miles and Directions

0.0 Start at the parking area on VA 613. Enter the woods and immediately turn right onto the War Spur Loop Trail.

1.0 Reach a junction with War Spur Overlook Trail.

1.2 War Spur Overlook Trail ends at an overlook. Return to War Spur Loop Trail.

1.4 Turn right onto War Spur Loop Trail.

1.8 Reach War Spur Branch. In this dark stream valley, turn left and follow the trail as it leads upstream beneath old-growth hemlocks. **Side trip:** Experienced hikers can bushwhack

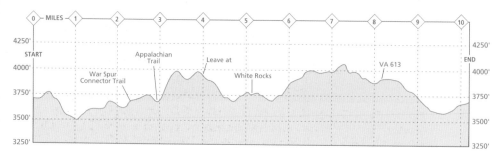

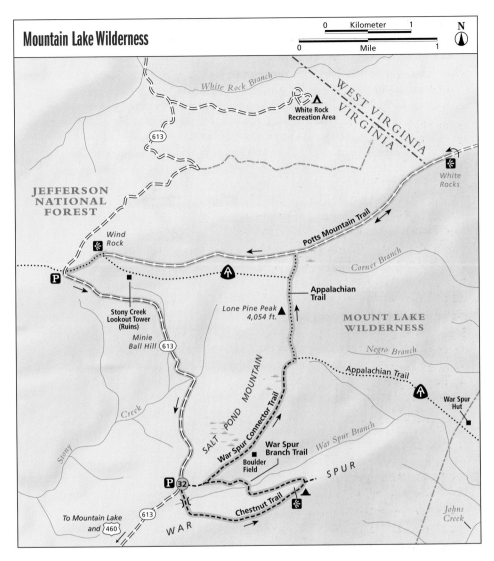

Mountain Lake Wilderness

Kilometer

0   Kilometer   1

0   Mile   1

N

White Rock Branch

WEST VIRGINIA
VIRGINIA

White Rock
Recreation Area

613

JEFFERSON
NATIONAL
FOREST

White
Rocks

Potts Mountain Trail

Corner Branch

Wind
Rock

P

Stony Creek
Lookout Tower
(Ruins)

Appalachian
Trail

Lone Pine Peak ▲
4,054 ft.

MOUNT LAKE
WILDERNESS

Minie
Ball Hill   613

Negro Branch

Appalachian Trail

Creek

SALT POND MOUNTAIN

War Spur Connector Trail

War Spur
Hut

Stony

War Spur
Branch Trail

War Spur Branch

Boulder
Field

P   32

SPUR

To Mountain Lake
and   460

613

Chestnut Trail

WAR

*Johns
Creek*

War Spur Branch downstream for 1.6 miles to the AT. Where War Spur Branch intersects with the AT, turn left onto the AT. In 75 yards, pass the War Spur Shelter on the right. The AT climbs steeply and, in 1 mile from the War Spur Shelter, intersects War Spur Connector Trail on the left. The first part of this side trip is a difficult bushwhack with many stream crossings. War Spur Branch is overgrown with mountain laurel and rhododendron, which hinders passage.

2.2   Reach a T junction of War Spur Loop Trail and War Branch Trail. Turn right onto the War Branch Trail. **Option:** A left turn leads 0.2 mile to the parking area on VA 613.

2.5   Scrub oak, Allegheny chinquapin, and witch hazel open onto a grassy, fern-ringed upland bog on the left side of the trail. A few feet past this on the right, a boulder field is visible through the trees. Large slabs of Tuscarora sandstone lay scattered over 3 or 4 acres. There are no tall cliffs or rock ledges—just disrupted, disjointed chunks of rock.

2.9 Turn left onto the AT and begin a short, steep ascent of Lone Pine Peak. You'll climb 335 feet in less than 0.5 mile to reach the wooded 4,054-foot summit.

3.7 Another upland bog opens up on the right side of the AT.

4.0 Double white blazes mark a hard left turn onto the AT. Instead of following the AT left, continue straight into the woods on a faint, unblazed path. In 0.1 mile, emerge from the woods onto Potts Mountain Trail, a wide, grassy forest road. A tall oak tree in the middle of the road marks this spot. Turn right onto Potts Mountain Trail and walk along the gently sloping ridgeline. **Note:** There are several campsites within the next mile.

5.2 Reach White Rocks, an exposed rock formation on Potts Mountain with overlooks onto Little Mountain and beyond to Stony Run. To the east you will see Johns Creek Mountain and the War Spur drainage. Turn and retrace your steps along Potts Mountain Trail.

6.3 Pass the tall oak that marks the spur trail to the AT; continue straight on Potts Mountain Trail. You may see faint white blazes on trees, leftovers from days when the AT followed Potts Mountain Trail.

7.1 Enter a large, sloping field overgrown with tall grass. The trail climbs from the bottom of the field to a clearing in the grass in the middle of the field. The trail then arcs gently right and reenters woods at the top of the field. Stay alert: There are no blazes or trail markers through this field. Several roads branch off from the clearing in the middle of the field.

7.3 Potts Mountain Trail passes through another clearing. Concrete pilings off the left side of the trail are all that remain of the Stony Creek lookout tower.

7.7 Potts Mountain Trail junctions with the AT, which enters from the left side. Off the right side of Potts Mountain Trail is Wind Rock, another overlook across to Fork Mountain and the West Virginia state line.

8.1 The AT ends at a gravel parking lot on VA 613. If you're shuttling, the hike ends here. If not, turn left and hike 2.1 miles on gravel VA 613 to the hike starting point.

10.2 Arrive back at the gravel parking area for the War Spur–Chestnut Loop.

Hike Information

Local Information

Giles County Administration, Pearisburg, (540) 921-2525, www.gilescounty.org

Lodging

Mountain Lake Hotel, Pembroke, (540) 626-7121, www.mountainlakehotel.com. The restaurant is open to the public.

White Rocks National Recreation Area Campground, Giles County, (540) 552-4641

Claytor Lake State Park, Montgomery County, (540) 643-2500

33 Crawfish/Channel Rock

Originating in the flat bottomland and old fields of Crawfish Valley, the Crawfish–Channel Rock Trail ascends Brushy Mountain on steep, narrow footpaths to run northeast parallel to Walker Mountain. En route, you'll cross the Tennessee Valley Divide, where Reed Creek and Bear Creek vividly illustrate the effects of the divide. Flowing off opposite sides of the divide, each enters separate, ever-expanding stream networks that eventually reach the Ohio River, albeit 100 miles distant from one another. Deer and raccoons forage along the stream edges; turkeys and ruffed grouse hunt for acorns on the slopes of Brushy and Walker Mountains. Beavers leave the most lasting impression: a two-stage dam you'll traverse on Bear Creek.

Start: Parking area at the dead end of FR 727 (Strawberry Road). As you enter the parking area, the trailhead is on a dirt road on the right.
Distance: 11.2-mile lollipop
Hiking time: About 6 hours
Difficulty: Moderate due to several steep climbs up Brushy Mountain
Trail surface: Dirt forest road and singletrack woods paths wind through stream valleys and old fields, along dry ridgetops, and up steep climbs.
Land status: National forest

Nearest town: Rural Retreat, VA
Other trail users: Mountain bikers, equestrians, and hunters (in season)
Accessibility: None
Canine compatibility: Dogs permitted
Trail contact: Eastern Divide Ranger District, Wytheville; (540) 552-4641
Schedule: Open year-round. Hunting is allowed in national forests, with the busiest season Nov through early Jan.
Fees/permits: None
Facilities/features: None
Map: USGS Rural Retreat

Finding the trailhead: From Rural Retreat, drive north on VA 90 for 0.8 mile to Staley Crossroads, where the road becomes VA 680. (If traveling on I-81, take exit 60 [Rural Retreat] and turn left on VA 680, 1.3 miles north of Rural Retreat). Take VA 680 for 2.6 miles, turn left onto VA 625, and follow it 4.2 miles to a fork in the road. Bear left onto FR 727, which is signed as Strawberry Road, a one-lane gravel road. Drive 1.8 miles and reach a large, circular turnaround area and parking for the trail. GPS: N36 57.916' / W81 18.916'. *DeLorme: Virginia Atlas & Gazetteer:* Page 23, A6.

The Hike

Traveling with surveyors into Cherokee Indian territory, eighteenth-century botanist William Bartram recorded a memorable scene while encamped northwest of Big Lick, Georgia: In a mountain stream, below a set of minor rapids, gold darters swarmed around small mounds made of rock and mud below the water surface. Periodically, crayfish rushed forth from the towers, "at which time a brilliant fight presented; the little gold-fish instantly fled from every side, darting through the transparent waters like streams of lightning," Bartram wrote.

A large bear print on the forest road leading to Crawfish Trail.

Crayfish, crawdads, freshwater lobsters, mud bugs—call them what you will, they're a fascinating part of a forest stream's ecology. The battle with "gold-fish" described by Bartram in his *Travels,* published in 1791, is a reminder of the surprisingly vicious underworld they inhabit. In a mountain stream, small fish regularly prey on one another. Around rock ledges near a creek's headwaters, chubs cannibalize their young. Trout circle in riffling water searching for lunch. A crayfish, sensing danger, flicks up a cloud of silt and scuttles backwards under a rock. When a predator approaches, schooling fish draw into a tight pack and flee upon sensing a chemical alarm emitted by one of their own. Tadpoles, too, scatter with a telltale odor. The alarmer, in doing so, cannot escape and sacrifices itself.

There's no guarantee that Reed Creek, a stocked trout stream running down Crawfish Valley between the steep slopes of Brushy and Walker Mountains, will yield the same battle royal Bartram observed. You'll see plenty of crawfish and their mud-and-rock mounds in the stream. It's these that make Reed Creek and Bear Creek—the two streams that define the lower elevations of this loop hike—great theater. By midsummer, the water level has dropped from spring highs, leaving isolated pools. Here, a myriad of life-forms—darters and shiners, crayfish, salamanders, and water bugs—play out their busy, and in some cases, very short lives.

Along stretches of these creeks, especially through Channel Rock Hollow, larger hemlock trees draw nourishment from the stream water. This evergreen splits and crumbles rocks with a tenacious root grip, contributing over time to a buildup of sediment in the small pools where the stream rests between cascades. Tennessee dace, a tiny fish with markings from olive to scarlet red, inhabit pools like this in Bear Creek. The dace is threatened; the only other community is on the Lick Creek in Bland County.

Easier to spot are the darts that return to the same pool in which they were born to lay eggs. Once it establishes residency, a fish will rarely venture from the area during spawning. One theory on the how and why of their return links the fish and the shoreline trees in a symbiotic relationship. Tree roots release organic molecules into the water and the fish may use the chemical as a homing signal.

Rising from the stream, the bottomlands in Crawfish Valley exhibit various stages of old-field succession. For 2 miles from the trailhead, fields drop gently left of the dirt road trail, reaching a fringe of trees that camouflage the stream. Ragweed grew tall the first year after the fields were abandoned. When it decomposes, this weed (the bane of hay fever sufferers) poisons the soil. Each subsequent year, the plant grows smaller and smaller until the stunted bunches of stalks, visible here, are all that remains. Queen Anne's lace with its telltale red spot—in folklore, a drop of Queen Anne's blood—sways on tall stalks. The flower is a member of the parsley family, with a tuber-like root resembling the carrot—it's also known as the wild carrot. Dig up the root in the autumn and it's the best carrot you've ever eaten. Beware, however: The plant looks similar to the water hemlock, an extremely poisonous (though tough to find) plant.

Black-eyed Susans bloom along the trail.

Along Bear Creek, the process of old-field succession is more advanced. This stream runs off the southwest side of the Tennessee Valley Divide. Skinny hardwoods and thickets of rhododendron grow alongside the stream. Poplar and its varieties, big tooth aspen and quaking aspen, are encroaching, step by step, on the old fields beyond the riverbanks. These hardwoods, disdained by lumber companies that wanted the harder chestnut and oaks, are pioneer species in the woody stage of old-field succession. Their tough seedlings can bear the exposure to sun and other elements that climax trees such as oak, hickory, or hemlock cannot. They reach top potential growth in fifty to sixty years, in the process creating the forest canopy that allows climax tree species to grow.

Overgrown fields are just one indicator along this hike that the land here was farmed. If you missed the more subtle clues—fruit trees, overgrown fields, barbwire, cut stone blocks—of past homesteaders, the board tacked onto an oak tree in a clearing near the trail's junction with the Appalachian Trail (AT) gives it away. The board reads Mozer's Place, marking the homesite of James Mozer, who farmed the upper reaches of Crawfish Valley at the turn of the last century. Lower in the valley, Simon Foglesong farmed 1,000 acres on Reed Creek in 1790; the family cemetery is on the south side of the stream on national forest land, as are the remnants of the homesite. Between these sites, plots of sorghum, a wild grain, dot the roadside. These are not indicators of someone following in the pioneer's footsteps. Rather, they're wildlife plots planted by the state Department of Conservation & Recreation for turkey and small songbirds.

From the valley floor, Brushy Mountain and its foothills frame Crawfish Valley on the east, and Walker Mountain rises to the west. The Wilderness Society calls this region one of the largest roadless areas in the Jefferson National Forest (referring to active forest roads, not the roads-turned-trails that comprise large parts of this loop). This and the presence of the Tennessee dace in lower Bear Creek make it a candidate for wilderness designation. The sense of isolation so often associated with a wilderness area creeps up on you on the steep climb up Brushy Mountain. Berry bushes crowd the narrow trail, scratching at your pant legs. Allegheny chinquapin and chestnut oak grow in the forest understory. Views in all directions are blocked by the dense understory of these thin trees. Your footsteps may flush a turkey. These

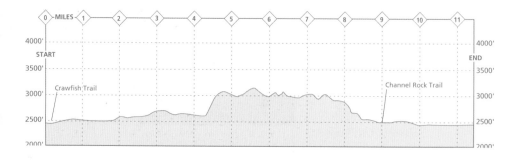

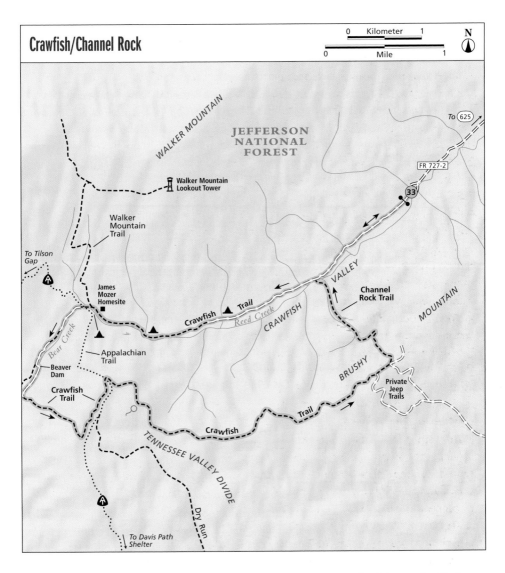

popular game birds awaken the hiker who camps on Brushy Mountain. Before sunrise, the birds call out to one another, a signal to head downslope to the river. And so, too, you rise, pack up your belongings, and head down the final stretch of trail off Brushy Mountain.

Miles and Directions

0.0 Start at a brown forest gate across the dirt road leading from the parking lot. Crawfish Trail begins at the forest gate and follows the dirt road as it runs along the base of Walker Mountain amid black-eyed Susans, asters, blackberries, and grasses. Wide fields open up left of the trail, and beyond the fields flows Reed Creek.

1.0 Come to a junction of Crawfish Trail and Channel Rock Trail; continue straight. **Note:** Channel Rock Trail branches left off the road through a field and crosses Reed Creek. This is the return leg of this loop hike.

1.5 Pass a good campsite amid pines and tulip poplar.

1.8 Pass through a grassy clearing. Crawfish Trail is now a dirt path. Blackberries are abundant in midsummer. Pass another campsite on the right within 0.2 mile.

2.6 Pass through a clearing dominated by a single large oak. A board nailed to the tree identifies this as the one-time homesite of James Mozer, a settler who farmed this valley in the early 1900s. Pieces of a home foundation lie in the overgrown grass.

2.8 Turn left onto the Crawfish Trail at a T junction with Walker Mountain Trail (Walker Mountain Trail continues straight). This junction is marked by orange arrows tacked onto a tree. A few feet after turning, cross Reed Creek and enter a clearing with a fire ring. From the clearing, turn right and enter the woods under a tunnel of rhododendron. A signboard marks where the white-blazed AT exits the clearing.

3.5 The trail passes several fields overgrown with grass. Past the second clearing, turn left and follow Crawfish Trail as it descends downhill into woods. **Note:** Be alert. This is an unmarked turn in the trail. If you hike more than 0.1 mile without seeing an orange blaze, turn around and search for the turn, which will now be on the right.

3.8 Crawfish Trail and Bear Creek finally run alongside one another amid tall hemlocks. Just as quickly as they join, however, they separate. Follow Crawfish Trail as it climbs a grassy road to a clearing. In this clearing, turn left and follow a grassy road downhill. **Note:** In this clearing, avoid a grassy road that continues uphill. It is marked with yellow blazes.

4.2 Reach a beaver dam across Bear Creek. This is a two-stage dam. **Note:** At high water, you will have to hike downstream and cross at a shallow bend in the stream. Return to a large maple tree on the trail. From this tree, walk up the grass road for 100 yards, turn right, and follow the faintly defined road. The trail is obscured by waist-high grass. Bear Creek flows in a deep gully on your right.

4.5 Turn left and follow Crawfish Trail as it climbs steeply up Brushy Mountain as a narrow dirt footpath.

5.9 Cross the AT and head downhill. The next mile brings more steep climbs along the spine of Brushy Mountain amid a ridge forest of chestnut oak, maple, scrub pines, and berry bushes.

7.8 Crawfish Trail steeply drops off the right side of the ridge, descending along the forest boundary marked by red paint slashes. The trail winds up and down the foothills of Brushy Mountain, straddling the forest boundary the entire way.

9.0 The trail converts to a grassy road as it descends into a clearing. Several old roads merge here. Avoid roads that are yellow blazed and posted private property. Instead, turn left onto Channel Rock Trail and follow plastic orange blazes downhill past rhododendron.

9.7 Reach the first of several points on the trail where Channel Rock Branch merges with the trail. (The stream's name is clear—the water has eroded a channel through the schist bedrock. Portions of the trail are very wet.)

10.2 Cross Reed Creek and rejoin Crawfish Trail. Turn right to return to the parking area.

11.2 Hike ends at the forest gate across Crawfish Trail. Walk past the gate to enter the parking area.

Hike Information

Local Information

Wythe Convention & Visitors Bureau, Wytheville, (877) 347-8307, http://visit
wytheville.com

Local Events/Attractions

The Settlers Museum of Southwest Virginia, Atkins, (276) 686-4401, www.settlers
museum.com. Dedicated to the mountain pioneers of southwest Virginia.

Lodging

Hungry Mother State Park, Smyth County, (276) 781-7400, (800) 933-7275 (reservations only), www.dcr.virginia.gov/state_parks/hun.shtml. Cabins and camping
are available.

Organizations

Appalachian Trail Conference, Harpers Ferry, WV, (304) 535-6331, www.appalachian
trail.org

34 Pine Mountain Trail

Pine Mountain Trail traces a razor's edge along the Virginia–Kentucky border. You're walking a geological fault line known as an overthrust plate—a chunk of the earth's crust that buckled, broke, and ramped up over another chunk hundreds of millions of years ago. The resulting terrain slopes gently east to Virginia, while to the west, sheer drops of 500 feet or more fall away into Kentucky. The stunning views, combined with the rugged terrain make this one of Virginia's most dramatic and scenic trails. The length of the trail and its remoteness make it one of the most challenging as well.

Start: Highlands Section trailhead on US 23 in Pound Gap

Distance: 15.7 miles point to point

Hiking time: 8–10 hours

Difficulty: Strenuous due to length and rugged terrain

Trail surface: Dirt footpaths and dirt roads lead to high escarpments, upland forest, and spectacular vistas off exposed rock faces.

Land status: National forest

Nearest cities: Pound, VA; Whitesburg, KY

Other trail users: Hunters (in season)

Accessibility: None

Canine compatibility: Dogs permitted

Trail contacts: Clinch Ranger District, Wise; (276) 328-2931; www.fs.usda.gov/gwj. Pine Mountain Trail Conference, PO Box 784, Whitesburg, KY 41858; (606) 633-2362; www.pinemountaintrail.com.

Schedule: Open year-round. Hunting is allowed on national forest property. Deer-hunting season in Wise and Dickenson Counties runs Oct through Jan. The national forest limits hiking groups to 10 people.

Fees/permits: None

Facilities/features: None

Maps: USGS Jenkins West, Jenkins East, Clintwood, Hellier, Elkhorn City

Finding the trailhead: From Pound, drive north on US 23 for 3 miles. In Pound Gap, just before passing into Kentucky, turn left into the Stateline Food Mart. Parking for hikers is provided on the side and in the back of this convenience store and gas station. GPS: N37 09.213' / W82 37.937'. *DeLorme: Virginia Atlas & Gazetteer:* Page 36, C2.

Shuttle point: From Pound Gap, drive north on US 23 for 1.3 miles to a junction with US 119 in Kentucky. Turn left onto US 119 and drive 10.8 miles to Whitesburg, Kentucky. At a junction with KY 15 in Whitesburg, turn left and continue on US 119 as it climbs Pine Mountain. In 4.9 miles, turn right into a trailhead parking area for the Pine Mountain Trail's Little Shepherd Trail section. There is parking for more than twenty cars and an interpretive sign. GPS: N37 04.581' / W82 48.644'. *DeLorme: Virginia Atlas & Gazetteer:* Page 37, B5.

The Hike

A short hike past Pine Mountain Trail's south trailhead lies some of the best this hike has to offer. Ravens Nest, with its smooth rock surface and soaring views east and west—to Virginia and Kentucky—is the first in a succession of high overlooks that culminate at Birch Knob (3,449 feet), 14.4 miles into the hike. The 30 miles between

Pound Gap and Breaks Interstate Park feature long views east and west off open rock faces, followed by long, torturous stretches through woodland. At trail's end, the feeling isn't so much that you completed Pine Mountain, but you survived.

The difficulty only heightens the rewards. Long the domain of horseback riders and ATVs (ATVs are now prohibited), Pine Mountain Trail enjoys a wider fame today thanks to enthusiastic hikers in Virginia and Kentucky. A group is working to make this trail the northern leg of a 120-mile-long trail through the Cumberland Mountains. Volunteers have rebuilt and reblazed sections of trail. When finished, the entire Pine Mountain Trail will run from Breaks Interstate Park to Cumberland Gap Historical Park. It should rank with other long trails, like the Bartram in North Carolina, Allegheny in West Virginia, and Tuscarora in Virginia, in offering some of the best long-distance trekking in the East.

Pine Mountain's story is the story of people who moved to southwest Virginia seeking isolation—from people, politics, and/or culture. Most settlers worked hard in the logging and mining industry. They were fiercely independent, to the point of suspecting any kind of authority. Some turned outlaw, others ran moonshine. Doc Taylor, aka "Red Fox," a notorious local outlaw, hid amid the caves and hollows of Pine Mountain. He was later hanged in Big Stone Gap for murder. In the gaps of Pine Mountain, settlers eked out a living—barely. Their cows grazed on rocky slopes. Cornfields cheapened already thin soil. Crop rotation simply meant clearing a few more acres and planting anew. Wherever they set roots, settlers guarded their holdings closely, often to protect their stills. Moonshine was the real cash crop of the region.

Knowing a bit of this history made meeting Henry Mullins special. Dusk had settled on our second day of hiking when Mullins stepped from the shadow of Birch Knob and introduced himself. He and his girlfriend, Penny, had driven up to Birch Knob to catch the sunset. (Newly improved FR 616 permits vehicle access to Pine Mountain's ridgetop from the Virginia side.) Together, the four of us climbed Birch Knob's final rocky upthrust (there are two approaches, one using a rope ladder, the other a scramble between huge boulders). Sitting atop the second-highest bump in the long Pine Mountain ridge, Henry pulled out a beverage and lit a cigarette. I figured this was as good a time as any to ask if he knew the Henry Mullins killed on Pine Mountain.

The Henry Mullins I had read about lived at Dutton Bottom Farm, one gap northwest of Birch Knob. Today a rusted metal bed frame marks the spot. As the story goes, deputized Virginians came upon Mullins's cabin while hunting for stills in the mountains. They had, earlier that day, found a still and partook in some of the spoils. Drunk and ornery, they found a bottle of moonshine on Mullins's front porch—which was located on the Virginia side of the Virginia-Kentucky border—and confronted him. Mullins protested his innocence. A scuffle broke out and a deputy shot and killed Mullins. Local authorities decided jurisdiction lay with Kentucky, and the deputies were tried and convicted, although they served minimal time.

Atop Birch Knob, the setting sun slipped behind the Kentucky mountains. The modern-day Henry Mullins confessed never having heard the story. His name, it

The Author walks the ridge that forms the boundary between Virginia and Kentucky.

turns out, is a pretty common name in the area. We climbed down off the peak and parted ways in the dark, Mary and I to our tent, Henry and Penny to civilization in a Ford Bronco.

Pine Mountain's past rests easy with the outlaws and homesteaders. Its future is in good hands, too. If the 120-mile Pine Mountain Trail can match the splendor of this inaugural leg, every backpacker, nature lover, and rock hound should count himself lucky. Distance alone makes this one of the most physically demanding hikes in Virginia. Scenery varies from upland bogs in the vicinity of The Doubles to wind-shaped rock formations between Blowing Rock Gap and Skegg Knob. Long stretches of trail pass through forestland, emerge for a length on sun-baked rock faces, then reenter the woods.

At its core, Pine Mountain is a geologic phenomenon called the Cumberland Overthrust Block. The mountain range formed when a piece of the earth's crust buckled and broke. The southeast chunk of rock (the Virginia piece) moved between 6 and 11 miles west and slid up and over the northwest rock (the Kentucky piece) at an angle of 30 to 40 degrees. The highest bits of rock on Pine Mountain are sandstone normally found 2,000 feet underground. And here's a kicker: It's thought that the Pine Mountain we see today is half its original size.

Miles and Directions

0.0 Start at a set of stone steps leading up a grass embankment next to the Stateline Food Mart. Climb the steps and bear left on a mowed path through a grass field.

0.1 Pass through a fence stile that keeps out horseback riders and motorized vehicles and continue downhill on the Pine Mountain Trail, which is blazed with florescent green markers.

0.7 Veer left onto an old forest road, a junction marked by a double blue blaze, and hike around a small knob in the Pine Mountain ridgeline. This pattern—the trail swerving south to work around the south side of small knobs—repeats itself numerous times in the first 5 miles along this hike.

0.8 Veer right and uphill at a double blaze as Pine Mountain Trail splits off the old forest road and climbs to a saddle as a singletrack woods path.

1.5 Reach the Jack Sautter Campsite and a turn-off for the Old Meade homesite. There is a fire ring and four established tent sites here. **Note:** There is a water source at the Old Meade homesite, a 0.2-mile hike off the trail via an old mountain road.

2.4 Pass through a stone cleft in the mountain ridge at Twin Cliffs. **Side trip:** Turn left and scale open rock to reach a perch atop one of the Twin Cliffs in less than 0.1 mile. Views from this high point stretch south and east into Virginia.

2.8 Stay alert as a double blaze marks a hard left turn and then skirts another knob.

2.9 Pass through Cold Spring Gap.

3.0 Stay alert for a hard left turn as the trail skirts another knob.

3.5 Turn left as Pine Mountain Trail merges with a forest road. Follow the wide two-track road downhill.

3.6 Stay straight on Pine Mountain Trail as the forest road forks. Pine Mountain climbs the ridge as a wide two-track dirt road.

Pine Mountain Trail

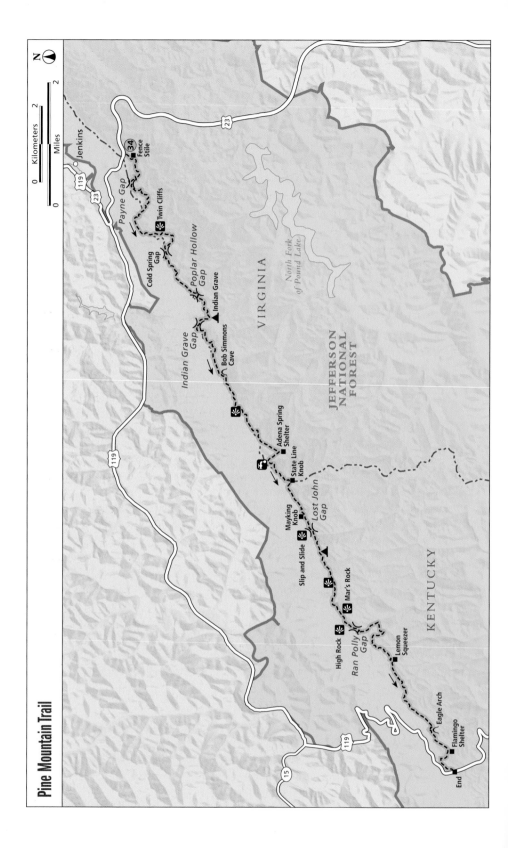

3.8   Turn left off the dirt road and follow the Pine Mountain Trail as it passes through rock outcrops. Where the trail briefly rejoins the dirt road, stay alert: Within a few feet, turn left again and follow the trail downhill to slip around another knob that rises uphill on the right. **Note:** This work-around is meant to avoid private property.

3.9   A double blaze and a wood sign with an arrow mark a sharp right turn in the trail. Turn right and climb up to Poplar Hollow Gap. In the gap, the trail reverts to an ATV trail.

4.7   In Indian Grave Gap, veer left off the ATV track and follow the trail as a footpath as it skirts another knob on Pine Mountain's ridgeline.

5.4   Reach Indian Grave campsite. (This is a primitive campsite with a seasonal water supply—no water flow in fall and winter months.) After the campsite, the trail rises to the ridgeline, finally offering views north into Kentucky.

5.9   Follow the trail as it drops left off the ridgeline to skirt Bob Simmons Cave, a small cavity in a large rock outcrop uphill on the right. After working around the exposed rock, regain the ridge and enjoy nice views off to the right (north) down into Kentucky.

6.4   After a steep descent through a tunnel of rhododendron, pass through Bear Track Gap (2,910 feet).

6.6   Finish the climb out of Bear Track Gap by turning right and uphill on a forest road. For the next mile, the trail follows a narrow two-track path.

7.5   Double blazes mark a right turn off the narrow two-track path onto a woods path as you begin a descent to Adena Spring shelter.

7.7   Reach Adena Spring shelter. Follow the trail as it swings right and downhill. In 0.1 mile, pass a natural spring. **Note:** Adena is an AT-style covered shelter with room to sleep six to eight people. There is a fire ring, a privy, and a bear pole to hang food.

8.5   Pass through State Line Knob (3,206 feet). From this point south, Pine Mountain Trail runs entirely within the state of Kentucky.

9.2   At a USGS benchmark, turn left and head downhill on an old forest road. After a short descent, the trail climbs steeply to another benchmark that marks the highpoint of Mayking Knob (3,273 feet), the highest point on Pine Mountain.

9.3   Just past a power substation, descend a tall ledge on a set of iron rungs drilled into the rock. The next 2 miles showcase Pine Mountain's famous cliff-lines and views west into Kentucky at places like Slip and Slide Rock, Box Rock, Mar's Rock, and High Rock.

9.9   Reach the Swindell campsite, a primitive camp with no water sources. Continue south on Pine Mountain Trail.

10.0   Follow the trail as it turns left off the ridgeline and descends.

10.5   Cross over The Cliff, an exposed rock-face with steep drop-offs off the trail to the right.

10.9   Continue on the green-blazed Pine Mountain Trail at a junction with the High Rock Loop Trail on the left. **Option:** High Rock Loop Trail descends into a hemlock grove around the headwaters of Bad Branch and rejoins Pine Mountain Trail at mile 12.0 below. The trail and land is protected as the Bad Branch State Nature Preserve.

11.1   Cross Mar's Rock, another exposed rock-face with ample views off the right side of the trail into Kentucky. Continue south on Pine Mountain Trail and begin a descent into Ran Polly Gap.

11.5 A house-size boulder marks Ran Polly Gap. Hikers can find shelter or shade in a rock overhang. In 0.1 mile beyond Ran Polly Gap, Pine Mountain Trail reverts to a wide graded forest road as it follows Bad Branch.

11.9 Turn right at a double green blaze, where the trail leaves the graded road and enters the woods as a footpath. Orange blazes are visible on the trail for 0.1 mile as Pine Mountain Trail shares the footpath with High Rock Loop Trail.

12.0 Continue straight on Pine Mountain Trail as High Rock Loop Trail splits left and downhill. **Note:** It is 1.9 miles on the High Rock Loop Trail to a parking area. En route, the trail passes by a 60-foot waterfall on Bad Branch.

13.0 "Squeeze" through the Lemon Squeezer, a narrow passage between tall rock outcrops.

14.7 Descend a set of stairs and pass a trail sign-in box.

15.1 Enter a clearing for the Flamingo Shelter. Pass straight through and continue on the Pine Mountain Trail.

15.3 Enter a wide clearing where two forest roads intersect. Bear left to follow a dirt road, avoiding the hard left turn as well as any road that branches right or south.

15.5 Veer right off the dirt road and follow a set of stairs downhill. At the foot of the stairs, cross US 119 and climb the roadside embankment via another staircase.

15.7 Hike ends at the Little Shepherd Trail trailhead of Pine Mountain Trail State Park.

Hike Information

Local Information

Heart of Appalachia, Big Stone Gap, (888) 798-2386, www.heartofappalachia.com

Local Events/Attractions

Hills of Home Bluegrass Festival, Memorial Day weekend, Coeburn, www.drralph stanley.com

Virginia Highlands Festival, Aug, Abingdon, (276) 623-5266, www.virginia highlandsfestival.org

Carter Fold Music Gathering and A. P. Carter Museum, Sat nights year-round, Hiltons, (276) 386-6054, www.carterfamilyfold.org

Lodging

Breaks Interstate Park, (276) 865-4413, www.breakspark.com

Gateway to the Breaks Motel, Breaks, (276) 531-8481

35 Chief Benge Scout Trail

Mountain Fork and Little Stony Creek thread the mountains of Wise and Scott Counties in wild and unpredictable fashion. Sticking with them faithfully is the 15-mile Chief Benge Scout Trail, a trek that links the cool waters of High Knob Lake with 30-foot falls, rapids, and small pools on the Little Stony. The trail follows old railroad grades at river level but makes several steep climbs up the ridges that make southwest Virginia such a rugged, wonderful place to hike. There is real variety of plants along this trail, from big-leaf magnolia to the huckleberries on the dry ridges. Bring a fishing pole and test stream waters or the wide Bark Camp Lake. With reliable water sources and only a few steep climbs, this hike is a highlight of any southwest trip.

Start: Parking lot for High Knob Lake in High Knob National Recreation Area (NRA)
Distance: 15.3 miles point to point
Hiking time: About 8 hours
Difficulty: Moderate due to the length and a number of unaided stream crossings
Trail surface: A combination of dirt footpaths, grassy forest roads, and gravel forest roads lead along streams and fern glades, through hardwood forests to two lakes and a craggy river gorge with three tall waterfalls.
Land status: National forest
Nearest town: Norton, VA
Other trail users: Hikers only
Accessibility: The Lakeshore Trail at Bark Camp Lake is paved
Canine compatibility: Dogs permitted
Trail contact: Clinch Ranger District, Wise; (276) 328-2931; www.fs.usda.gov/gwj

Schedule: Open year-round. Hunting is permitted on national forest land. Deer-hunting season in Wise and Scott Counties runs Oct through Jan. The national forest limits hiking groups to 10 people.
Fees/permits: High Knob Recreation Area day-use and campsite fees; Bark Camp Lake Recreation Area day-use and tent-site fees
Facilities/features: There are restrooms, picnic areas and camping at High Knob Recreation Area, open May 15–Sept. 15, at the beginning of the hike. Bark Camp Lake, about midway on the trail, has camping, restrooms and a lake. There are no facilities at Hanging Rock at the eastern terminus of the trail.
Maps: USGS Wise, Fort Blackmore, Coeburn, Dungannon, Norton, East Stone Gap

Finding the trailhead: To High Knob, start of Chief Benge Scout Trail: From Big Stone Gap, take VA 23/Alt US 58 East to exit 1. At a stop sign, turn right on 619 (good signage for High Knob). It's a curvy, uphill, hairpin road. At 1.9 miles, pass the Flag Rock Recreation Area. At 3.1 miles, enter the national forest (signed). At 3.8 miles, turn left on FR 238 (no sign for High Knob). At 4.2 miles, make a sharp, hairpin right to go up to High Knob. A sign says gate is closed 10 p.m. to 6 a.m. (straight would take you to the camping area). Go 0.1 mile to the parking area and sign for trails. Before you head out, walk up the stairs a few hundred feet to the panoramic view from High Knob. GPS: N36 53.621' / W82 37.710'.

To Bark Camp Lake (the midway point, if want to break hike into two days): From Alt 58 in Tacoma, take VA 706 south (Stone Mountain Road) and cross a railroad track almost immediately. There is a sign for Bark Camp Lake. At 7.5 miles is national forest sign. At 8.2 miles, turn left on FR 699 (Pine Camp Road). At 8.5 miles, turn right on VA 822 (good signage). At 10.2 miles, turn right into Bark Camp Lake Recreation Area. Pay Station is at 11 miles. GPS: N36 52.017' / W82 31.446'.

To Hanging Rock (end of Chief Benge/Little Stony Falls hike): From Coeburn, take VA 72 south 8.8 miles and turn right into Hanging Rock National Recreation Area. GPS: N36 51.681' / W82 26.769'. *DeLorme: Virginia Atlas & Gazetteer:* Page 20, A3-A4.

The Hike

Mountain Fork creek swallows the sunlight with each step along the Chief Benge Scout Trail, as hills on either side steepen and the valley narrows. Thick patches of laurel, small trees, and an earthy smell fill the valley. Downed trees force water into narrow channels that spill over small rock ledges. Rushing water is always audible, even when the stream itself is obscured by vine and shrub entanglements. Soon trail and stream meet, cross, meet again, and cross again—before the wide, flat trail narrows and climbs the left hillside.

At this point, where mountain laurel gives way to oak and maple, we part ways with Mountain Fork—and the spirit who's been stalking silently behind since High Knob Lake. The ghost of Chief Bob Benge won't be following us up Bark Camp Branch; instead, he'll steer right along Big Stony Creek. Painted in warrior colors and traveling by night, he'll head south to the Livingston Farm on the North Fork Holston. He'll return this way, with prisoners and booty, evading militia by traveling obscure mountain passes. Eleven miles north of here, in a gap overlooking the city of Norton, he'll die as he did in 1794, of a bullet to the head.

Chief Benge entered southwest Virginia in April 1777 leading a band of Cherokee and Shawnee, marking the start of an eighteen-year reign of terror. A man who had, in his youth, lived with his Native American mother and English stepfather at Dorton's Fort on the Copper River, would kill between forty to fifty settlers as retribution for their encroachment on Native American land. Hunting parties fell prey to his ambushes. Farmers looked up from work to find him standing over them. Women peered from their homes, saw nothing . . . looked again . . . and saw Benge. Like a ghost, he materialized, murdered, plundered, and moved on.

What caused a man with an English father, trader John Benge, and Cherokee mother, Elizabeth Watts Dorton, to strike out so?

Benge came of age in the 1770s, a tense time in the colonies. City folk on the Eastern Seaboard were ruffled by such concepts as taxation without representation. In southwest Virginia, a more tangible threat occupied settlers. Local Native American tribes were lashing out against settlers' land gains down the Clinch, Powell, and Holston Valleys. When the American Revolution broke out in 1776, British-instigated Cherokee and Shawnee war parties returned to southwest Virginia for revenge. Virginia's Holston Militia retaliated by burning Cherokee towns in Tennessee. Bob Benge, who had run away from Dorton's Fort as a teenager to live out his

The view from High Knob near the trailhead for Chief Benge Scout Trail.

days as a Cherokee, lost his home twice in these raids. Neighbors from his childhood years helped pillage his village.

With his red head and fair complexion, Benge could pass as a settler. He spoke flawless English and knew the mountains of the Clinch, Holston, and Powell Valleys like few others. His discovery of a pass between Stone and Powell Mountains enabled him to move in and out of the region undetected.

The morning of April 6, 1794, found Benge at the Livingston family home near Mendota on the North Fork Holston River. A daughter of Elizabeth Livingston later described the scene:

> One bright morning after the sun had risen and the men had gone to the clearings and the women were busy at their wheels and looms, all joyous and jovial amid the fragrance of wild flowers and the music of songbirds, and not dreaming of coming danger, Benge and his painted warriors stealthily approached and surrounded the cabins.

In short order, Benge's band killed a woman and three children, burned the house, and carried off eight prisoners, including the wife of Henry Livingston, Susannah.

Falls at Little Stony.

Runners carried the alarm northeast to Castlewood (then Castle's Wood) and northwest to Yoakum's Station near present-day Dryden. Militias moved to predetermined mountain passes Benge might use. A small group started out after Benge and tracked him down the North Fork Holston River to Hilton, across Clinch Mountain at Hamilton Gap, and north to the Clinch River. Yet as hours slipped past, the Cherokee's trail grew faint.

At the Clinch River just south of present-day Dungannon, Benge's raiding party made a fateful misstep—literally. Author Lawrence Fleenor recounts in his book *Benge!* how a wet moccasin print on a dry stone tipped pursuers to his route. Benge moved downstream to the confluence of Big Stony Creek near Fort Blackmore, turned upstream, and followed Big Stony up Powell Mountain, his pursuers closing ground.

In late afternoon, the sun slips behind Powell Mountain, shrouding one entire side of the Mountain Fork stream valley in dusk. The opposite bank remains bathed in warm light, although the hiker still feels vulnerable to ever-encroaching shadows. At this point, Chief Benge Scout Trail climbs up the left hill, first gradually, then at a steeper grade. Mountain Fork is 200 feet below you. Sunlight baths a large fern glade on the valley floor. It's tempting to imagine Benge walking here on April 7, 1794. He would have kept one prisoner, Susannah Livingston, wife of Henry Livingston, out in front. The remaining prisoners would be behind him. In single file, the party would pass out of the light into the shadows of the stream valley, picking their way upstream to High Knob and spending the night at Camp Rock.

Benge did spend his last night alive at Camp Rock, but best evidence shows he followed a more direct route up Powell Mountain, one roughly approximated by VA 619. He was headed for a gap in the mountains overlooking a town called Prince's Flats (present-day Norton). At this pass, now called Benge's Gap, the party turned west and entered Hoot Owl Hollow.

Benge's pursuers set an ambush in Little Stony Gap, a deep mountain pass flanked by steep ridges and a valley floor covered with large rocks. Militia men watched as Benge hustled his prisoners up the trail. One man took aim, but noise in lifting his rifle alerted Benge to danger. The Cherokee ran and, as he fled, stepped in a hole. The bullet intended to hit him square in the back lodged in his head.

Benge's death is a watershed event in southwest Virginia; raids on settlers ceased with his passing. The Cherokee, already pushed far beyond their homelands, never threatened the region again in any material way.

The Chief Benge's Scout Trail touches only briefly on its namesake. Still, the warrior lingers with you on a 15-mile trek to the falls at Little Stony. The trail is a fitting tribute to a Native American whose hidden paths along dark mountain stream valleys enabled him to make a statement, however destructive, against the expansion of white settlers into Cherokee land.

Miles and Directions

0.0 Start at the High Knob Lake parking area. Walk 0.2 mile downhill, turn left in front of a shower house, and cross a small bridge spanning Mountain Branch (on USGS topo quadrant Wise, this stream is labeled Stony Creek but has been renamed). **Note:** There is a water spigot near the shower house. Stock up on water here. The trail follows streams almost its entire route, but this is the only treated water source for 9.5 miles.

0.5 Cross a concrete dam at the top of High Knob Lake and turn right on Chief Benge Trail, a wide, flat dirt trail along the left bank of Mountain Fork Creek. Through this ever-deepening stream valley, you'll hop the rough-and-tumble creek five times in the next 2 miles.

1.9 Pass a nice campground amid hemlocks on the right side of the trail.

2.4 Cross FR 704 and drop down the opposite bank. The trail keeps its wide, flat course while Mountain Fork Creek runs through some wild stretches, obscured by rhododendron, other times nearly dammed by tree debris.

3.5 Climb out of the stream valley up the left slope and wrap around a small hill. (Mountain Fork takes a much longer route around the base of this hill.) The climb, at first gradual, steepens considerably as a drainage forms downslope on the right.

4.2 Cross Bark Camp Branch and climb out of this stream gully to a large field within 0.5 mile.

4.6 Pass by a natural gas well and enter a young hardwood forest. The trail, ascending on a gentle slope, is wide, grassy, and dry.

5.2 Turn left onto a gravel road (FR 2570). Within 20 paces, turn right and hike along a wide grassy road.

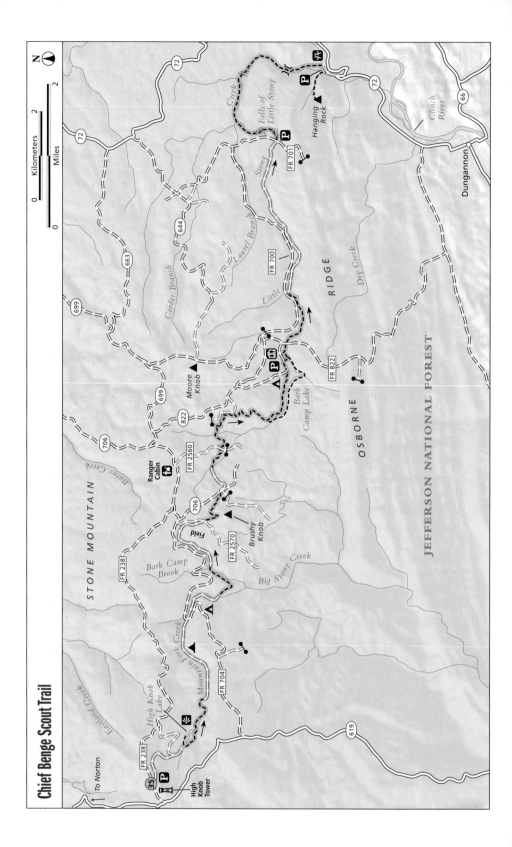

Chief Benge Scout Trail

N

0   Kilometers   2
0   Miles   2

72

Stony Creek

Falls of
Little Stony

P

FR 701

P

Hanging
Rock

72

Clinch
River

66

Dungannon

72

644

663

Corder Branch

Laurel Branch

FR 700

Little

Stony

RIDGE

Dry Creek

699

699

822

Moore
Knob

P

Bark
Camp Lake

FR 822

OSBORNE

JEFFERSON NATIONAL FOREST

706

Burns Creek

Ranger
Cabin

FR 2560

706

FR 2570

Brushy
Knob

Field

Big Stony Creek

STONE MOUNTAIN

FR 238

Bark Camp
Brook

Eastland Creek

High Knob
Lake

Mountain Fork Creek

FR 704

619

FR 238

35

P

To Norton

High Knob
Tower

5.8 The trail reverts to a singletrack woods path as it descends off a small hill, crossing by the headwaters of Little Stony Creek.

6.1 Cross VA 706 and descend on another grassy woods road. Between here and Little Stony Creek, two trails branch right off this road. Stay left each time.

6.9 Cross Little Stony Creek and hike along the left stream bank. After a short distance, the trail climbs the hill on your left to meet a forest road.

7.3 Cross a gravel road (FR 2560) and reenter woods directly opposite on a narrow woods path. Ferns line the trail and there are several large specimens of big-leaf magnolias. From here, the trail drops back to Little Stony Creek and you'll follow the right stream bank for a short distance, then hop it to follow the left streamside.

8.4 Reach the Lakeshore Loop Trail encircling Bark Camp Lake. Signs show the Chief Benge Trail turns right and traces the backside of the lake. Turn left for a nice respite at Bark Camp Lake Recreation Area.

9.5 After wrapping in and out of the lake's marshy fingers, enter the picnic area. (There are bathrooms, a water spigot, and picnic tables.) Reconnect with the Chief Benge Trail by following the Lakeshore Loop Trail to a dam on the lower end of Bark Camp Lake. Cross the concrete portion of the dam, then immediately turn left and follow the right stream bank of Little Stony Creek. This is a difficult stretch of trail, obscured by tall shrubs and poorly marked. Cues for the turnoff include several rusted metal posts and a rotted stump slashed with double yellow blazes found on the earthen embankment just after the concrete portion of the dam.

9.7 Reach FR 822, a gravel road. Turn right and walk along the road for less than 0.1 mile. A sign on the left side reads FALLS OF LITTLE STONY, 4.9 MILES. Turn left and drop back into woods. The river is on your left side. Seven stream crossings follow in quick succession.

10.4 After the ninth stream crossing, look for a nice campsite on the right side of the trail. Ahead, the trail skips across Little Stony eight more times.

12.2 Look right immediately after crossing Little Stony Creek. There is a campsite under hemlocks on a small bluff at a bend in the river. Large stream boulders are ideal for lounging.

12.5 Reach FR 701. Follow the gravel road right, enter a vehicle turnaround, and look for the trailhead for Little Stony National Recreation Trail at a signboard at the back of the parking lot.

12.7 Cross over the top of a spectacular 25-foot waterfall. Two other falls (10 feet and 30 feet) follow in quick succession. After this, the trail drops to stream level and passes through hemlock and cove forests.

15.3 Reach Hanging Rock Picnic Area and the southern terminus of the Chief Benge and Little Stony Trails.

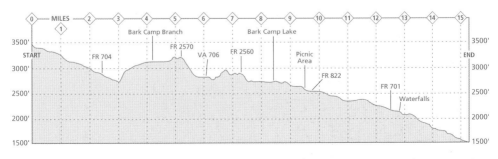

Hike Information

Local Information

Wise County Chamber of Commerce, Norton, (276) 679-0961, www.wisecounty chamber.org

Heart of Appalachia, Big Stone Gap, (276) 762-0011, www.heartofappalachia.com

Town of Big Stone Gap, (276) 523-0115, www.bigstonegap.org

Local Events / Attractions

Carter Family Fold, Hiltons, (276) 386-9480, www.carterfamilyfold.org

Country Cabin, Norton, (276) 679-3541. Live bluegrass by local performers.

Lodging

High Knob Recreation Area, Norton, (276) 679-1754. Camping is available May 15–Sept. 15.

Bark Camp Lake, Coeburn, (276) 328-2931. Camping is available May 15–Sept. 15.

Natural Tunnel State Park, Duffield, (276) 940-2674. Camping is available.

Jessie Lea RV Park, Big Stone Gap, (276) 523-0055, www.jessielearv.com

Other Resources

Benge! by Lawrence J. Fleenor. Biography of Chief Benge. Call (276) 523-1600 for ordering information.

36 Devils Fork Loop

Devils Fork is a luxuriant streamscape of rocks, cliffs, and small cascades that grow in size and frequency as you hike. It all comes together at the Devils Bathtub, where a long waterfall trips step by step over shale bedrock and crashes in a swirl of currents into a bowl-like pool—the bathtub. Framed by tall hemlocks and rhododendron, this scenery is as lush and abundant as the landscape a few hundred feet upslope is simple and unadorned.

Start: Forest gate at the end of FR 2631
Distance: 7.1-mile loop
Hiking time: About 4 hours
Difficulty: Moderate due to the unaided stream crossings and one steep climb
Trail surface: Dirt footpaths and dirt roads lead through hardwood forest slopes and hemlock groves along streams.
Land status: National forest
Nearest town: Norton, VA
Other trail users: Hikers only
Accessibility: None
Canine compatibility: Dogs permitted

Trail contact: Clinch Ranger District, Wise; (276) 328-2931; www.fs.usda.gov/gwj
Schedule: Open year-round. Hunting is allowed on national forestland. Deer hunting season in Scott County runs Oct through Jan. The national forest limits hiking groups to 10 people.
Fees/permits: High Knob Recreation Area day-use and campsite fees; Bark Camp Lake Recreation Area day-use and tent-site fees
Facilities/features: None
Maps: USGS East Stone Gap, Fort Blackmore

Finding the trailhead: From VA 72 North near Fort Blackmore, turn left on VA 619 (Big Stoney Creek Road). Go 3.6 miles to the community of "Ka" (right turn-off goes to High Knob). In 0.6 mile, turn left on "High Knob SC" (it is still VA 619). In 0.3 mile, see an abandoned house on the left, surrounded by a chain-link fence, and a very rough dirt road to the left of the house. There are No Trespassing signs, so no parking here. You can drive this forest road, but 4WD or high clearance is recommended. Go 0.2 mile to a clearing to park. There's evidence of camping here. Look to right of the clearing for wooden steps up an incline with fluorescent green trail blazes. GPS: N36 49.107' / W82 37.602'. *DeLorme: Virginia Atlas & Gazetteer:* Page 20, B3.

The Hike

The trip up Devils Run hollow is 3 miles of tricky hiking. At each stream crossing, shrubs and ferns hide where the trail might climb the opposite bank. The deeper into the hollow, the more damp and shaded the scenery. The rocky, uneven trail creeps up in elevation until stream banks become small cliffs, and the river froths 20 feet below your feet.

This ruggedness makes it hard to fathom how a railroad once ran along this stream. It's been seventy years or more since private landowners carted oak, beech, chestnut, and poplar trees off the mountain slopes around Devils Fork. These were

A stream cascades into a shady pool on Devils Fork Loop.

old-growth trees, described by one nineteenth-century traveler as "walls and buttresses, square structures like the titanic ruins of castles." As had been the case throughout much of southwest Virginia, companies from New York and Philadelphia owned the timber. A sawmill could produce 12,000 board feet from just three of these trees. (A small home uses about 6,000 board feet of timber—which means three of these trees could supply the lumber needed for two homes.) At the other end of the scale, Singer Manufacturing Company bought and removed all black walnut of a certain size in neighboring Wise County for their sewing machine cabinets and base plates.

Halfway between Straight Branch and Devils Bathtub, a rusted coal car lies half-buried in trailside brambles. Uphill from this, speculators dug a mining prospect in search of coal. These were "punch mines," small dents dug out of hills in hopes of finding a vein. Coal's era has passed, while natural gas production is rising. The return leg of Devils Fork Loop crosses a dirt road high on Stone Mountain. Embedded in the dirt road path are signs of modern prospecting. Exploratory drilling for natural gas produces long pieces of smooth, round stones—as large as a silver dollar and broken into 2- or 3-inch pieces.

When coal miners worked this area, they did so exclusively on the north bank of Devils Fork. The stream follows a geologic fault between sandstone on the north stream bank, which holds coal deposits, and limestone on the south bank. On its north stream bank, acid soil supports the hemlock and rhododendron that lend the hollow its lush setting. There are few, if any, of these type plants on the south stream bank, where the soil is less hospitable.

The hemlocks along Devils Fork are second- and third-growth. Rhododendron, which seems to grow hand in hand with hemlock, fills the gaps in the forest floor. A spring hike here, while certain to net you wet feet, also leaves a lasting impression of both these evergreens. As you climb, the hemlock and rhododendron decrease in number until, on well-

A rocky outdrop on Devils Fork Loop Trail.

drained mountain slopes, white oak and hickory trees form the forest canopy. Off the slope run five streams and numerous seasonal runoffs, all of which feed Devils Fork. A century ago, when chestnut trees grew tall and wide, loggers would range throughout this forest, cutting rings around the trunk at certain intervals. Using tools called spuds, they ripped bark from the tree in sheets, piled it high onto wagons, and hauled it to tanneries. Before railroads and on-site sawmills, the trees were too difficult to remove. More often than not, they were left to rot.

At times, the route across Stone Mountain's slope pitches sharply downhill and right. This pitch is what, in part, led Appalachian Power in the mid-1970s to propose flooding Devils Fork and creating a reservoir out of the stream valley. Using a pipeline, the company could have generated electricity by directing the flow of water between the proposed reservoir and Big Cherry Reservoir on Long Mountain. Opposition from local residents was swift, and Appalachian Power abandoned the plan. The idea of protecting Devils Fork persisted, however. When the national forest proposed a road up the side of Little Mountain, a local trail club rose to the cause. Roadwork progressed to the point where a survey crew cut a first pass through the forest, but then the project was dropped. Sensing an opportunity, the trail club made use of the crew's work. Today, the road that would have opened the Devils Fork watershed up for timber harvest and natural gas production is one section of this loop.

Devils Fork Loop

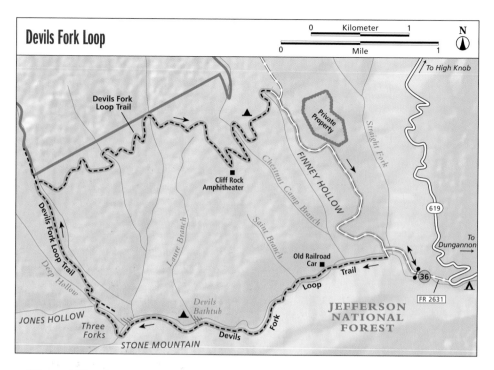

Miles and Directions

0.0   Start at a parking area on FR 2631. Depart the parking area by walking up a flight of tall stairs and turning left on the dirt and gravel forest road.

0.1   Cross Straight Fork. In a few feet, bear left at a double yellow blaze, avoiding a trail that branches right. **Note:** The yellow-blazed dirt road that arcs right and uphill from this clearing is the return leg of this loop.

0.3   Cross Devils Fork, the first of ten crossings in the next 2 miles. The trail alternates between wide, flat stretches and narrow, eroded footpaths. Sections of trail often merge with the streambed itself. After spring floods, parts of the trail may be washed out or blocked by downed trees.

0.6   After crossing Devils Fork several times, stay alert for ruins of a small railcar on the right side of the trail. (A narrow-gauge railroad once ran alongside Devils Fork, used to haul out lumber from the stream valley.)

1.4   Arrive at a scenic crossing of Devils Fork. Just downstream, the river bends and the stratified layers of bedrock are visible where the stream has eroded and undercut the stream bank.

1.5   In an area of fallen rocks strewn around the trail, a tall cliff face rises five stories high on the left side of the trail. Descend along the trail to the stream and the first of the "tubs" that comprise the "Devils Bathtub." (Devils Bathtub's name derives from the way the stream pours down a V-shaped cut in the shale streambed and swirls in whirlpool fashion into a round "tub," or basin at the foot of the falls.)

2.1   The trail takes a sharp right turn and heads northwest out of the Devils Fork gorge. Deep Hollow forms below on the right.

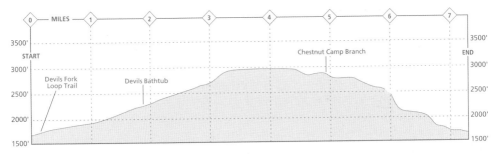

2.3 After a steep climb on a woods path, the trail merges with an old roadbed, which is a wide, graded, and grassy path. In 0.1 mile after this merge, turn right at a double yellow blaze and descend into Deep Hollow on a footpath. Cross the small stream and climb the opposite hillside.

2.8 Switchback over a shoulder ridge separating Deep and Corder Hollows. The footpath will climb, then drop off this ridge into Corder Hollow.

3.6 Cross a streambed (dry in late summer) and begin a traverse of Little Mountain's undulating slope. A number of streams run down this hill to Devils Fork. **Note:** Blazes are infrequent on this stretch of trail, and it shows little use by hikers. As a result, stay alert where the woods path may be unmarked and obscured by leaf litter.

4.1 Veer left and downhill at a double yellow blaze on the trail.

4.6 Crest a small knoll and note the six-trunked tree. (Trees with two or more trunks are common in woodlands that were once logged. It is evidence of *girdling*, or removing a ring of bark between knee and waist high. This kills the tree above the girdle mark but not below. The still-living trunk will often sprout two or more trunks as it grows again.)

4.8 Turn right at a double blaze and descend right off the hillside into a gully. There is a natural rock amphitheater here along the right side of the trail.

4.9 Bear right as the trail merges with a faint road trace.

5.6 Turn right and begin a descent to Straight Branch.

6.0 Bear right as the trail merges with another grassy road. Uphill is private property.

7.0 Enter a clearing alongside Straight Fork. Cross the stream and hike up a small knoll on the dirt/gravel forest road.

7.1 Arrive back at the parking area on FR 2631.

Hike Information

Local Information

Wise County Chamber of Commerce, Norton, (276) 679-0961, www.wisecounty chamber.org

Heart of Appalachia, Big Stone Gap, (276) 762-0011 or (888) 798-2386, www .heartofappalachia.com

Town of Big Stone Gap, (276) 523-0115, www.bigstonegap.org

Lodging

Natural Tunnel State Park, Duffield, (276) 940-2674. Camping is available.

Jessie Lea RV Park, Bit Stone Gap, (276) 523-0055, www.jessielearv.com

37 Stone Mountain Trail

The 12.5-mile Stone Mountain Trail begins with the long climb from Cave Springs. The tall cliffs and boulders that crop out from the mountain slope make for a dramatic introduction to the ridge, and soon give way to whopping views off Stone Mountain's ridgetop. From the last of these overlooks, High Butte, it's possible to see the bumpy profile of Kentucky's Black Mountains to the west, while eastward run Virginia's narrow ridges and valleys. The final leg of the Stone Mountain Trail down Roaring Run is tailor-made for people who save the best for last. The stream cascades through small gorges beneath hemlock and rhododendron.

Start: Cave Springs Recreation Area
Distance: 12.5 miles point to point, with a 14.5-mile overnight option
Hiking time: About 7 hours
Difficulty: Moderate to difficult with steep climbs up Stone Mountain
Trail surface: Dirt footpaths and dirt forest roads lead to exposed cliff lines, stream gorges, old-growth hemlocks, and expansive views.
Land status: National forest
Nearest town: Big Stone Gap, VA
Other trail users: Hunters (in season)
Accessibility: None

Canine compatibility: Dogs permitted
Trail contact: Clinch Ranger District, Wise; (276) 328-2931; www.fs.usda.gov/gwj
Schedule: Open year-round. Hunting is permitted on national forestland. Deer-hunting season in Wise and Lee Counties runs Oct through Jan. The national forest limits hiking groups to 10 people.
Fees/permits: Cave Springs Campground fee
Facilities/features: Cave Springs Campground has restrooms
Maps: USGS Keokee, Big Stone Gap, Appalachia

Finding the trailhead: For start point at Cave Springs: From Big Stone Gap, take Alt US 58 south for 7.1 miles and turn right on VA 982 (Seminary Lane). Go 0.7 mile and turn left on VA 621 (Cave Springs Road). In 1.3 miles the road becomes VA 622 but is still Cave Springs Road (just go straight). In 0.6 mile the road becomes VA 621 again. In 1 mile, cross a railroad track. Go 3 miles and turn right into Cave Springs Recreation Area (VA 845). In the off season, there may be a gate across the road. Park on the road shoulder, but do not block the gate. GPS: N36 48.118' / W82 55.284'. *DeLorme: Virginia Atlas & Gazetteer:* Page 19, B7.

Shuttle point at Roaring Branch: From Big Stone Gap, go north on US 23 toward Appalachia. In 1.4 miles, on a curve, you'll see the trailhead and stream coming down on the left. For safety, proceed up to a safe place to turn around and come back down. There's very limited parking here, enough for one or two cars, but overnight is not recommended. Be very careful getting in and out of the car, as there's very little shoulder. For overnight parking, go south from the trailhead 0.8 mile to the Auto World/Jeep Chrysler dealership (721 E. Fifth St. North, Big Stone Gap, 276-523-4667) and ask permission to park there. GPS: N36 53.015' / W82 47.276'. *DeLorme: Virginia Atlas & Gazetteer:* Page 20, A1.

A dozen years later: the author walking beneath the Stone Mountain overhang, 2011. ▶

The Hike

A view off High Butte spans the Powell Valley and reaches into folds and contours on Wallen Ridge. These shady nooks are the "dark hollows" made famous in stories such as John Fox Jr.'s *Trail of the Lonesome Pine*. Fox's heroine, a mountain girl named June Tolliver, left a closely guarded mountain home and close-knit family for schooling in Big Stone Gap. In the hills, her family grappled with changes brought by discovery of coal and the clash of mountain culture with the law and order of civil society.

Hiking Stone Mountain Trail, it's difficult to separate characters, real and imagined, from the natural wonders. The model for Fox's June Tolliver, a woman named Elizabeth Morris, hailed from Keokee. At Olinger Gap, the Olinger Gap Trail descends to Lake Keokee, a remote, man-made lake stocked with bass and muskie. Fox based other characters on colorful real-life personalities such as "Devil John" Wright, a desperado, and "Red Fox," a preacher, herb doctor, and moonshiner. Both were publicly hanged in 1893 for killing three members of the Mullins family in an ambush on Pine Mountain.

Recent history takes the form of carved stone steps alongside Roaring Branch. Local masons, out of work and destitute from the boom-bust cycle of the coal industry, carved the steps while working for the Civilian Conservation Corps (CCC). (In the 1960s, the Forest Service completed similar stonework at Cave Springs Recreation Area, where this hike begins.) The beauty of the moss-covered steps and shady hemlocks makes the Roaring Run stretch of Stone Mountain Trail a "rangers' choice"—national forest district rangers compete for maintenance duty on this section of the trail!

Roaring Run gurgles and tumbles into the Powell River, which flows to nearby Big Stone Gap. The Gap was built by Eastern industrialists who made—and lost—fortunes on coal. Stone Mountain, centrally located in a region known for coal production, never yielded the deposits that made nearby Dickenson, Wise, and Buchanan Counties famous. Stone Mountain did, however, supply lumber by the railroad-car full. Chestnut and oak came off the dry ridgetops. From the slopes, lumbermen took oak, poplar, ash, and beech. Out of the coves came thick-trunked hemlocks. Today, every species has returned in quantity, if not size, among the present-day forests of Stone Mountain—except the chestnut tree, which suffered a debilitating blight in the early twentieth century.

The mountain itself originated from a cycle of oceanic, sedimentary, and mountain-building events, repeated several times. Walking the high, exposed cliff lines to High Butte, it defies rational thought to imagine that, hundreds of millions of years ago, this land appeared as shoals and beaches of the prehistoric Iapitus Ocean. Two and a half miles up the Stone Mountain Trail, an up-close inspection of massive rock cliffs shows a pebbly conglomerate. The rocks are the size of loose change—dimes, nickels, and quarters—melded together in a stucco-like consistency. Streaks of colors indicate the layering that built this rock over millions of

Roaring Branch near the end of the trail.

years. Here and there, red streaks mark hematite, an iron oxide.

This rock outcrop punctuates a steep climb out of Cave Springs. Along twenty-five switchbacks, the trail traces Stone Mountain's contours, running from moist drainages to dry, exposed slopes. As it climbs, the trail takes an increasingly narrow, precipitous route. Green spleenwort fern adds color to the orange and brown carpet of leaves in moist areas. In fall, acorns litter the trail. Large, isolated boulders appear amid the trees; these blocks of rock were split from formations higher upslope by a process of freezing and thawing that expanded cracks until large chunks fell away and tumbled downhill.

Departing from the old Olinger fire tower (only four concrete corner post bases remain, resting in the overgrowth off the left side of the trail), the wide, undulating road serves as nice relief from the first 4 miles of the hike—though you still have a steep climb in and out of Low Gap. Past Low Gap, the trail follows a cliff line with overlooks onto the Powell River Valley. The Powell River, along with the Clinch, runs a southwest course between Stone Mountain and Wallen Ridge. The river is home to the odd-looking species known as the paddlefish. Scaleless, with a large head and a body measuring up to 64 inches, the paddlefish is currently threatened nationwide, a result of overfishing by the caviar industry. In Virginia, the fish suffers from high levels of sediment in the Powell River, a problem that has placed a number of fish, mussels, snails, and mollusks that inhabit the river on the threatened and endangered list.

The Powell name extends beyond the river to one of the region's prominent landforms, Powell Mountain. In Virginia, a unique mountain culture thrived here and radiated into surrounding hills, including Stone Mountain. The Melungeon, a mixed-race group of mountain inhabitants, were once thought to be part Portuguese and part Cherokee. Today, tracing their race and ethnicity is a cottage industry. Melungeon gatherings celebrate the heritage of a people long discriminated against because of their dark complexion. Genetic and language analysis explore links between the Melungeons and Mediterranean, Middle Eastern, and Central Asian immigrants.

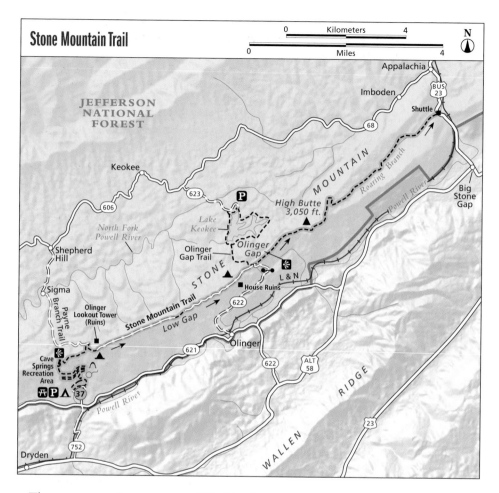

Stone Mountain Trail

These were not, however, your Ellis Island–variety newcomers. A theory currently in vogue traces their arrival to Sir Francis Drake, an English privateer who deposited several hundred Turkish and Moorish sailors onto Roanoke Island, on the coast of North Carolina, in 1586. When Drake returned to resupply, there were no signs of the sailors. Survivors, it's assumed, mixed with the Native American population. How their ancestors reached the hidden coves and folds of Appalachia makes for dandy daydreaming as you stare off the high outcrops of Stone Mountain.

Miles and Directions

0.0 Start at the Cave Springs Overlook trailhead between campsites 24 and 21. The dirt footpath is flanked by rhododendron, and within a few feet of starting, veers right and uphill where an unmarked trail branches left. In 0.1 mile, there is a spur trail on the left leading a few feet to the Cave Springs.

0.2 Reach a four-way junction and turn right on the yellow-blazed Stone Mountain Trail. **Option:** Turn left at this junction to visit Cave Springs Overlook, a round, elevated earthen dais with, unfortunately, poor summertime views of Powell Valley. From here, the Stone Mountain Trail climbs via twenty-five switchbacks through a hardwood forest to reach the crest of Stone Mountain.

1.9 Pass by the first of several imposing rock outcrops and tall cliffs. Red streaks in this rock indicate the presence of iron ore. Close inspection reveals the rock's composite of dime- and quarter-size pebbles melded together.

2.3 The trail turns left, and the forest understory grows denser with rhododendron, sassafras, and mountain maple. The trail will achieve the top of Stone Mountain in 0.1 mile and bear right to follow the ridgeline in a north-northeast direction.

3.0 The trail arcs left around a small knob and, after 0.1 mile, pops over an earthen embankment onto a wide dirt forest road. Follow the road right and uphill. At the top, in woods off the left side of the trail, are remnants of the old Olinger lookout tower.

4.7 A long descent off the ridgeline marks the approach to Low Gap. In the gap, a dirt road continues downhill to the left, while the blazed Stone Mountain Trail goes straight uphill through a tunnel of mountain laurel. For the next 0.3 mile, Stone Mountain Trail is steep and poorly blazed and requires you scale several tall rock ledges. The road downhill to the left is a longer work-around to this difficult stretch of trail.

6.0 Excellent views open up from a cliff on the right side of the trail.

6.6 A clearing on the right shows signs of heavy campsite use. A road exits the right side of the trail, leading to the ruins of a cabin with a sheet-metal roof 100 feet or so downslope.

7.1 Trail enters Olinger Gap and a four-way junction. Continue straight through the gap on the yellow-blazed Stone Mountain Trail heading uphill. **Option:** Turn left on blue-blazed Olinger Gap Trail, which descends to Lake Keokee in 1 mile. There is primitive camping and water at the lake. A right onto a dirt road takes you 0.5 mile to parking at the end of VA 622.

7.4 Finish the climb out of Olinger Gap and begin walking along a narrow open rock-face with steep drop-offs on either side. Views to the right span Powell Valley.

7.8 The trail drops off the ridgeline to the left as it passes by several large rock outcrops.

8.0 Begin a short, steep descent into a saddleback.

8.2 Finish a climb out of the saddleback to an open rock-face with soaring views east over Powell Valley.

8.9 After a series of small dips and ever-steeper climbs, the trail opens onto High Butte (3,050 feet), the highest point on the hike, with views east across Powell Valley and west to the Black Mountain range.

9.6 Reach the summit of Stonega. The Stone Mountain Trail enters a young, mixed hardwood forest of chestnut oak and maple, leaving behind the exposed ridgetop vegetation of

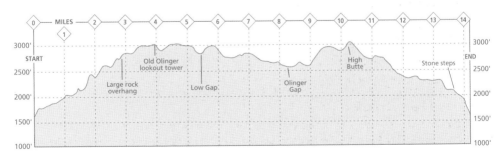

berries, shrubs, and scrub oak. The 3-mile descent to US 23 passes through three distinct Appalachian forests types: the heaths, oaks, and hickories on the ridge; mixed hardwoods of tulip poplars, maples, and buckeyes midway down the slope; and finally eastern hemlock and mountain laurel in the moist soil along Roaring Branch.

10.9 Complete your descent into the Roaring Branch valley by crossing the stream to the right bank. In the next 0.5 mile, the Appalachian hardwood forest gives way to towering hemlocks.

11.9 Climb up and over three spur ridges. As you top out on the third, the rushing waters of Roaring Branch are audible. The forest has a primeval feel, with tall hemlocks blocking sunlight and large rocks coated in lush green moss. The forest floor is carpeted with ferns and rotted leaves. Roaring Branch descends over a series of picturesque waterfalls.

12.4 Begin descending on stone steps. **Note:** Steps are slick and mossy.

12.5 Hike ends at US 23.

Hike Information

Local Information
Town of Big Stone Gap, (276) 523-0115, www.bigstonegap.org

Local Events/Attractions
Coal/Railroad Days, first weekend in Aug, Appalachia, (276) 565-0055

Trail of the Lonesome Pine Outdoor Drama, late June through Aug, Big Stone Gap, (800) 362-0149, www.trailofthelonesomepine.com. Virginia's official state outdoor theater is a retelling of John Fox Jr.'s novel about mountain folk.

Southwest Virginia Museum, Big Stone Gap, (276) 523-1322. Majestic stone home that ably chronicles the boom and bust of Big Stone Gap.

June Tolliver House, Big Stone Gap, (276) 523-4707

Lodging
Cave Springs Recreation Area, Wise, (540) 328-2931. Campground.

Jessie Lea RV Park, Bit Stone Gap, (276) 523-0055, www.jessielearv.com

Other Resources
My Melungeon Heritage, by Mattie Ruth Johnson, Overmountain Press

Honorable Mentions: Southwest Highlands

EE. Bald Mountain

A remote hike situated northwest of New Castle on VA 617. The Pines Recreation Area serves as a base camp for exploring the streams that lead up Bald and Potts Mountains. Recent clearing activity on the ridges has opened up views into West Virginia. (540) 864-5195. GPS: N37 36.300' / W80 04.571'. *DeLorme: Virginia Atlas & Gazetteer:* Page 52, D2.

FF. North Mountain-AT Loop

A long hike northwest of Roanoke. Take exit 140 off I-81 and follow VA 311 to trailhead parking opposite the intersection of VA 311 and VA 624. Volunteers have recently cleared the North Mountain leg of this difficult 28.7-mile loop. An added bonus is the proximity of Dragons Tooth, one of Virginia's most impressive short hikes. (540) 864-5195. GPS: N37 22.514' / W80 08.935'. *DeLorme: Virginia Atlas & Gazetteer:* Page 42, B1.

GG. The Rice Fields

From Blacksburg, take VA 460 west to VA 641; make a right onto VA 641 and follow to a parking lot (within 0.5 mile of where the Appalachian Trail [AT] crosses the road). The Rice Fields are open meadows on top of Peters Mountain accessed via the AT. For 10 miles along this stretch, the AT follows the Virginia–West Virginia border. Where it intersects the Allegheny Trail, the AT descends back into Virginia. This is an out-and-back hike with no loop possibilities. (540) 552-4641. GPS: N37 21.306' / W.80 45.944'. *DeLorme: Virginia Atlas & Gazetteer:* Page 40, B3. (Also see page 342.)

HH. Hungry Mother State Park

A gem of a park located 3 miles north of Marion on VA 16. There are 12 miles of trails in this 2,180-acre state park. Highlights include inspired views from the Lake Trail of early morning mist rising off Hungry Mother Lake against a backdrop of brilliant fall foliage. Molly's Pioneer Trail and Molly's Knob Trail lead 2.2 miles to a 3,270-foot peak with views of Mount Rogers. (540) 783-3422. GPS: N36 53.036' / W81 31.597'. *DeLorme: Virginia Atlas & Gazetteer:* Page 23, A5.

II.   Guest River Gorge Trail

A 6-mile point-to-point on a former railroad grade along the Guest River west of St. Paul. Starting at the northern end, this pleasant walk is a gradual and scenic descent into the gorge. The railway hauled the coal and saltpeter mined in the gorge, leaving behind sheer cliffs. The area harbors several threatened and endangered animals and plants. (540) 328-2931. GPS: N36 55.378' / W82 27.053'. *DeLorme: Virginia Atlas & Gazetteer:* Page 20, A4.

Mount Rogers National Recreation Area

In Virginia, the Blue Ridge escarpment culminates in a large concentration of peaks and ridges near the North Carolina border. Here, Mount Rogers pokes a tree-shrouded summit above neighboring mountains to lay claim as the state's highest point. Competition is stiff, with only a 200-foot difference between it and nearby Whitetop Mountain. Striking about both—other than their size—is how little these peaks and the rural landscape around them resemble the more dramatic and sharply etched mountains in the northern Blue Ridge. The difference reflects forces that have shaped each. Folding and faulting characterized late-era mountain-building activity to the north. Here in southwest Virginia, the Blue Ridge's sweeping mountain slopes and rounded stream valleys resulted from hundreds of millions of years of erosion.

Little about Mount Rogers's high country resembles Virginia's other mountain regions. The spruce-fir forest at the highest elevations contains plants and animals typical of northern boreal forests, a result of the last ice age, which pushed plants and animals southward in its path. Mount Rogers's volcanic bedrock contains rhyolite, a mineral found nowhere else in Virginia. Even views seem otherworldly. Looking west from a wide meadow between Cabin Ridge and Mount Rogers appears more Big Sky, Montana, than Southern Appalachian.

In the high-mountain meadows that slope away from Mount Rogers, horses graze in knee-high grass. A hiker's approaching footsteps may stir a foal that lies hidden in the overgrowth on Wilburn Ridge. Hawthorn trees and large, house-size boulders scattered randomly across the fields above. Scales break up the smooth lines of these meadows. The fields here are entirely man-made, created after clear-cut logging and since maintained, first by grazing and now through periodic burning done by the Forest Service.

Given the popularity of climbing Mount Rogers, visitors would do well to disperse their activity over as wide an area as possible. In a recreation area of 117,000 acres, it's easy to find other attractions, be it the laurel-choked streams on Iron Mountain or the rugged backcountry in Little Dry Run Wilderness, in the often-overlooked eastern section of Mount Rogers National Recreation Area.

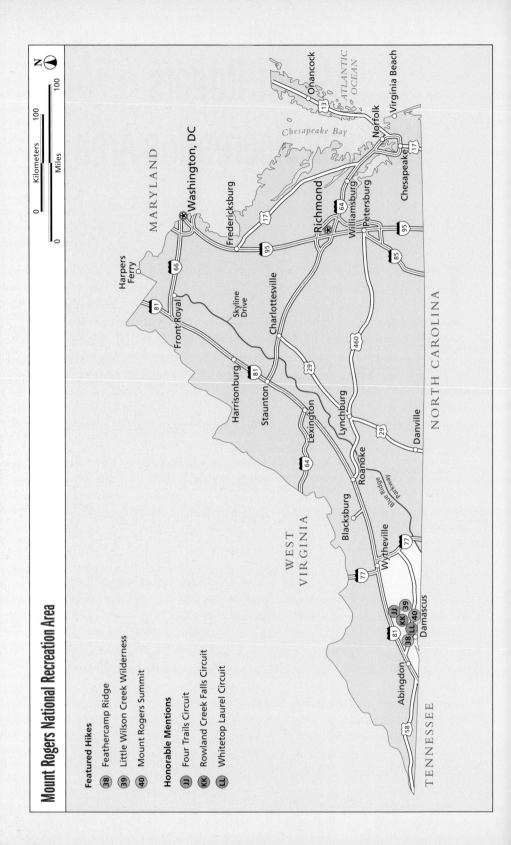

The Hikes

38. Feathercamp Ridge
39. Little Wilson Creek Wilderness
40. Mount Rogers Summit

Honorable Mentions

JJ. Four Trails Circuit
KK. Rowland Creek Falls Circuit
LL. Whitetop Laurel Circuit

38 Feathercamp Ridge

If Mount Rogers's summit is the heart, Iron Mountain is the backbone of southwest Virginia's mountain playground. Its breadth, 80 miles from the Tennessee-Virginia state line to the New River, makes it one of Virginia's longest ridges. The natural resources it holds made it a target of mineral and timber industries in earlier times. Now it simply offers miles of uninterrupted hiking and access to remote, less-visited parts of Mount Rogers National Recreation Area. On Feathercamp Branch, the scenery rivals any along Virginia's many mountain streams. As it ducks under thick rhododendron, it gathers speed between the steep shoulders of Iron Mountain and drops into shallow pools deep enough to wade.

Start: Appalachian Trail (AT) at US 58
Distance: 8.1-mile loop
Hiking time: About 5 hours
Difficulty: Moderate due to well-graded trails, good signage, gentle ascents, and only a few steep sections of trail
Trail surface: Dirt woodland paths and old roads lead to dry ridges, cove forests, and streams.
Land status: National recreation area
Nearest town: Damascus, VA
Other trail users: Mountain bikers and equestrians
Accessibility: You can access the accessible Virginia Creeper trail at Straight Branch
Canine compatibility: Dogs permitted
Trail contact: Mount Rogers National Recreation Area, Marion; (276) 783-5196 or (800)

628-7202; www.fs.usda.gov/gwj. The visitor center is 10 miles north of Troutdale on VA 16.
Schedule: Open year-round. Hunting permitted, with the busiest season between Nov and Jan. Forest rangers conduct prescribed burns outside the wilderness in fall and spring.
Fees/permits: No permits required. Tent site fee (backcountry camping is free); shower fee for nonregistered campers; day-use parking fee at some areas.
Facilities/features: Toilet and parking at trailhead
Maps: USGS Konnarock; Mount Rogers High Country & Wilderness map available at Mount Rogers Visitor Center; Appalachian Trail Map 1: Mount Rogers National Recreation Area available from Appalachian Trail Conference, Harpers Ferry, WV

Finding the trailhead: From Damascus, take VA 91/US 58 east. At 0.6 miles, VA 91 splits to the right. Turn left to stay on US 58. Go 3.1 miles and turn right into the Straight Branch NRA parking area (there's a sign for Virginia Creeper Trail parking), with a restroom and access to the AT and Virginia Creeper Trail (the Iron Mountain Trailhead is across the highway.) From Grayson Highlands SP, take US 58 west 22.7 miles to the Straight Branch NRA parking area on left. GPS: N36 38.639' / 81 44.405'. *DeLorme: Virginia Atlas & Gazetteer:* Page 22, D2.

The Hike

As mountain ridges go, Iron Mountain is classic—undulating and, as you huff up and over your umpteenth knob, seemingly never-ending. Small peaks punctuate the long

Mountain bikers on the multi-use Feathercamp Branch Trail.

ridgeline. Hikers know a day spent "up on the ridge" is both an exhilarating and exasperating experience. The latter emotion results, unfortunately, from sheer monotony. Woods-covered ridges lack the glamour of a peak, or the drama, say, of a canyon. After the sixth knob (was it the sixth or was that last one the sixth?), they start to resemble a popular television rabbit: They keep going and going and going . . .

The Iron Mountain Trail would suffer this unkind judgment, if not for some key redeeming features. Among them, in my humble opinion, are blackberry thickets near Clark Mountain. One hundred yards of trailside thickets hold blackberries so juicy and plump, a mere touch stains the fingers with dark juice. No one should ever become so busy walking that she ignores the fruits of her labor.

Iron Mountain's other treasure lies in the many coves formed by ridge spurs that intersect it from all directions. Streams, torturous in their route, cut down these narrow, lush valleys. In the shade of tall trees, layers of leaf rot make a fertile bed for an array of mushrooms. The scaly vase chanterelle is an eye-catcher. Orange or yellow in color, its shape looks suspiciously like a waffle cone. Unlike waffle cones, however, tasting this mushroom is not recommended. It's not poisonous, but has a bitter taste

Signage showing horses use the trail too.

and may cause indigestion. Other mushrooms pop up unexpectedly as you hike: slickners (poisonous), American Caesars (edible, but not choice), and yellow and violet corals, as well as milky mushrooms.

The abundance of mushrooms on the Iron Mountain section of the Appalachian Trail makes the plant worth a closer look. Technically, mushrooms are plants. Unlike green plants, however, they do not contain chlorophyll; their food source is organic material. Where a mushroom grows not only helps identify the type, but also the food source. The thick, pink beefsteak polypore grows on dead trees and extracts food from the rotting wood. The largest and most-studied mushroom type, the mycorrhizal, has a symbiotic relationship with their host plant. Out of sight, beneath the earth, a mycorrhizal mushroom coats root stems of plants with threadlike strands; this helps the host plant grow. In exchange, the mushroom receives food. Of course, most people identify a mushroom by its cap—technically the fruit of a mushroom. And while tracking edible wild mushrooms is a booming hobby (remember, never eat a wild mushroom unless absolutely sure it is edible), their plentiful shapes and colors on Iron Mountain approach the beauty of wildflowers in spring.

The wildflowers on Feathercamp Branch emerge in April. The white blossom of mayapple hides away beneath umbrella-shaped leaves on a single, delicate stem (only plants with two leaves produce a flower). Appearances notwithstanding, this small wildflower is cousin to barberry, a thorny bush favored by professional landscapers—the link between them is berries. Anyone familiar with the orange and yellow barberry fruit will see a resemblance in the mayapple, which bears a single, red fruit three months after the flower blossoms. Herbalists use crushed barberry root for treating pink eye, diarrhea, and giardiasis (which hikers know as the infection contracted from drinking untreated stream or spring water). The unripe mayapple fruit isn't poisonous, but it will give you a stomachache.

Feathercamp Branch is a beauty of a stream, decked out in rhododendron, mountain laurel, and shrubby trees. After a rainstorm, shrubs and thickets fairly burst with chirps and peeps of warblers and songbirds. The stream sings as well, running a gentle grade between two steep ridges. An impenetrable thicket of rhododendron camouflages the stream near its headwaters. Farther downstream, you can sit on boulders and watch buds fall from rhododendron and float past. If they were seaworthy, they'd eventually reach the Gulf of Mexico via Laurel Creek, the New River, the Kanawha River, the Ohio River, and, finally, the great Mississippi. Across Iron Mountain, Rush Creek flows off in the opposite direction of Feathercamp Branch; it empties into the South Fork Holston River. It, too, will reach the Gulf of Mexico someday, but because the ridge of Iron Mountain marks the Tennessee Divide, these two streams follow very different routes. That's the effect of the divide: Streams that begin a mere 2,500 feet apart empty into the Ohio River more than 100 miles distant from one another.

The Ohio and Mississippi Rivers and the Gulf of Mexico are distant thoughts as you nestle into your sleeping bag on Feathercamp Ridge. Leaves rustle, twigs crack, tree branches sway. If you're straining your ears, trying to attach size and shape to the noises (Feathercamp Ridge is home to deer, turkeys, a host of other animals, and a good number of bears as well), take comfort that you're not alone. Somewhere above you, in the trees, a great horned owl swivels its head. The owl's eyes are encased in bone. To compensate for little eye movement, they turn their heads on very flexible necks, with a rotation range of 270 degrees in some species. The great horned owl is among the largest of owls, and streamsides such as Feathercamp Branch make ideal hunting ground for live prey. But before you ever hear it swoop for a mouse or frog, you'll hear its signature call: three to eight hoots, the second and third rapid and doubled. Superstition labels owls as harbingers of ghosts and omens of death—in part due to their silent flight and stalking nature. It's also true, however, that when salted and eaten, the owl was thought to cure gout. I prefer to think of them as sentinels, sitting stock-still on a branch. If I'm feeling spooked, I mimic their call. There's a good chance the owl will respond.

Miles and Directions

0.0 Start from a pull-off on US 58 at the confluence of Laurel Creek and Straight Branch. Cross US 58, enter the woods, and hike upstream following white AT blazes. **Note:** The Forest Service built a large earthen mound where the trail enters woods to block off-road vehicles.

0.1 The blue-blazed Feathercamp Branch Trail continues straight. Turn left and follow the AT for a 2-mile climb to Iron Mountain Trail through rich hardwood forests.

0.6 The AT intersects with a dirt road (FR 4552). Cross the road and continue straight along the AT. **Option:** A right turn on FR 4552 will take you up to the top of Iron Mountain, making for a shorter hike. The trail is nicely constructed to dip in and out of Iron Mountain's folds. You'll pass under white oak, chestnut oak, hickory, and dogwood. The ground is covered with several types of mosses and numerous mushrooms.

2.0 Turn right onto an unnamed blue-blazed trail that connects the AT and Iron Mountain Trail. In 0.1 mile, turn right onto yellow-blazed Iron Mountain Trail. **Note:** Iron Mountain Trail skirts a knob to the right, passing by the wavy fronds of black snakeroot.

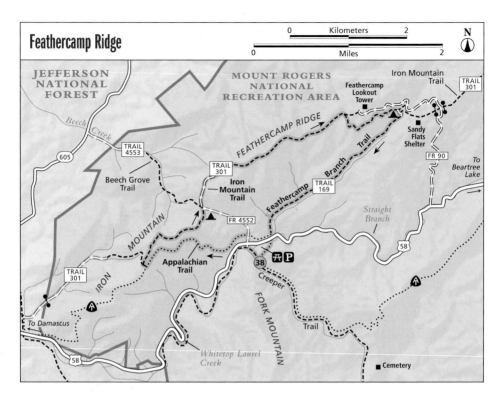

Feathercamp Ridge

JEFFERSON NATIONAL FOREST

MOUNT ROGERS NATIONAL RECREATION AREA

Iron Mountain Trail

Feathercamp Lookout Tower

TRAIL 301

Sandy Flats Shelter

FEATHERCAMP RIDGE

TRAIL 4553

Beech Creek

605

Branch Trail

TRAIL 301

FR 90

To Beartree Lake

Beech Grove Trail

Iron Mountain Trail

TRAIL 169

Feathercamp

Straight Branch

FR 4552

58

MOUNTAIN

IRON

Appalachian Trail

TRAIL 301

38

To Damascus

Creeper

FORK MOUNTAIN

Trail

58

Whitetop Laurel Creek

Cemetery

3.1   Enter a clearing where the trail becomes a wide, grassy road. There are blueberry thickets on your left. Follow the road straight. Ahead on the right you'll find a fire ring that sees frequent use.

3.4   Iron Mountain Trail reenters woods, climbing amid bear oak, poplar, and table mountain pine to skirt right of another knob. There are lots of mountain laurel here and a large dogwood tree.

5.0   Arrive at a fork in the trail; bear right and continue on Iron Mountain Trail up a small knob. **Side trip:** If you bear left at the fork, you can take Feathercamp Ridge Trail 0.2 mile to FR 90 and Feathercamp Lookout Tower.

5.9   Take a hard right and follow Iron Mountain Trail downhill through a grove of hemlock. Within 0.1 mile, it drops you onto blue-blazed Feathercamp Branch Trail, which begins as a doubletrack dirt road. Turn right to return to US 58. **Side trip:** Sandy Flats Shelter is 0.3 mile up Iron Mountain Trail.

6.0   Pass through a clearing with a fire ring. As you reenter the woods, Feathercamp Branch Trail reverts to a singletrack woods path.

7.0   The stream on your left, Feathercamp Branch, has gained enough strength at this point to create nice toe-dipping pools at the bottom of small cascades.

7.6   Cross a feeder stream that enters Feathercamp Branch from the right. This marks the start of a series of stream crossings between here and the AT.

8.0   Feathercamp Branch Trail merges with the AT trail. Follow the white-blazed AT trail straight.

8.1   Arrive back at US 58.

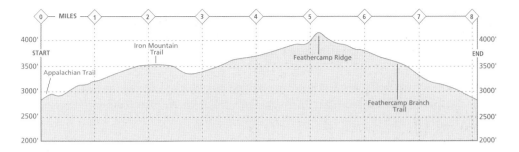

Hike Information

Local Information

Town of Damascus Tourism, (276) 475-3542, www.damascus.org

Grayson County Tourism, Independence, (276) 773-3711, www.graysoncounty va.com

Abingdon Convention & Visitors Bureau, Abingdon, (800) 435-3440, www .abingdon.com/tourism

Local Events/Attractions

Blue Ridge Backroads at the Rex Theater, Galax, (276) 236-0668. Live radio music show every Fri from Galax's downtown theater. Programs air on 98.1 WBRC-FM.

Galax Old Time Fiddlers Convention, second week in Aug, Galax, (276) 238-8130. Attracts national and international recording acts. Grayson Highlands State Park and the town of Fries also host bluegrass, old-time, and country music festivals every year.

Grayson County Fiddlers Convention, last full weekend in June, Elk Creek, (276) 655-4740

Naturalist Rally, second weekend in May, Mount Rogers, (276) 579-7092

Whitetop Mountain Ramp Festival, third Sun in May, Whitetop, (276) 773-3711. *Ramp* is a term for wild leek, and this festival features an eating contest that can bring you to tears—from laughter or from the onion itself.

Grayson Highlands Fall Festival, last full weekend of Sept, Grayson Highlands State Park, Mouth of Wilson, (276) 579-7092. Just one of many fall festivals in the area. Independence, Fries, Baywood, and Marion all hold fall festivals through Sept and Oct.

Appalachian Trail Days, third week in May, Damascus, (276) 475-3831. Annual gathering of AT thru-hikers in the town dubbed "friendliest town on the AT."

Grandfather Mountain Country Store, Damascus, (423) 739-2557. Hams, jellies, syrups, and jerky—it's all authentic handmade or homemade mountain food. A nice collection of mountain crafts, T-shirts, and books as well.

Lodging

The Enchanted Lodge, White Top, (276) 466-4044, www.enchantedlodge.com. Log lodge surrounded by mountain views and 17 acres with hiking trails. Spa treatments available.

More than a half-dozen Damascus residents have turned their homes into bed-and-breakfasts to accommodate the many hikers and bikers who frequent the small town. Call (276) 475-3381 or visit www.damascus.org.

Abingdon has numerous bed-and-breakfasts, motels, and the famed Camberley's Martha Washington Inn, (800) 555-8000, www.marthawashingtoninn.com.

For other lodging in Abingdon, contact the Convention & Visitors Bureau, (800) 435-3440, www.abingdon.com/visitors/lodging/htm.

North of the Mount Rogers area, the town of Marion has several motels. Call Smyth County Chamber of Commerce, (276) 783-3161, or visit www.smyth chamber.org.

Grayson Highlands State Park has camping on the southern boundary of the Mount Rogers area, (800) 933-PARK.

Restaurants

Side Track Computer Cafe, Damascus, (276) 475-6106. A favorite hangout for hikers.

Damascus Old Mill, (276) 475-3745, www.damascusoldmill.com. A recently renovated 1912 mill turned restaurant and sports bar with outdoor seating on the banks of Laurel Creek.

Cowboys, Damascus, (276) 475-5444. This deli, located inside a service station, has great Southern breakfasts.

In the Country, Damascus, (276) 475-5319. Bakery, eatery, and ice cream shop.

Organizations

Appalachian Trail Conference, Harpers Ferry, WV, (304) 535-6331, www.appalachian trail.org

Virginia's Southwest Blue Ridge Highlands, Inc., Abingdon, (800) 446-9670, www.virginiablueridge.org. A regional tourism agency with information on festivals and attractions throughout southwest Virginia.

Other Resources

Appalachian Trail Guide to Southwest Virginia, Appalachian Trail Conference, Harpers Ferry, WV

39 Little Wilson Creek Wilderness

Most hikers enter Little Wilson Creek Wilderness on trails out of Grayson Highlands State Park. Scales, an area named for the livestock scales once located here, makes a great alternate starting point. You not only avoid crowds but get a high-country fix that much faster. Scales sits smack-dab in the midst of Mount Rogers' crest zone, flanked by Stone Mountain and Wilburn Ridge. Huckleberry bushes bloom profusely (there are reports of folks carrying three gallons or more out of thickets along Scales Trail). On Stone Mountain, wild horses graze. As you approach them, young foals bolt from cover of tall grass and dart behind their mothers. In the words of a passerby, "It's as wild as it gets up here."

Start: Corralled campground at Scales

Distance: 7.6-mile loop

Hiking time: About 5 hours

Difficulty: Moderate due to some long climbs and several muddy, eroded sections of trail

Trail surface: A combination of dirt footpaths, old dirt wagon roads, and railroad grades lead through high-altitude meadows, mountain balds, and mixed hardwood forests.

Land status: National recreation area

Nearest town: Troutdale, VA

Other trail users: Equestrians

Accessibility: None

Canine compatibility: Dogs permitted

Trail contact: Mount Rogers National Recreation Area, Marion; (276) 783-5196 or (800) 628-7202. The visitor center is 10 miles north of Troutdale on VA 16. Grayson Highlands State Park; (276) 579-7092; www.dcr.state.va.us/parks/graysonh.htm.

Schedule: Open year-round. Hunting permitted, with the busiest season between Nov and Jan. Forest rangers conduct prescribed burns outside the wilderness in fall and spring.

Fees/permits: No permits required. Tent site fee (backcountry camping is free); shower fee for nonregistered campers; day-use parking fee at some areas.

Facilities/features: None

Maps: USGS Trout Dale; Mount Rogers High Country & Wilderness map available at the Mount Rogers Visitor Center; Appalachian Trail Map 1: Mount Rogers National Recreation Area available from Appalachian Trail Conference, Harpers Ferry, WV

Finding the trailhead: Four-wheel-drive vehicles with high clearance: From Troutdale, take VA 603 west from its intersection with VA 16. In 2.8 miles, turn left onto FR 613, a dirt road. (Look for a sign on the right-hand side of the road.) Road conditions are rocky, rutted, and sometimes wet. Once on FR 613, you'll pass a fork at 0.7 mile. Turn left. Turn left at the second fork at 2 miles. At 2.8 miles, turn right at the fork. In 3.8 miles, pass through a metal gate (the gate may be closed, but not locked). In 0.2 mile past the gate, enter the campground at Scales. GPS: N36 40.165' / W81 29.224'. *DeLorme: Virginia Atlas & Gazetteer:* Page 23, C5.

Two-wheel-drive or low-clearance vehicles: From Troutdale: Drive south on VA 16. In 7 miles, turn right onto US 58. It is another 7.6 miles on US 58 to the Grayson Highlands State Park entrance road, VA 362. Turn right onto VA 362 and, in 3.1 miles, turn right onto the Grayson Highlands State Park campground access road. It dead-ends at the campground in 1.3 miles. The Wilson Creek trailhead is clearly marked near the ranger station. Follow it downhill and, in 1.8

The Hike

They stare at you from a black-and-white photograph, fourteen men in dirty overalls wearing brimmed hats, saws and poles gripped firmly in hand. Remember them as you soak in the high-country meadows around Scales, a swale in Pine Mountain tucked between Wilburn Ridge and Stone Mountain. If not for loggers like them, this landscape wouldn't exist.

Transformation of Scales, once a weigh-in site for livestock, took a mere twenty years. Starting around 1900, lumber companies and private landowners stripped virgin spruce and fir, chestnut, maple, and oak from the hillsides. What's developed since is a product of man and nature. Erosion carried away fertile soil and exposed portions of volcanic bedrock. Livestock grazing and periodic fires set by the Forest Service keep the forest at bay. From this, Virginia's most striking landscape evolved: miles of meadow awash in green, orange, red, and purple cresting against a horizon filled with Virginia's highest peaks, fading into the haze of North Carolina's Blue Ridge.

First Peak Trail climbs through just this type of landscape en route to Little Wilson Creek Wilderness, a 3,900-acre tract protecting three peaks and five creek watersheds, including the dual headwaters of Little Wilson Creek. As you pass just under the summit of Third Peak, isolated clumps of hawthorn, buckeye, and beech grow increasingly thick and dense. This is how all of the Mount Rogers's crest zone—land 4,000 feet or more above sea level—would look if left to nature. Huckleberry grows in ever-larger thickets. Scrubby witch hazel (the divining rod of choice for modern-day dowsers), flame azaleas, and mountain laurel grow head-high. Small American chestnut intersperse with beech and chinquapin oak.

A blight has stunted the chestnut from growing even big enough to produce its burr-like fruit. Only one hundred years ago, it grew so large, residents of Troutdale, a boomtown at the foot of Pine Mountain, cut 12-by-12-by-2-inch-thick pieces for stepping stones across their muddy roads. C. P. Greer, a Troutdale resident, logged trees so big in this wilderness that, with his daughter perched on his shoulders, the base of a felled tree dwarfed them both. Greer is the man responsible for the faint trace of railroad grades visible on Hightree Rock Trail, one of the wilderness's less-traveled footpaths. He built a small-grade railroad on his own land to carry logs to his mill on Fox Creek, where he processed it for furniture and building material. (Ever the entrepreneur, Greer later converted the mill into a dynamo, or power plant, and supplied Troutdale's first electricity.) It was in the vicinity of Hightree Rock that Greer felled his largest trees. A mile and a half past where it splits from First Peak Trail, the Kabel Trail takes on the appearance of an old railroad grade: wide and flat with high banks. What might have been a rail spur angles left and peters out in thick woods.

Rocks buttress the underside of the trail here, the masonry work visible by looking downslope off the left side.

Locomotives crossed grades like this daily during the boom years on Pine Mountain, traveling from Fairwood, a company town on FR 613. Before a fire destroyed it in 1911, Fairwood served as base of operations for the U.S. Spruce Lumber Company's Pine Mountain operations. Life there and in nearby Troutdale hummed along with the lumber business. Two furniture manufacturers employed any able-bodied man not working in timber. Farmers traveled the dirt roads between their homes and town, carrying livestock and produce to a rail depot at Troutdale. On their return trip, they were loaded with chairs from the factory for their wives and children to cane. Passenger trains ran twice a day from Troutdale south to Sugar Grove and Marion. For a time, Troutdale families rode the rails to Fairwood every Fourth of July for an annual baseball game, since the Spruce Lumber Company had built the finest baseball diamond in the valley.

It was for Spruce Lumber Company that engineer Kent Steffey worked on the fateful September day he took a Shay Locomotive No. 9 up Pine Mountain. After uncoupling a boxcar and reversing the engine, he started downhill. The train gathered speed and Steffey blew two sharp whistles, signaling for brakes. Nothing happened. The train careened on. Steffey's repeated whistle blows pealed across the mountain. The conductor and fireman jumped, but Steffey stayed aboard. Workers later found his body under the smoking wreckage of the 65-ton Shay. All that's left today is his tombstone in Rural Retreat, Virginia, and a ballad, "The Wreck of Ole Number Nine."

Longhorn cattle.

Little Wilson Creek tumbles over rocks.

Still on the rails the bell / Began its pondering clang / And out upon the mountain air / the mourning whistle rang / "Farewell, farewell," it seemed to say / And the wheels like death did sing / It struck the curve with an awful shock / And from the rails she sprang.

They stare at you, men in dirty overalls and brimmed hats sitting atop Steffey's wrecked Shay No. 9. Say what you will about habitats destroyed, species lost, trees gone forever. But don't forget their faces.

Miles and Directions

0.0 Start from the trail board at Scales, an enclosed campground on Pine Mountain. Past the trail board, exit the corral via a pass-thru in the fence. Turn left, keep the fence to your left, and round the next corner of the corral. Bear right and uphill at a signboard for First Peak Trail. **Note:** Avoid the Appalachian Trail (AT), which also ascends through these fields. The AT is clearly marked with white blazes.

0.8 Pass a junction with Third Peak Trail; continue straight.

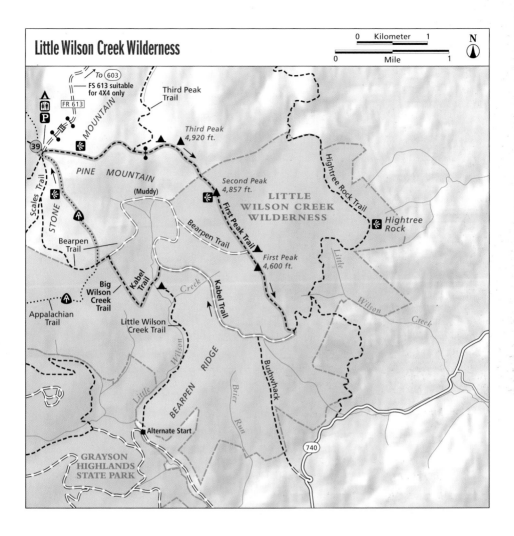

Little Wilson Creek Wilderness

To (603)

FS 613 suitable for 4X4 only

FR 613

Third Peak Trail

MOUNTAIN

39

PINE MOUNTAIN

STONE

(Muddy)

Bearpen Trail

Third Peak 4,920 ft.

Second Peak 4,857 ft.

LITTLE WILSON CREEK WILDERNESS

Bearpen Trail

First Peak Trail

First Peak 4,600 ft.

Hightree Rock Trail

Hightree Rock

Scales Trail

Kabel Trail

Big Wilson Creek Trail

Appalachian Trail

Little Wilson Creek Trail

Creek

Kabel Trail

Little Wilson

Little

Wilson Creek

BEARPEN RIDGE

Brier Run

Bushwhack

Alternate Start

740

GRAYSON HIGHLANDS STATE PARK

1.0   Pass a campsite on the left side of the trail. This is an ideal spot for anyone looking for a sheltered evening under red spruce and hardwoods.

1.1   Pass to the right of 4,920-foot Third Peak.

1.8   Near the top of Second Peak, look out for several footpaths, unblazed, that branch left and disappear into the low forest cover. These trails lead a few hundred feet to a rock outcrop with views. Continue straight on First Peak Trail.

2.3   Enter a clearing. A fire ring marks this as an established backwoods campsite and there are signs of heavy use. Pass straight through the clearing on the First Peak Trail. **Note:** Bearpen Trail departs this clearing to the right. It descends to Little Wilson Creek before climbing to a junction with Big Wilson Creek Trail.

3.0   Reach a T junction and turn right onto Kabel Trail. **Note:** Hightree Rock Trail leads left from this T junction to an overlook in 2 miles.

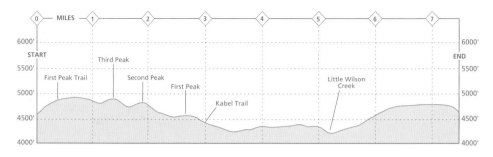

4.8 After passing over some wet ground, climb on Kabel Trail as the route widens from a footpath into a dirt road.

4.9 Turn sharply left and downhill, still on the Kabel Trail.

5.2 Cross a fork of Little Wilson Creek. There's a prime camping spot on the left in a grassy meadow before you cross.

5.5 Kabel Trail ends at Big Wilson Creek Trail. Turn right onto Big Wilson Creek Trail.

6.2 Leave the Little Wilson Creek Wilderness. Just beyond the wilderness sign, Big Wilson Creek Trail intersects Bearpen Trail at a T junction. Turn left onto Bearpen Trail. **Note:** A right turn onto Bearpen leads back to First Peak Trail. Hiking on this trail is not advisable in wet weather because of eroded and muddy trail conditions.

6.4 At a four-way intersection, turn right onto the AT and climb. The trail crosses a barbed-wire fence on a step-up and enters high-country meadows. The grass is waist-high in spots, tall enough to hide young foals resting on the ground. This stretch of the AT is one of the best to see the wild horses of Mount Rogers high country, in part because it is less traveled than trails near the Mount Rogers summit.

7.6 Hike ends at Scales. **Note:** If your hike began in Grayson Highlands State Park, it's another 3.1 miles on the Scales Trail and Wilson Creek Trail to the campground and parking area.

Hike Information

Local Information

Town of Damascus Tourism, (276) 475-3831, www.damascus.org

Grayson County Tourism, Independence, (276) 773-2471, www.graysoncounty va.com

Local Events/Attractions

Blue Ridge Backroads at the Rex Theater, Galax, (276) 236-0668. Live radio music show every Fri from Galax's downtown theater. Programs air on 98.1 WBRC-FM.

Galax Old Time Fiddlers Convention, second week in Aug, Galax, (276) 238-8130. Attracts national and international recording acts. Grayson Highlands State Park and the town of Fries also host bluegrass, old-time, and country music festivals every year.

Whitetop Mountain Ramp Festival, third Sun in May, Whitetop, (276) 773-3711. *Ramp* is a term for wild leek, and this festival features an eating contest that can bring you to tears—from laughter or from the onion itself.

Grayson Highlands Fall Festival, last full weekend of Sept, Grayson Highlands State Park, Mouth of Wilson, (276) 579-7092. Just one of many fall festivals in the area. Independence, Fries, Baywood, and Marion all hold fall festivals through Sept and Oct.

Appalachian Trail Days, third week in May, Damascus, (276) 475-3831. Annual gathering of AT thru-hikers in the town dubbed "friendliest town on the AT."

Lodging

Damascus Old Mill Inn, (276) 475-3745, www.damascusinn.com. A renovated 1912 mill turned hotel with casual fine dining and outdoor seating on the banks of Laurel Creek.

More than a half-dozen Damascus residents have turned their homes into bed-and-breakfasts to accommodate the many hikers and bikers who frequent the small town. Call (276) 475-3831 or visit www.damascus.org.

Grayson Highlands State Park has camping on the southern boundary of the Mount Rogers area, (800) 933-PARK.

Restaurants

Cowboys, Damascus, (276) 475-5444. This deli, located inside a service station, has great Southern breakfasts to eat in or to go for your hike.

Organizations

Appalachian Trail Conference, Harpers Ferry, WV, (304) 535-6331, www.appalachiantrail.org

Other Resources

The Virginia Creeper: Remembering the Virginia-Carolina Railway, by Doug McGuinn, Bamboo Books

The Switchback Scenic Route: A History of the Marion and Rye Valley Railway, by Gary P. Price, Mallicote Printing Inc.

40 Mount Rogers Summit

Dispense with the suspense right off: This 5,729-foot monolith of volcanic rock—third loftiest mountain in the Southern Appalachians—is not hard to climb. Yes, you must hike 7 miles to reach it from Grindstone Campground, and, yes, the elevation change hovers around 2,000 feet. This, however, only ranks somewhere between climbing Flat Top Mountain at Peaks of Otter and Three Ridges near Lexington, both mountains 4,000 feet or smaller. In other words, there are tougher climbs out there. But what Mount Rogers lacks in mountaineering daring-do, it easily compensates for in sheer presence, the diversity of its plant and animal life, the breathtaking views across high-country meadows, and, of course, its wild ponies. And to those eager for bragging rights, it affords the modest claim: "I climbed the highest mountain in Virginia."

Start: From the Massie Gap parking area on VA 362 in Grayson Highlands State Park

Distance: 9.0 miles out and back.

Hiking time: About 5 hours

Difficulty: Moderate to easy due to open rock face and uneven footing along Wilburn Ridge.

Trail surface: Dirt footpaths and open rock lead to Virginia's highest peak, grassy highlands, cove forests, and wooded slopes.

Land status: Federal wilderness and national recreation area

Nearest town: Troutdale, VA

Other trail users: Equestrians

Accessibility: Grayson Highlands State Park has some accessible facilities

Canine compatibility: Dogs permitted

Trail contact: Mount Rogers National Recreation Area, Marion; (276) 783-5196; www .southernregion.fs.fed.us/gwj. The visitor center is 10 miles north of Troutdale on VA 16.

Schedule: Open year-round. Hunting permitted, with the busiest season between Nov and Jan. Forest rangers conduct prescribed burns of 100 to 500 acres outside the wilderness in fall and spring.

Fees/permits: No permits required. Tent site fee (backcountry camping is free); shower fee for nonregistered campers; day-use parking fee at some areas.

Facilities/features: [AU: Please provide.]

Maps: USGS Whitetop; Mount Rogers High Country & Wilderness map available at the Mount Rogers Visitor Center on VA 16 north of Troutdale; Appalachian Trail Map 1: Mount Rogers National Recreation Area available from Appalachian Trail Conference, Harpers Ferry, WV

Finding the trailhead: From Troutdale: Drive south on VA 16. In 7 miles, turn right onto US 58. It is another 7.6 miles on US 58 to the Grayson Highlands State Park entrance road, VA 362. Turn right onto VA 362 and, in 3.3 miles, turn right into the Massie Gap parking area. There is parking for 50 cars, picnic tables and interpretive signs. If you are backpacking in the High Country, park in a seperate lot accessed via the campground road. GPS: N36 38.404' / W81 30.541'. *DeLorme: Virginia Atlas & Gazetteer:* Page 23, D5.

A stunning mountain in Grayson Highlands.

The Hike

You reach a point climbing Mount Rogers's north slope where nature gets a little giddy. A relatively tame, wooded mountainside slips into a jumble of cliff and rock outcrops. In a short span of trail, large boulders appear. Down a steep grade on the right is a cliff and, at the base of the cliff, a shallow cave formed by the overhanging rocks. A birch tree grafts on exposed roots of another birch. A cleaved rock exposes the entire root system of a hemlock growing out its top side. The trail becomes more streambed than dirt footpath. On rainy days, runoff will trickle underfoot. All that's missing, really, is a big sign: WELCOME TO 5,000 FEET. ENJOY YOUR STAY.

That's a magic number, 5,000. In the whole Blue Ridge chain, from southern Pennsylvania to north Georgia, only seven peaks exceed that threshold. Two of them stand in Virginia. One, Whitetop Mountain, has a road leading to the top. It's tempting to say the same about Mount Rogers, judging by the number of people who climb it every year. In truth, Mount Rogers, namesake for the 117,000-acre national recreation area, harbor for remnant boreal forests and threatened species, is in a class all its own.

A wild pony on Mount Rogers Trail.

Mount Rogers hasn't always enjoyed fame. For two centuries after colonial settlement in Virginia, it was just another obstacle to westward travel. During his 1728 survey of the "dividing line" between Virginia and North Carolina, Colonel William Byrd never reached the peak, thwarted as he was by the Blue Ridge Mountains, which he described from afar as "ranges of blue clouds." Byrd's group turned for home, frustrated by slow progress through "troublesome thickets and underwood," and the Southern Appalachians remained the "back of the beyond," as Horace Kephart described them, until a series of scientific explorations in the early 1800s. Not that the mountains remained unsettled. Pioneers were followed by mining and logging, but the region as a whole remained a place where people in neighboring hollows could pass a lifetime meeting only once or twice.

As it happens, the honor for mapping Mount Rogers goes to William Barton Rogers, Virginia's first state geologist. Rogers climbed the mountain during his geologic survey of Virginia in 1836, a mission ordered by the state legislature. These first decades of the 1800s were a busy time for scientists. States up and down the East Coast were interested in exploiting their mineral, plant, and animal resources. Rogers's brother, Henry Darwin Rogers, had conducted a geologic survey for Pennsylvania. Based on information gathered, the Rogers brothers published their famous theory on the Appalachian Mountains, a theory that generated some controversy for its assumption that the earth was at least several million years old. It's a notion few question today, but in the 1800s, the scientists who believed in creationism—that God created the world in a single moment—condemned Rogers's work. As it turns out, the criticism proved merely a warm up for Charles Darwin's *The Origin of Species,* published in 1859, and the work of biologist Asa Grey, who wrote of similarities between plants found in East Asia and North America.

Rogers didn't need to span continents in search of similar flora among regions far-removed from one another. Atop Mount Rogers, the fir-spruce forest indicates a mixing of temperate and cold-weather plants. At its highest points grow northern hardwoods, red spruce, and mountain wood sorrel wildflower. There are northern flying squirrels and birds such as the chestnut-sided warbler (its call: a slow *please, please, pleased to meet you*) and Swainson's thrush (its call: a *whit* and a *heep*). These species, normally associated with northern forests, arrived with the last ice age in North America, when encroaching ice and cold weather pushed habitats south into Virginia. Eventually, the ice receded and so did the flora and fauna—except on high peaks such as Mount Rogers. Naturalists like to describe this peak as a southern sentinel for plants and animals more common to America's northeast. The summit also supports stands of Fraser fir, an evergreen that grows no farther north than the crest zone of Mount Rogers.

Mount Rogers, then, stands as a link in a north–south chain of ecosystems, those typically found on cool, moist mountaintops such as Mount Mitchell in North Carolina and the 6,000-foot-plus peaks of the Great Smoky Mountains. It's a stepping stone, especially for such birds as the magnolia warbler (its call: *weetee weetee weeteo*), which has extended its range out of New York and Pennsylvania and into North Carolina and Tennessee.

Mount Rogers is a threatened ecosystem. Many people worry about air pollution, which weakens a tree's resistance to disease. Survival of Mount Rogers's spruce-fir trees is fiercely debated, given the almost total obliteration of Fraser fir on Mount Mitchell, 75 miles to the south. The firs on Mount Rogers show resistance to the balsam woolly adelgid, a microscopic pest that coats the crowns of fir trees, leading to defoliation and eventually death. Nonetheless, eerie parallels exist between the trees on Mount Rogers and the hemlocks in Ramsey's Draft Wilderness and Shenandoah National Park, where the hemlock woolly adelgid is defoliating Eastern hemlock at such a rate that park rangers predict virgin stands will disappear within twenty years. Mount Rogers's foresters say reports of the fir tree's demise in Virginia are greatly exaggerated, but it's difficult, when staring at the bleached spikes of dead conifers scattered across the summit, not to wonder.

It's worth looking back over your shoulder as you hike up the Appalachian Trail (AT) toward Wilburn Ridge, savoring another view of a special mountain. Colonel Byrd, the surveyor who never made it this far west, couldn't help but do so. His reaction rings true today.

> We could not forbear now and then facing about to survey them (the mountains), as if unwilling to part with a prospect which at the same time . . . was very wild and very agreeable.

Miles and Directions

0.0 Start at Massie Gap parking area in Grayson Highlands State Park. Follow the blue-blazed Rhododendron Trail through an open field. The route is initially a mowed grass path. Within a few hundred yards, cross straight over a graded dirt and gravel path, which is the Virginia Highlands Horse Trail, pass through a gate in a fence, and continue walking north on the

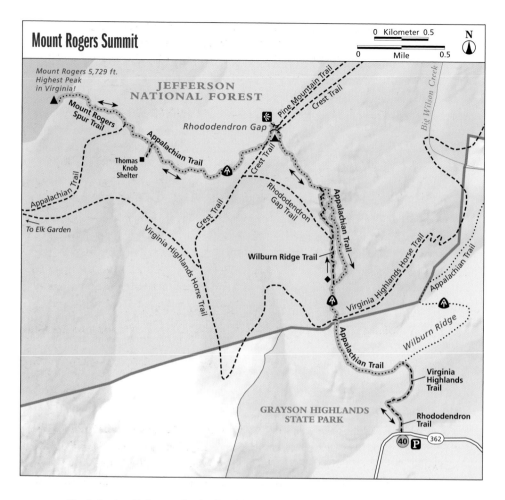

Mount Rogers Summit

Rhododendron Trail. **Note:** For the first 1.2 miles, this route crosses the horse trail and, very briefly, merges with it..

0.4 Veer left onto the Virginia Highlands Horse Trail, which remains a wide dirt and gravel trail.

0.6 Turn left onto the white-blazed Appalachian Trail. **Note:** There is a wooden trail sign with mileage for Mount Rogers summit, Rhododendron Gap, and Thomas Knob Shelter.

1.2 Cross a fence stile and enter the Mount Rogers National Recreation Area. Immediately, cross straight over the Virginia Highlands Horse Trail and continue north on the Appalachian Trail. There is a primitive campsite in this area.

1.5 Turn left onto Wilburn Ridge Trail. **Note:** The AT continues straight and both trails will merge in 0.8 miles, just prior to Rhododendron Gap.

1.8 Cross over Rhododendron Gap Trail and continue north on Wilburn Ridge Trail.

2.3 Wilburn Ridge Trail merges with the AT. Continue straight on white-blazed AT. **Note:** Between here and Rhododendron Gap, there are numerous primitive campsites.

2.7 Cross over Crest Trail and continue straight on the AT. Within a few hundred feet, reach Rhododendron Gap, a trails crossroads marked by a house-sized rock outcrop. Bear left and continue following the AT. **Note:** Keep a sharp eye out for white blazes marking the AT; avoid the Crest Trail and Pine Mountain Trail.

3.2 Cross a fence that marks the boundary of the Lewis Fork Wilderness Area.

3.8 Cross another fence and approach Thomas Knob shelter on the left. **Note:** A blue-blazed trail leads 0.1 miles to a spring.

4.2 Turn right onto the Mount Rogers Spur Trail.

4.7 Reach the tree-shrouded summit of Mount Rogers, Virginia's highest point (5,729 feet elevation). Turn around and retrace the trail to Massie Gap.

6.9 **Option:** Continue straight on the AT to cross Wilburn Ridge for an alternate return route to Massie Gap.

9.0 Hike ends at Massie Gap parking area.

Hike Information

Local Information

Town of Damascus Tourism, (276) 475-3542, www.damascus.org

Grayson County Tourism, Independence, (276) 773-3711, www.graysoncounty va.com

Abingdon Convention & Visitors Bureau, Abingdon, (800) 435-3440, www .abingdon.com/tourism

Local Events/Attractions

Galax Old Time Fiddlers Convention, second week in Aug, Galax, (276) 238-8130. Attracts national and international recording acts. Grayson Highlands State Park and the town of Fries also host bluegrass, old-time, and country music festivals every year.

Grayson County Fiddlers Convention, last full weekend in June, Elk Creek, (276) 655-4740

Naturalist Rally, second weekend in May, Mount Rogers, (276) 579-7092

Whitetop Mountain Ramp Festival, third Sun in May, Whitetop, (276) 773-3711. *Ramp* is a term for wild leek, and this festival features an eating contest that can bring you to tears—from laughter or from the onion itself.

Grayson Highlands Fall Festival, last full weekend of Sept, Grayson Highlands State Park, Mouth of Wilson, (276) 579-7092. Just one of many fall festivals in the area. Independence, Fries, Baywood, and Marion all hold fall festivals through Sept and Oct.

Appalachian Trail Days, third week in May, Damascus, (276) 475-3831. Annual gathering of AT thru-hikers in the town dubbed "friendliest town on the AT."

Grandfather Mountain Country Store, Damascus, (423) 739-2557. Hams, jellies, syrups, and jerky—it's all authentic handmade or homemade mountain food. A nice collection of mountain crafts, T-shirts, and books as well.

Lodging

Damascus Old Mill Inn, (276) 475-3745, www.damascusinn.com. A renovated 1912 mill turned hotel with casual fine dining and outdoor seating on the banks of Laurel Creek.

Fox Hill Inn, Troutdale, (276) 677-3313, (800) 874-3313, www.bbonline.com/va/foxhill

Sugar Grove Bed & Breakfast, Sugar Grove, (276) 677-3351. Offers hiker discount and shuttles; ask for "Peggy." Restaurant and lodging. Each room has a kitchen, sitting area, bed, and bath.

The Enchanted Lodge, White Top, (276) 466-4044, www.enchantedlodge.com. Log lodge surrounded by mountain views and 17 acres with hiking trails. Spa treatments available.

More than a half-dozen Damascus residents have turned their homes into bed-and-breakfasts to accommodate the many hikers and bikers who frequent the small town. Call (276) 475-3831, or visit www.damascus.org.

Abingdon has numerous bed-and-breakfasts, motels, and the famed Camberley's Martha Washington Inn, (800) 555-8000, www.marthawashingtoninn.com.

For other lodging in Abingdon, contact the Convention & Visitors Bureau, (800) 435-3440, www.abingdon.com/visitors/lodging/htm.

North of the Mount Rogers area, the town of Marion has several motels. Call Smyth County Chamber of Commerce, (276) 783-3161, or visit www.smythchamber.org.

Grayson Highlands State Park has camping on the southern boundary of the Mount Rogers area, (800) 933-PARK.

Restaurants

Cowboys, Damascus, (276) 475-5444. This deli, located inside a service station, has great Southern breakfasts to eat in or to go for your hike.

Other Resources

The Dying of the Trees, by Charles E. Little, Penguin Books, New York
Appalachian Trail Guide to Southwest Virginia, Appalachian Trail Conference, Harpers Ferry, WV

Honorable Mentions: Mount Rogers

JJ. Four Trails Circuit

Located near Hurricane Campground. Head south of Sugar Grove on VA 16, turn right onto VA 650, and then left onto FR 84 to Hurricane Campground. This moderately difficult 9.6-mile loop uses a portion of the Appalachian Trail (AT) and three other trails. Terrain varies from the dry ridgetop of Iron Mountain to cool waterfalls on Comers Creek. (800) 628-7202. GPS: N36 43.319' / W81 29.243'. *DeLorme: Virginia Atlas & Gazetteer: Page 23, C5.*

KK. Rowland Creek Falls Circuit

Located west of Sugar Grove. From VA 16, turn right onto VA 601, which after 3.5 miles turns into VA 670 in Teas. Continue on VA 670 for 4.4 miles and then fork left onto VA 656. (If you pass the Butler Fish Culture Station on the right, you've missed this left turn. Go back 1 mile and look for the turnoff.) Stay on VA 656 for 1.7 miles, then turn left onto VA 668, which turns into dirt FR 643. Park at the first trailhead on the right-hand side. After following Jerry's Creek Trail to Iron Mountain, hikers can return via Rowland Creek or head west and explore Skulls Gap for a total hike of 11.8 miles. Rowland Creek Falls is a highlight of this trip. (800) 628-7202. GPS: N36 43.986' / W81 33.675'. *DeLorme: Virginia Atlas & Gazetteer: Page 22, B4.*

LL. Whitetop Laurel Circuit

From Damascus, take US 58 east and turn right onto VA 728 to Creek Junction parking lot. This 11.5-mile loop uses portions of the Appalachian Trail (AT) and the Virginia Creeper Trail, and includes a number of crossings over the cascading Whitetop Laurel Creek. (800) 628-7202. GPS: N36 38.876' / W81 40/328'. *DeLorme: Virginia Atlas & Gazetteer: Page 22, C3.* (Also see page 340.)

The Great Escape: The Appalachian Trail through Virginia

The Appalachian Trail through Virginia

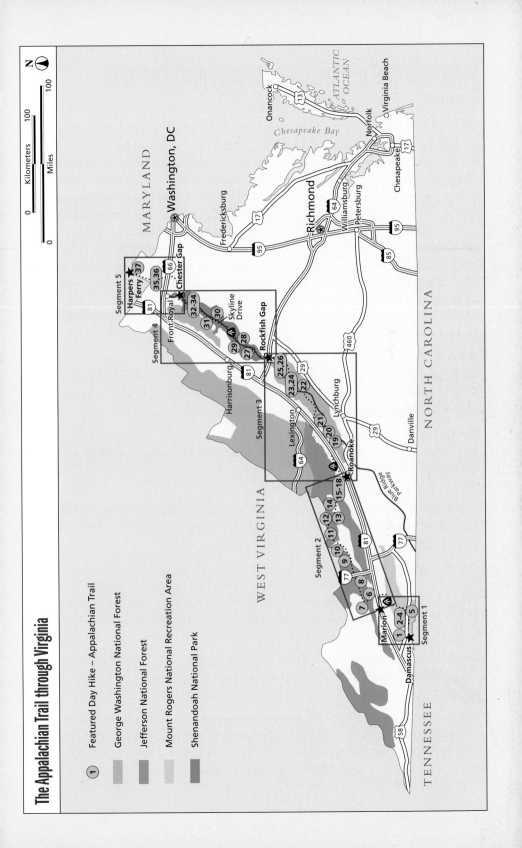

Legend

- ① Featured Day Hike – Appalachian Trail
- George Washington National Forest
- Jefferson National Forest
- Mount Rogers National Recreation Area
- Shenandoah National Park

N

Kilometers
0   100

Miles
0   100

MARYLAND

Washington, DC

Fredericksburg

Chesapeake Bay

Onancock

ATLANTIC OCEAN

Richmond

Norfolk

Virginia Beach

Williamsburg

Petersburg

Chesapeake

WEST VIRGINIA

Harrisonburg

Lynchburg

Danville

NORTH CAROLINA

Lexington

Roanoke

Blue Ridge Parkway

TENNESSEE

Damascus

Marion

Harpers Ferry

Chester Gap

Front Royal

Skyline Drive

Rockfish Gap

Segment 1

Segment 2

Segment 3

Segment 4

Segment 5

TRAVELING GREEN: PUBLIC TRANSPORTATION TO THE AT IN VIRGINIA

The "leave no trace" ethic goes beyond the trailhead. Choosing not to drive farther reduces the footprint you leave on the environment. Taking a bus or train also eliminates the hassle of shuttling two cars at opposite ends of the trail. Remember that these services are infrequent, so it's best to call ahead and plan carefully. The Appalachian Trail Conference (ATC) also publishes names of drivers who will shuttle thru-hikers and section-hikers to major transportation centers. For more information contact the ATC at (304) 535-6331 or visit www.appalachiantrail.org.

The major transit carriers that access towns all close to Virginia's AT are Greyhound Bus Lines, (800) 229-9424 or www.greyhound.com, and AMTRAK, (800) 872-7245 or www .amtrak.com. Often you may want to use a combination of the two. AMTRAK can get you to Lynchburg, Staunton, Charlottesville, Culpepper, and Harpers Ferry—all of which provide access, whether by bus or by shuttle, to the AT.

The following towns are accessible by bus or by train and lie within a reasonable walking distance of the AT. This is not a complete list, but it is the most practical.

Abingdon (accesses Segment 1)
Greyhound services Abingdon. It's a 16-mile hike via the Virginia Creeper Trail to access the AT in Damascus. Or, you can seek out one of the several private shuttle services in town, which will take you directly to the Damascus trailhead.

Roanoke (accesses Segment 2)
Greyhound services Roanoke. It's 7 miles to the AT trailhead at the US 220 crossing. Local taxi services will take you there.

Buena Vista (accesses Segment 3)
Greyhound has limited services to Buena Vista (no ticketing available). It's 5 miles up VA 607 (east) to the Blue Ridge Parkway (south) to access the AT trailhead. Local taxi services will take you there.

Roseland (accesses Segment 3)
JAUNT commuter van services Roseland from Charlottesville weekdays, during commuting times only. Call (434) 296-3184 or visit www.commuterinformation.com for rates and schedules. Once in Roseland, it's a 5-mile walk up VA 56 to the AT trailhead at the Tye River swinging bridge.

Waynesboro (accesses Segment 4)
Greyhound services Waynesboro. It's 4 miles up US 250 (east) to the AT trailhead at Rockfish Gap. Local taxi services will take you there.

Harpers Ferry (accesses Segment 5)
AMTRAK services Harpers Ferry, with connections to Washington, Pittsburgh, and Chicago. From Washington, DC, hikers can take the more frequent (and cheaper) MARC commuter rail, (866) RIDE-MTA or www.mtamaryland.com. From the train station in Harpers Ferry, take a left onto Potomac Street and head down to Shenandoah Street, where you'll find the AT.

The Appalachian Trail through Virginia

It takes a northbound thru-hiker about six weeks to reach Virginia on the Appalachian Trail. Once here, there are another six weeks of difficult and rewarding trail ahead before the hiker exits Virginia at Harpers Ferry. The Old Dominion holds nearly a quarter of the AT's 2,173 miles—more miles than any other state along the trail. A half-million day hikers hit Virginia's portion of the AT each year. Most follow the south–north direction we've chosen to feature. Since hiking the entire length of the trail is a luxury most of us cannot afford, we've included a list of suggested day hikes or short overnight trips that capture Virginia's greatest natural highlights. And so, whether you choose one long trip, or small bite sizes, plan on a showcase of some of the East's most beautiful mountain scenery.

Start: Damascus, VA
End: Harpers Ferry, WV
Distance: 549.1 miles
Hiking time: About 40 days
Difficulty: Difficult
Trail surface: The trail climbs Virginia's highest mountain range; crosses the Great Valley and a succession of steep, narrow ridges and valleys; rejoins the Blue Ridge crest; crosses several steep, outlying mountains; parallels Skyline Drive through Shenandoah National Park; and, from Stony Man, descends through the northern Blue Ridge to the Potomac River.
Land status: National scenic trail
Other trail users: Hikers only
Canine compatibility: Dogs permitted (must be on a leash in Mount Rogers National Recreation Area and in Shenandoah National Park)

GREAT RESOURCES FOR HIKING THE AT

Appalachian Trail Guides, available for purchase from the ATC at (800) AT-STORE or at www .atctrailstore.org

Appalachian Trail Thru-hikers' Companion, available for purchase from the ATC at (800) AT-STORE

Story Line: Exploring the Literature of the Appalachian Trail, by Ian Marshall, University Press of Virginia

MAPTECH Appalachian Trail set, an exhaustive resource, with digital coverage of the entire AT, featuring complete versions of official AT guides. Visit www.maptech.com for more information.

A Walk in the Woods, by Bill Bryson, Broadway Books

A Walk for Sunshine, by Jeff Alt, Dreams Shared Publications

Segment 1 Damascus to Marion

As an introduction to Virginia, it's hard to top Mount Rogers National Recreation Area. The Appalachian Trail passes near the tallest mountains in the state. Close to the summit of Mount Rogers, wild ponies graze in the high-country meadows. There are steep climbs up Iron Mountain, past small waterfalls and tunnels of rhododendron. The hike seems over too soon. Longer lasting are memories of wide-open sky, jagged rock outcrops, and a refreshing dip below the falls on Comers Creek.

Start: Damascus Town Hall
Distance: 63.8 miles point to point
Difficulty: Difficult
Trail surface: Using dirt footpaths and abandoned dirt roads, hike along rocky peaks, cliffs, and steep ridges; through deep valley hollows; and across high-altitude meadows.
Nearest towns: Damascus, VA (south access); Marion, VA (north access)

Canine compatibility: Dogs permitted (must be on a leash in the Mount Rogers National Recreation Area)
Trail contacts: Appalachian Trail Conference, Harpers Ferry, WV, (304) 535-6331, www.appalachiantrail.org; Piedmont Appalachian Trail Hikers, www.path-at.org; Mount Rogers Appalachian Trail Club, Abingdon, www.geocities.com/Yosemite/Geyser/2539
Map: ATC #1: Mount Rogers National Recreation Area

Finding the trailhead: To the Damascus Trailhead: In Damascus, locate the Damascus Town Hall, 208 W. Laurel Ave., between Smith Street and Reynolds Avenue. You can use on-street parking or park at Mount Rogers Outfitters, 110 West Laurel Ave.—there's a per-day fee and a shower available. Begin walking east on Laurel Avenue (US 58). *DeLorme: Virginia Atlas & Gazetteer:* Page 22, C2. To Marion Trailhead: See Segment 2: Marion to Roanoke.

The Hike

A few miles north of the Tennessee-Virginia border, the Appalachian Trail (AT) wraps around Holston Mountain, part of the Iron Mountain range, and descends into Damascus. The small town, first visible from an overlook high atop the ridge, bills itself as the "friendliest town on the AT." Its downtown strip, Laurel Avenue, doubles as the trail route. Shopkeepers and restaurants welcome AT hikers as friends. The hospitality really shows itself each May during the Appalachian Trail Days festival, when hundreds of hikers converge on Damascus and swap stories about the 2,173-mile trail.

Surrounding Damascus is scenery unlike any you've seen in Virginia. In Mount Rogers National Recreation Area (NRA), herds of wild ponies roam expansive mountain meadows. A strong spruce-fir scent lingers around the tree-capped Mount Rogers (5,729 feet), Virginia's tallest peak. Colorful mushrooms and large patches of wild berries brighten the slope and crest of Iron Mountain. Rhododendron's pink

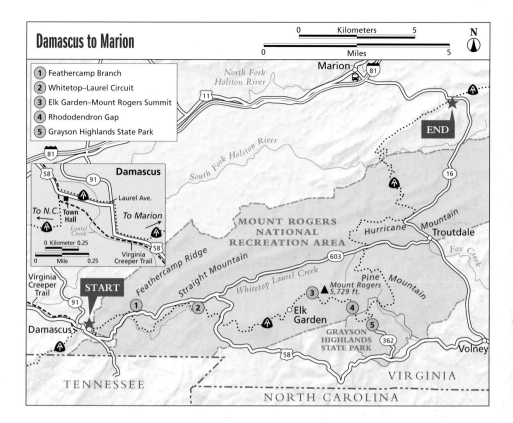

Kilometers 5

Miles 5

N

1 Feathercamp Branch
2 Whitetop–Laurel Circuit
3 Elk Garden–Mount Rogers Summit
4 Rhododendron Gap
5 Grayson Highlands State Park

Marion

END

North Fork Holston River

South Fork Holston River

Damascus

Laurel Ave.

To N.C. Town Hall

To Marion

Laurel Creek

Virginia Creeper Trail

Virginia Creeper Trail

Damascus

START

Feat
ercamp Ridge

Straight Mountain

MOUNT ROGERS NATIONAL RECREATION AREA

Hurricane

Mountain

Troutdale

Fox Creek

Whitetop Laurel Creek

Mount Rogers 5,729 ft.

Elk Garden

Pine Mountain

GRAYSON HIGHLANDS STATE PARK

Volney

TENNESSEE

VIRGINIA

NORTH CAROLINA

and purple blooms seem ever-present in June. Turk's cap lily, orange and delicate, is one of an array of wildflowers seen spring through fall.

The route north from Damascus begins with a 1,000-foot ascent of Feathercamp Ridge. The next 14 miles of AT bring two more steep climbs up Straight Mountain and Lost Mountain. Between each ridge, rhododendrons choke stream valleys cut by Straight Branch and Whitetop Laurel Creek. As the AT climbs and descends each ridge, flashes of yellow and red amid the drab-colored leaf rot signal mushroom colonies. Chanterelles, waxy caps, and a host of other types grow along the trail. Occasionally, a view of the rooftop of Virginia, as the high country is nicknamed, breaks out through the heavy oak forest atop the ridges.

From Elk Garden, the AT begins an ascent past Virginia's three tallest mountains—Mount Rogers, Whitetop, and Pine. All three peaks exceed 5,000 feet, and the AT slips past without actually crossing any of them. Whitetop Mountain (5,520 feet) has a road leading to its top. When the Virginia Creeper Railroad operated one hundred years ago, the Whitetop station had the distinction of being the highest railroad depot east of the Rockies. Past Whitetop, the AT enters Lewis Fork Wilderness, which surrounds and covers Mount Rogers. Elevation is above 5,000 feet, and the forested summit of Mount Rogers appears a mere bulge in the high ridge. A spur trail leads 0.5 mile from the AT up to Rogers's summit area. It's a cool, moist woodland that covers Mount Rogers, with dangling bunches of moss and rotted logs everywhere. Many of the trees, plants, and animals at the summit are vestiges of a northern forest environment that developed here during the last glacial period in North America some 10,000 years ago.

Pine Mountain, the third in Mount Rogers NRA's triumvirate of 5,000-foot peaks, is a series of rocky promontories rising sharply from the sweeping meadows. This gray-purplish rock is rhyolite, formed 800 million years ago when the

Blue Ridge was volcanically active. The trail passes several jagged piles of rock on Wilburn Ridge, then disappears into tunnels of rhododendron. When the AT reenters meadows, stunted hawthorn trees offer shade and a rest spot for watching wild horses graze. Meadow grass grows knee-high. Wildflowers wash the fields with orange and red. The meadows are burned regularly by the Forest Service in order to hold back total reforestation, creating conditions ideal for fireweed. Were it not for the fires, a new forest of hardwoods would reclaim the meadows.

A descent from Scales (an old cattle-weighing station dating back one hundred years) to Fox Creek signals the end of the Mount Rogers high country. From Fox Creek, the AT climbs again to the crest of Iron Mountain (4,200 feet). Yellow blossoms of the Indian cucumber root put on a spring show along streams. Absent its blooms, which appear in May and June, the cucumber root is identified by a distinct double-decker whorl of leaves. The tuber is edible, but should only be collected if they're found in abundance. As it crosses Iron Mountain Trail (which used to be the AT until it was relocated), the AT follows sections of old logging roads. There's little in the way of forest canopy, but the constant exposure to sunlight makes the blackberries that grow along the trail especially plump and juicy, much like the huckleberries that grow off the trail in the high-country meadows.

The route north from Iron Mountain might seem anticlimactic when compared with the high country; that is, until the AT crosses Comers Creek. As it runs down Hurricane Mountain, the stream forms a 10-foot waterfall. There's a small swimming

AT SHELTERS/HUTS
(MILEAGE ON THE AT NORTH FROM DAMASCUS TO VA 16)

Mile 9.4 – Saunders Shelter

Mile 15.8 – Lost Mountain Shelter

Mile 28.0 – Thomas Knob Shelter

Mile 33.1 – Wise Shelter

Mile 39.0 – Old Orchard Shelter

Mile 50.7 – Raccoon Branch Shelter

Mile 53.2 – Trimpi Shelter

Mile 63.7 – Partnership Shelter

hole here that is popular with hikers. It's a nice spot to tarry, dip your feet in cool water, and contemplate the remaining 483 miles of Virginia's AT.

Miles and Directions

0.0 Start at Damascus Town Hall and head east on Laurel Avenue, following US 58/VA 91 out of town.

1.0 Turn left off US 58 and enter the woods. Look for the white blazes on the left, or west-bound side, of US 58.

3.5 Turn right and descend. **Note:** Blue-blazed connector trail leads to yellow-blazed Iron Mountain Trail.

5.6 Cross US 58. Immediately descend to Straight Branch and cross. After crossing, turn right and follow Straight Branch downstream.

9.4 ▶ Pass a side trail that leads left 300 yards to Saunders Shelter.

11.7 Pass a T junction with Bear Tree Gap–Shaw Gap Trail on the left; continue straight on the AT.

14.0 Cross the Luther Hassinger Memorial Bridge over Green Cove and Whitetop Laurel Creeks. (The bridge is named in honor of a lumberman who clear-cut the woodland around Damascus in the early 1900s.)

15.8 ▶ Pass Lost Mountain Shelter on the right.

20.6 Reach Buzzard Rock with views of Iron Mountain to the north, and Grandfather Mountain (North Carolina) to the south. Follow the AT as it descends off Buzzard Rock and skirts an open area below the summit of Whitetop Mountain.

21.3 Cross Whitetop Road and enter the woods on the opposite side. **Note:** Whitetop Road leads left uphill to the top of Whitetop Mountain (5,520 feet).

24.4 Enter Lewis Fork Wilderness Area; continue climbing on the AT.

27.6 Turn right at a T junction with the Mount Rogers Spur Trail. A few feet past this junction, exit Lewis Fork Wilderness. **Note:** The Mount Rogers Spur Trail leads 0.5 mile to the tree-shrouded summit of Mount Rogers (5,729 feet).

28.0 ▶ Pass the Thomas Knob Shelter on the right.

29.8 Cross through the open fields. Wilburn Ridge rises to points of exposed rock to the right.

30.4 Enter Grayson Highlands State Park by passing over a wooden fence.

33.1 ▶ Pass Wise Shelter on the right. In 0.1 mile, exit Grayson Highlands State Park and reenter Mount Rogers NRA.

35.1 Cross Stone Mountain. Wild horses graze in the open meadows that cover this mountain.

35.6 Descend to Scales, a corralled campground open to four-wheel-drive vehicle traffic via VA 613. Walk around the campsite and follow the AT as it climbs Pine Mountain.

39.0 ▶ Pass the Old Orchard Shelter.

40.7 Cross VA 603. On the opposite side, cross Fox Creek.

47.1 At a T junction with a blue-blazed trail, turn right and climb. **Note:** The blue-blazed trail leads 0.5 mile to Hurricane Campground.

48.0 Cross Comers Creek at the base of a 10-foot waterfall.

50.7 ▶ Pass a blue-blazed trail that branches right to the Raccoon Branch Shelter.

51.3 Continue straight past a blue-blazed trail that branches right to a view off High Point (4,040 feet).

53.2 At a fork in the trail, bear left on the AT. ⚑ A blue-blazed trail leads right to Trimpi Shelter in 0.1 mile.

55.9 Cross the South Fork Holston River on a 12-foot-long footbridge.

63.7 ⚑ Pass the Partnership Shelter.

63.8 Hike ends at VA 16 in front of the Mount Rogers Visitor Center.

Hike Information

Local Information

Damascus website, www.damascus.org

Abingdon Convention & Visitors Bureau, Abingdon, (800) 435-3440, www.abingdon.com/tourism

Local Events / Attractions

Appalachian Trail Days, May, Damascus, www.traildays.org

Lodging

The Place, 200 E. Laurel Ave., Damascus; (276) 475-5572. Run by the Damascus United Methodist Church, the hostel accommodates roughly 35 hikers with tent space in the yard. Has hot showers but no heat. Open seasonally, usually Apr through Nov. Donations appreciated.

Segment 2 Marion to Roanoke

The Appalachian Trail through southwest Virginia forsakes the Blue Ridge for the valley and ridge region, but loses none of the beauty or steep climbs. Open cliffs on Tinker Mountain and overlooks from McAfee Knob and Dragons Tooth are popular day hikes. More remote is Wind Rocks in Mountain Lake Wilderness or a perch on Angels Rest, near Pearisburg, with views of the New River. It's been sixty-plus years since volunteers moved the AT off the Blue Ridge, in hopes of saving the trail's remote character. It's safe to say they succeeded.

Start: Mount Rogers Visitor Center
Distance: 190.3 miles point to point
Difficulty: Difficult
Trail surface: Using dirt footpaths and abandoned dirt roads, hike along steep ridge crests, through deep valley hollows and bogs, and across high-altitude meadows.
Nearest towns: Marion, VA (south access); Roanoke, VA (north access)
Canine compatibility: Dogs permitted

Trail contacts: Appalachian Trail Conference, Harpers Ferry, WV, (304) 535-6331, www .appalachiantrail.org; Roanoke ATC, c/o Bob Peckman, (540) 366-7780; Outdoor Club at Virginia Tech, filebox.vt.edu/org/outing; Piedmont Appalachian Trail Hikers, www.path-at .org; Mount Rogers National Recreation Area Headquarters, Marion, (276) 783-5196, www .southernregion.fs.fed.us/gwj
Maps: ATC #2: Wythe Ranger District; ATC #3: Blacksburg Ranger District

Finding the trailhead: To Marion Trailhead: From Marion, proceed south on VA 16 to the Mount Rogers Visitor Center (6 miles from VA 16's junction with I-81). Turn right into the visitor center parking lot and park. Follow a sidewalk to the front of the visitor center, walk to VA 16, and cross the highway. The Appalachian Trail (AT) enters the woods on the northbound side of VA 16. *DeLorme: Virginia Atlas & Gazetteer:* Page 23, B5. To Roanoke Trailhead: See Segment 3: Roanoke to Rockfish Gap.

The Hike

From the point where it leaves the Great Valley, north of the Mount Rogers National Recreation Area, the AT crosses seven mountain ridges. Little Brushy Mountain is the first. Beyond it stand Big Walker, Lynn Camp, and Garden Mountain. Each ridge rises sharply, then drops into stream valleys. Crawfish Valley, at the base of Big Walker, is secluded and overgrown. Across Big Walker, Rich Valley is wide and busy, with the North Fork Holston River and VA 42 running along its bottomland.

Burkes Garden breaks the valley and ridge pattern in scenic fashion. Garden Mountain forms the southern boundary of this bowl-shaped valley, and the AT follows its crest for 5 miles. At Chestnut Knob and again at Davis Field Campsite, views west drop 900 feet into the valley, which formed millions of years ago when a basement rock of limestone eroded and washed away. The resulting claylike soil makes

A family sets out for an easy overnight hike on the AT from Grayson Highlands State Park.

for prime farmland. Local lore says James Burke, the first white man to settle in the Garden, tossed a few potato peels on the ground during his first visit here in the mid-1700s. The next season, Burke returned and found potato plants. True or not, a small community of farmers continues a tradition of farming that dates back centuries. They've also managed to keep the commercial world at bay, with prohibitions on billboards and neon signs.

Northwest of Burkes Garden, the AT crosses three more ridges. On the last, Pearis Mountain, an overlook called Angels Rest provides beautiful views across the New River to the slope of Peters Mountain. The AT crosses the New on a highway bridge and follows Stillhouse Branch up the steep side of Peters Mountain. On the ridgetop, the West Virginia border and AT crisscross for 12 miles through grass fields and a portion of the Peters Mountain Wilderness.

Like Catawba Mountain to the north, which derives its name from the Catawba rhododendron, Peters Mountain shares its name with a plant. Peters Mountain mallow grows only in Giles County, Virginia. The single known community of this purple-blossoming herb is protected on land owned by the Nature Conservancy. The AT is partly to blame for its earlier decline. In the late 1960s, a section of the trail ran along the mountain's sandstone outcrops, a favored habitat of the mallow. Heavy foot traffic took its toll. Virginia and the federal government now list the plant as endangered. What communities exist are fenced in and tended carefully. Trail relocation remedied encroachment by AT hikers.

The descent off Peters Mountain marks a turn in the AT. Its direction is now once again northeast, a course that will eventually intersect with the Blue Ridge Mountains, beyond Roanoke. For the intervening 74 miles, the AT crosses eight more ridges, each with a corresponding stream valley. The first, Potts Mountain, caps out at a rocky point called Wind Rocks in Mountain Lake Wilderness. The 10,753-acre federal wilderness, like Burkes Garden, is a welcome respite to the valley-and-ridge routine. Gently graded trail leads across two flat-topped mountains, Salt Pond and Lone Pine, and their upland bogs. The descent off Salt Pond steepens and ends at Johns Creek. In quick succession, the AT then crosses Johns Creek, Sinking Creek, Brush, and Cove Mountains. Cove Mountain makes a U shape around the headwaters of Trout Creek and rises to the pointed, skin-your-knee-rough rock on Dragons Tooth.

The wide valley east of Dragons Tooth is part of the Great Valley system that runs down the Appalachian chain from southern New Jersey into Tennessee. Views of Roanoke, the largest city in southwest Virginia, signal the approaching end of this leg of the AT.

Before leaving the valley and ridge region, the AT crosses Tinker Cliffs. Blocks of sandstone in Devils Kitchen and the overhangs at Snack Bar Rock and Rock Haven make striking formations. Tinker Cliffs itself is reminiscent of another high-mountain ridge, Pine Mountain, on the Virginia-Kentucky border. Like Pine Mountain, the edge of Tinker and Catawba Mountains were, millions of years ago, a leading edge of a thrust fault—essentially a piece of the earth's crust that slid up and over another piece of the earth. The resulting topography is steep and often sheer to the west, while more graded and sloping eastward.

The subdivisions and farms visible on the last 6.5 miles of the AT signal the descent into the Great Valley. From a final rock outcrop, Hay Rock, the view reaches west across the heavily populated valley to the Blue Ridge, and another leg of the AT.

Miles and Directions

0.0 Start at the Mount Rogers Visitor Center. Cross VA 16 and enter the woods on the opposite side of the visitor center, following white blazes.

4.1 Cross FR 86 and reenter woods on the opposite side. **Note:** A spring is located 100 yards on FR 86 to the right.

7.0 ▶ Pass Chatfield Shelter.

11.5 Trail empties onto US 11. Turn right and hike east along the highway. Turn left onto VA 638 and cross under I-81. Follow the AT as it enters a field on the right side of VA 638 after passing under I-81.

14.2 ▶ Come to Davis Path Shelter. Turn right at the shelter and climb on the AT.

17.8 Descend off Brushy Mountain into a clearing and campsite in Crawfish Valley. (See Hike 33 for a detailed description of the Crawfish/Channel Rock loop hike.)

Marion to Roanoke

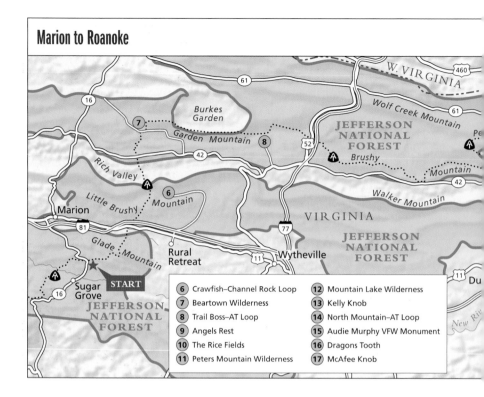

W. VIRGINIA

JEFFERSON NATIONAL FOREST

Burkes Garden

Garden Mountain

Rich Valley

Little Brushy

Marion

Sugar Grove

JEFFERSON NATIONAL FOREST

Glade Mountain

Rural Retreat

Wytheville

VIRGINIA

JEFFERSON NATIONAL FOREST

Wolf Creek Mountain

Brushy Mountain

Walker Mountain

Du

New Ri

6 Crawfish–Channel Rock Loop		**12** Mountain Lake Wilderness	
7 Beartown Wilderness		**13** Kelly Knob	
8 Trail Boss–AT Loop		**14** North Mountain–AT Loop	
9 Angels Rest		**15** Audie Murphy VFW Monument	
10 The Rice Fields		**16** Dragons Tooth	
11 Peters Mountain Wilderness		**17** McAfee Knob	

25.4 Come to Knot Maul Branch Shelter. Turn right at the shelter. After crossing several streams, climb Lynn Camp Mountain.

29.8 Begin ascent of Chestnut Mountain. The AT here traces a border of Beartown Wilderness. (See the "Great Day Hikes along the Appalachian Trail" section for a brief description of this hike.) At the summit of Chestnut Mountain, pass the Chestnut Knob Shelter.

36.7 Follow the ridgetop of Garden Mountain as it traces a rim of Burkes Garden. **Note:** The summit of Garden Mountain (4,052 feet) offers more views of Burkes Garden.

41.4 Pass a blue-blazed trail that branches left 0.5 mile to Davis Farm Campsite; continue straight on the AT.

44.4 Pass Jenkins Shelter on the left.

48.9 Cross VA 615; enter the woods on the opposite side and climb. **Note:** The Trail Boss Trail begins 100 yards to the left on VA 615. See the "Great Day Hikes along the Appalachian Trail" section for a brief description of a loop hike using Trail Boss and the AT.

55.9 Turn left onto paved US 21/52 and follow the road downhill. In 0.2 mile, follow VA 612 straight as US 21/52 makes a hard left switchback. Cross I77 on a road bridge. At a fork on the opposite side of the bridge, bear right onto a gravel road.

56.7 Turn right off the gravel road and enter woods on white-blazed AT.

58.2 Pass a trail on the right that leads 0.3 mile to Helveys Mill Shelter.

68.0 Pass Jenny Knob Shelter on the right.

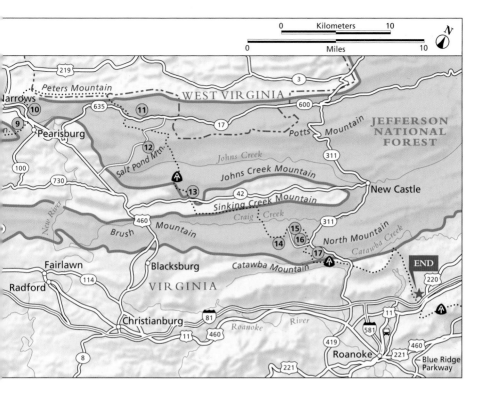

69.2 Turn left onto paved VA 608 and hike 0.1 mile. Cross the road and enter woods at the back of a small gravel parking lot, following white blazes.

76.9 Pass White Pine Horse Camp. There is a hand pump for water located in the camp.

80.0 Cross Dismal Creek. Hike past the blue-blazed Ribble Trail on the left; continue straight on the AT.

82.2 ▶ Pass a blue-blazed trail that branches right and leads 100 yards to Wapiti Shelter. Continue straight as the AT climbs Sugar Run Mountain.

86.7 Proceed straight through a four-way intersection with the blue-blazed Ribble Trail. **Note:** The Ribble Trail leads right to Honey Spring Picnic Area.

90.6 ▶ Pass Doc's Knob Shelter.

96.4 Pass a blue-blazed trail on the left; continue straight on the AT. **Note:** The blue-blazed trail leads 100 yards to Angels Rest. See the "Great Day Hikes along the Appalachian Trail" section for a brief description of this hike.

97.9 After a steep descent, cross paved VA 634. Cross a fence stile on the opposite side. Pass a blue-blazed trail that branches right. **Note:** The blue-blazed trail leads to downtown Pearisburg in 1 mile.

98.9 Cross the New River on the Senator Shumate Bridge (US 460). At the opposite side, turn right and cross US 460. Follow a paved road 80 yards, then turn left onto a gravel road.

AT SHELTERS/HUTS
(MILEAGE ON THE AT FROM VA 16 NORTH TO US 220)

Mile 0.0 – Partnership Shelter (at Mount Rogers Visitor Center on VA 16)

Mile 7.0 – Chatfield Shelter

Mile 14.2 – Davis Path Shelter

Mile 25.4 – Knot Maul Branch Shelter

Mile 34.4 – Chestnut Knob Shelter

Mile 44.4 – Jenkins Shelter

Mile 58.2 – Helveys Mill Shelter

Mile 68 – Jenny Knob Shelter

Mile 82.2 – Wapiti Shelter

Mile 90.6 – Doc's Knob Shelter

Mile 105.7 – Rice Field Shelter (also called Star Haven Shelter)

Mile 118.0 – Pine Swamp Branch Shelter

Mile 121.9 – Bailey Gap Shelter

Mile 130.7 – War Spur Shelter

Mile 136.5 – Laurel Creek Shelter

Mile 142.9 – Sarver Hollow Shelter

Mile 148.9 – Niday Shelter

Mile 157.8 – Pickle Branch Shelter

Mile 171.7 – Boy Scout Shelter

Mile 172.7 – Catawba Mountain Shelter

Mile 174.9 – Campbell Shelter

Mile 180.9 – Lamberts Meadow Shelter

105.1 Enter the Rice Fields atop Peters Mountain. (See the "Great Day Hikes along the Appalachian Trail" section for a brief description of this hike.)

105.7 ⬛ Pass Rice Field Shelter (also called Star Haven Shelter) on the left.

115.5 Reach a fork with the yellow-blazed Allegheny Trail, which enters from the left; bear right on the AT and descend Peters Mountain. (See Hike 31 for a detailed description of trails in this section of Peters Mountain.)

118.0 ⬛ Pass Pine Swamp Branch Shelter on the right.

120.4 Cross Stony Creek, and, in 100 yards, cross paved VA 635.

121.9 ⬛ Pass Bailey Gap Shelter on the left.

125.6 Cross gravel VA 613 and enter Mountain Lake Wilderness. In 0.3 mile, pass Wind Rock on the right. Bear right on the AT as it skirts the east slope of Potts Mountain.

128.7 Turn left at a T intersection. **Note:** The War Spur Connector Trail leads right to a parking area on VA 613. (See Hike 32 for a detailed description of hikes in the wilderness.)

130.7  Pass War Spur Shelter on the left. The trail descends and crosses Johns Creek in 0.8 mile.

134.0 Johns Creek Trail branches left off the AT; continue straight. **Note:** Blue-blazed Johns Creek Trail leads 3.5 miles to VA 658.

135.3 Pass a trail on the right that leads 100 yards to overlooks on White Rock; continue straight on the AT. In 0.3 mile, reach the summit

The author takes a day hike on the AT near Iron Mountain and the Virginia Creeper Trail.

of Kelly Knob. (See the "Great Day Hikes along the Appalachian Trail" section for a brief description of this hike.)

136.5 Pass Laurel Creek Shelter on the right. Descend on the AT to cross Sinking Creek.

142.9 After climbing Sinking Creek Mountain, pass a blue-blazed trail that leads right 0.3 mile to Sarver Hollow Shelter.

148.9 Pass a trail that leads 50 yards right to Niday Shelter.

150.2 Cross paved VA 621 and enter woods on the other side, following white blazes. The AT soon crosses Craig Creek and climbs Brush Mountain.

154.0 Pass a blue-blazed trail that climbs left to the Audie Murphy VFW Monument; continue straight on the AT. (See the "Great Day Hikes along the Appalachian Trail" section for a brief description of this hike.)

157.8 After crossing VA 620, begin ascent of Cove Mountain. In 1 mile, pass a blue-blazed trail that leads right for 0.5 mile to the Pickle Branch Shelter.

161.4 At a T junction, turn left and begin a difficult descent on the AT past Devils Seat and Rawies Rest. At this junction, a blue-blazed trail continues straight to Dragons Tooth in 200 yards. (See the "Great Day Hikes along the Appalachian Trail" section for a brief description of this hike.)

166.5 Cross Catawba Creek and begin an ascent of Catawba Mountain. At the top, the AT turns left and traces the ridge crest.

170.7 Descend steeply and cross VA 311. On the opposite side of the highway, enter the woods, following white blazes.

171.7 ▪ Pass Boy Scout Shelter.

172.7 ▪ Pass Catawba Mountain Shelter on the right.

174.2 After a difficult, rocky climb, reach the summit of McAfee Knob. (See the "Great Day Hikes along the Appalachian Trail" section for a brief description of this hike.)

174.9 ▪ Pass Campbell Shelter on the right.

179.8 Begin a traverse of Tinker Cliffs.

180.9 ▪ Pass Lamberts Meadow Shelter on the right. The next 7 miles trace the ridge of Tinker Mountain, past Julius Knob, Chimney Rocks, and Hay Rock.

190.3 Hike ends at US 220.

Hike Information

Local Information

Roanoke Valley Convention & Visitors Bureau, Roanoke, (800) 635-5535, www.Visit RoanokeVA.com

Montgomery County Chamber of Commerce, Blacksburg, (540) 552-4503 or (540) 382-4010, www.montgomerycc.org

Segment 3 Roanoke to Rockfish Gap

The Appalachian Trail once ran the crest of the Blue Ridge from Roanoke north to Rockfish Gap, until construction of the Blue Ridge Parkway pushed sections onto outlying peaks. That's good news for hikers who like climbing. From heights of 4,000 feet atop The Priest and Cold Mountain, the trail descends to an elevation of 659 feet at the James River. The Blue Ridge, Virginia's oldest mountains, show weathered knobs of resistant bedrock at Humpback Rocks, Spy Rock, and Fullers Rocks. Views from each seem better than the last.

Start: Shoulder of US 220 west of I-81
Distance: 133.4 miles point to point
Difficulty: Difficult
Trail surface: Using dirt footpaths and abandoned dirt roads, hike along ridge crests, peaks, and rock outcrops and through open meadows, virgin hemlock, and the James River Gorge.
Nearest towns: Roanoke, VA (south access); Waynesboro, VA (north access)
Canine compatibility: Dogs permitted

Trail contacts: Appalachian Trail Conference, Harpers Ferry, WV, (304) 535-6331, www.appalachiantrail.org; Old Dominion ATC, www.odatc.org; Tidewater ATC, www.tidewateratc.com; Natural Bridge ATC, www.nbatc.org; Shenandoah National Park, Luray, (540) 999-3500, www.nps.gov/shen; George Washington and Jefferson National Forests, www.southern region.fs.fed.us/gwj
Maps: ATC #4: Glenwood Ranger District/Newcastle Ranger District; ATC #5: Pedlar Ranger District

Finding the trailhead: To Roanoke Trailhead: From Roanoke, drive north on combined I-581/US 220 to I-81 north. Drive north on the combined routes of I-81/US 220 for 6 miles and take exit 150. Turn left at the bottom of the exit ramp onto US 220. In 0.2 mile, turn left onto VA 816 and park in the park-and-ride lot. Walk the few steps back to US 220 and turn left (north). In 0.2 mile, reach the Appalachian Trail (AT) where it crosses US 220. *DeLorme: Virginia Atlas & Gazetteer:* Page 42, B3. To Rockfish Gap Trailhead: See Segment 4: Rockfish Gap to Chester Gap.

The Hike

The AT route north of Roanoke begins with a steep climb up Fullhardt Knob. In Tollhouse Gap, the main trunk of the Blue Ridge is visible slightly east. It will be another 10 miles before the trail and the mountain crest intersect at the Blue Ridge Parkway, a scenic highway that runs south into the North Carolina Smokies.

Like Skyline Drive in Shenandoah National Park to the north, construction of the Blue Ridge Parkway followed a route AT volunteers blazed decades earlier. Subsequent trail relocations moved the AT off the main Blue Ridge. On the outlying mountains, like The Priest and Three Ridges, the AT gains and loses 3,000 feet in elevation in a few miles. Bumpy terrain—AT thru-hikers call them PUDs (pointless

The Thomas Knob Shelter near Mount Rogers.

up-and-downs)—along Cove Mountain's ten small knobs are punishing, as are the short sprints up Spy Rock and Humpback Rocks.

The newest section of AT falls within James River Face Wilderness. The James is Virginia's longest river, running 450 miles from its mountain headwaters into Hampton Roads harbor on the Chesapeake Bay. Between Buena Vista and Lynchburg, the river breaches the Blue Ridge in a deep gorge. Land south of the river falls inside Virginia's first and largest wilderness area, the James River Face. Inside the wilderness boundaries the newly constructed AT follows tall river cliffs and a scenic stream, Matts Creek. A pedestrian footbridge across the James, opened in 2000, made the relocation possible. The footbridge honors the memory of Bill Foot, a Natural Bridge ATC president who pioneered construction of the James River Foot Bridge, but passed away before seeing it completed.

On the north bank of the James River, the AT enters the Pedlar district of the George Washington/Jefferson National Forest. A series of fires dating from the 1890s, including one as recently as 1963, consumed thousands of acres of woodland in this area. The 1963 fire stopped at Little Rocky Row (reached via twenty-one switchbacks out of the gorge). It's here, from a vista on Fullers Rocks, that the last—and perhaps best—view of the James and the gorge unfolds south and west. More climbing awaits for northbound hikers to Bluff Mountain (3,372 feet) and Rice Mountain, (2,228 feet). Past Rice Mountain, the trail gains 2,000 feet to the summit of Bald Knob (4,059 feet), which is actually crowned with a healthy head of trees. After dipping into Cow Camp Gap, the AT climbs again to Cold Mountain (4,022 feet), a grassy peak once grazed by livestock. The Forest Service, swayed by the beautiful views from the peak, keeps it clear with controlled burns.

The view from Cold Mountain includes the Religious Range—a series of peaks named by Robert Rose, a large landowner in the area. There is The Priest and Little Priest, as well as the Friar and Cardinal Ridge. The Priest stands within Virginia's newest wilderness area, designated in 2000. Because of the prohibition on mechanical tools for trail maintenance in a wilderness, the board of the Natural Bridge ATC opposed this initiative. Instead, they sought a special management area designation, like that which covers Mount Pleasant. Special management areas offer similar protection as wilderness, but with relaxed rules that allow chain saws. But wilderness advocates prevailed, and, in November 2000, President Clinton announced creation of Virginia's seventeenth wilderness, The Priest–Three Ridges Wilderness Area.

Humpback Rocks (3,080 feet) is the AT's last hurrah before it descends to Rockfish Gap and enters the Shenandoah National Park. With views in all directions, it's a perfect spot to get a glimpse of how far you've come. And what lies ahead.

Miles and Directions

0.0. Start on the shoulder of US 220 west of I-81. Cross the highway to the northbound side and enter the woods, following white blazes.

2.6 Begin a series of switchbacks up the side of Fullhardt Knob leading to Tollhouse Gap.

5.0 ⛺ Pass a blue-blazed trail that leads right to Fullhardt Knob Shelter. Continue on the white-blazed AT.

8.6 Curry Creek intersects the AT on the left; continue straight on the AT.

11.2 ⛺ Pass a trail on the left that leads to Wilson Creek Shelter.

13.6 Cross FR 186 and enter woods on the opposite side. **Note:** To the left as you cross FR 186, in 100 yards, is the Blue Ridge Parkway (milepost 97.7).

14.4 Cross the Blue Ridge Parkway at Taylors Mountain Overlook. The AT and parkway run beside one another and cross several times for the next 6.7 miles.

18.5 ⛺ Pass a blue-blazed trail on the left that leads 0.2 mile downhill to Bobbletts Gap Shelter. Continue straight on the AT.

19.2 Cross the parkway at the overlook (milepost 92.5).

21.7 At Bearwallow Gap, the AT and parkway separate. Follow the AT as it branches left to follow the ridge of Cove Mountain. **Note:** The Blue Ridge Parkway continues along the main ridge of the Blue Ridge to Peaks of Otter Recreation Area in 4.9 miles. There is a restaurant, lodge, bathrooms, and campground.

23.5 Pass Little Cove Mountain Trail, a blue-blazed trail that branches right off the AT. (See the "Great Day Hikes along the Appalachian Trail" section for more information on a loop hike using Little Cove Mountain Trail.)

24.9 ▶ Pass Cove Mountain Shelter on the right.

28.1 Descend off Cove Mountain; cross VA 614 and, soon after, cross Jennings Creek. Past the creek, the AT climbs Fork Mountain (2,042 feet).

31.8 ▶ Bryant Ridge Shelter. From this clearing, follow the AT right and uphill as it ascends Bryant Ridge and Floyd Mountain.

36.8 ▶ Pass a blue-blazed trail that leads right 0.1 mile to Cornelius Creek Shelter.

37.7 Pass a side trail that leads left to Black Rock, a rocky lookout with views of Floyd and Pine Mountains; continue straight on the AT.

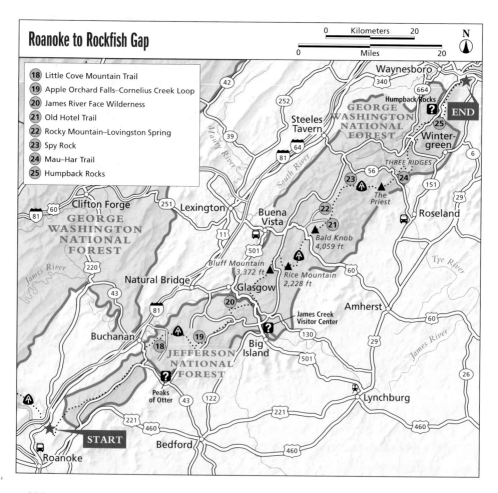

Roanoke to Rockfish Gap

18 Little Cove Mountain Trail
19 Apple Orchard Falls–Cornelius Creek Loop
20 James River Face Wilderness
21 Old Hotel Trail
22 Rocky Mountain–Lovingston Spring
23 Spy Rock
24 Mau–Har Trail
25 Humpback Rocks

38.3 Pass the blue-blazed Cornelius Creek Trail on the left; continue straight on the AT. (See the "Great Day Hikes along the Appalachian Trail" section for information on a loop hike along Cornelius Creek and Apple Orchard Falls.)

39.4 Pass blue-blazed Apple Orchard Falls Trail on the left; continue straight on the AT.

40.9 Cross Apple Orchard Mountain (4,222 feet), the highest point on the AT between Chestnut Knob 200 miles south and Mount Moosilauke in New Hampshire. On a clear day, there are views of Natural Bridge to the northwest.

42.1 ◗ Pass Thunder Hill Shelter on the left. **Note:** Except for a short section where the AT crosses the 3,683-foot peak of Thunder Ridge, the trail and Blue Ridge Parkway run beside each other for the next 5 miles.

46.8 Enter the James River Face Wilderness at Petites Gap. (See the "Great Day Hikes along the Appalachian Trail"section for a brief description of trails in this wilderness area.)

48.0 Cross Highcock Knob (3,073 feet).

54.5 ◗ Pass Matts Creek Shelter on the left. In 0.1 mile, reach a T intersection with Matts Creek Trail on the right. Continue straight on the AT. (This leg of the AT opened in 2000. The old AT followed Matts Creek Trail to the Snowden Bridge on the James River.)

55.3 Turn right at the mouth of Matts Creek. The James River is on the left, high cliffs walls on the right; follow the AT downstream.

56.5 Turn left and cross the James River Foot Bridge. On the opposite side, cross US 501/VA 130. A newly constructed section of the AT climbs on Rocky Row, crossing it twice. (The new bridge across the James River is named in honor of Bill Foot, a former president of the Natural Bridge ATC, who led efforts to have it built.)

58.4 ◗ Pass a blue-blazed trail on the left to Johns Hollow Shelter. Continue straight on the AT as it climbs to Fullers Rocks, a lookout with views back onto the James River gorge.

65.6 Cross Bluff Mountain (3,372 feet).

67.2 Turn right at a T intersection with an old road. ◗ Straight ahead on the road is Punchbowl Shelter in 0.2 mile.

67.6 Cross the Blue Ridge Parkway at mile 51.7 and follow the AT as it descends the road embankment on the opposite side. The AT soon crosses a stream and climbs Rice Mountain (2,228 feet).

71.6 Enter a clearing after crossing Little Irish Creek. Beyond the clearing, turn right onto gravel FR 39. For the next 2 miles, the AT skirts Pedlar Lake, a man-made reservoir that supplies water to Lynchburg, Virginia.

76.0 ◗ Pass Brown Mountain Creek Shelter on the right.

77.8 Cross US 60 and enter Long Mountain Wayside. Follow the AT as it reenters the woods next to a dirt road on the left, or west, end of the wayside.

81.6 After climbing Bald Knob (4,059 feet), descend into Cow Camp Gap. ◗ Blue-blazed trail leads right 0.6 mile to Cow Camp Gap Shelter. Not very practical, though, given that Brown Mountain Creek Shelter (mile 76.0) is right on the AT.

82.8 ◗ Cross Cold Mountain (4,022 feet). The summit is a mountain bald with views of Mount Pleasant and the Religious Range. (See Hike 30 for a detailed description of hiking on Mount Pleasant.)

91.8 ◗ Pass Seeley-Woodworth Shelter on the right. In 0.3 mile, pass two unprotected springs.

92.1 Pass a blue-blazed trail (old road) on the left. It leads 2.2 miles to a campsite at Lovingston Spring. (See the "Great Day Hikes along the Appalachian Trail" section for a brief description of a loop hike in this area.)

94.6 Pass a campsite in a grassy gap. A trail leads right 150 feet to Spy Rock. (See the "Great Day Hikes along the Appalachian Trail" section for a brief description of this hike.)

99.2 Cross over The Priest (4,063 feet). ☛ Access to The Priest Shelter is on any of the unmarked trails that branch right off of the AT as it approaches the summit.

103.5 Cross VA 56; on the opposite side, descend to the Tye River and cross on a suspension bridge.

106.1 Turn right and cross Harpers Creek to begin a steep climb up Three Ridges. ☛ To reach Harpers Creek Shelter, continue straight where the AT turns right. The shelter stands about 400 yards uphill.

109.4 Cross Three Ridges. (See Hike 29 for a detailed description of a loop hike on Three Ridges.)

112.3 ☛ Pass a blue-blazed trail that branches left to Maupin Field Shelter.

114.6 Cross the Blue Ridge Parkway near Three Ridges Overlook. On the opposite side, enter the woods and descend the road embankment.

AT SHELTERS/HUTS
(MILEAGE ON THE AT FROM US 220 NORTH TO ROCKFISH GAP)

Mile 5.0 – Fullhardt Knob Shelter

Mile 11.2 – Wilson Creek Shelter

Mile 18.5 – Bobbletts Gap Shelter

Mile 24.9 – Cove Mountain Shelter

Mile 31.8 – Bryant Ridge Shelter

Mile 36.8 – Cornelius Creek Shelter

Mile 42.1 – Thunder Hill Shelter

Mile 54.5 – Matts Creek Shelter

Mile 58.4 – Johns Hollow Shelter

Mile 67.2 – Punchbowl Shelter

Mile 76.0 – Brown Mountain Creek Shelter

Mile 91.8 – Seeley-Woodworth Shelter

Mile 99.2 – The Priest Shelter

Mile 106.1 – Harpers Creek Shelter

Mile 112.3 – Maupin Field Shelter

Mile 128.4 – Paul C. Wolfe Shelter

Hikers on Wilburn Ridge in Mount Rogers NRA.

122.9   Cross the highest point on Humpback Mountain (3,600 feet).

124.3   Pass beneath Humpback Rocks. (See the "Great Day Hikes along the Appalachian Trail" section for a brief description of this hike.)

128.4   ▸ Pass the Paul C. Wolfe Shelter on the left.

133.4   Hike ends at Rockfish Gap.

Hike Information

Local Information

Greater Lynchburg Convention & Visitors Bureau, Lynchburg, (800) 732-5821, www.lynchburgchamber.org

     Roanoke Valley Convention & Visitors Bureau, Roanoke, (800) 635-5535, www.VisitRoanokeVA.com

Segment 4 Rockfish Gap to Chester Gap

Shenandoah National Park and the Appalachian Trail grew up together. Civilian Conservation Corps crews built Skyline Drive on right-of-ways carved by AT trail volunteers. The routes stay within a half mile of each other as they pass through mountain gaps, past old farms and orchards, and over rocky mountaintops. Recent fires, ice-storm damage, and gypsy moth infestation have decimated large areas of the forest in Shenandoah. In these areas, the AT gives hikers a view of the shrubby plants, small trees, wildflowers, and vines that mark early stages of reforestation.

Start: Blue Ridge Parkway south of I-64
Distance: 107.1 miles point to point
Difficulty: Moderate
Trail surface: Using dirt footpaths and abandoned dirt roads, hike along ridges and outcrops; down steep wooded slopes; and through old fields, red spruce, and balsam fir at highest elevations.
Nearest towns: Waynesboro, VA (south access); Front Royal, VA (north access)
Canine compatibility: Dogs permitted (must be on a leash at all times)
Trail contacts: Appalachian Trail Conference, Harpers Ferry, WV, (304) 535-6331, www .appalachiantrail.org; Potomac Appalachian Trail Club (PATC), Vienna, (703) 242-0693, patc.net; Shenandoah National Park, Luray, (540) 999-3500, www.nps.gov/shen; Skyland

Lodge, Skyline Drive, (800) 778-2851, www .visitshenandoah.com
Schedule: Open year-round. Skyline Drive may close without advance notice due to inclement weather. Portions of this road are also closed during hunting season to discourage poachers. Call (540) 999-3500 for closures.
Fees/permits: Entrance fee (honor boxes at north and south park boundaries). Appalachian Trail (AT) hikers must register for a free backcountry permit at Tom Floyd Wayside (north district) and Rockfish Gap entrance station (south district).
Maps: PATC #9: Shenandoah National Park, Northern District; PATC #10: Shenandoah National Park, Central District; PATC #11: Shenandoah National Park, South District

Finding the trailhead: To Rockfish Gap Trailhead: From Waynesboro, at the junction of US 340 and I-64, take I-64 east for 5.1 miles to the Afton Mountain exit 99. At the bottom of the exit ramp, turn right onto US 250. In 0.2 mile, turn right onto the Skyline Drive/Blue Ridge Parkway access road. Park at the Augusta County Visitor Center at Rockfish Gap, which is behind the Chevron gas station. The AT is located on the east side of the Blue Ridge Parkway. **Note:** If leaving a car for multiple nights, inform the visitor center staff. *DeLorme: Virginia Atlas & Gazetteer:* Page 67, D5. To Chester Gap Trailhead: See Segment 5: Chester Gap to Harpers Ferry.

The Hike

The AT just north of Rockfish Gap passes little in the way of rock formations, gorges, and waterfalls that draw millions of visitors to Shenandoah National Park. There are, instead, acres of farmland and meadow. Cattle graze and views spill off the mountains onto farms and towns of the Shenandoah Valley.

As introductions go, this pastoral entry into Shenandoah National Park feels right. The parkland was, for hundreds of years, privately owned. Much of it was farmed. Every meadow and mountain gap, every peak, pass, and hollow holds a story or mystery about the people who lived there. At Blackrock, 20 miles north of Rockfish Gap, legend says a friend of Thomas Jefferson hid Virginia's state seal and records of the General Assembly in a cave during the Revolutionary War. The cave has never been identified (although the records and state seal survived the British raid that prompted the stash). Mystery aside, Blackrock commands attention on its own merits. This formation was once a cliff that collapsed after the soft limestone beneath it dissolved. Limestone, by its very nature, erodes faster than granite and greenstone. Where it underlies harder rock, erosion can result in the formation of talus, or large rock piles, at the base of cliffs.

North of Jarmans Gap, mountain laurel spreads roots into the cracks of exposed rock. Rhododendron grow tall and lush around stream headwaters near Moormans River Overlook. Taken together, these plants signal that more rugged, rocky terrain lies ahead. At Ivy Creek, the AT drops into a small canyon (2.7 miles north of Loft Mountain camp store). Briefly, it follows the hemlock-lined stream. The forest undergrowth is lush with mountain laurel, a plant that prefers the shade of pines and hemlocks. If it's been a mild winter, look for an extra spectacular spring laurel bloom. The many white, cup-shaped laurel flowers make this short stretch of the AT one of a kind in the park.

On the approach to Big Meadows (17.4 miles north of Swift Run Gap), a cemetery and pieces of a pasture fence are visible from the AT. Periwinkle blooms in spring. The wildflower, with small, waxy-looking leaves that spread like a ground ivy, is not a naturally occurring mountain wildflower. Its presence usually indicates that a homesite once stood in the area. Nearby, on Tanner's Ridge, residents refused to leave their homes after President Franklin D. Roosevelt dedicated the park in 1936. Old pictures show sheriff deputies carrying a woman away from her house, a vivid example of forced eviction.

Not every mountain settler resisted. Some left willingly. North of Rock Spring Hut, where the AT passes beneath the cliffs of Hawksbill Mountain (4,051 feet), a view opens north onto Ida Valley. This is where the federal government built its first resettlement community for park residents in 1937. Hawksbill is the tallest mountain in Shenandoah National Park, but the AT passes below, not over, the summit. The trail reaches its highest point in this section a few miles north on Stony Mountain. Stony is followed in quick succession by the Pinnacles and Little Stony Mountain. These peaks, short on tree-cover, offer great views from rock summits and cliffs. They are also within easy reach of Skyland Lodge, a hotel and restaurant that draws flocks of visitors.

Skyland is famous for its founder, George Freeman Pollack, who opened the resort in the 1880s. In 1924 Pollack helped sell the idea of making the Blue Ridge, from Front Royal to Rockfish Gap, America's first national park east of the Mississippi

River. "A national park near our nation's capital" became the group's slogan. After twelve years, they succeeded. There is a story about local boys who climbed from the valley to watch tourists drive Skyline Drive and counted as many as six cars in a day. In 2002 Shenandoah National Park recorded 1.4 million visitors, making it the fourteenth most visited national park in the nation.

Like periwinkle, an orchard tree—apple, pear, cherry, or other fruit—signals that a homesite or farm once stood in the area. Apples were prized for making moonshine brandy in Gravel Spring Gap (14.5 miles north of Thornton Gap). Nicholson Hollow, south of Mary's Rock, was renowned for its apple brandy. Jarmans Gap, at the southern end of the park, was known for corn whiskey. Moonshine, though illegal, offered poor mountaineers extra income. If a man had the skills, nature provided the ingredients: clean, running water, fruit or corn, and yeast. Stills were hidden and well protected from suspicious strangers who wandered nearby. This included early AT trail volunteers. Stories tell of how settlers chased Potomac Appalachian Trail Club (PATC) volunteers by setting fires.

Today, the AT hiker in Shenandoah National Park is a herald of spring. Thousands of men and women begin the AT at Springer Mountain in Georgia in March. The bulk of them hit this park in May. Many have their hearts—or stomachs—set on a good meal at one of the park's three restaurants. As their thoughts wander ahead to Harpers Ferry, West Virginia—the official halfway point on the 2,173-mile trail—their feet pass over storied ground. In Shenandoah, there's a tale around every turn in the trail.

Miles and Directions

0.0 Start on the Blue Ridge Parkway south of I-64. Walk north across a bridge spanning the interstate. **Note:** For its first 8 miles, the AT runs on a narrow strip of land owned by the National Park Service. Land a few feet off either side of the trail is private property.

5.0 Cross Bear Den Mountain (2,885 feet). In another 1.4 miles, cross Calf Mountain (2,974 feet).

7.0 Pass a blue-blazed trail that leads left 0.2 mile to Calf Mountain Shelter.

8.0 Pass through Jarmans Gap. The AT now traverses land in Shenandoah National Park.

13.7 Pass Wildcat Ridge Trail on the left. (See the "Great Day Hikes along the Appalachian Trail" section for a brief description of a loop hike using Wildcat Ridge Trail.)

20.0 A trail leads right 200 yards to Blackrock Hut. In another 0.5 mile, the AT circles around Blackrock (3,092 feet), a rock formation.

21.9 Reach a four-way intersection with Jones Run Trail; continue straight on the AT. (See the "Great Day Hikes along the Appalachian Trail" section for a brief description of a loop using Jones Run Trail and Doyles River Trail.)

23.6 Pass blue-blazed Big Run Loop Trail on the left; continue straight on the AT. (See the "Great Day Hikes along the Appalachian Trail" section for a brief description of this trail.)

27.4 Pass a trail on the left that climbs uphill to the Loft Mountain camp store, open May to October.

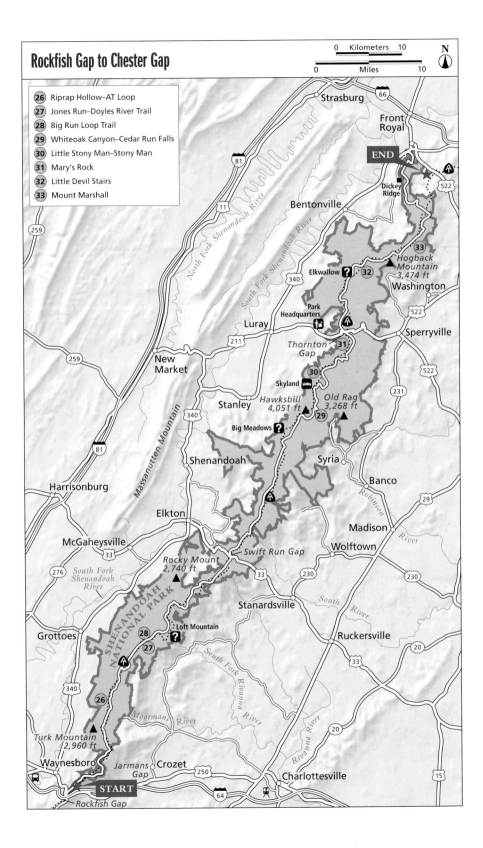

Rockfish Gap to Chester Gap

0 — Kilometers — 10
0 — Miles — 10

N

26 Riprap Hollow–AT Loop
27 Jones Run–Doyles River Trail
28 Big Run Loop Trail
29 Whiteoak Canyon–Cedar Run Falls
30 Little Stony Man–Stony Man
31 Mary's Rock
32 Little Devil Stairs
33 Mount Marshall

Strasburg
66
Front Royal
81
END
522
Dickey Ridge
Bentonville
33
Hogback Mountain 3,474 ft
Elkwallow
32
Washington
340
522
Park Headquarters
Sperryville
Luray
211
Thornton Gap
31
522
259
New Market
30
Skyland
231
Hawksbill 4,051 ft
Old Rag 3,268 ft
Stanley
29
Big Meadows
340
81
Shenandoah
Syria
Banco
Robinson River
Harrisonburg
29
Elkton
Madison River
McGaheysville
33
Wolftown
230
230
Rocky Mount 2,740 ft
Swift Run Gap
33
230
276
South Fork Shenandoah River
Stanardsville
South River
SHENANDOAH NATIONAL PARK
Loft Mountain
28
Ruckersville
Grottoes
27
20
33
340
26
South Fork Rivanna River
Turk Mountain 2,960 ft
Rivanna River
20
Waynesboro
Jarmans Gap
Crozet
250
Charlottesville
15
START
64
Rockfish Gap

North Fork Shenandoah River
South Fork Shenandoah River
Massanutten Mountain
Moormans River

29.5 Cross Ivy Creek, turn right, and follow the AT downstream. The hollow is shaded in hemlock with thick undergrowth of mountain laurel.

33.2 Cross a road and continue straight on the AT. ▐ The road leads right 0.1 mile to Pinefield Hut.

41.4 Descend from Flattop Mountain (3,325 feet) and cross a service road. ▐ The road leads left to Hightop Hut in 0.1 mile; continue straight on the AT.

44.7 Cross above US 33 on a bridge on Skyline Drive. Walk north until you pass an entrance road from US 33 on the left. Past this entrance road, turn right and reenter the woods following white blazes.

53.1 A concrete post on the left signals a connector trail leading left to Lewis Mountain Campground; continue straight on the AT.

53.8 ▐ Pass a road on the right that leads 0.1 mile to Bearfence Hut.

56.8 Pass Laurel Prong Trail on the right. **Note:** Laurel Prong Trail leads 2.8 miles to Camp Hoover, a vacation retreat used by President Herbert Hoover.

61.6 Pass below the cliffs of Blackrock, a tall rock formation that signals the approach of Big Meadows Campground. The AT soon passes an amphitheater and skirts around the campground.

65.3 ▐ Pass a trail leading left to Rock Spring Hut in 0.2 mile.

65.6 Pass the trail to Hawksbill (4,051 feet) that branches right off the AT; continue straight on the AT. The AT runs along the base of cliffs below Hawksbill's summit. (Hawksbill is the highest point in Shenandoah National Park. The highest point on the AT in Shenandoah comes 6 miles to the north, on Stony Man.)

69.9 Cross a paved entrance road to Skyland Resort and enter a parking area for the Stony Man Nature Trail. Follow white-blazed AT as it climbs Stony Man. (See the "Great Day Hikes along the Appalachian Trail" section for a brief description of hikes in this area.)

76.2 Pass Byrds Nest #3, a day-use only shelter with a water supply. Follow the AT a short distance on a dirt road, then turn left to re-enter the woods following white blazes.

77.5 Pass a trail on the left to a lookout off Mary's Rock; continue straight on the AT as it descends and crosses US 211 in Thornton Gap, near the Panorama Restaurant. (See the" Great Day Hikes along the Appalachian Trail" section for a brief description of this trail.)

80.6 ▐ A blue-blazed trail branches right off the AT and leads 0.2 mile to Pass Mountain Hut.

87.9 Reach a four-way intersection with Elkwallow Trail; continue straight on the AT. **Note:** Elkwallow trail leads left to Matthews Arm Campground in 1.9 miles.

90.1 Tuscarora Trail intersects with the AT on the left; continue straight on the AT. (See Hike 22 for a history of the Tuscarora Trail.)

92.0 A dirt road leads right 50 yards to Skyline Drive and Little Hogback Overlook. (See the "Great Day Hikes along the Appalachian Trail" section for a brief description of a hike that begins at this overlook.)

93.7 The Bluff Trail intersects the AT; bear left on the AT. ▐ Gravel Springs Shelter is 0.2 mile to the right on Bluff Trail.

96.2 Cross the summit of Mount Marshall (3,369 feet). (See Hike 15 for a detailed description of this trail.)

103.5 Exit Shenandoah National Park at Compton Gap. The AT follows a corridor of land owned by the National Park Service.

104.2 A path leads left off the AT to Tom Floyd Wayside; continue straight on the AT.

105.7 Enter land owned by the Smithsonian Institute's Conservation & Research Center. A few feet off the trail is private property. Camping is prohibited. In 0.2 mile, pass a blue-blazed trail leading right 0.1 mile to the Northern Virginia Trail Center; continue straight on the AT.

107.1 Hike ends at US 522 in Chester Gap.

Hike Information

Local Information

Front Royal Visitor Center, Front Royal, (800) 338-2576, www.frontroyalchamber .com

Luray-Page County Chamber of Commerce, Luray, (540) 743-3915 or (888) 743-3915, www.luraypage.com

Staunton/Augusta County Visitor Center at Rockfish Gap, Afton Mountain, (540) 943-5187

AT SHELTERS/HUTS (MILEAGE ON THE AT FROM ROCKFISH GAP NORTH TO CHESTER GAP)

Mile 7.0 – Calf Mountain Shelter

Mile 20.0 – Blackrock Hut

Mile 33.2 – Pinefield Hut

Mile 41.4 – Hightop Hut

Mile 53.8 – Bearfence Hut

Mile 65.3 – Rock Spring Hut

Mile 80.6 – Pass Mountain Hut

Mile 93.7 – Gravel Springs Shelter

Mile 104.2 – Tom Floyd Wayside (primitive site)

Segment 5 Chester Gap to Harpers Ferry

The Blue Ridge of northern Virginia have none of the 4,000-foot-plus heights so plentiful on the Appalachian Trail farther south. Still, the northern Virginia leg is one exhausting climb after another. On open mountain balds, views drop west onto the Great Valley. The bumpy spine of the Blue Ridge runs southward, and to the east lie the rolling meadows of Virginia's hunt country. Come fall and winter, the mountains here harbor quiet moments, interrupted occasionally by the thrashing of birds foraging among the hornbeam, dogwood, spicebush, and sassafras.

Start: Parking lot on the southbound side of US 522

Distance: 54.5 miles

Difficulty: Moderate

Trail surface: Using dirt footpaths and abandoned dirt roads, hike along low ridges, cliffs, and rock lookouts and through fields, meadows, and stream hollows.

Nearest towns: Front Royal, VA (south access); Harpers Ferry, WV (north access)

Canine compatibility: Dogs permitted

Trail contacts: Appalachian Trail Conference, Harpers Ferry, WV, (304) 535-6331, www .appalachiantrail.org; Potomac Appalachian Trail Club (PATC), Vienna, (703) 242-0693, patc.net; Harpers Ferry National Historical Park, Harpers Ferry, WV, (304) 535-6298, www .nps.gov/hafe

Schedule: Open year-round. Hunting season in G. R. Thompson Wildlife Management Area, mid-Nov through first week in Jan.

Maps: PATC #7 (AT–Northern VA); PATC #8 (AT–Northern VA)

Finding the trailhead: To Chester Gap Trailhead: From Front Royal, drive south 3.4 miles on US 522 from its intersection with VA 55. The Appalachian Trail (AT) crosses US 522 here. There's parking for several cars on the southbound side of the highway. *DeLorme: Virginia Atlas & Gazetteer:* Page 74, A3.

To Harpers Ferry Trailhead: From Harpers Ferry, WV, cross the Shenandoah River bridge and drive west 0.9 mile on US 340 to the Harpers Ferry National Historical Park Visitor Center. There's an entrance fee. A free shuttle runs every ten to fifteen minutes into Lower Town, where the AT is located. Notify park rangers if you intend on leaving the car for multiple nights. Alternate parking for day hikers is located at the junction of US 340 and VA 671 (in Virginia), at an unsecured roadside parking area near the Tri-State Amoco gas station. From the east end of the Shenandoah River bridge, proceed east 1.6 miles on US 340 to the parking area, on the left. On foot, backtrack 0.3 mile on US 340 to the Loudoun Heights Trail on the southbound side of the road. *DeLorme: Virginia Atlas & Gazetteer:* Page 79, B7.

The Hike

Small as it appears on a map, Chester Gap looms big on the AT. The Blue Ridge tapers suddenly into this gap, located east of Front Royal. Northward, the range becomes a chain of low, rounded ridges. After hundreds of miles of exposed ridges, mountain balds, and towering cliffs, this section shrinks into short, vigorous climbs. From Manassas Gap to Snickers Gap, it's either steep up, or steep down, with little in between. Thru-hikers nickname it the roller coaster for its many breath-stealing bumps.

The story of Chester Gap touches on the mystery of Virginia's first white explorer who crossed the Blue Ridge. John Lederer explored the mountains for Virginia's colonial government and, in 1670, wrote of the inspiring view from the mountains. Where exactly he stood is still debated. The AT passes a monument in Linden, Virginia, at Manassas Gap, in honor of his explorations. Some historians say he climbed the Swift Run Gap in Shenandoah National Park. Others say Mount Marshall, also in Shenandoah. Because Lederer's mission was to locate the headwaters of the Rappahannock River, many believe Chester Gap is where he broke through the Blue Ridge in 1670. The Rappahannock starts as a small mountain stream east of Chester Gap, eventually to become a major tributary of the Chesapeake Bay.

Wherever he stood, Lederer's first impression of the mountains speaks volumes about how early explorers and settlers viewed the Blue Ridge. It was, for the English, terra incognito. Lederer, maybe feeling lightheaded from his long climb, initially described the blue haze covering the western mountain slope as some kind of great western ocean. When the haze lifted, he moved across the Great Valley and explored present-day West Virginia.

It's nostalgic, as you hike this 54-mile stretch of the AT, to imagine how volunteers in 1927 plotted the first miles of the world-famous long trail in this region. Only a few stretches of original trail remain intact north of Chester Gap. Trail relocations peaked in the 1950s, when private landowners blocked access. With Washington, DC, only 60 miles east, and because of the many gaps that permit short hikes, the AT in this region has historically received heavy day use. Landowners' protest is now a moot point. The AT passes near homes and uses several dirt and paved roads south of Manassas Gap. But there are also long stretches through heavy forestland where the scarlet tanager's song floats down from tall treetops.

Birds make much racket in the overgrowth of spicebush, honeysuckle, and Virginia creeper along the trail. Redstarts, vireos, wood thrush, bluebirds, robins, and thrushes flit branch to branch, wavering for a second or two on a twig that can barely hold their weight. If they're lucky, the noisy forage for food ends with a prize: the grapelike fruit of Virginia creeper. Any hiker who has violently pitched forward, tripped up by a camouflaged creeper, knows this vine deserves to be pruned rather than admired. The vine grows adhesive discs on its tendrils that cement to the surfaces of trees, fence posts, and all forms of climbable surfaces. Perhaps we would all have higher regard for the creeper if Virginia's General Assembly had enshrined it as the state flower. Instead, by a one-vote margin, the vine lost to the flowering dogwood.

The climb on the AT north from Snickers Gap follows a rocky switchback ascent. After topping out, the trail drops and crosses a boulder-lined stream in Pigeon Hollow. Sounds of water bubble up from beneath the rocks. The trail will climb again, descend to another stream, and then climb once more to Crescent Rock. Beyond this folded section of Catoctin greenstone, the trail continues its roller-coaster route.

Three times between Snickers Gap and Ashby Gap, the AT climbs to high points: Lookout Point, Tomblin Hill, and Buzzard Hill. Three times the trail drops, first into a valley formed by a branch of Spout Run, then into Fent Willey Hollow and Reservoir Hollow.

During the Civil War, the mountain hollows of northern Virginia sheltered a group of Confederate raiders known as Mosby's Rangers. John Singleton Mosby led the group and coordinated his soldiers' guerilla-style tactics. They sprang upon Union soldiers in the mountain passes, took clothes, weapons, and money, then led prisoners into Confederate strongholds. By the end of the war, Mosby ruled a small fiefdom in Loudoun County, from Bull Run Mountain to the crest of the Blue Ridge. Ruled isn't too strong a word, either. His rangers were not allowed to leave the boundaries of the Confederacy without permission. Any man who missed two roll calls without good reason was discharged. At war's end, Mosby received a pardon (as did most Confederate soldiers), and then supported his old battlefield enemy Ulysses S. Grant in the presidential election.

Few towns are richer in Civil War history than Harpers Ferry, West Virginia. This national historic park is the end of the AT in Virginia, at the bridge crossing on US 340. The Shenandoah River thunders below this symbolic crossing. The Blue Ridge extends into Maryland and southern Pennsylvania. In that region, the chain goes by the name South Mountain. Not until the White Mountains of New Hampshire does the AT reach heights equal to Virginia's mountains. From Weaver Cliffs, north of Harpers Ferry, the AT hiker can look back south along the Blue Ridge. If conditions are right, you might see (or believe you see), if only for a whimsical moment, what John Lederer saw in 1670, an endless ocean of blue haze.

Miles and Directions

0.0 Start in a parking lot on the southbound side of US 522. Cross the highway and enter the woods following the white blazes. In this area, the AT passes through land owned by the Smithsonian Institute's Conservation & Research Center. Camping is not allowed.

2.3 Leave the Conservation & Research Center property.

5.2 ◣ A trail branches left to the Denton Shelter.

8.1 Cross a set of railroad tracks and, in 0.1 mile, reach VA 55. Cross and follow VA 725 as it passes under I-66. **Note:** The town of Linden and the Discovery Monument in honor of John Lederer are 0.1 mile left on VA 55.

8.5 Reach a Potomac Appalachian Trail Conference parking lot on the right. Follow the AT as it enters the woods from the back of the lot.

10.2 Enter the G. R. Thompson Wildlife Management Area, which is managed by the state. Use caution, especially during fall hunting season.

10.7 ◣ A blue-blazed footpath leads left to Manassas Gap Shelter. Don't confuse the shelter trail with the blue-blazed Ted Lake Trail, also in the vicinity. (See Hike 10 for a detailed description of these trails.)

15.1 ◣ Begin a descent that leads to Dicks Dome Shelter on the right side of the trail.

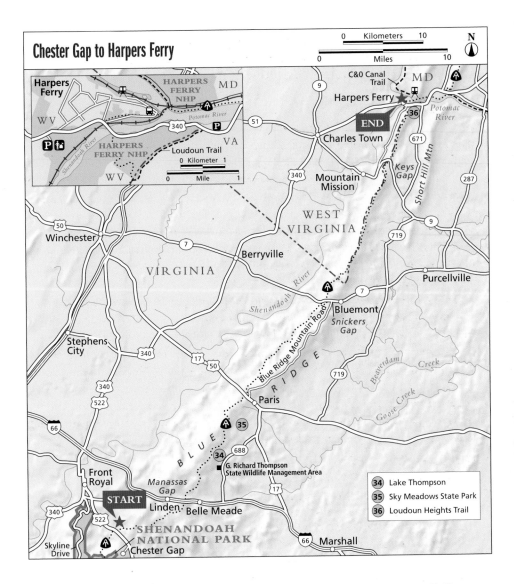

Chester Gap to Harpers Ferry

0   Kilometers   10

0   Miles   10

N

Harpers Ferry

HARPERS FERRY NHP   MD

WV

Potomac River

340

51

VA

HARPERS FERRY NHP   Loudoun Trail

0 Kilometer 1

0   Mile   1

WV

C&0 Canal Trail   MD

9

Harpers Ferry

36

Potomac River

END

Charles Town

671

Mountain Mission

340

Keys Gap

Short Hill Mtn

287

WEST VIRGINIA

9

719

Winchester

50

7

Berryville

Purcellville

VIRGINIA

Shenandoah River

7

Bluemont

Snickers Gap

Blue Ridge Mountain Road

BLUE RIDGE

Beaverdam Creek

Stephens City

340

17

50

719

Goose Creek

340

522

Paris

66

35

34   688

G. Richard Thompson State Wildlife Management Area

Front Royal

Manassas Gap

17

34 Lake Thompson

35 Sky Meadows State Park

36 Loudoun Heights Trail

340

522

START

Linden   Belle Meade

SHENANDOAH NATIONAL PARK

66   Marshall

Skyline Drive   Chester Gap

17.4   Enter Sky Meadows State Park. (See the "Great Day Hikes along the Appalachian Trail" section for a brief description of trails in the state park.)

20.5   Cross US 50 in Ashby Gap. As you cross, bear to the right and re-enter the woods at a PATC parking area on US 50.

24.1   ▄ A blue-blazed trail on the left leads to Rod Hollow Shelter. The roller-coaster ride through northern Virginia's Blue Ridge begins as the AT climbs in and out of four hollows.

31.0   Turn left at a T intersection. ▄ A blue-blazed trail leads straight from the junction to reach Sam Moore Shelter. Soon after turning left, you'll cross Spout Run. From here, the AT ascends to Lookout Point.

37.2   Reach Crescent Rock and Pulpit Rock; continue straight on the AT. A footpath descends to the base of a cliff, where this geologic formation is visible.

AT SHELTERS/HUTS (MILEAGE NORTH FROM CHESTER GAP)

Mile 5.2 – Denton Shelter

Mile 10.7 – Manassas Gap Shelter

Mile 15.1 – Dicks Dome Shelter

Mile 24.1 – Rod Hollow Shelter

Mile 31.0 – Sam Moore Shelter

Mile 45.1 – David Lesser Shelter

42.8 Pass a grassy field on the left, the site of an old homestead.

44.5 A trail on the left leads to Buzzard Rocks; continue straight on the AT. Buzzard Rocks has views over the Shenandoah Valley and room for a tent.

45.1 ▶ Pass the David Lesser Shelter on the right.

48.1 Cross the paved West VA 9 at Keys Gap. Reenter the woods on the opposite side at a trail bulletin board near a gravel parking area.

52.0 At a T intersection with the Loudoun Heights Trail, turn left and descend the AT. The trail now crosses land inside Harpers Ferry National Historical Park. (See the "Great Day Hikes along the Appalachian Trail" section for a brief description of this area.) **Note:** If using the alternate trailhead described in the "Finding the trailhead" section of this chapter, proceed straight on Loudoun Heights Trail to its intersection with US 340.

53.6 Cross the Shenandoah River on a bridge on US 340.

54.5 The hike ends in Lower Town of Harpers Ferry National Historical Park. **Note:** The Park Service runs a shuttle every ten to fifteen minutes to the secure parking lot at the park visitor center.

Hike Information

Local Information

Loudoun Tourism Council, Leesburg, (703) 771-2617 or (800) 752-6118, www.visit loudoun.org

Front Royal Visitor Center, Front Royal, (800) 338-2576, www.frontroyal chamber.com

Great Day Hikes along the Appalachian Trail

Compiled here is an index of great day hikes along the Appalachian Trail (AT) in Virginia. Some are featured hikes in this book, others are Honorable Mentions, and the rest are great sections of the AT that should be hiked at one time or another.

Segment 1 Damascus to Marion

1 Feathercamp Branch

See Hike 38: Feathercamp Ridge.

2 Whitetop Laurel Circuit

For nearly 6 miles, the AT follows the ridge of Straight Mountain with overlooks onto wild Whitetop Laurel Creek. At either end, it junctions with the Virginia Creeper Trail, a multiuse trail for hikers and mountain bikers. Together, the AT and Creeper Trail make a vigorous 10-mile loop. The Creeper Trail is a model for the Rails-to-Trails effort. Its total length along the former Abingdon Branch of the Virginia-Carolina Railroad measures 34 miles. The stretch used in this loop is noted for its pathway along scenic Whitetop Laurel Creek. Begin and end the loop at a parking area on VA 728, south of US 58 near Beartree Day Use Area. Mount Rogers NRA/JNF. (276) 579-7092. *DeLorme: Virginia Atlas & Gazetteer:* Page 22, C3.

3 Elk Garden-Mount Rogers Summit

See Hike 40: Mount Rogers Summit.

4 Rhododendron Gap

See Hike 40: Mount Rogers Summit.

5 Grayson Highlands State Park

There are 3 miles of the AT in this popular state park. The quickest link to the long trail is via the Highlands Horse Trail from the park ranger station at Massie Gap. From there, the AT goes north to Little Wilson Creek Wilderness and high-country meadows overlooking Scales. In the other direction, the AT ascends along Wilburn Ridge to amazing rock outcrops, deep thickets of rhododendron, and finally the Mount Rogers Spur Trail. Grayson Highlands State Park and Mount Rogers NRA/JNF. (276) 579-7092 or (276) 783-5196. *DeLorme: Virginia Atlas & Gazetteer:* Page 23, C5.

Segment 2 Marion to Roanoke

6 Crawfish-Channel Rock Loop

See Hike 33: Crawfish/Channel Rock.

7 Beartown Wilderness

It's an easy 2.4-mile hike up the AT from FR 222 (an extension of VA 625) and the boundary of Beartown Wilderness. The AT skirts the south edge of this 6,375-acre federal wilderness until Chestnut Knob. From the mountain, views drop into Burkes Garden, a pocket of agricultural bliss formed when subsurface limestone eroded. Beartown Wilderness has no marked trails besides the AT, but old logging roads allow for exploring Roaring Branch and a sphagnum bog at the headwaters of Cove Branch. Eastern Divide Ranger District, (540) 552-4641. *DeLorme: Virginia Atlas & Gazetteer:* Page 39, D5.

8 Trail Boss-AT Loop

Trail crews rerouted 2.1 miles of the AT to descend off Brushy Mountain as it approaches VA 615. The old section was renamed Trail Boss in honor of a dedicated volunteer. Combined, they make a 5.1-mile loop hike. The AT's route up Brushy Mountain is steep, with ten switchbacks and several overlooks. This is, however, primarily a woodland hike through an oak-hickory forest. There are mountain laurel and rhododendron. In the dark hollows, look for the bloodroot wildflower, plus many mosses and ferns. Eastern Divide Ranger District, (540) 552-4641. *DeLorme: Virginia Atlas & Gazetteer:* Page 39, C7.

9 Angels Rest

South of the New River from Pearisburg, the AT makes a steep, switchback-heavy trip up Pearis Mountain. In 1.5 miles, a trail leads a few hundred yards to Angels Rest. This 3,550-foot perch has views into the New River's passage through the Narrows, a rock fault between Devonian shale and Cambrian limestone. The trailhead for this 3-mile in-and-out hike is on VA 634 (Morris Avenue) in Pearisburg. A turnaround at Angels Rest makes a 3-mile day hike. Eastern Divide Ranger District, (540) 552-4641. *DeLorme: Virginia Atlas & Gazetteer:* Page 40, B3.

10 The Rice Fields

From Pearisburg, the AT climbs Peters Mountain and traces the crest to a mountain meadow called the Rice Fields. The oddity of open farm meadows atop a tall ridge is matched by the beauty of views off the west slope into West Virginia. Begin the hike on VA 624 (Stillhouse Branch Road) north of US 460 between Pearisburg and Narrows. An AT hut 5 miles from the trailhead marks a reasonable turnaround point for this 10-mile in-and-out hike. Eastern Divide Ranger District, (540) 552-4641. *DeLorme: Virginia Atlas and Gazetteer:* Page 40, B3.

11 Peters Mountain Wilderness

See Hike 31: Huckleberry Loop.

12 Mountain Lake Wilderness

See Hike 32: Mountain Lake Wilderness.

13 Kelly Knob

A 3.3-mile trek from Sinking Creek and VA 42 to Kelly Knob ends with views off this 3,742-foot peak. The AT crosses privately owned farmland near the trailhead. Be sure to follow all posted signs regarding parking and hiking. Past Kelly Knob, the AT dips to Big Pond; a side trail here leads 100 yards to views from White Rocks. For an 8.5-mile point-to-point hike, continue hiking up the AT and descend Johns Creek Mountain Trail. Park a shuttle at the Johns Creek trailhead on VA 658 west of Twin Oaks. Eastern Divide Ranger District, (540) 552-4641. *DeLorme: Virginia Atlas & Gazetteer:* Page 41, B6.

14 North Mountain–AT Loop

See Honorable Mention FF (North Mountain–AT Loop).

15 Audie Murphy VFW Monument

The AT rises steeply from VA 620 to the spine of Brush Mountain. In 3.8 miles, the trail passes a monument to Audie Murphy, erected by the VFW on the site of Murphy's plane crash in 1971. Murphy was a recipient of the Congressional Medal of Honor and twenty-eight wartime medals from the United States, France, and Belgium. From the memorial, the AT continues north for another 3.8 miles to cross VA 620. Eastern Divide Ranger District, (540) 552-4641. *DeLorme: Virginia Atlas & Gazetteer:* Page 42, A1.

16 Dragons Tooth

It is a steep and rugged climb on the AT for 2.6 miles to Dragons Tooth, a craggy rock that juts 35 feet above the summit of Cove Mountain. En route, the AT traces the razor edge of Tuscarora sandstone in an area called Rawies Rest. Use the blue-blazed Dragons Tooth Trail to make a loop hike that begins and ends at VA 624. There is alternate parking and trail access on VA 311 north at the Dragons Tooth parking lot past Catawba Grocery. Eastern Divide Ranger District, (540) 552-4641. *DeLorme: Virginia Atlas & Gazetteer:* Page 42, B1.

17 McAfee Knob

The AT leads 3.5 miles uphill to McAfee Knob, a 3,197-foot high point on Catawba Mountain. The southern trailhead is on VA 311, west of Salem, Virginia. For a longer day hike, continue past McAfee for another 6 miles along Tinker Mountain with its gorgeous cliff overlooks. A junction with the blue-blazed Andy Lane Trail leads 2.3 miles left to VA 600. Highlights of this trip include views of Catawba Valley, boulders in the Devils Kitchen area, and a half mile of exposed, cliff trail on Tinker Cliffs. Appalachian Trail Conference corridor, NPS, (540) 961-5551. *DeLorme: Virginia Atlas & Gazetteer:* Page 42, A/B2.

Segment 3   Roanoke to Rockfish Gap

18 Little Cove Mountain Trail

South of Jennings Creek, the AT rides a high ridge called Cove Mountain. In total, there are ten small knobs en route, from the trailhead on VA 614 to the blue-blazed Little Cove Mountain Trail. Cove Mountain (2,720 feet) marks the highest point. A return hike on Little Cove Mountain Trail passes through the watershed of Cove Creek and Little Cove Creek. Where the Little Cove trail ends at VA 614, turn left and walk 0.7 mile up gravel VA 614 to the trailhead. This hike features a shale barren, a rare ecosystem hosting prickly pear and other fragile plants, located off the AT near VA 614. Glenwood-Pedlar Ranger District, (540) 291-2188. *DeLorme: Virginia Atlas & Gazetteer:* Page 53, D5.

19 Apple Orchard Falls-Cornelius Creek Loop

The AT measures only 1.1 miles between Apple Orchard Falls National Recreation Trail and Cornelius Falls Trail. This short stint, however, makes possible a delight of a hike alongside two beautiful streams replete with waterfalls, pools, and thick stands of rhododendron and mountain laurel. There is considerable elevation loss and gain on this 7.6-mile loop—as much as 2,000 feet difference from the AT to FR 59, where you pick up the Cornelius Falls Trail for a return to the AT. Begin the trip at a parking area on the Sunset Field Overlook on the Blue Ridge Parkway (milepost 78.4). Glenwood-Pedlar Ranger District, (540) 291-2188. *DeLorme: Virginia Atlas & Gazetteer:* Page 53, D6.

20 James River Face Wilderness

The AT through this mountainous, 8,903-acre wilderness area was reconstructed in 2000. It now begins at the James River Foot Bridge, on the north bank of the James on US 501/VA 130 (the bridge is named in honor of Bill Foot, a Natural Bridge ATC volunteer who passed away in 2000). After crossing, the AT passes beneath high cliff walls in the river gorge, then climbs gradually up Matts Creek to the Matts Creek Shelter. (The old AT route has been renamed.) Several trails branch off the AT in the wilderness. Belfast Trail leads to Devil's Marbleyard, an 8-acre boulder field with rocks the size of cars. From an alternate trailhead on the Blue Ridge Parkway (milepost 71), hike the AT 1.2 miles to Highcock Knob (3,073 feet). Views from the top are limited in summer. Glenwood-Pedlar Ranger District, (540) 291-2188. *DeLorme: Virginia Atlas & Gazetteer:* Page 53, D7.

21 Old Hotel Trail

See Hike 30: Mount Pleasant.

22 Rocky Mountain/Lovingston Spring

A 5.8-mile stretch of the AT runs from Salt Log Gap on FR 63 (extension of VA 634) to the Seeley-Woodworth AT shelter. A return on Lovingston Spring Trail makes an 11.7-mile loop. Wildflowers, mosses, and ferns grow thick around the many springs on these trails. There are signs of an old apple orchard near the AT uphill from Salt Log Gap. Wolf Rocks is a scenic overlook with views of The Priest (northeast) and Rocky Mountain (west). The return trip includes a 0.8-mile side trip (0.4 mile each way) up Rocky Mountain, a summit with views west over the Shenandoah Valley. Glenwood-Pedlar Ranger District, (540) 291-2188. *DeLorme: Virginia Atlas & Gazetteer:* Page 54, B2.

23 Spy Rock

There are two access points on the AT for this overlook, famous for its wide views of the Cardinal, The Priest, Little Priest, and the Friar. If time is short, use the 0.4 mile of the AT that links Fish Hatchery Trail (a 1.2-mile extension of VA 690 east of Montebello) with the 0.1-mile Spy Rock Trail. This makes a total loop of 3.4 miles. (Ask permission to park at the state-run fish hatchery.) For a longer trip, hike the AT for 3.2 miles between VA 826 (Crabtree Farm Road) and Spy Rock. Access to the AT is 0.5 mile uphill from Crabtree Campground on VA 826. Glenwood-Pedlar Ranger District, (540) 291-2188. *DeLorme: Virginia Atlas & Gazetteer:* Page 54, B2.

24 Mau-Har Trail

See Hike 29: Three Ridges.

25 Humpback Rocks

The AT departs the Humpback Rocks parking area on the Blue Ridge Parkway (milepost 6) and in 1 mile, passes a spur trail to Humpback Rocks. This 3,080-foot outcrop offers wide views of the Blue Ridge and Shenandoah Valley. Another mile on the AT brings the summit of Humpback Mountain (3,600 feet). A return to the parking lot makes a 4-mile hike. Blue Ridge Parkway, (828) 271-4779. *DeLorme: Virginia Atlas & Gazetteer:* Page 55, A4.

Segment 4 Rockfish Gap to Chester Gap

26 Riprap Hollow-AT Loop

There is a 2.7-mile stretch of the AT between the Riprap Trail parking area (milepost 90) and Wildcat Ridge parking (milepost 92.1). To make a 10-mile loop hike, begin at the Riprap Trail parking area and descend Riprap Trail past Chimney Rock and Calvary Rock. Climb from the hollow on Wildcat Ridge Trail. Signs of a recent forest fire date from 1998 blaze that originated in the area of Calvary Rock. This a great hike for witnessing nature's regenerative powers. SNP South District, (540) 999-3500. *DeLorme: Virginia Atlas & Gazetteer:* Page 67, C5.

27 Jones Run-Doyles River Trail

The AT runs for 3.5 miles alongside Skyline Drive between Jones Run Trail and the Doyles River Trail. Using all three trails makes for a nice 8.2-mile hike, with small waterfalls and rock outcrops on Jones Run and the Doyles River. Begin the hike at Doyles River parking area (milepost 81.1). Descend Jones Run and ascend Jones Run Trail to Skyline Drive, then hike north on the AT. Brown Gap Road is a cutoff for a shorter 6.6-mile loop. SNP South District, (540) 999-3500. *DeLorme: Virginia Atlas & Gazetteer:* Page 67, C6.

28 Big Run Loop Trail

A 1.6-mile stretch of the AT links either end of Big Run Loop Trail. The hike begins at Big Run Loop Overlook (milepost 82.2), drops into the Big Run stream valley, and returns to the AT in 4.2 miles. A forest fire torched parts of the Big Run watershed. Finish the 5.8-mile loop by hiking north on the AT to the Doyles River trailhead, then uphill 200 yards to Skyline Drive. SNP South District, (540) 999-3500. *DeLorme: Virginia Atlas & Gazetteer:* Page 67, B6.

29 Whiteoak Canyon-Cedar Run Falls

This is an extremely popular hike that uses 3.3 miles of the AT. Popular, however, does not mean easy. At 11 miles, this loop takes the better part of the day. There are steep drop-offs and difficult climbs. Payoff comes with 40-foot cascades in Whiteoak Canyon, and the many falls and pools along Cedar Run. Use the Stony Man Nature Trail parking area (milepost 41.7) at Skyland as a starting point, and the Whiteoak-Cedar Run Link Trail to complete the loop. SNP Central District, (540) 999-3500. *DeLorme: Virginia Atlas & Gazetteer:* Page 74, D1.

30 Little Stony Man–Stony Man

Stony Man (3,387 feet) is a popular site thanks to Skyland, a park resort. This route uses a northern approach from the Little Stony Man parking area (milepost 39.1). The 1.2-mile hike on the AT traces tall cliffs and intersects the 0.4-mile loop trail around Stony Man's summit. Past Stoney Man, leave the AT and descend on Stony Man Horse Trail and Furnace Spring Trail. Return via the Passamaquoddy Trail. SNP Central District, (540) 999-3500. *DeLorme: Virginia Atlas & Gazetteer:* Page 74, D2.

31 Mary's Rock

An easy 2-mile hike on the AT leads to a 360-degree view off Mary's Rock. From the Panorama Restaurant at Thornton Gap, the AT climbs 1.9 miles on switchbacks to the overlook spur trail. Samples of rock called granodiorite from this area were carbon dated to more than one billion years, making it officially the oldest rock known in the park. Retrace the AT to the Panorama for a 4-mile hike. Parking is permitted at the restaurant. SNP Central District, (540) 999-3500. *DeLorme: Virginia Atlas & Gazetteer:* Page 74, C2.

32 Little Devil Stairs

Three miles of AT run between Little Hogback Overlook (milepost 19.7) and Rattlesnake Point Overlook (milepost 21.9). En route, the AT crosses Hogback Mountain (3,474 feet). Begin this hike at Little Hogback Overlook and use the Piney Branch Trail and Pole Bridge Link Trail to reach Little Devil Stairs, a 2-mile route down Keyser Run under sheer cliff walls and past picturesque waterfalls. Little Devil Stairs is a popular route, but dangerous. Use caution in icy or wet weather. Hike back up Little Devil Stairs and return to the Little Hogback Overlook on Keyser Fire Road for a 10.5-mile loop. SNP Northern District, (540) 999-3500. *DeLorme: Virginia Atlas & Gazetteer:* Page 74, B2.

33 Mount Marshall

See Hike 15: Mount Marshall Loop.

Segment 5 Chester Gap to Harpers Ferry

34 Lake Thompson

See Hike 10: G. Richard Thompson Wildlife Management Area.

35 Sky Meadows State Park

A 3.6-mile piece of the AT runs through this beautiful Virginia state park set hard against the eastern foothills of the Blue Ridge. Large meadows lend the area a pastoral feel, but steep climbs await hikers on North Ridge Trail. Gap Run Trail follows a woodland stream, and Piedmont Overlook Trail features nice views of the meadows that sweep off the mountainside. Sky Meadows operated as a farm in the mid-1800s. A stone farmhouse now serves as a visitor center (seasonal) and there are several outbuildings, including stables for horseback riders. Entrance to the park is on US 17, 1.2 miles south of US 50. An entrance fee varies by season. Call (800) 933-PARK for camping reservations. *DeLorme: Virginia Atlas & Gazetteer:* Page 75, A5.

36 Loudoun Heights Trail

A 2.4-mile stretch of the AT joins the Loudoun Heights Trail for a moderately difficult day hike. There are views over the Potomac from Split Rock, a promontory on Loudoun Heights Trail. (The view also explains why Stonewall Jackson bombarded Harpers Ferry, West Virginia, from this hill in 1862.) This hike requires some roadside trekking on busy US 340 and navigation through Harpers Ferry National Historical Park. There are two access points: Harpers Ferry National Historical Park (fee charged for parking in a secure overnight lot) or a road-side pull-off on US 340 at VA 671 in Virginia (unsecured and suitable for day hikes only). Call the park at (304) 535-6298 or the ATC at (304) 535-6068. In wintertime, the ATC headquarters is closed on weekends. Outfitter at Harpers Ferry, 189 High St., Harpers Ferry, WV (888-535-2087) sells maps. *DeLorme: Virginia Atlas & Gazetteer:* Page 79, B7.

Contact Information

Statewide

State Travel Information, (800) VISIT-VA, www.virginia.org
Department of Conservation & Recreation (DCR), Division of State Parks, (804) 786-1712, www.dcr.state.va.us/parks
DCR, State Park Reservation Line, (800) 933-PARK (7275)
DCR, Natural Heritage Program, (804) 786-7951,www.dcr.state.va.us/dnh
Department of Game and Inland Fisheries, (804) 367-1000, www.dgif.state.va.us
Department of Mines, Minerals and Energy, (276) 523-8146, www.mme.state.va.us
Department of Forestry, (434) 977-6555, www.vdof.org/stforest
Cumberland HQ, (804) 492-4121
Appomattox/Buckingham HQ, (434) 983-2175

National Forests

Supervisor's Office, Roanoke, (888) 265-0019, www.southernregion.fs.fed.us/gwj
Massanutten Visitors Center, New Market, (540) 740-8310
Mount Rogers National Recreation Area, Marion, (276) 783-5196

Ranger Districts

Clinch, Wise, (276) 328-2931
Deerfield, Staunton, (540) 885-8028
Dry River, Bridgewater, (540) 828-2591
Eastern Divide, Blacksburg, (540) 552-4641; Wytheville, (540) 228-5551
Glenwood/Pedlar, Natural Bridge Station, (540) 291-2188; Buena Vista (540) 261-6105
Highlands Gateway Visitors Center, Max Meadows, (800) 446-9670
James River, Covington, (540) 962-2214
Lee, Edinburg, (540) 984-4101
Warm Springs, Hot Springs, (540) 839-2521

National Parks

www.nps.gov
Blue Ridge Parkway, Asheville, NC, (828) 271-4779
George Washington Memorial Parkway, McLean, VA, (703) 289-2500
Great Falls Park, Great Falls, VA, (703) 285-2966
Prince William Forest Park, (703) 221-7181
Shenandoah National Park, Luray, VA, (540) 999-3500

Hike Index

Apple Orchard Falls–Cornelius Creek
    Loop Trail, 227
Bad Mountain, 277
Beaverdam Park, 49
Belle Isle (Richmond), 115
Belle Isle State Park , 39
Big Run Portal–Rockytop Loop, 166
Big Schloss , 170
Bull Run-Occoquan Trail, 89
Caledon Natural Area State Park, 65
Chester Gap to Harpers Ferry (Segment
    5), 334, 348
Chief Benge Scout Trail, 257
Chincoteague National Wildlife
    Refuge, 12
Crabtree Falls, 227
Crawfish/Channel Rock, 243
Damascus to Marion (Segment 1),
    308, 340
Devils Fork Loop, 265
Fairy Stone State Park, 115
False Cape State Park/Back Bay Wildlife
    Refuge, 19
Feathercamp Ridge, 282
First Landing State Park , 26
Four Trails Circuit, 303
Fridley Gap , 183
G, Richard Thompson Wildlife
    Management Area, 75
Great Dismal Swamp National Wildlife
    Refuge, 49
Great Falls Park, 67
Guest River Gorge Trail, 278
Hazel Mountain, 127
Hickory Hollow Natural Area
    Preserve, 49

Huckleberry Loop, 231
Humpback Rocks, 227
Hungry Mother State Park, 277
James River State Park, 110
Jeremy's Run, 166
Laurel Fork Area , 189
Little Wilson Creek Wilderness, 289
Manassas National Battlefield Park, 89
Marion to Roanoke (Segment 2),
    313, 341
Mason Neck, 89
Massanutten Mountain East/Duncan
    Hollow, 201
Massanutten Mountain West/Signal
    Knob, 201
Mount Marshall Loop, 120
Mount Pleasant, 222
Mount Rogers Summit, 296
Mountain Lake Wilderness, 237
Newport News Park, 44
Nicholson Hollow, 166
North Fork Moormans River, 148
North Mountain–AT Loop, 277
Old Rag, 134
Overall Run, 155
Pine Mountain Trail, 250
Piney River, 160
Prince William Forest Park, 54
Ragged Mountain Natural Area, 116
Riprap Hollow–Appalachian Trail
    Loop, 166
Rivanna Trails, 115
Roanoke to Rockfish Gap (Segment 3),
    321, 344
Roaring Run/Hoop Hole, 195
Rock Castle Gorge, 205

Rock Creek Park, 81

Rockfish Gap to Chester Gap (Segment 4), 328, 346

Rocky Mount/Gap Run, 141

Rowland Creek Falls Circuit, 303

Sandy Bottom Nature Preserve, 49

Scotts Run Nature Preserve, 61

Shawl Gap–Massanutten East Trail, 201

Shenandoah Mountain Trail/South, 201

Sky Meadows State Park, 90

St, Mary's Wilderness, 210

Stephens Trail , 177

Stone Mountain Trail, 270

The Rice Fields, 277

Three Ridges, 216

Torry Ridge–Mill Creek Loop, 227

Trout Trail, 94

Twin Lakes State Park, 115

Whetstone Ridge, 227

Whiteoak Canyon, 166

Whitetop Laurel Circuit, 303

Wild Oak National Recreation Trail, 201

Wildcat Mountain Preserve, 89

Willis River Trail, 101

York River State Park, 33

About the Authors

Bill and Mary Burnham, aka "Burnham Guides," are guidebook authors and outdoor guides who have penned four books on Virginia travel. They live on the Eastern Shore of Virginia, within easy reach of their sources of inspiration: ocean and mountains. Bill began hiking with friends in New York's Adirondack Mountains in the 1980s. Mary came aboard a few years later, and together they have hiked and traveled America. Their first-ever trip as a couple came in Shenandoah National Park. After they married, they led adventure trips for youth in West Virginia. They paddle and hike throughout Virginia spring through fall and spend the coldest months guiding multiday kayak adventure in the Florida Keys and Everglades. Their *Florida Keys Paddling Atlas* (FalconGuides) is a National Outdoor Book Award winner. Follow along the authors' adventures at BurnhamGuides.com.

Books by Bill and Mary Burnham:

Best Hikes Near Washington, D.C., 2010, FalconGuides
Knack Kayaking for Everyone, 2010, FalconGuides
Knack Car Camping for Everyone, 2009, FalconGuides
Florida Keys Paddling Atlas, 2007, FalconGuides

APR   2013

Your next adventure begins here.

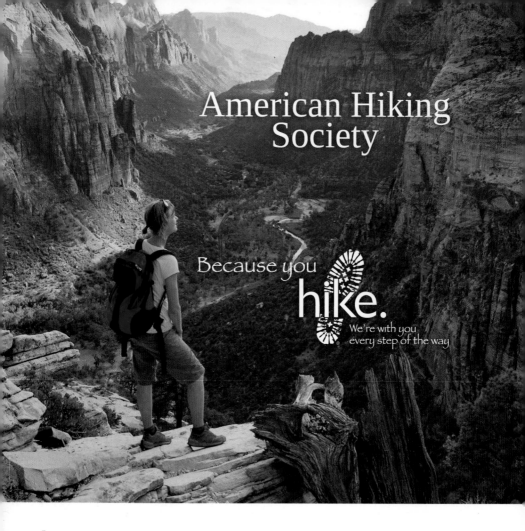

American Hiking Society

Because you hike.
We're with you every step of the way

As a national voice for hikers, **American Hiking Society** works every day:

- Building and maintaining hiking trails
- Educating and supporting hikers by providing information and resources
- Supporting hiking and trail organizations nationwide
- Speaking for hikers in the halls of Congress and with federal land managers

Whether you're a casual hiker or a seasoned backpacker, become a member of American Hiking Society and join the national hiking community! You'll enjoy great member benefits and help preserve the nation's hiking trails, so tomorrow's hike is even better than today's. We invite you to join us now!

American Hiking Society